# UNDERSTANDING FINANCIAL CRISES

# Understanding Financial Crises

FRANKLIN ALLEN
and
DOUGLAS GALE

OXFORD

UNIVERSITY PRESS

# OXFORD
UNIVERSITY PRESS

Great Clarendon Street, Oxford OX2 6DP

Oxford University Press is a department of the University of Oxford.
It furthers the University's objective of excellence in research, scholarship,
and education by publishing worldwide in

Oxford New York

Auckland Cape Town Dar es Salaam Hong Kong Karachi
Kuala Lumpur Madrid Melbourne Mexico City Nairobi
New Delhi Shanghai Taipei Toronto

With offices in

Argentina Austria Brazil Chile Czech Republic France Greece
Guatemala Hungary Italy Japan Poland Portugal Singapore
South Korea Switzerland Thailand Turkey Ukraine Vietnam

Oxford is a registered trade mark of Oxford University Press
in the UK and in certain other countries

Published in the United States
by Oxford University Press Inc., New York

The moral rights of the authors have been asserted
Database right Oxford University Press (maker)

First published 2007

British Library Cataloguing in Publication Data

Data available

Library of Congress Cataloging in Publication Data

Data available

Typeset by Newgen Imaging Systems (P) Ltd., Chennai, India
Printed in Great Britain
on acid-free paper by
Biddles Ltd., King's Lynn, Norfolk

ISBN 978–0–19–925141–4

1 3 5 7 9 10 8 6 4 2

# Preface

This book has grown out of a series of papers written over a number of years. Our paper "Liquidity Preference, Market Participation, and Asset Price Volatility" was actually begun by one of us in 1988, although it appeared in 1994. Our interest in bank runs and financial crises began with "Optimal Financial Crises," and this led to further studies on the welfare economics of crises. Each paper seemed to leave questions unanswered and led to new papers which led to new questions.

When one of us was invited to give the Clarendon Lectures in Finance, it seemed the right time to begin the task of synthesizing the ideas presented in a variety of different places using different models. Our aim was to make these ideas accessible to a wider audience, including undergraduates and policy makers in central banks and international organizations, and also to put them in a coherent framework that might make them more useful for graduate students and researchers. This is far from being the last word on the subject, but it may provide a set of tools that will be helpful in pursuing the many open questions that remain.

Over the years we have had many opportunities to present our work in seminars and at conferences and have benefited from the comments and suggestions of many economists. In particular, we would like to thank Viral Acharya, Christina Bannier, Michael Bordo, Patrick Bolton, Mike Burkart, Mark Carey, Elena Carletti, Michael Chui, Marco Cipriani, Peter Englund, Prasanna Gai, Gary Gorton, Antonio Guarino, Martin Hellwig, Marcello Pericoli, Glen Hoggarth, Jamie McAndrews, Robert Nobay, Önür Ozgur, João Santos, Massimo Sbracia, Hyun Song Shin, Giancarlo Spagnolo, Xavier Vives, David Webb, Andrew Winton, and Tanju Yorulmazer.

We have included some of these topics in graduate courses we taught at New York University and Princeton University. Once we began writing the book, we were fortunate to have the opportunity to present lecture series at the Bank of England, the Banca d'Italia, the Stockholm School of Economics, and the University of Frankfurt. We developed an undergraduate course on financial crises at NYU based on the manuscript of the book. We are very grateful to the undergraduates who allowed us to experiment on them and rose to the challenge presented by the material. Antonio Guarino used several chapters for an undergraduate course at University College London and offered us many comments and corrections.

We are sure there are others whom we may have forgotten, but whose contributions and encouragement helped us greatly. Thanks to all of you.

# Contents

1. **History and institutions**                                             1

  1.1    Introduction                                              1
  1.2    Historical crises in Europe and the US                     2
  1.3    Crises and stock market crashes                           5
  1.4    Currency and twin crises                                  9
  1.5    Crises in different eras                                  10
  1.6    Some recent crises                                       14
       1.6.1  The Scandinavian crises                          14
       1.6.2  Japan                                            15
       1.6.3  The Asian crisis                                 15
       1.6.4  The Russian crisis and long term capital
              management (LTCM)                                16
       1.6.5  The Argentina crisis of 2001–2002                17
  1.7    The costs of crises                                       18
  1.8    Theories of crises                                        19
  1.9    Concluding remarks                                        23

2. **Time, uncertainty, and liquidity**                                      27

  2.1    Efficient allocation over time                            27
       2.1.1  Consumption and saving                           27
       2.1.2  Production                                       36
  2.2    Uncertainty                                               40
       2.2.1  Contingent commodities and risk sharing          40
       2.2.2  Attitudes toward risk                            44
       2.2.3  Insurance and risk pooling                       48
       2.2.4  Portfolio choice                                 49
  2.3    Liquidity                                                 52
  2.4    Concluding remarks                                        57

3. **Intermediation and crises**                                             58

  3.1    The liquidity problem                                     59
  3.2    Market equilibrium                                        60
  3.3    The efficient solution                                    64
  3.4    The banking solution                                      72
  3.5    Bank runs                                                 74

3.6   Equilibrium bank runs                                      76
3.7   The business cycle view of bank runs                       82
3.8   The global games approach to finding a unique
      equilibrium                                                90
3.9   Literature review                                         94
3.10  Concluding remarks                                        96

4. Asset markets                                                 99
4.1   Market participation                                      99
4.2   The model                                                103
4.3   Equilibrium                                              104
      4.3.1  Market-clearing at date 1                         107
      4.3.2  Portfolio choice                                  109
4.4   Cash-in-the-market pricing                               110
4.5   Limited participation                                    114
      4.5.1  The model                                         116
      4.5.2  Equilibrium                                       117
      4.5.3  Equilibrium with full participation               120
      4.5.4  Full participation and asset-price volatility     120
      4.5.5  Limited participation and asset-price volatility  121
      4.5.6  Multiple Pareto-ranked equilibria                 123
4.6   Summary                                                  124

5. Financial fragility                                          126
5.1   Markets, banks, and consumers                            128
5.2   Types of equilibrium                                     132
      5.2.1  Fundamental equilibrium with no aggregate
             uncertainty                                       133
      5.2.2  Aggregate uncertainty                             135
      5.2.3  Sunspot equilibria                                140
      5.2.4  Idiosyncratic liquidity shocks for banks          142
      5.2.5  Equilibrium without bankruptcy                    144
      5.2.6  Complete versus incomplete markets                146
5.3   Relation to the literature                               147
5.4   Discussion                                               148

6. Intermediation and markets                                   153
6.1   Complete markets                                         155
6.2   Intermediation and markets                               164
      6.2.1  Efficient risk sharing                            165
      6.2.2  Equilibrium with complete financial markets       167

|       | 6.2.3 | An alternative formulation of complete markets | 170 |
|       | 6.2.4 | The general case | 172 |
|       | 6.2.5 | Implementing the first best *without* complete markets | 177 |
| 6.3   | Incomplete contracts | | 181 |
|       | 6.3.1 | Complete markets and aggregate risk | 182 |
|       | 6.3.2 | The intermediary's problem with incomplete markets | 186 |
| 6.4   | Conclusion | | 188 |

**7. Optimal regulation**    **190**

| 7.1   | Capital regulation | | 191 |
|       | 7.1.1 | Optimal capital structure | 194 |
|       | 7.1.2 | Models with aggregate uncertainty | 199 |
| 7.2   | Capital structure with complete markets | | 201 |
| 7.3   | Regulating liquidity | | 204 |
|       | 7.3.1 | Comparative statics | 206 |
|       | 7.3.2 | Too much or too little liquidity? | 209 |
| 7.4   | Literature review | | 213 |
| 7.5   | Concluding remarks | | 213 |

**8. Money and prices**    **216**

| 8.1   | An example | 218 |
| 8.2   | Optimal currency crises | 223 |
| 8.3   | Dollarization and incentives | 226 |
| 8.4   | Literature review | 228 |
| 8.5   | Concluding remarks | 232 |

**9. Bubbles and crises**    **235**

| 9.1   | Agency problems and positive bubbles | | 237 |
|       | 9.1.1 | The risk-shifting problem | 238 |
|       | 9.1.2 | Credit and interest rate determination | 243 |
|       | 9.1.3 | Financial risk | 245 |
|       | 9.1.4 | Financial fragility | 246 |
| 9.2   | Banking crises and negative bubbles | | 247 |
|       | 9.2.1 | The model | 247 |
|       | 9.2.2 | Optimal risk sharing | 248 |
|       | 9.2.3 | Optimal deposit contracts | 251 |
|       | 9.2.4 | An asset market | 252 |
|       | 9.2.5 | Optimal monetary policy | 256 |
| 9.3   | Concluding remarks | | 258 |

**10. Contagion**                                                    260

    10.1   Liquidity preference                                  263
    10.2   Optimal risk sharing                                 266
    10.3   Decentralization                                     268
    10.4   Contagion                                            274
          10.4.1  The liquidation "pecking order"           275
          10.4.2  Liquidation values                        276
          10.4.3  Buffers and bank runs                     277
          10.4.4  Many regions                              280
    10.5   Robustness                                           280
    10.6   Containment                                          281
    10.7   Discussion                                           282
    10.8   Applications                                         284
          10.8.1  Upper and Worms (2004)                    284
          10.8.2  Degryse and Nguyen (2004)                 290
          10.8.3  Cifuentes, Ferrucci, and Shin (2005)      291
    10.9   Literature review                                    293
    10.10  Concluding remarks                                  295

**Index**                                                            299

# 1

# History and institutions

## 1.1 INTRODUCTION

What happened in Asia in 1997? Countries such as South Korea, Thailand, Indonesia, Singapore, and Hong Kong whose economies had previously been the envy of the world experienced crises. Banks and other financial intermediaries were put under great strain and in many cases collapsed. Stock markets and currencies plunged. Their real economies were severely affected and their GDPs fell significantly. What were the causes of these dramatic events?

To many people these crises were a new phenomenon. There had been crises in other countries such as Mexico and Brazil but these could be attributed to inconsistent government macroeconomic policies. In those cases taxes were too small relative to government expenditures to maintain a fixed exchange rate. This was not the case for the Asian crisis. Other causes were looked for and found. The institutions in these countries were quite different from those in the US. Many had bank-based financial systems. There was little transparency either for banks or corporations. Corporate governance operated in a quite different way. In many cases it did not seem that managers' interests were aligned with those of shareholders. In some countries such as Indonesia corruption was rife. These factors were seen by many as the cause of the crises. However, they had all been present during the time that these countries were so successful.

Others blamed guarantees to banks and firms by governments or implicit promises of "bail-outs" by organizations such as the International Monetary Fund (IMF). Rather than inconsistent macroeconomic policies being the problem, bad microeconomic policies were the problem. Either way it was governments and international organizations that were to blame.

In this book we will argue that it is important not to take too narrow a view of crises. They are nothing new. They have not been restricted to emerging economies even in recent times. The Scandinavian crises of the early 1990's are examples of this. Despite having sophisticated economies and institutions, Norway, Sweden and Finland all had severe crises. These were similar in many ways to what happened in the Asian crisis of 1997. Banks collapsed, asset prices plunged, currencies came under attack and their value fell. Output was severely affected.

Taking an historical view the period from 1945–1971 was exceptional. There were no banking crises anywhere in the world, apart from one in Brazil in 1962. There were currency crises when exchange rates were pegged at the wrong levels but that was all. Going back to the first half of the twentieth century and before there were many examples of financial crises. The stock market crash of 1929, the banking crises of the early 1930's and the Great Depression were some of the most dramatic episodes. There were many others, particularly in the US in the last half of the nineteenth century when it had no central bank. In Europe crises were much less frequent. The Bank of England had learned to prevent crises and the last one there was the Overend & Gurney crisis of 1866. Other central banks also learned to prevent crises and their incidence was significantly reduced. Prior to that crises were endemic in Europe as well.

Particularly after the experience of the Great Depression in the period prior to 1945–1971, crises were perceived as a market failure. It was widely agreed they must be avoided at all costs. The reform of the Federal Reserve System in the early 1930's and the extensive regulation of the financial system that was put in place in the US were part of this mindset. In other countries financial regulation went even farther. Governments controlled the allocation of funds to different industries through state-owned banks or heavily regulated banks. This extensive regulation was the cause of the virtual disappearance of banking crises from 1945–1971.

However, the elimination of crises came at a cost. Because of the extensive regulation and government intervention the financial system ceased to perform its basic function of allocating investment. There were many inefficiencies as a result. This led to calls for deregulation and the return of market forces to the allocation of investment. As a result crises have returned. Bordo et al. (2000) find that the frequency of crises in the recent period since 1971 is not that different from what it was before 1914.

We start in this chapter with an historical review of crises and the institutions involved. This provides a background for the theories that are subsequently developed.

## 1.2 HISTORICAL CRISES IN EUROPE AND THE US

Prior to the twentieth century banking panics occurred frequently. Kindle-berger (1993, p. 264) in his book recounting the financial history of Western Europe points out that financial crises have occurred at roughly 10 year intervals over the last 400 years. Panics were generally regarded as a bad thing because they were often associated with significant declines in economic activity. Over time one of the main roles of central banks has become to eliminate panics and ensure financial stability. It has been a long and involved process. The first central bank, the Bank of Sweden, was established over 300 years ago in 1668. The Bank of England was established soon after. It played an especially important role in the development of effective stabilization policies in the eighteenth and nineteenth centuries. The last true panic in the UK was the Overend & Gurney crisis of 1866.

In his influential book *Lombard Street*, Bagehot (1873) laid out his famous principles of how a central bank should lend to banks during a crisis.

- Lend freely at a high rate of interest relative to the pre-crisis period but only to borrowers with good collateral (i.e. any assets normally accepted by the central bank).
- The assets should be valued at between panic and pre-panic prices.
- Institutions without good collateral should be allowed to fail.

Bordo (1986) documents that for the period 1870–1933 there were very few banking panics in the UK, Germany, and France. Kindleberger (1993) points out that many British economists ascribe the absence of crises in the UK to central banking experience gained by the Bank of England and their ability to skillfully manipulate discount rates. However, France also experienced no financial crises from 1882–1924 despite leaving its discount rate constant for many decades. Kindleberger suggests that France was perhaps stabilized by England.

The US took a different tack. Alexander Hamilton was influenced by British experience with the Bank of England and after the revolution advocated a large federally chartered bank with branches all over the country. This led to the foundation of the First Bank of the United States (1791–1811) and later the Second Bank of the United States (1816–1836). However, there was considerable distrust of the concentration of power these institutions represented. In a report on the Second Bank, John Quincy Adams wrote "Power for good, is power for evil, even in the hands of Omnipotence" (Timberlake 1978, p. 39). The controversy came to a head in the debate on the re-chartering of the Second Bank in 1832. Although the bill was passed by Congress it was vetoed by President Jackson and the veto was not overturned. Since then there has been a strong bias toward decentralization of the banking system and an aversion to powerful institutions of any kind. There was no central bank in the US from 1836 until 1914.

Throughout the nineteenth century the US banking system was highly frag-
mented and unlike every other industrializing country the US failed to develop
nationwide banks with extensive branch networks. Prior to the Civil War, states
were free to regulate their own banking systems and there was no national system. Many states adopted a "free banking" system which allowed free entry.
There were serious banking panics in 1837 and 1857 and both were followed
by depressions and significant economic disruption.

The advent of the Civil War in 1861 and the need to finance it significantly changed the role of the Federal Government in the financial
system. The National Bank Acts of 1863 and 1864 set up a national banking system. They granted limited powers to banks. In particular, the 1864
Act was interpreted as confining each to a single location. When the
question of whether banks could hold equity arose, the Supreme Court
ruled that since the 1864 Act had not specifically granted this right they
could not.

The creation of the National Banking system did not prevent the problem
of panics and the associated economic disruption and depressions. There were
panics in 1873, 1884, 1893 and 1907. Table 1.1, which is from Gorton (1988),
shows the banking crises that occurred repeatedly in the US during the National
Banking Era from 1863–1914. The first column shows the business cycles
identified by the National Bureau of Economic Research (NBER). The first
date is the peak of the cycle and the second is the trough. The second column
shows the date on which panics occurred. In a banking panic people worry

Table 1.1. National Banking Era panics.

| NBER cycle Peak–Trough | Panic date | %Δ(Currency/ deposit)* | %Δ Pig iron[†] |
|---|---|---|---|
| Oct. 1873–Mar. 1879 | Sep. 1873 | 14.53 | −51.0 |
| Mar. 1882–May 1885 | Jun. 1884 | 8.80 | −14.0 |
| Mar. 1887–Apr. 1888 | No Panic | 3.00 | −9.0 |
| Jul. 1890–May 1891 | Nov. 1890 | 9.00 | −34.0 |
| Jan. 1893–Jun. 1894 | May 1893 | 16.00 | −29.0 |
| Dec. 1895–Jun. 1897 | Oct. 1896 | 14.30 | −4.0 |
| Jun. 1899–Dec. 1900 | No Panic | 2.78 | −6.7 |
| Sep. 1902–Aug. 1904 | No Panic | −4.13 | −8.7 |
| May 1907–Jun. 1908 | Oct. 1907 | 11.45 | −46.5 |
| Jan. 1910–Jan. 1912 | No Panic | −2.64 | −21.7 |
| Jan. 1913–Dec. 1914 | Aug. 1914 | 10.39 | −47.1 |

*Percentage change of ratio at panic date to previous year's average.
[†]Measured from peak to trough.
(Adapted from Table 1, Gorton 1988, p. 233)

about the soundness of the banks they have deposited their funds in. As a result they withdraw their money and hold it in the form of currency. The third column shows the percentage change in the ratio of currency to deposits. It is a measure of the severity of a banking panic. The higher the change in the currency/deposit ratio, the more serious is the crisis. It can be seen that the panics of 1873, 1893, 1896, and 1907 were particularly severe. The final column shows how much the production of pig iron changed from the peak of the cycle to the trough. GDP figures for this period have not been reliably compiled. Economic historians often use production of pig iron as a proxy for GDP. The final column is therefore meant to indicate how serious the recessions were. It can be seen that the troughs occurring after the panics of 1873, 1890, 1893, 1907, and 1914 were particularly severe.

After the crisis of 1907, a European banker summed up European frustration with the inefficiencies of the U.S. banking system by declaring the US was "a great financial nuisance" (Studenski and Krooss 1963, p. 254). The severity of the recession following the 1907 banking panic led to a debate on whether or not a central bank should be established in the US. The National Monetary Commission investigated this issue and finally in 1914 the Federal Reserve System was established.

The initial organization of the Federal Reserve System differed from that of a traditional central bank like the Bank of England. It had a regional structure and decision making power was decentralized. During the years after its creation it did not develop the ability to prevent banking panics. In 1933 there was another major banking panic which led to the closing of banks for an extended period just after President Roosevelt took office. The problems faced by the banking system led to the Glass–Steagall Act of 1933, which introduced deposit insurance and required the separation of commercial and investment banking operations. The Banking Act of 1935 extended the powers of the Federal Reserve System and changed the way it operated. These reforms finally eliminated the occurrence of banking panics almost seventy years after this had happened in the UK.

## 1.3 CRISES AND STOCK MARKET CRASHES

So far we have focused on banking crises. Often banking crises and stock market crashes are closely intertwined. For example, Wilson et al. (1990) consider four major banking panics accompanied by stock market crashes in the US during the National Banking Era. These are the crises of September 1873, June 1884, July 1893, and October 1907.

Why was there a link between banking panics and stock market crashes? As mentioned above banks were not able to hold equity so it might be thought that movements in the stock market would be independent of banks' policies. In fact this was not the case. To see why, it is necessary to have some understanding of the link between banks and the stock market during this period.

Banks must hold liquid reserves in case customers wish to withdraw cash from their accounts. All banks hold some reserves in the form of currency. In addition a large proportion of reserves were held in the form of interbank balances. In practice, most banks had deposits in New York City banks. The reason banks held interbank deposits rather than cash was that they paid interest. The New York City banks could pay attractive rates of interest because they lent a large proportion of these funds in the call loan market at the stock exchange in New York. The loans were used to buy stocks on margin (i.e. the stocks were bought with borrowed money). They were referred to as call loans because they were payable on demand. The borrowers could either obtain funds to repay their call loans by taking out other loans or if necessary they could sell the securities the original call loans were used to purchase. These call loans constituted a large part of New York banks' assets. For example, Sprague (1910, p. 83) reports that on September 12, 1873, 31 percent of New York banks' loans were call loans.

Agriculture was much more important during the National Banking Era than it is today. During the Spring planting and Autumn harvesting banks in farming areas required cash. Because of the random nature of these demands for cash it was difficult for the New York City banks to plan with certainty what their liquidity needs would be. When liquidity needs were high the New York City banks would demand repayment of their call loans. The borrowers might be forced to sell the securities they had purchased on margin. A wave of selling could cause prices to fall if those participating in the market on the buy side had limited amounts of cash. In other words there could be a crash in prices.

Wilson, Sylla, and Jones investigate stock returns and their volatility during the panic and crash periods of 1873, 1884, 1893, and 1907. Table 1.2 shows the 25 lowest and 25 highest stock monthly price changes between 1866 and 1913. Four of the eight lowest returns occurring during this period were during panic months. Apart from May 1880, which is not associated with a banking panic, all the others from the nine lowest returns are around panics. Notice also from the highest stock returns that there is some tendency for stocks to rally two or three months after a crisis. December 1873

**Table 1.2.** The 25 lowest and 25 highest stock price changes 1866–1913 (from Table 1 of Wilson et al. 1990).

| Year | Month | Lowest return | Rank | Year | Month | Highest return |
|------|-------|---------------|------|------|-------|----------------|
| 1907 | 10 | −10.8514% | 1 | 1879 | 10 | 10.8824% |
| 1907 | 3 | −9.7987 | 2 | 1901 | 6 | 9.9678 |
| 1893 | 7 | −9.4340 | 3 | 1873 | 12 | 9.5385 |
| 1893 | 5 | −8.8993 | 4 | 1901 | 4 | 8.4437 |
| 1873 | 10 | −8.6721 | 5 | 1891 | 9 | 8.0605 |
| 1884 | 5 | −8.5575 | 6 | 1900 | 11 | 7.8512 |
| 1880 | 5 | −7.9137 | 7 | 1899 | 1 | 7.6923 |
| 1873 | 9 | −7.7500 | 8 | 1906 | 8 | 7.4074 |
| 1907 | 8 | −7.4809 | 9 | 1877 | 8 | 6.9869 |
| 1890 | 11 | −7.3350 | 10 | 1898 | 5 | 6.8120 |
| 1877 | 6 | −7.1730 | 11 | 1893 | 9 | 6.6869 |
| 1877 | 4 | −7.0588 | 12 | 1897 | 8 | 6.6852 |
| 1899 | 12 | −6.7308 | 13 | 1896 | 11 | 6.6667 |
| 1901 | 7 | −6.7251 | 14 | 1908 | 11 | 6.6066 |
| 1896 | 7 | −6.6092 | 15 | 1884 | 8 | 6.4067 |
| 1869 | 9 | −6.4913 | 16 | 1885 | 11 | 6.3131 |
| 1884 | 6 | −6.4171 | 17 | 1898 | 12 | 6.3084 |
| 1876 | 9 | −6.0127 | 18 | 1877 | 9 | 6.1224 |
| 1877 | 2 | −5.9441 | 19 | 1881 | 1 | 5.9574 |
| 1907 | 11 | −5.8052 | 20 | 1904 | 10 | 5.9423 |
| 1895 | 12 | −5.6911 | 21 | 1900 | 12 | 5.9387 |
| 1903 | 6 | −5.5556 | 22 | 1885 | 10 | 5.8824 |
| 1896 | 8 | −5.5385 | 23 | 1895 | 5 | 5.6980 |
| 1911 | 9 | −5.4201 | 24 | 1882 | 7 | 5.6893 |
| 1877 | 3 | −5.2045 | 25 | 1885 | 8 | 5.5710 |

is the third highest return, September 1993 is the eleventh highest, and August 1884 is the fifteenth highest. It is not just stocks where this effect is found. Bonds and commercial paper show similar patterns of returns. Returns are low during the panic and then rebound in the months after the panic.

Table 1.3 shows the top 50 months of volatility for stocks between 1866 and 1913. These volatilities are calculated by including the annualized standard deviation of returns using the current month and nine of the previous 11 months with the two discarded being the ones with the highest and lowest returns. The greatest volatility seems to occur in the year following the panic with peak stock price volatility coming 2–7 months after the panic.

**Table 1.3.** The top 50 months of volatility for stocks 1866–1913 (from Table 5 of Wilson et al. 1990).

| Rank | Stocks | | |
|---|---|---|---|
| | Year | Mo. | Stocks |
| 1 | 1908 | 5 | 16.2433 |
| 2 | 1908 | 6 | 15.6801 |
| 3 | 1908 | 7 | 15.6239 |
| 4 | 1908 | 4 | 15.4590 |
| 5 | 1908 | 2 | 15.0509 |
| 6 | 1908 | 1 | 15.0179 |
| 7 | 1901 | 7 | 15.0078 |
| 8 | 1878 | 1 | 14.2182 |
| 9 | 1877 | 10 | 14.1960 |
| 10 | 1877 | 12 | 14.1921 |
| 11 | 1877 | 11 | 14.1841 |
| 12 | 1873 | 12 | 14.1461 |
| 13 | 1908 | 3 | 13.9722 |
| 14 | 1901 | 8 | 13.7695 |
| 15 | 1901 | 10 | 13.7645 |
| 16 | 1877 | 8 | 13.7459 |
| 17 | 1877 | 9 | 13.7238 |
| 18 | 1907 | 12 | 13.5497 |
| 19 | 1893 | 9 | 13.5273 |
| 20 | 1908 | 9 | 13.0782 |
| 21 | 1908 | 8 | 13.0658 |
| 22 | 1901 | 9 | 13.0519 |
| 23 | 1878 | 2 | 13.0206 |
| 24 | 1896 | 11 | 12.8153 |
| 25 | 1894 | 4 | 12.5641 |
| 26 | 1901 | 5 | 12.4214 |
| 27 | 1894 | 3 | 12.3836 |
| 28 | 1901 | 11 | 12.3543 |
| 29 | 1891 | 9 | 12.2079 |
| 30 | 1884 | 8 | 12.1837 |
| 31 | 1898 | 5 | 12.0430 |
| 32 | 1901 | 12 | 12.0014 |
| 33 | 1901 | 6 | 11.9526 |
| 34 | 1902 | 1 | 11.8947 |
| 35 | 1878 | 3 | 11.8415 |
| 36 | 1893 | 12 | 11.8154 |
| 37 | 1874 | 8 | 11.8127 |
| 38 | 1902 | 2 | 11.8042 |
| 39 | 1880 | 5 | 11.7880 |
| 40 | 1898 | 6 | 11.7863 |

**Table 1.3.** *(Continued)*

| Rank | Stocks | | |
|------|--------|------|--------|
| | Year | Mo. | Stocks |
| 41 | 1874 | 7 | 11.7802 |
| 42 | 1874 | 6 | 11.7571 |
| 43 | 1874 | 5 | 11.7442 |
| 44 | 1874 | 4 | 11.7132 |
| 45 | 1893 | 11 | 11.7040 |
| 46 | 1874 | 3 | 11.5068 |
| 47 | 1894 | 2 | 11.5040 |
| 48 | 1874 | 2 | 11.4914 |
| 49 | 1901 | 4 | 11.4480 |
| 50 | 1902 | 3 | 11.4422 |

## 1.4 CURRENCY AND TWIN CRISES

Many of the crises in the nineteenth and early twentieth century were international in scope. For example, the crisis of 1873 had an extensive impact in Austria and Germany as well as in the US and in a number of emerging countries such as Argentina. In fact the 1873 crisis ended a wave of lending that occurred in the 1850's and 1860's to finance railroads in Latin America (Bordo and Eichengreen 1999). These international dimensions led to a flow of funds between countries and this in turn could cause a currency crisis. When banking crises and currency crises occur together there is said to be a twin crisis.

Prior to the First World War countries had a strong commitment to the gold standard. If a country suffered an outflow of funds it might leave the gold standard but it was generally expected to resume after some time had passed. This lessened the effect of currency crises as investors believed the value of the currency would eventually be restored. Between the wars, commitment to the gold standard was weakened. As a result banking and currency crises frequently occurred together. These twin crises are typically associated with more severe recessions than banking or currency crises occurring on their own.

After the Second World War the Bretton Woods system of fixed exchange rates was established. Strong banking regulations and controls were put in place that effectively eliminated banking crises. Currency crises continued to occur. Due to the extensive use of capital controls their nature changed. During this period they were typically the result of macroeconomic and financial policies that were inconsistent with the prevailing exchange rate. After the collapse of the Bretton Woods system in the early 1970's banking crises and twin crises reemerged as capital controls were relaxed and capital markets became global.

## 1.5 CRISES IN DIFFERENT ERAS

Bordo et al. (2000, 2001) have addressed the question of how recent crises such as the European Monetary System crisis of 1992–1993, the Mexican crisis of 1994–1995, the Asian crisis of 1997–1998, the Brazilian crisis of 1998, the Russian crisis of 1998, and the Argentinian crisis of 2001 compare with earlier crises. They identify four periods.

1. Gold Standard Era 1880–1913
2. The Interwar Years 1919–1939
3. Bretton Woods Period 1945–1971
4. Recent Period 1973–1997

As we shall see there are a number of similarities between the periods but also some important differences. They consider 21 countries for the first three periods and then for the recent period give data for the original 21 as well as an expanded group of 56.

The first issue is how to define a crisis. They define a banking crisis as financial distress that is severe enough to result in the erosion of most or all of the capital in the banking system. A currency crisis is defined as a forced change in parity, abandonment of a pegged exchange rate or an international rescue. The second issue is how to measure the duration of a crisis. To do this they compute the trend rate of GDP growth for five years before. The duration of the crisis is the amount of time before GDP growth returns to its trend rate. Finally, the depth of the crisis is measured by summing the output loss relative to trend for the duration of the crisis.

Figure 1.1 shows the frequency of crises in the four periods. Comparing the data with the original 21 countries it can be seen that the interwar years are the worst. This is perhaps not surprising given that this was when the Great Depression occurred. Banking crises were particularly prevalent during this period relative to the other periods.

It can be seen that the Bretton Woods period is very different from the other periods. As mentioned above, after the Great Depression policymakers in most countries were so determined not to allow such an event to happen again that they imposed severe regulations or brought the banks under state control to prevent them from taking much risk. As a result banking crises were almost completely eliminated. There was one twin crisis in Brazil in 1962 but apart from that there were no other banking crises during the entire period. There were frequent currency crises but as we have seen these were mostly situations where macroeconomic policies were inconsistent with the level of the fixed exchange rates set in the Bretton Woods system.

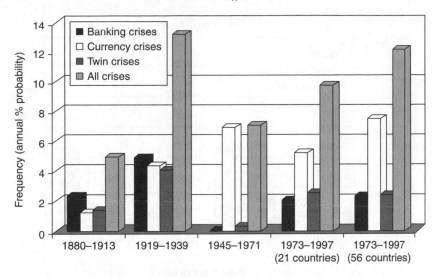

**Figure 1.1.** Crisis frequency, 1880–1997 (from Figure 1 of Bordo et al. 2001).

Interestingly the most benign period was the Gold Standard era from 1880 to 1913. Here banking crises did occur but were fairly limited and currency and twin crises were limited compared to subsequent periods. Since the global financial system was fairly open at this time, the implication is that globalization does not inevitably lead to crises.

The recent period is not as bad as the interwar period but is nevertheless fairly bad. Banking and twin crises are more frequent than in every period except the interwar years and currency crises are much more frequent. This is especially true if the sample of 56 countries is used as the basis of comparison rather than the 21 countries used in the other periods. The countries that are added to create the larger sample are mostly emerging countries. This suggests that emerging countries are more prone to crises and particularly to currency crises.

Figure 1.2 confirms this. It breaks the sample into industrial countries and emerging markets. In recent years emerging countries have been particularly prone to currency crises and twin crises. The other interesting observation from Figure 1.2 is that during the interwar period it was the industrial countries that were particularly hard hit by crises. They were actually more prone to currency and twin crises than the emerging countries.

Table 1.4 shows the average duration and depth of crises broken out by type of crisis and for the different periods and samples. Perhaps the most striking feature of Table 1.4 is the short duration and mild effect of crises during the

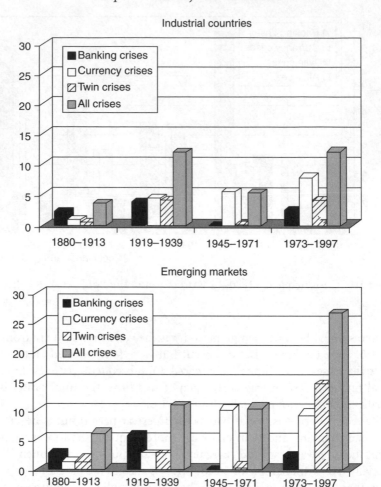

**Figure 1.2.** Frequency of crises – distribution by market (from Figure 2 of Bordo et al. (2000)).

Bretton Woods period. The second distinctive feature is that twin crises are much worse than other crises in terms of the output lost. As might be expected during the interwar period the effect of crises was much more severe than in the other periods. Although they did not last longer the cumulative loss in output is higher than in the other periods. During the Gold Standard Era the duration and cumulative loss were not remarkable compared to the other periods. In recent years twin crises have lasted for a particularly long time and the lost output is significant.

**Table 1.4.** Duration and depth of crises (from Table 1 of Bordo et al. 2001).

| All countries | 1880–1913 | 1919–1939 | 1945–1971 | 1973–1997 21 nations | 1973–1997 56 nations |
|---|---|---|---|---|---|
| | Average duration of crises in years | | | | |
| Currency crises | 2.6 | 1.9 | 1.8 | 1.9 | 2.1 |
| Banking crises | 2.3 | 2.4 | a | 3.1 | 2.6 |
| Twin crises | 2.2 | 2.7 | 1.0 | 3.7 | 3.8 |
| All crises | 2.4 | 2.4 | 1.8 | 2.6 | 2.5 |
| | Average crisis depth (cumulative GDP loss in %) | | | | |
| Currency crises | 8.3 | 14.2 | 5.2 | 3.8 | 5.9 |
| Banking crises | 8.4 | 10.5 | a | 7.0 | 6.2 |
| Twin crises | 14.5 | 15.8 | 1.7 | 15.7 | 18.6 |
| All crises | 9.8 | 13.4 | 5.2 | 7.8 | 8.3 |

*Notes:* [a] indicates no crises.
*Source:* Authors' calculations.

Finally, Figure 1.3 shows the effect of crises on recessions. It can be seen that recessions with crises have a much higher loss of GDP than recessions without crises. This was particularly true in the interwar period. Also the average recovery time is somewhat higher in recessions with crises rather than recessions without crises.

In summary, the analysis of Bordo et al. (2000, 2001) leads to a number of conclusions. Banking crises, currency crises, and twin crises have occurred under a variety of different monetary and regulatory regimes. Over the last 120 years crises have been followed by economic downturns lasting on average from 2 to 3 years and costing 5 to 10 percent of GDP. Twin crises are associated with particularly large output losses. Recessions with crises were more severe than recessions without them.

The Bretton Woods period from 1945 to 1971 was quite special. Countries either regulated bank balance sheets to prevent them from taking very much risk or owned them directly to achieve the same aim. These measures were successful in that there were no banking crises during this time and only one twin crisis.

The interwar period was also special. Banking crises and currency crises were widespread. Moreover the output losses from these were severe particularly when they occurred together and there was a twin crisis.

The most recent period does indeed appear more crisis prone than any other period except for the interwar years. In particular, it seems more crisis prone than the Gold Standard Era, which was the last time that capital markets were as globalized as they are now.

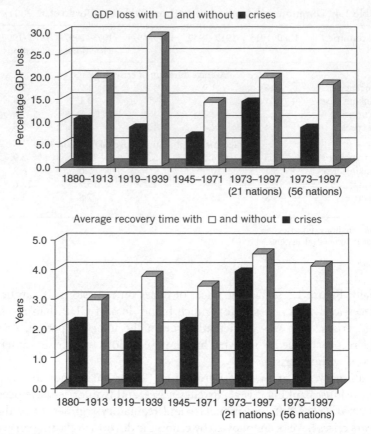

**Figure 1.3.** Recessions with and without crises (from Figure 2 of Bordo et al. 2001).

## 1.6 SOME RECENT CRISES

Now that we have seen a comparison of recent crises with crises in other eras, it is perhaps helpful to consider some of the more recent ones in greater detail. We start with those that occurred in Scandinavia in the early 1990's.

### 1.6.1 The Scandinavian crises

Norway, Finland and Sweden experienced a classic boom–bust cycle that led to twin crises (see Heiskanen 1993 and Englund and Vihriälä 2006). In Norway lending increased by 40 percent in 1985 and 1986. Asset prices soared while investment and consumption also increased significantly. The collapse in oil prices helped burst the bubble and caused the most severe banking crisis and recession since the war. In Finland an expansionary budget in 1987 resulted in massive credit expansion. Housing prices rose by a total of 68 percent in 1987 and 1988. In 1989 the central bank increased interest rates and imposed reserve requirements to moderate credit expansion. In 1990 and 1991 the economic situation was exacerbated by a fall in trade with the Soviet Union. Asset prices collapsed, banks had to be supported by the government and GDP shrank by 7 percent. In Sweden a steady credit expansion through the late 1980's led to a property boom. In the fall of 1990 credit was tightened and interest rates rose. In 1991 a number of banks had severe difficulties because of lending based on inflated asset values. The government had to intervene and a severe recession followed.

### 1.6.2 Japan

In the 1980's the Japanese real estate and stock markets were affected by a bubble. Financial liberalization throughout the 1980's and the desire to support the United States dollar in the latter part of the decade led to an expansion in credit. During most of the 1980's asset prices rose steadily, eventually reaching very high levels. For example, the Nikkei 225 index was around 10,000 in 1985. On December 19, 1989 it reached a peak of 38,916. A new Governor of the Bank of Japan, less concerned with supporting the US dollar and more concerned with fighting inflation, tightened monetary policy and this led to a sharp increase in interest rates in early 1990 (see Frankel 1993; Tschoegl 1993). The bubble burst. The Nikkei 225 fell sharply during the first part of the year and by October 1, 1990 it had sunk to 20,222. Real estate prices followed a similar pattern. The next few years were marked by defaults and retrenchment in the financial system. Three big banks and one of the largest four securities firms failed. The real economy was adversely affected by the aftermath of the bubble and growth rates during the 1990's and 2000's have mostly been slightly positive or negative, in contrast to most of the post-war period when they were much higher. Using the average growth rate of GDP of 4 percent from 1976–1991, the difference between trend GDP and actual GDP from 1992–1998 is around ¥340 trillion or about 68 percent of GDP (Mikitani and Posen 2000, p. 32).

### 1.6.3 The Asian crisis

From the early 1950's until the eve of the crisis in 1997 the "Dragons" (Hong Kong, Singapore, South Korea, and Taiwan) and the "Tigers" (Indonesia, Malaysia, the Philippines, and Thailand) were held up as models of successful economic development. Their economies grew at high rates for many years. After sustained pressure, the Thai central bank stopped defending the baht on July 2, 1997 and it fell 14 percent in the onshore market and 19 percent in the offshore market (Fourçans and Franck 2003, Chapter 10). This marked the start of the Asian financial crisis.

The next currencies to come under pressure were the Philippine peso and the Malaysian ringitt. The Philippine central bank tried to defend the peso by raising interest rates but it nevertheless lost $1.5 billion of foreign reserves. On July 11 it let the peso float and it promptly fell 11.5 percent. The Malaysian central bank also defended the ringitt until July 11 before letting it float. The Indonesian central bank defended the rupee until August 14.

The Dragons were also affected. At the beginning of August, Singapore decided not to defend its currency and by the end of September it had fallen 8 percent. Taiwan also decided to let their currency depreciate and were not much affected. Hong Kong's exchange rate, which was pegged to the dollar came under attack. However, it was able to maintain the peg. Initially the South Korean won appreciated against the other South East Asian currencies. However, in November it lost 25 percent of its value. By the end of December 1997 which marked the end of the crisis the dollar had appreciated by 52, 52, 78, 107, and 151 percent against the Malaysian, Philippine, Thai, South Korean, and Indonesian currencies, respectively.

Although the turbulence in the currency markets was over by the end of 1997, the real effects of the crisis continued to be felt throughout the region. Many financial institutions, and industrial and commercial firms went bankrupt and output fell sharply. Overall, the crisis was extremely painful for the economies involved.

### 1.6.4 The Russian crisis and long term capital management (LTCM)

In 1994 John Meriwether who had previously worked for Salomon Brothers and had been a very successful bond trader founded LTCM. In addition to Meriwether, the other partners included two Nobel-prize winning economists, Myron Scholes and Robert Merton, and a former vice-chairman of the Federal Reserve Board, David Mullins. The fund had no problem raising $1.3 billion initially (see http://www.erisk.com/Learning/CaseStudies/ref_case_ltcm.asp and Lowenstein 2000).

The fund's main strategy was to make convergence trades. These involved finding securities whose returns were highly correlated but whose prices were slightly different. The fund would then short (i.e. borrow) the one with the high price and use the proceeds to go long in the one with the low price. The convergence trades that were taken included the sovereign bonds of European countries that were moving towards European Monetary Union, and on-the-run and off-the-run US government bonds. Since the price differences were small the strategy involved a large amount of borrowing. For example, at the beginning of 1998 the firm had equity of about \$5 billion and had borrowed over \$125 billion.

In the first two years the fund was extremely successful and earned returns for its investors of around 40 percent. However, 1997 was not as successful with a return of 27 percent which was about the same as the return on equities that year. By this time LTCM had about \$7 billion under management. Meriwether decided to return about \$2.7 billion to investors as they were not able to earn high returns with so much money under management.

On August 17, 1998 Russia devalued the rouble and declared a moratorium on about 281 billion roubles (\$13.5 billion) of government debt. Despite the small scale of the default, this triggered a global crisis with extreme volatility in many financial markets. Many of the convergence trades that LTCM had made started to lose money as the flight to quality caused prices to move in unexpected directions. By September 22, 1998 the value of LTCM's capital had fallen to \$600 million. Goldman Sachs, AIG, and Warren Buffet offered to pay \$250 million to buy out the partners and to inject \$4 billion into the business so that it would not be forced to sell out its positions. Eventually the Federal Reserve Bank of New York coordinated a rescue whereby the banks that had lent significant amounts to LTCM would pay \$3.5 million for 90 percent of the equity of the fund and take over the management of the portfolio. The reason the Fed did this was to avoid the possibility of a meltdown in global asset markets and the systemic crisis that would follow.

### 1.6.5 The Argentina crisis of 2001–2002

During the 1970's and 1980's Argentina's economy did poorly. It had a number of inflationary episodes and crises. In 1991 it introduced a currency board that pegged the Argentinian peso at a one-to-one exchange rate with the dollar. This ushered in a period of low inflation and economic growth. Despite these favorable developments, a number of weaknesses developed during this period including an increase in public sector debt and a low share of exports in output and a high concentration of these in a limited number of sectors (see IMF 2003).

In the last half of 1998 a number of events including the crisis in Brazil and the resulting devaluation and the Russian crisis triggered a sharp downturn in Argentina's economy. The public debt the government had accumulated limited the amount of fiscal stimulation that the government could undertake. Also the currency board meant that monetary policy could not be used to stimulate the economy. The recession continued to deepen. At the end of 2001, it began to become clearer that Argentina's situation was not sustainable. The government tried to take a number of measures to improve the situation such as modifying the way that the currency board operated. Exporters were subject to an exchange rate that was subsidized and importers paid a tax. The effect of these kinds of measures was to lower confidence rather than raise it. Despite an agreement with the IMF in September 2001 to inject funds of $5 billion immediately and the prospect of another $3 billion subsequently the situation continued to worsen. There were a number of attempts to restructure the public debt but again this did not restore confidence.

During November 28–30 there was a run on private sector deposits. The government then suspended convertibility in the sense that it imposed a number of controls including a weekly limit of 250 pesos on the amount that could be withdrawn from banks. In December 2001, the economy collapsed. Industrial production fell 18 percent year-on-year. Imports fell by 50 percent and construction fell 36 percent. In January 2002 the fifth president in three weeks introduced a new currency system. This involved multiple exchange rates depending on the type of transaction. In February this was abolished and the peso was allowed to float and it soon fell to 1.8 pesos to the dollar.

Overall the crisis was devastating. Real GDP fell by about 11 percent in 2002 and inflation in April 2002 went to 10 percent a month. The government defaulted on its debt. Although the economy started to recover in 2003 and has done well since then, it will be some time before it retains its pre-crisis activity.

## 1.7 THE COSTS OF CRISES

There is a large literature on the costs of crises and their resolution (see, e.g. Bordo et al. 2001; Hoggarth et al. 2002; Roubini and Setser 2004; Boyd et al. 2005; and Honohan and Laeven 2005). Much of the debate has been concerned with how exactly to measure costs. A large part of the early literature focused on the fiscal costs. This is the amount that it costs the government to recapitalize banks and reimburse insured depositors. However, these are mostly transfers rather than true costs. The subsequent literature has focused more on the lost output relative to a benchmark such as trend growth rate.

There are two important aspects of the costs of crises. The first is the high average cost and the second is the large variation in the amount of costs. Boyd et al. (2005) estimate the average discounted present value of losses in a number of different ways. Depending on the method used the mean loss is between 63 percent and 302 percent of real per capita GDP in the year before the crisis starts. The distribution of losses is very large. In Canada, France, Germany, and the US, which experienced mild nonsystemic crises, there was not any significant slowdown in growth and costs were insignificant. However, at the other extreme the slowdown and discounted loss in output were extremely high. In Hong Kong the discounted PV of losses was 1,041 percent of real output the year before the crisis.

It is the large average costs and the very high tail costs of crises that makes policymakers so averse to crises. This is why in most cases they go to such great lengths to avoid them. However, it is not clear that this is optimal. There are significant costs associated with regulations to avoid crises and in many cases crises are not very costly. An important theme of this book is that the costs of avoiding crises must be traded off against the costs of allowing crises.

## 1.8 THEORIES OF CRISES

The contrast between the majority view concerning the cause of crises in the 1930's and the view of many today is striking. In the 1930's the market was the problem and government intervention through regulation or direct ownership of banks was the solution. Today many argue that inconsistent government macroeconomic policies or moral hazard in the financial system caused by government guarantees is at the root of recent crises. Here the view is that government is the cause of crises and not the solution. Market forces are the solution.

In this book we aim to provide some perspective on this debate by developing a theoretical approach to analyze financial crises. In each chapter we will develop the basic ideas and then provide a brief account of the theoretical and empirical literature on the topic.

We start in Chapter 2 with some background material. In particular, we review the basics of time, uncertainty, and liquidity. For many readers who are quite familiar with this material it will be better to proceed straight to Chapter 3. For those who are not, or who need a refresher on models of resource allocation over time and with uncertainty, Chapter 2 will provide an introduction. The first part of the chapter develops basic ideas related to consumption and saving, and production, such as dated commodities and forward markets. The second part considers uncertainty and introduces states of nature, contingent commodities, complete markets, and Arrow securities. Attitudes toward risk, and the roles of insurance and risk pooling are also introduced. The final part of the chapter considers how liquidity and liquidity preference can be modeled.

Chapter 3 considers intermediation. In order to understand how banking crises arise it is first necessary to develop a theory of banking or more generally of intermediation. The approach adopted is to model intermediaries as providing liquidity insurance to consumers. Using this foundation two approaches to crises can be developed. Both views of crises have a long history. One view, well expounded by Kindleberger (1978), is that they occur spontaneously as a panic. The modern version was developed by Bryant (1980) and Diamond and Dybvig (1983). The analysis is based on the existence of multiple equilibria. In at least one equilibrium there is a panic while in another there is not.

The business cycle theory also has a long history (see, e.g. Mitchell 1941). The basic idea is that when the economy goes into a recession or depression the returns on bank assets will be low. Given their fixed liabilities in the form of deposits or bonds they may unable to remain solvent. This may precipitate a run on banks. Gorton (1988) showed empirically that in the US in the late nineteenth and early twentieth centuries, a leading economic indicator based on the liabilities of failed businesses could accurately predict the occurrence of banking crises. The second part of Chapter 3 develops this approach to crises.

One of the most important causes of crises is a dramatic collapse in asset prices. One explanation for this drop in prices, which is the basis for the business cycle view of crises examined in Chapter 3, is that expected future cash flows fall. Another possibility is that prices are low because of a shortage of liquidity. Chapter 4 investigates the operation of asset markets where asset price volatility is driven by liquidity shocks. The model is similar to that in Chapter 3, except there are no intermediaries. In addition there is a fixed cost to participating in markets and this can lead to limited market participation. When liquidity is plentiful, asset prices are driven by expected future payoffs in the usual way. However, when there is a scarcity of liquidity there is "cash-in-the-market pricing." In this case, an asset's price is simply the ratio of the amount sold to the amount of cash or liquidity that buyers have. Ex post buyers would like to have more liquidity when there is cash-in-the-market pricing. Ex ante they balance the opportunity cost of holding liquidity when liquidity is plentiful against the profits to be made when liquidity is scarce. This theory of asset price determination is consistent with significant asset price volatility. It is shown that there can be multiple Pareto-ranked equilibria. In one equilibrium, there is limited participation and asset prices are volatile. In another, which is Pareto-preferred, there is complete participation and asset prices are not very volatile.

Although in some crises the initial trigger is a large shock, in others it appears the trigger is a small event. For example, in the Russian crisis of 1998 discussed above, the moratorium on debt payments that triggered the crisis involved a tiny proportion of the world's assets. Nevertheless it had a huge impact on the world's financial markets. There was subsequently a period of extreme turbulence in financial markets. Understanding how this type of financial fragility can arise is the topic of Chapter 5. Rather than just focusing on banks as in Chapter 3, or on markets as in Chapter 4, here the interaction of banks and markets is considered. The markets are institutional markets in the sense that they are for banks and intermediaries to share risks and liquidity. Individuals cannot directly access these markets but instead invest their funds in banks that have access to the markets. As in Chapter 4, the key to understanding the form of equilibrium is the incentives for providing liquidity to the market. In order for banks to be willing to hold liquidity, the opportunity cost of doing this in states where the liquidity is not used must be balanced by the profits to be made when liquidity is scarce and there is cash-in-the-market pricing. It is possible to show that if such events are rare then very large changes in prices can be triggered by small changes in liquidity demand. These price changes can cause bankruptcy and disruption. There is financial fragility.

While in Chapters 3–5 the focus is on understanding the *positive* aspects of how various types of crisis can arise, in Chapter 6 we develop a general framework for understanding the *normative* aspects of crises. The model is a benchmark for investigating the welfare properties of financial systems. Similarly to Chapter 5, there are both intermediaries and markets. However, whereas in Chapter 5 markets were incomplete in the sense that hedging opportunities were limited, here we assume financial markets are complete. In particular, it is possible for intermediaries to hedge all aggregate risks in the financial markets. Under these ideal circumstances it can be shown that Adam Smith's invisible hand works. The allocation of resources is efficient in the following sense. If the contracts between intermediaries and consumers are complete in that they can also be conditioned on aggregate risks, then the allocation is (incentive) efficient.

Many contracts observed in practice between intermediaries and consumers such as debt and deposit contracts are incomplete. Provided financial markets are complete, then even if contracts between intermediaries and consumers are incomplete, it can be shown the allocation is constrained efficient. In other words, a planner subject to the same constraints in terms of incomplete contracts with consumers could not do better. What is more it is shown that the equilibrium with incomplete contracts often involves there being financial crises. For example, if a bank uses a deposit contract then there can be a banking crisis. This demonstrates that crises are not everywhere and always bad. In some cases they can increase effective contingencies and improve the allocation of resources. Of course, we are not saying that crises are always good, only that in some cases they can be, in particular when financial markets are complete and contracts between intermediaries and consumers are incomplete. If financial markets are incomplete then crises can indeed be bad. For example, as mentioned the financial fragility considered in Chapter 5 occurs because markets are incomplete. Thus the contribution of Chapter 6 is to identify when there are market failures that potentially lead to a loss of welfare.

Having identified when there is a market failure, the natural question that follows is whether there exist policies that can correct the undesirable effects of such failures. This is the topic of Chapter 7. Two types of regulation are considered. The first is the regulation of bank capital and the second is the regulation of bank liquidity. Simple examples with constant relative risk aversion consumers are analyzed when financial markets are incomplete. It is shown that the effect of bank and liquidity regulation depend critically on the degree of relative risk aversion. When relative risk aversion is sufficiently low (below 2) increasing levels of bank capital above what banks would voluntarily hold can make everybody better off. For bank liquidity regulation, requiring banks to hold more liquidity than they would choose to is welfare improving if relative risk aversion is above 1. The informational requirements for these kinds of intervention are high. Thus it may be difficult to improve welfare through these kinds of regulation as a practical matter.

The analysis in Chapters 6 and 7 stresses the ability of investors to share different risks. Risk sharing to the extent it is possible occurs because of explicit contingencies in contracts or effective contingencies that can occur if there is default. Liquidity is associated with supplies of the consumption good. There has been no role for money or variations in the price level. Chapter 8 considers the effect of allowing for money and the denomination of debt and other contracts in nominal terms. It is shown that if the central bank can vary the price level then this provides another way for risk to be shared. This is true for risks shared within a country. It is also true for risks shared between countries. By varying the exchange rate appropriately a central bank can ensure risk is shared optimally with the rest of the world. However, such international risk sharing creates a moral hazard because of the possibility that a country will borrow a lot in domestic currency and then expropriate the lenders by inflating away the value of the currency.

The final two chapters in the book consider two forms of crisis that appear to be particularly important but which were not considered earlier. In many instances financial crises occur after a bubble in asset prices collapses. How these bubbles form and collapse and their effect on the financial system is the subject of Chapter 9. The most important recent example of this phenomenon is Japan which was discussed above. In the mid 1980's the Nikkei stock index was around 10,000. By the end of the decade it had risen to around 40,000. A new governor of the Bank of Japan who was concerned that a loose monetary policy had kindled prospects of inflation decided to increase interest rates substantially. This pricked the bubble and caused stock prices to fall. Within a few months they had fallen by half. Real estate prices continued to rise for over a year however they then also started to fall. Fifteen years later both asset prices and real estate are significantly lower with stocks and real estate at around a quarter of their peak value. The fall in asset prices has led to a fall in growth and a banking crisis. Japan is by no means the only example of this phenomenon. It can be argued the Asian crisis falls into this category. In the US the Roaring 1920's and the Great Depression of the 1930's are another example.

The Asian crisis illustrated another important phenomenon, contagion. The episode started in Thailand and spread to many other countries in the region including South Korea, Malaysia, Indonesia, Hong Kong, the Philippines and Singapore. Interestingly it did not affect Taiwan nearly as much. Other regions, particularly South America, were also affected. Understanding the contagious nature of many crises has become an important topic in the literature. There are a number of theories of contagion. One is based on trade and real links, another is based on interbank markets, another on financial markets and one on payments systems. Contagion through interbank markets is the subject matter of Chapter 10.

## 1.9 CONCLUDING REMARKS

The word crisis is used in many different ways. This naturally raises the question of when a situation is a crisis and when it is not. It is perhaps helpful to consider the definition of crises. According to the dictionary (dictionary.com) a crisis is:

1. (a) the turning point for better or worse in an acute disease or fever
   (b) a paroxysmal attack of pain, distress, or disordered function
   (c) an emotionally significant event or radical change of status in a person's life

2. the decisive moment (as in a literary plot)
3. (a) an unstable or crucial time or state of affairs in which a decisive change is impending; especially : one with the distinct possibility of a highly undesirable outcome
   (b) a situation that has reached a critical phase.

This gives a range of the senses in which the word is used in general. With regard to financial crises it is also used in a wide range of situations. Banking crises usually refer to situations where many banks simultaneously come under pressure and may be forced to default. Currency crises occur when there are large volumes of trade in the foreign exchange market which can lead to a devaluation or revaluation. Similarly it is used in many other situations where big changes, usually bad, appear possible. This is the sense in which we are using the word in this book.

Historically, the study of financial crises was an important field in economics. The elimination of banking crises in the post-war period significantly reduced interest in crises and it became an area for economic historians. Now that crises have reemerged much work remains to be done using modern theoretical tools to understand the many aspects of crises. This book is designed to give a brief introduction to some of the theories that have been used to try and understand these complex events.

There is a significant empirical literature on financial crises. Much of this work is concerned with documenting regularities in the data. Since the theory is at a relatively early stage there is relatively little work trying to distinguish between different theories of crises. In the chapters below the historical and empirical work is discussed as a background to the theory. Much work remains to be done in this area too.

There is a tendency in much of the literature on crises to argue that the particular theory being presented is "THE" theory of crises. As even the brief discussion in this chapter indicates crises are complex phenomena in practice. One of the main themes of this book is that there is no one theory of crises that can explain all aspects of the phenomena of interest. In general, the theories of crises that we will focus on are not mutually exclusive. Actual crises may contain elements of some combination of these theories.

## REFERENCES

Bagehot, W. (1873). *Lombard Street: A Description of the Money Market*, London: H. S. King.

Bordo, M. (1986). "Financial Crises, Banking Crises, Stock Market Crashes and the Money Supply: Some International Evidence, 1870-1933," in F. Capie and G. Wood (eds.), *Financial Crises and the World Banking System*. New York: St. Martin's Press, 1986, 190–248.

Bordo, M. and B. Eichengreen (1999). "Is Our Current International Economic Environment Unusually Crisis Prone?" Working paper, Rutgers University.

Bordo, M., B. Eichengreen, D. Klingebiel and M. Martinez-Peria (2000). "Is the Crisis Problem Growing More Severe?" Working paper, University of California, Berkeley. Updated version of previous paper. http://emlab.berkeley.edu/users/eichengr /research.html – this link also allows you to download the figures: scroll down the page until you reach the link to the paper and figures – see also http://www.haas.berkeley.edu/ arose/BEKSc.pdf

Bordo, M., B. Eichengreen, D. Klingebiel and M. Martinez-Peria (2001). "Is the Crisis Problem Growing More Severe?" *Economic Policy*, April 2001, 53–82 + Web Appendix.

Boyd, J., S. Kwak, and B. Smith (2005). "The Real Output Losses Associated with Modern Banking Crises," *Journal of Money, Credit, and Banking* 37, 977–999.

Bryant, J. (1980). "A Model of Reserves, Bank Runs, and Deposit Insurance," *Journal of Banking and Finance* 4, 335–344.

Diamond, D. and P. Dybvig (1983). "Bank Runs, Deposit Insurance, and Liquidity," *Journal of Political Economy* 91, 401–419.

Englund, P. and V. Vihriälä (2006). "Financial Crises in Developed Economies: The Cases of Finland and Sweden," Chapter 3 in Lars Jonung (ed.), *Crises, Macroeconomic Performance and Economic Policies in Finland and Sweden in the 1990s: A Comparative Approach*, forthcoming.

Fourçans, A. and R. Franck (2003). *Currency Crises: A Theoretical and Empirical Perspective*, Northampton, MA: Edward Elgar.

Frankel, J. (1993). "The Japanese Financial System and the Cost of Capital," in S. Takagi (ed.), *Japanese Capital Markets: New Developments in Regulations and Institutions*, Oxford: Blackwell, 21–77.

Gorton, G. (1988). "Banking Panics and Business Cycles," *Oxford Economic Papers* 40, 751–781.

Heiskanen, R. (1993). "The Banking Crisis in the Nordic Countries," *Kansallis Economic Review* 2, 13–19.

Hoggarth, G., R. Reis, and V. Saporta (2002). "Costs of Banking System Instability: Some Empirical Evidence," *Journal of Banking and Finance* 26, 825–855.

Honohan, P. and L. Laeven (2005). *Systemic Financial Crises: Containment and Resolution*, Cambridge, UK: Cambridge University Press.

IMF (2003). "Lessons form the Crisis in Argentina," Washington, DC: IMF, http://www.imf.org/external/np/pdr/lessons/100803.pdf.

Kindleberger, C. (1978). *Manias, Panics, and Crashes: A History of Financial Crises*, New York: Basic Books.

Kindleberger, C. (1993). *A Financial History of Western Europe* (second edition), New York: Oxford University Press.

Lowenstein, R. (2000). *When Genius Failed: The Rise and Fall of Long-Term Capital Management*, New York: Random House.

Mikitani, R. and A. Posen (2000). *Japan's Financial Crisis and its Parallels to U.S. Experience*, Washington, DC: Institute for International Economics, Special Report 13.

Mitchell, W. (1941). *Business Cycles and Their Causes*, Berkeley: University of California Press.

Roubini, N. and B. Setser (2004). *Bailouts or Bail-Ins? Responding to Financial Crises in Emerging Economies*, Washington, DC: Institute for International Economics.

Sprague, O. (1910). *A History of Crises Under the National Banking System*, National Monetary Commission, Washington DC: U.S. Government Printing Office.

Studenski, P. and H. Krooss (1963). *Financial History of the United States* (second edition), New York: McGraw Hill.

Timberlake, R. (1978). *The Origins of Central Banking in the United States*, Cambridge MA: Harvard University Press.

Tschoegl, A. (1993). "Modeling the Behaviour of Japanese Stock Indices," in S. Takagi (ed.), *Japanese Capital Markets: New Developments in Regulations and Institutions*, Oxford: Blackwell, 371–400.

Wilson, J., R. Sylla and C. Jones (1990). "Financial Market Panics and Volatility in the Long Run, 1830–1988," in E. White (ed.), *Crashes and Panics*, Illinois: Dow-Jones Irwin, 85–125.

# 2

## Time, uncertainty, and liquidity

Financial economics deals with the allocation of resources over time and in the face of uncertainty. Although we use terms like "present values," "states of nature," and "contingent commodities" to analyze resource allocation in these settings, the basic ideas are identical to those used in the analysis of consumer and producer behavior in ordinary microeconomic theory. In this chapter we review familiar concepts such as preferences, budget constraints, and production technologies in a new setting, where we use them to study the intertemporal allocation of resources and the allocation of risk. We use simple examples to explain these ideas and later show how the ideas can be extended and generalized.

### 2.1 EFFICIENT ALLOCATION OVER TIME

We begin with the allocation of resources over time. Although we introduce some new terminology, the key concepts are the same as concepts familiar from the study of efficient allocation in a "timeless" environment. We assume that time is divided into two periods, which we can think of as representing the "present" and the "future." We call these periods **dates** and index them by $t = 0, 1$, where date 0 is the present and date 1 is the future.

#### 2.1.1 Consumption and saving

Suppose a consumer has an **income stream** consisting of $Y_0$ units of a homogeneous consumption good at date 0 and $Y_1$ units of the consumption good at date 1. The consumer's utility $U(C_0, C_1)$ is a function of his **consumption stream** $(C_0, C_1)$, where $C_0$ is consumption at date 0 and $C_1$ is consumption at date 1. The consumer wants to maximize his utility but first has to decide which consumption streams $(C_0, C_1)$ belong to his **budget set**, that is, which streams are feasible for him. There are several ways of looking at this question. They all lead to the same answer, but it is worth considering each one in turn.

*Borrowing and lending*

One way of posing the question (of which consumption streams the consumer can afford) is to ask whether the income stream $(Y_0, Y_1)$ can be transformed into a consumption stream $(C_0, C_1)$ by borrowing and lending. For simplicity, we suppose there is a bank that is willing to lend any amount at the fixed interest rate $i > 0$ per period, that is, the bank will lend one unit of present consumption today in exchange for repayment of $(1 + i)$ units in the future. Suppose the consumer decided to spend $C_0 > Y_0$ today. Then he would have to borrow $B = C_0 - Y_0$ in order to balance his budget today, and this borrowing would have to be repaid with interest $iB$ in the future. The consumer could afford to do this if and only if his future income exceeds his future consumption by the amount of the principal and interest, that is,

$$(1 + i)B \leq Y_1 - C_1.$$

We can rewrite this inequality in terms of the consumption and income streams as follows:

$$C_0 - Y_0 \leq \frac{1}{1 + i}(Y_1 - C_1).$$

Conversely, if the consumer decided to consume $C_0 \leq Y_0$ in the present, he could save the difference $S = Y_0 - C_0$ and deposit it with the bank. We suppose that the bank is willing to pay the same interest rate $i > 0$ on deposits that it earns on loans, that is, one unit of present consumption deposited with the bank today will be worth $(1 + i)$ units in the future. The consumer will receive his savings with interest in the future, so his future consumption could exceed his income by $(1 + i)S$, that is,

$$C_1 - Y_1 \leq (1 + i)S.$$

We can rewrite this inequality in terms of the consumption and income streams as follows:

$$C_0 - Y_0 \leq \frac{1}{1 + i}(Y_1 - C_1).$$

Notice that this is the same inequality as we derived before. Thus, any feasible consumption stream, whether it involves saving or borrowing, must satisfy the same constraint. We call this constraint the **intertemporal budget constraint** and write it for future reference in a slightly different form:

$$C_0 + \frac{1}{1 + i}C_1 \leq Y_0 + \frac{1}{1 + i}Y_1. \tag{2.1}$$

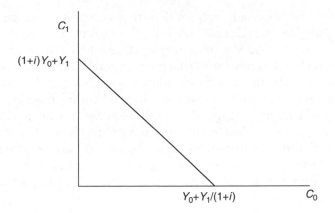

**Figure 2.1.** Intertemporal budget constraint.

Figure 2.1 illustrates the set of consumption streams $(C_0, C_1)$ that satisfy the intertemporal budget constraint. It is easy to see that the income stream $(Y_0, Y_1)$ must satisfy the intertemporal budget constraint. If there is neither borrowing nor lending in the first period then $C_0 = Y_0$ and $C_1 = Y_1$. The endpoints of the line represent the levels of consumption that would be possible if the individual were to consume as much as possible in the present and future, respectively. For example, if he wants to consume as much as possible in the present, he has $Y_0$ units of income today and he can borrow $B = Y_1/(1 + i)$ units of the good against his future income. This is the maximum he can borrow because in the future he will have to repay the principal $B$ plus the interest $iB$, for a total of $(1 + i)B = Y_1$. So the maximum amount he can spend today is given by

$$C_0 = Y_0 + B = Y_0 + \frac{Y_1}{1 + i}.$$

Conversely, if he wants to consume as much as possible in the future, he will save his entire income in the present. In the future, he will get his savings with interest $(1 + i)Y_0$ plus his future income $Y_1$. So the maximum amount he can spend in the future is

$$C_1 = (1 + i)Y_0 + Y_1.$$

Suppose now that consumption in the first period is increased by $\Delta C_0$. By how much must future consumption be reduced? Every unit borrowed in the first period will cost $(1 + i)$ in the second because interest must be paid. So the decrease in second period consumption is $\Delta C_1 = -(1 + i)\Delta C_0$. This shows that he can afford any consumption stream on the line between the two endpoints with constant slope $= -(1 + i)$. (See Figure 2.1.)

We have shown that any consumption stream that can be achieved by borrowing and lending must satisfy the intertemporal budget constraint. Conversely, we can show that any consumption stream $(C_0, C_1)$ that satisfies the intertemporal budget constraint can be achieved by some feasible pattern of borrowing or lending (saving). To see this, suppose that the intertemporal budget constraint is satisfied by the consumption stream $(C_0, C_1)$. If $C_0 > Y_0$ we assume the consumer borrows $B = C_0 - Y_0$. In the future he has to repay his loan with interest, so he only has $Y_1 - (1 + i)B$ left to spend on consumption. However, the intertemporal budget constraint ensures that his planned future consumption $C_1$ satisfies

$$C_1 \leq (1 + i)(Y_0 - C_0) + Y_1$$
$$= Y_1 - (1 + i)(C_0 - Y_0).$$

So the consumer can borrow $B$ units today and repay it with interest tomorrow and still afford his planned future consumption. The other case where $C_0 \leq Y_0$ is handled similarly. Thus, we have seen that the income stream $(Y_0, Y_1)$ can be transformed into the consumption stream $(C_0, C_1)$ through borrowing or lending at the interest rate $i$ if and only if it satisfies the intertemporal budget constraint (2.1).

## Wealth and present values

Another way of thinking about the set of affordable consumption streams makes use of the concept of present values. The present value of any good is the amount of present consumption that someone would give for it. The present value of one unit of present consumption is 1. The present value of one unit of future consumption is $1/(1 + i)$, because one unit of present consumption can be converted into $1 + i$ units of future consumption, and vice versa, through borrowing and lending. Thus, the present value of the income stream $(Y_0, Y_1)$, that is, the value of $(Y_0, Y_1)$ in terms of present consumption is

$$PV(Y_0, Y_1) \equiv Y_0 + \frac{1}{1 + i}Y_1$$

and the present value of the consumption stream $(C_0, C_1)$ is

$$PV(C_0, C_1) \equiv C_0 + \frac{1}{1 + i}C_1.$$

The intertemporal budget constraint says that the present value of the consumption stream $(C_0, C_1)$ must be less than or equal to the present value of the consumer's income stream.

The present value of the income stream $(Y_0, Y_1)$ is also called the consumer's **wealth**, denoted by $W \equiv Y_0 + \frac{1}{1+i}Y_1$. The intertemporal budget constraint allows the consumer to choose any consumption stream $(C_1, C_2)$ whose present value does not exceed his wealth, that is,

$$C_0 + \frac{C_1}{1+i} \leq W. \tag{2.2}$$

### Dated commodities and forward markets

There is still a third way to interpret the intertemporal budget constraint (2.1). We are familiar with the budget constraint of a consumer who has to divide his income between two goods, beer and pizza, for example. There is a price at which each good can be purchased and the value of consumption is calculated by multiplying the quantity of each good by the price and adding the two expenditures. The consumer's budget constraint says that the value of his consumption must be less than or equal to his income. The intertemporal budget constraint (2.1) can be interpreted in this way too. Suppose we treat present consumption and future consumption as two different commodities and assume that there are markets on which the two commodities can be traded. We assume these markets are perfectly competitive, so the consumer can buy and sell as much as he likes of both commodities at the prevailing prices. The usual budget constraint requires the consumer to balance the value of his purchases and expenditures on the two commodities. If $p_0$ is the price of present consumption and $p_1$ is the price of future consumption, then the ordinary budget constraint can be written as

$$p_0 C_0 + p_1 C_1 \leq p_0 Y_0 + p_1 Y_1.$$

Suppose that we want to use the first-period consumption good as our **numeraire**, that is, measure the value of every commodity in terms of this good. Then the price of present consumption is $p_0 = 1$, since one unit of the good at date 0 is worth exactly one (unit of the good at date 0). How much is the good at date 1 worth in terms of the good at date 1? If it is possible to borrow and lend at the interest rate $i$, the price of the good at date 1 will be determined by **arbitrage**. If $p_1 > \frac{1}{1+i}$, then anyone can make a riskless arbitrage profit by selling one unit of future consumption for $p_1$, using the proceeds to buy $\frac{1}{1+i}$ units of present consumption, and investing the $\frac{1}{1+i}$ units at the interest rate $i$

to yield $(1+i)\frac{1}{1+i} = 1$ unit of future consumption. This strategy yields a profit of $p_1 - \frac{1}{1+i}$ at date 0 and has no cost since the unit of future consumption that is sold is provided by the investment at date 0. Such a risk free profit is incompatible with equilibrium, since anyone can use this arbitrage to generate unlimited wealth. Thus, in equilibrium we must have $p_1 \leq \frac{1}{1+i}$.

A similar argument can be used to show that if $p_1 < \frac{1}{1+i}$, it is possible to make a risk free profit by borrowing $\frac{1}{1+i}$ units of present consumption, buying one unit of future consumption at the price $p_1$, and using it to repay the loan at date 1. Thus, in equilibrium, we must have $p_1 \geq \frac{1}{1+i}$.

Putting these two arbitrage arguments together, we can see that, if it is possible to borrow and lend at the interest rate $i$ and present consumption is the numeraire, the only prices consistent with equilibrium are $p_0 = 1$ and $p_1 = \frac{1}{1+i}$.

Substituting the prices $p_0 = 1$ and $p_1 = \frac{1}{1+i}$ into the budget constraint above, we see that it is exactly equivalent to the intertemporal budget constraint (2.1). Borrowing and lending at a constant interest rate is equivalent to having a market in which present and future consumption can be exchanged at the constant prices $(p_0, p_1)$. The same good delivered at two different dates is two different commodities and present and future consumption are, in fact, simply two different commodities with two distinct prices. From this point of view, the intertemporal budget constraint is just a new interpretation of the familiar consumer's budget constraint.

## Consumption and saving

Since the consumer's choices among consumption streams $(C_0, C_1)$ are completely characterized by the intertemporal budget constraint, the consumer's decision problem is to maximize his utility $U(C_0, C_1)$ by choosing a consumption stream $(C_0, C_1)$ that satisfies the budget constraint. We represent this decision problem schematically by

$$\max \quad U(C_0, C_1)$$
$$\text{s.t.} \quad C_0 + \frac{C_1}{1+i} = W.$$

Note that here we assume the budget constraint is satisfied as an equality rather than an inequality. Since more consumption is preferred to less, there is no loss of generality in assuming that the consumer will always spend as much as he can on consumption. The solution to this maximization problem is illustrated in Figure 2.2, where the optimum occurs at the point on the budget constraint where the indifference curve is tangent to the budget constraint.

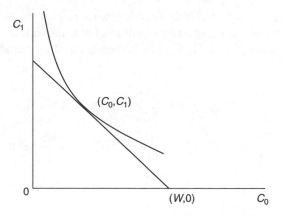

**Figure 2.2.** Consumption and saving.

The slope of the budget constraint is $-(1+i)$ and the slope of the indifference curve at the optimum point is

$$-\frac{\frac{\partial U}{\partial C_0}(C_0^*, C_1^*)}{\frac{\partial U}{\partial C_1}(C_0^*, C_1^*)},$$

so the tangency condition can be written as

$$\frac{\frac{\partial U}{\partial C_0}(C_0^*, C_1^*)}{\frac{\partial U}{\partial C_1}(C_0^*, C_1^*)} = (1+i).$$

It is easy to interpret the first-order condition by rewriting it as

$$\frac{\partial U}{\partial C_0}(C_0^*, C_1^*) = (1+i)\frac{\partial U}{\partial C_1}(C_0^*, C_1^*).$$

The left hand side is the marginal utility of consumption at date 0. The right hand side is the marginal utility of $(1+i)$ units of consumption at date 1. One unit of the good at date 0 can be saved to provide $1+i$ units of the good at date 1. So the first-order condition says that the consumer is indifferent between consuming one unit at date 0 and saving it until date 1 when it will be worth $(1+i)$ units and then consuming the $(1+i)$ units at date 1.

An alternative to the graphical method of finding the optimum is to use the method of Lagrange, which requires us to form the Lagrangean function

$$\mathcal{L}(C_0, C_1, \lambda) = U(C_0, C_1) - \lambda\left(C_0 + \frac{1}{1+i}C_1 - W\right)$$

and maximize the value of this function with respect to $C_0$, $C_1$, and the Lagrange multiplier $\lambda$. A necessary condition for a maximum at $(C_0^*, C_1^*, \lambda^*)$ is that the derivatives of $\mathcal{L}(C_0, C_1, \lambda)$ with respect to these variables should all be zero. Then

$$\frac{\partial \mathcal{L}}{\partial C_0}(C_0^*, C_1^*, \lambda^*) = \frac{\partial U}{\partial C_0}(C_0^*, C_1^*) - \lambda^* = 0,$$

$$\frac{\partial \mathcal{L}}{\partial C_1}(C_0^*, C_1^*, \lambda^*) = \frac{\partial U}{\partial C_0}(C_0^*, C_1^*) - \frac{\lambda^*}{1+i} = 0,$$

$$\frac{\partial \mathcal{L}}{\partial \lambda}(C_0^*, C_1^*, \lambda^*) = C_0^* + \frac{1}{1+i}C_1^* - W = 0.$$

The first two conditions are equivalent to the tangency condition derived earlier. To see this, eliminate $\lambda^*$ from these equations to get

$$\frac{\partial U}{\partial C_0}(C_0^*, C_1^*) = \lambda^* = (1+i)\frac{\partial U}{\partial C_0}(C_0^*, C_1^*).$$

The last of the three conditions simply asserts that the budget constraint must be satisfied.

As before, the optimum $(C_0^*, C_1^*)$ is determined by the tangency condition and the budget constraint.

Clearly, the optimal consumption stream $(C_0^*, C_1^*)$ will be a function of the consumer's wealth $W$ and the rate of interest $i$. If the pattern of income were $(W, 0)$ instead of $(Y_1, Y_2)$ the value of wealth would be the same and hence the budget line would be the same. So the same point $(C_1^*, C_2^*)$ would be chosen. In fact $(Y_1, Y_2)$ could move to any other point on the budget line without affecting consumption. Only savings or borrowing would change.

On the other hand, an increase in $W$ to $W'$, say, will shift the budget line out and increase consumption. The case illustrated in Figure 2.3 has the special property that the marginal rate of substitution is constant along a straight line OA through the origin. The slope of the budget line does not change so in this case the point of tangency moves along the line OA as $W$ changes. In this special case, $C_1$ is proportional to $W$.

## Problems

1. An individual consumer has an income stream $(Y_0, Y_1)$ and can borrow and lend at the interest rate $i$. For each of the following data points, determine whether the consumption stream $(C_0, C_1)$ lies within the consumer's budget

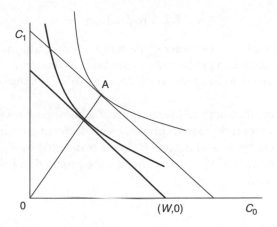

**Figure 2.3.** The effect of an increase in wealth.

set (i.e. whether it satisfies the intertemporal budget constraint).

| $(C_0, C_1)$ | $(Y_0, Y_1)$ | $(1 + i)$ |
|---|---|---|
| $(10, 25)$ | $(15, 15)$ | 2 |
| $(18, 11)$ | $(15, 15)$ | 1.1 |
| $(18, 11)$ | $(15, 15)$ | 1.5 |
| $(10, 25)$ | $(15, 15)$ | 1.8 |

Draw a graph to illustrate your answer in each case.

2. An individual consumer has an income stream $(Y_0, Y_1) = (100, 50)$ and can borrow and lend at the interest rate $i = 0.1\dot{1}$. His preferences are represented by the additively separable utility function

$$U(C_0, C_1) = \log C_0 + 0.9 \log C_1.$$

The marginal utility of consumption in period $t$ is

$$\frac{d \log C_t}{dC_t} = \frac{1}{C_t}.$$

Write down the consumer's intertemporal budget constraint and the first-order condition that must be satisfied by the optimal consumption stream. Use the first-order condition and the consumer's intertemporal budget constraint to find the consumption stream $(C_0^*, C_1^*)$ that maximizes utility. How much will the consumer save in the first period? How much will his savings be worth in the second period? Check that he can afford the optimal consumption $C_1^*$ in the second period.

## 2.1.2 Production

Just as we can cast the consumer's intertemporal decision into the familiar framework of maximizing utility subject to a budget constraint, we can cast the firm's intertemporal decision into the form of a profit- or value-maximization problem.

Imagine a firm that can produce outputs of a homogeneous good in either period subject to a production technology with decreasing returns. Output at date 0 is denoted by $Y_0$ and output at date 1 is denoted by $Y_1$. The possible combinations of $Y_0$ and $Y_1$ are described by the production possibility curve illustrated in Figure 2.4.

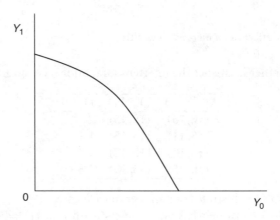

**Figure 2.4.** The production possibility curve.

Note the following properties of the production possibility curve:

- the curve is downward sloping to the right because the firm must reduce output tomorrow in order to increase the output today;
- the curve is convex upward because of the diminishing returns – as the firm decreases output today, each additional unit of present output foregone adds less to output tomorrow.

The production technology can be represented by a transformation function $F(Y_0, Y_1)$. A pair of outputs $(Y_0, Y_1)$ is feasible if and only if it satisfies the inequality

$$F(Y_0, Y_1) \leq 0.$$

The function $F$ is said to be **increasing** if an increase in $Y_0$ or $Y_1$ increases the value $F(Y_0, Y_1)$. The function $F$ is said to be **convex** if, for any output streams

$(Y_0, Y_1)$ and $(Y_0', Y_1')$ and any number $0 < t < 1$,

$$F\left(t\,(Y_0, Y_1) + (1 - t)\,(Y_0', Y_1')\right) \leq tF\,(Y_0, Y_1) + (1 - t)\,F\left(Y_0', Y_1'\right).$$

If $F$ is increasing, then the production possibility curve is downward sloping. If the function $F$ is convex, the production possibility curve is convex upward. In other words, if $(Y_0, Y_1)$ and $(Y_0', Y_1')$ are feasible, then any point on the line segment between them is feasible.

To illustrate the meaning of the transformation curve, suppose that the firm's past investments produce an output of $\bar{Y}_0$ at the beginning of period 0. The firm can re-invest $K_0$ units and sell the remaining $Y_0 = \bar{Y}_0 - K_0$. The investment of $K_0$ units today produces $Y_1 = G(K_0)$ in the future (assume there is no investment in the future because the firm is being wound up). Then the firm can produce any combination of present and future goods $(Y_0, Y_1)$ for sale that satisfies $Y_0 \leq \bar{Y}_0$ and $Y_1 = G(\bar{Y}_0 - Y_0)$. Then the transformation curve $F(Y_0, Y_1)$ can be defined by

$$F(Y_0, Y_1) = Y_1 - G(\bar{Y}_0 - Y_0).$$

Which combination of outputs $Y_0$ and $Y_1$ should the firm choose? In general, there may be many factors that will guide the firm's decision, but under certain circumstances the firm can ignore all these factors and consider only the market value of the firm. To see this, we need only recall our discussion of the consumer's decision. Suppose that the firm is owned by a single shareholder who receives the firm's outputs as income. If the consumer can borrow and lend as much as he wants at the rate $i$, all he cares about is his wealth, the present value of the income stream $(Y_0, Y_1)$. The exact time-profile of income $(Y_0, Y_1)$ does not matter. So if the firm wants to maximize its shareholder's welfare, it should maximize the shareholder's wealth. To make these ideas more precise, suppose that the firm has a single owner-manager who chooses both the firm's production plan $(Y_0, Y_1)$ and his consumption stream $(C_0, C_1)$ to maximize his utility subject to his intertemporal budget constraint. Formally, we can write this decision problem as follows:

$$\max \quad U(C_0, C_1)$$
$$\text{s.t.} \quad F(Y_0, Y_1) \leq 0$$
$$C_0 + \tfrac{1}{1+i}C_1 \leq W \equiv Y_0 + \frac{1}{1+i}Y_1.$$

Then it is clear that the choice of $(Y_0, Y_1)$ affects utility only through the intertemporal budget constraint and that anything that increases the present value of the firm's output stream will allow the consumer to reach a more desirable consumption stream. Thus, the joint consumption and production decision above is equivalent to the following two-stage procedure. First, have the firm maximize the present value of outputs:

$$\max \quad W \equiv Y_0 + \frac{1}{1+i} Y_1$$
$$\text{s.t.} \quad F(Y_0, Y_1) \leq 0.$$

The present value of outputs is also known as the **market value of the firm**, so this operational rule can be rephrased to say that firms should always maximize market value. Then have the consumer maximize his utility taking the firm's market value as given:

$$\max \quad U(C_0, C_1)$$
$$\text{s.t.} \quad C_0 + \frac{1}{1+i} C_1 \leq W,$$

where $W = Y_0 + \frac{1}{1+i} Y_1$. Figure 2.5 illustrates this principle for the case of a single shareholder.

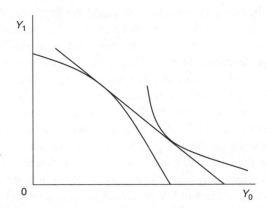

**Figure 2.5.** Value maximization and utility maximization.

In fact, this argument extends to the case where there are many shareholders with different time preferences. Some shareholders may be impatient and want to consume more in the present while others are more patient and are willing to postpone consumption, but all will agree that a change in production that increases the present value of output must be a good thing, because it increases the consumers' wealth. Figure 2.6 illustrates the case of two shareholders with equal shares in the firm. Then they have identical budget constraints with

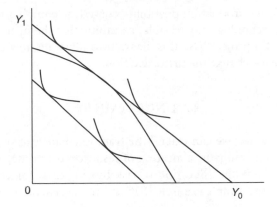

**Figure 2.6.** The separation theorem.

slope $-(1 + i)$, i.e. their budget constraint is parallel to the maximum value line that is tangent to the production possibility frontier. Each shareholder will choose to consume the bundle of goods $(C_0, C_1)$ that maximizes his utility subject to the budget constraint. Because they have different time preferences, represented here by different indifference curves, each shareholder will choose a different bundle of goods, as indicated by the different points of tangency between indifference curves and budget constraint. Nonetheless, both agree that the firm should maximize its market value, because maximizing the value of the firm has the effect of putting both shareholders on the highest possible budget constraint. This is known as the **separation theorem** because the firm's decision to maximize its value is separate from shareholders' decisions to maximize their utility.

**Problem**

3. A firm has 100 units of output at the beginning of period 0. It has three projects that it can finance. Each project requires an input of $I$ units of the good at date 0 and produces $Y_1$ units of the good at date 1. The projects are defined in the following table:

| Project | Investment $I$ | Output $Y_1$ |
|---------|---------------|--------------|
| 1 | 20 | 30 |
| 2 | 30 | 48 |
| 3 | 50 | 70 |

Which projects should the firm undertake when the interest factor is

$$1 + i = 2, 1.5, 1.1?$$

Trace the firm's production possibility curve (the combinations of $Y_0$ and $Y_1$ that are technologically feasible) assuming that the firm can undertake a fraction of a project. Use this diagram to illustrate how changes in the discount factor change the firm's decision.

## 2.2 UNCERTAINTY

In the same way that we can extend the traditional analysis of consumption and production to study the allocation of resources over time, we can use the same ideas to study the allocation of risk bearing under uncertainty. Once again we shall use a simple example to illustrate the general principles.

### 2.2.1 Contingent commodities and risk sharing

We assume that time is divided into two periods or dates indexed by $t = 0, 1$. At date 0 (the present) there is some uncertainty about the future. For example, an individual may be uncertain about his future income. We can represent this uncertainty by saying that there are several possible **states of nature**. A state of nature is a complete description of all the uncertain, exogenous factors that may be relevant for the outcome of an individual's decision. For example, a farmer who is planting a crop may be uncertain about the weather. The size of his crop will depend on choices he makes about the time to plant, the use of fertilizers, etc., as well as the weather. In this case, we identify the weather with the state of nature. Each state would be a complete description of the weather – the amount of rainfall, the temperature, etc. – during the growing season. The outcome of the farmer's choices will depend on the parameters he determines – time to plant, etc. – and the state of nature. In other words, once we know the farmer's choices and the state of nature, we should know the size of the crop; but even after the farmer has determined all the parameters that he controls, the fact that the state is still unknown means that the size of the crop is uncertain.

In what follows we assume that the only uncertainty relates to an individual's income, so income is a function of the state of nature. The true state of nature is unknown at date 0 and will be revealed at date 1. For simplicity, suppose that there are two possible states indexed by $s = H, L$. The letters $H$ and $L$ stand for "high" and "low."

Commodities are distinguished by their physical characteristics, by the date at which they are delivered, and by the state in which they are delivered. Thus, the consumption good in state $H$ is a different commodity from the consumption good in state $L$. We call a good whose delivery is contingent on the occurrence of a particular state of nature a **contingent commodity**. By adopting this convention, we can represent uncertainty about income and consumption in terms of a bundle of contingent commodities. If $Y_H$ denotes future income in state $H$ and $Y_L$ denotes income in state $L$, the ordered pair $(Y_H, Y_L)$ completely describes the future uncertainty about the individual's income. By treating $(Y_H, Y_L)$ as a bundle of different (contingent) commodities, we can analyze choices under uncertainty in the same way that we analyze choices among goods with different physical characteristics. We assume that $Y_H > Y_L$, that is, income is higher in the "high" state.

An individual's preferences over uncertain consumption outcomes can be represented by a utility function that is defined on bundles of contingent commodities. Let $U(C_H, C_L)$ denote the consumer's utility from the bundle of contingent commodities $(C_H, C_L)$, where $C_H$ denotes future consumption in state $H$ and $C_L$ denotes future consumption in state $L$. Later, we introduce the notion of a state's probability and distinguish between an individual's probability beliefs and his attitudes to risk. Here, an individual's beliefs about the probability of a state and his attitudes towards risk are subsumed in his preferences over bundles of contingent commodities.

*Complete markets*

There are two equivalent ways of achieving an efficient allocation of risk. One approach to the allocation of risk assumes that there are **complete markets** for contingent commodities. An economy with complete markets is often referred to as an Arrow–Debreu economy. In an Arrow–Debreu economy, there is a market for each contingent commodity and a prevailing price at which consumers can trade as much of the commodity as they like subject to their budget constraint. Let $p_H$ and $p_L$ denote the price of the contingent commodities corresponding to states $H$ and $L$, respectively. The consumer's income consists of different amounts of the two contingent commodities, $Y_H$ units of the consumption good in state $H$ and $Y_L$ units of the consumption good in state $L$. We can use the complete markets to value this uncertain income stream and the consumer's wealth is $p_H Y_H + p_L Y_L$. Then the consumer's budget constraint, which says that his consumption expenditure must be less than or equal to his wealth, can be written as

$$p_H C_H + p_L C_L \leq p_H Y_H + p_L Y_L.$$

The consumer can afford any bundle of contingent commodities $(C_H, C_L)$ that satisfies this constraint. He chooses the consumption bundle that maximizes his utility $U(C_H, C_L)$ subject to this constraint. We illustrate the consumer's decision problem in Figure 2.7.

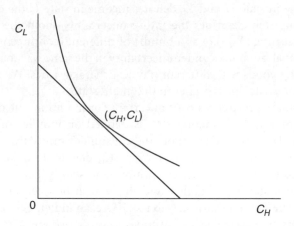

**Figure 2.7.** Maximizing utility under uncertainty.


## Arrow securities

The assumption of complete markets guarantees efficient allocation of risk, but it may not be realistic to assume that every contingent commodity, of which there will be a huge number in practice, unlike in our example, can literally be traded at the initial date. Fortunately, there exists an alternative formulation which is equivalent in terms of its efficiency properties, but requires far fewer markets. More precisely, it requires that securities and goods be traded on spot markets at each date, but the total number of spot markets is much less than the number of contingent commodities.

The alternative representation of the allocation of risk makes use of the idea of **Arrow securities**. We define an Arrow security to be a promise to deliver one unit of money (or an abstract unit of account) if a given state occurs and nothing otherwise. In terms of the present example, there are two types of Arrow securities, corresponding to the states $H$ and $L$ respectively. Let $q_H$ denote the price of the Arrow security corresponding to state $H$ and let $q_L$ denote the price of the Arrow security in state $L$. In other words, $q_H$ is the price of one unit of account (one "dollar") delivered in state $H$ at date 1 and $q_L$ is the price of one unit of account delivered in state $L$ at date 1. A consumer can trade Arrow securities at date 0 in order to hedge against income risks at date 1. Let $Z_H$ and $Z_L$ denote the excess demand for the Arrow securities corresponding to states $H$ and $L$ respectively.[1] If $Z_s > 0$ then the consumer is taking a long position (offering to buy) in the Arrow security and if $Z_s < 0$ the consumer is taking a short position (offering to sell). We assume the consumer has no income at date 0 – this period exists only to allow individuals to hedge risks that occur at date 1 – so the consumer has to balance his budget by selling one security in order to purchase the other. Suppose that the consumer chooses a portfolio $Z = (Z_H, Z_L)$ of Arrow securities. Then at date 1, once the true state has been revealed, his budget constraint will be

$$\hat{p}_H C_H \leq \hat{p}_H Y_H + Z_H, \tag{2.3}$$

if state $H$ occurs, and

$$\hat{p}_L C_L \leq \hat{p}_L Y_L + Z_L, \tag{2.4}$$

if state $L$ occurs. The consumer will choose the portfolio $Z$ and the consumption bundle $(C_H, C_L)$ to maximize $U(C_H, C_L)$ subject to the date-0 budget constraint

$$q_H Z_H + q_L Z_L \leq 0$$

and the budget constraints (2.3) and (2.4). Since $Z_H = \hat{p}_H (C_H - Y_H)$ and $Z_L = \hat{p}_L (C_L - Y_L)$, the budget constraint at date 0 is equivalent to $q_H \hat{p}_H (C_H - Y_H) + q_L \hat{p}_L (C_L - Y_L) \leq 0$ or

$$q_H \hat{p}_H C_H + q_L \hat{p}_L C_L \leq q_H \hat{p}_H Y_H + q_L \hat{p}_L Y_L.$$

This looks just like the standard budget constraint in which we interpret $p_H = q_H \hat{p}_H$ and $p_L = q_L \hat{p}_L$ as the prices of contingent commodities and $C_H$ and $C_L$ as the demands for contingent commodities.

Now that we have seen how to interpret the allocation of risk in terms of contingent commodities, we can use the standard framework to analyze efficient risk sharing. Figure 2.8 shows an Edgeworth box in which the axes correspond to consumption in state $H$ and consumption in state $L$. A competitive equilibrium in which consumers maximize utility subject to their budget constraint leads to an efficient allocation of contingent commodities, that is, an efficient allocation of risk.

As usual, the conditions for efficiency include the equality of the two consumers' marginal rates of substitution, but here the interpretation is different.

---

[1] Each agent begins with a zero net supply of Arrow securities. Then agents issue securities for one state in order to pay for their purchase of securities in the other. The vector $Z$ represents the agent's net or excess demand of each security: a component $Z_s$ is negative if his supply of the security (equals minus the excess demand) is positive and positive if his net demand is positive.

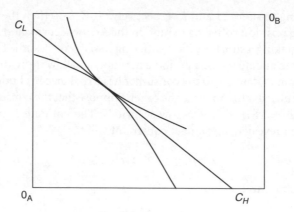

**Figure 2.8.** Efficient allocation of risk between two agents.

We are equating the marginal rates of substitution between consumption in the two states rather than two different (physical) goods. The marginal rate of substitution will reflect an individual's subjective belief about the probability of each state as well as his attitude toward risk.

### 2.2.2 Attitudes toward risk

To characterize individuals' attitudes toward risk we introduce a special kind of utility function, which we call a **von Neumann–Morgenstern** (VNM) utility function. Whereas the standard utility function is defined on bundles of contingent commodities, the VNM utility is defined on quantities of consumption in a particular state. Von Neumann and Morgenstern showed that, under certain conditions, a rational individual would act so as to maximize the expected value of his VNM utility function. If individuals satisfy the assumptions of the VNM theory, they will always make choices so as to maximize the value of their expected utility. To see what this means in practice, let $U(C)$ denote the VNM utility of consuming $C$ units of the good at date 1 and suppose that the probability of state $s$ occurring is $\pi_s > 0$ for $s = H, L$. Then the expected utility of a consumption plan $(C_H, C_L)$ is $\pi_H U(C_H) + \pi_L U(C_L)$. The decision problem of the consumer we encountered above can be re-written as

$$\max \quad \pi_H U(C_H) + \pi_L U(C_L)$$
$$\text{s.t.} \quad q_H C_H + q_L C_L \leq q_H Y_H + q_L Y_L.$$

The first-order conditions for this problem are

$$\pi_s U'(C_s) = \mu q_s,$$

for $s = H, L$, where $U'(C_s)$ is the marginal utility of consumption in state $s$ and $\mu$ (the Lagrange multiplier associated with the budget constraint) can be interpreted as the marginal utility of money. Notice that the marginal utility of consumption in state $s$ is multiplied by the probability of state $s$ and it is the product – the *expected* marginal utility – which is proportional to the price of consumption in that state. Then the first-order condition can be interpreted as saying that the expected marginal utility of one unit of consumption in state $s$ is equal to the marginal utility of its cost.

We typically think of individuals as being **risk averse**, that is, they avoid risk unless there is some advantage to be gained from accepting it. The clearest evidence for this property is the tendency to buy insurance. We can characterize risk aversion and an individual's attitudes to risk generally in the shape of the VNM utility function. Figure 2.9 shows the graph of a VNM utility function. Utility increases with income (the marginal utility of consumption is positive) but the utility function becomes flatter as income increases (diminishing marginal utility of consumption).

A VNM utility function has diminishing marginal utility of consumption if and only if it is strictly concave. Formally, a VNM utility function $U$ is **strictly concave** if, for any consumption levels $C$ and $C'$ ($C \neq C'$) and any number $0 < t < 1$, it satisfies the inequality

$$U\left(tC + (1 - t)\,C'\right) > tU(C) + (1 - t)U(C'). \tag{2.5}$$

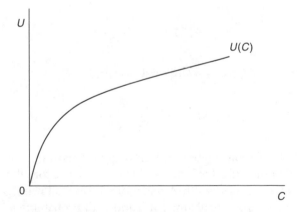

**Figure 2.9.** The von Neumann–Morgenstern utility function.

Concavity of the VNM utility function can be interpreted as an attitude towards risk. To see this, suppose that an individual is offered a gamble in which he receives $C$ with probability $t$ and $C'$ with probability $1 - t$. If his VNM utility is strictly concave, he will prefer to receive the expected value $tC + (1 - t)C'$ for sure, rather than take the gamble. This is because the expected utility of the gamble (the right hand side of the inequality) is less than the utility of the sure thing. The utility function will always be strictly concave if the individual exhibits diminishing marginal utility of income. An individual who satisfies the assumption of diminishing marginal utility of income is said to be **risk averse**. (Draw the graph of a utility function with increasing marginal utility of income and see how the comparison of the two options changes. An individual with these preferences is called a **risk lover**.)

The conclusion then is that, faced with a choice between a risky income distribution and a degenerate distribution with the same expected value, a risk averse individual will always choose the one without risk. In what follows, we assume that the VNM utility function is concave and, hence, individuals are risk averse.

We have seen that risk aversion is associated with the curvature of the utility function, in particular, with the fact that the marginal utility of income is decreasing. Mathematically, this means that the second derivative of the utility function $U''(C)$ is less than or equal to zero. It would be tempting to take the second derivative $U''(C)$ to be the measure of risk aversion. Unfortunately, the VNM utility function is only determined up to an affine transformation, that is, for any constants $\alpha$ and $\beta > 0$, the VNM utility function $\alpha + \beta U$ is equivalent to $U$ in terms of the attitudes to risk that it implies. Thus, we must look for a measure that is independent of $\alpha$ and $\beta > 0$. Two such measures are available. One is known as the degree of *absolute risk aversion*

$$A(C) = -\frac{U''(C)}{U'(C)}$$

and the other is the degree of *relative risk aversion*

$$R(C) = -\frac{U''(C)C}{U'(C)}.$$

There is a simple relationship between the degree of risk aversion and the risk premium that an individual will demand to compensate for taking risk. Suppose that an individual has wealth $W$ and is offered the following gamble. With probability 0.5 he wins a small amount $h$ and with probability 0.5 he loses $h$. Since the expected value of the gamble is zero, the individual's expected income is not changed by the gamble. Since a risk averse individual would rather have $W$ for sure than have an uncertain income with the same expected value, he will reject the gamble. The risk premium $a$ is the amount he would have to be given in order to accept the gamble. That is, $a$ satisfies the equation

$$U(W) = \frac{1}{2}U(W + a - h) + \frac{1}{2}U(W + a + h).$$

A Taylor expansion of the right hand side shows that, when $h$ is small,

$$U(W) \approx U(W) + U'(W)a + \frac{1}{2}U''(W)h^2.$$

Thus,

$$a \approx -\frac{U''(W)}{U'(W)}\frac{h^2}{2} = A(W)\frac{h^2}{2}.$$

So the risk premium $a$ is equal to the degree of absolute risk aversion times one-half the variance of the gamble (a measure of the risk). A similar interpretation can be given for the degree of relative risk aversion when the gamble consists of winnings of $hW$ and $-hW$ with equal probability.

If the degree of absolute risk aversion is constant, the VNM utility function must have the form

$$U(C) = -e^{-AC},$$

and $A > 0$ is the degree of absolute risk aversion. If the degree of relative risk aversion is constant and different from 1, then

$$U(C) = \frac{1}{1 - \sigma}C^{1-\sigma},$$

where $\sigma > 0$ is the degree of relative risk aversion. This formula is not defined when the degree of relative risk aversion is $\sigma = 1$; however, the limiting value of the utility function as $\sigma \to 1$ is well defined and given by

$$U(C) = \ln C,$$

where $\ln C$ denotes the natural logarithm of $C$.

The higher the degree of (relative or absolute) risk aversion, the more risk averse the individual with the VNM utility function $U(C)$ is.

### 2.2.3 Insurance and risk pooling

Returning to the example of efficient risk sharing studied earlier, we can use the assumption that consumers have VNM utility functions to characterize the efficient risk sharing allocation more precisely. Suppose that there are two individuals $A$ and $B$ with VNM utility functions $U_A$ and $U_B$ and income distributions $(Y_{AH}, Y_{AL})$ and $(Y_{BH}, Y_{BL})$ respectively. If the efficient allocation of consumption in the two states is given by $\{(C_{AH}, C_{AL}), (C_{BH}, C_{BL})\}$, then the condition for equality between the marginal rates of substitution can be written as

$$\frac{U_A'(C_{AH})}{U_A'(C_{AL})} = \frac{U_B'(C_{BH})}{U_B'(C_{BL})}.$$

The probabilities do not appear in this equation because, assuming $A$ and $B$ have the same probability beliefs, they appear as multipliers on both sides and so cancel out.

It is interesting to consider what happens in the case where one of the consumers is **risk neutral**. We say that a consumer is risk neutral if his VNM utility function has the form

$$U(C) \equiv C.$$

A risk neutral consumer cares only about the expected value of his income or consumption. In other words, his expected utility is just the expected value of consumption. Suppose that consumer $B$ is risk neutral. Then his marginal utility is identically equal to 1 in each state. Substituting this value into the efficiency condition, we see that

$$\frac{U_A'(C_{AH})}{U_A'(C_{AL})} = 1,$$

which implies that $C_{AH} = C_{AL}$. All the risk is absorbed by the risk neutral consumer $B$, leaving consumer $A$ with a certain level of consumption.

Risk neutrality is a very special property, but there are circumstances in which risk averse consumers can achieve the same effects. First, let us consider more carefully the way in which the optimal consumption allocation depends on income. First, note that the efficiency equation implies that $U_A'(C_{AH}) < U_A'(C_{AL})$ if and only if $U_B'(C_{BH}) < U_B'(C_{BL})$. Since marginal utility is decreasing in consumption, this implies that $C_{AH} > C_{AL}$ if and only if $C_{BH} > C_{BL}$. This immediately tells us that the optimal consumption allocation depends only on the aggregate income of the pair. Let $Y_s = Y_{As} + Y_{Bs}$ for

$s = H, L$. Then feasibility requires that total consumption equals total income in each state:

$$C_{As} + C_{Bs} = Y_s,$$

for $s = H, L$. Thus, the consumption of each consumer rises if and only if aggregate income rises. This property is known as coinsurance between the two consumers: they provide insurance to each other in the sense that their consumption levels go up and down together. In particular, if the aggregate income is the same in the two states, $Y_H = Y_L$, then $C_{AH} = C_{AL}$ and $C_{BH} = C_{BL}$. So if aggregate income is constant, the consumption allocation will be constant too, no matter how individual incomes fluctuate.

When there are only two consumers, constant aggregate income depends on a rather remarkable coincidence: when $A$'s income goes up, $B$'s income goes down by the same amount. When there is a large number of consumers, however, the same outcome occurs quite naturally, thanks to the law of large numbers, as long as the incomes of the different consumers are assumed to be **independent**. This is, in fact, what insurance companies do: they pool large numbers of independent risks, so that the aggregate outcome becomes almost constant, and then they can ensure that each individual gets a constant level of consumption. Suppose there is a large number of consumers $i = 1, 2, \ldots$ with random incomes that are independently and identically distributed according to the probability distribution

$$Y_i = \begin{cases} Y_H & \text{with probability } \pi_H \\ Y_L & \text{with probability } \pi_L. \end{cases}$$

Then the law of large numbers ensures that the average income is equal to the expected value of an individual's income $\bar{Y} = \pi_H Y_H + \pi_L Y_L$ with probability one, that is, with certainty. Then an insurance company could ensure every one a constant consumption level because the average aggregate income is almost constant.

### 2.2.4 Portfolio choice

The use of Arrow securities to allocate income risk efficiently is a special case of the portfolio choice problem that individuals have to solve in order to decide how to invest wealth in an uncertain environment. We can gain a lot of insight into the portfolio choice problem by considering the special case of two securities, one a safe asset and the other a risky asset.

As before, we assume there are two dates $t = 0, 1$ and two states $s = H, L$ and a single consumption good at each date. Suppose that an investor has an initial income $W_0 > 0$ at date 0 and that he can invest it in two assets. One is a **safe asset** that yields one unit of the good at date 1 for each unit invested at date 0. The other is a **risky asset**: one unit invested in the risky asset at date 0 yields $R_s > 0$ units of the good in state $s = H, L$. We assume that the investor's risk preferences are represented by a VNM utility function $U(C)$ and that the probability of state $s$ is $\pi_s > 0$ for $s = H, L$.

The investor's portfolio can be represented by the fraction $\theta$ of his wealth that he invests in the risky asset. That is, his portfolio will contain $\theta W_0$ units of the risky asset and $(1 - \theta) W_0$ of the safe asset. His future consumption will depend on his portfolio choice and the realized return of the risky asset. Let $C_H$ and $C_L$ denote consumption in the high and low states, respectively. Then

$$C_s = R_s \theta W_0 + (1 - \theta) W_0,$$

for $s = H, L$. The investor chooses the portfolio that maximizes the expected utility of his future consumption. That is, his decision problem is

$$\max_\theta \quad \pi_H U(C_H) + \pi_L U(C_L)$$
$$\text{s.t.} \quad C_s = R_s \theta W_0 + (1 - \theta) W_0, \; s = H, L.$$

Substituting the expressions for $C_H$ and $C_L$ into the objective function we see that the expected utility is a function of $\theta$, say $V(\theta)$. The optimal portfolio $0 < \theta^* < 1$ satisfies the first-order condition $V'(\theta^*) = 0$, or

$$\pi_H U'(C_H)(R_H - 1) + \pi_L U'(C_L)(R_L - 1) = 0.$$

The optimum is illustrated in Figure 2.10. The set of attainable consumption allocations $(C_H, C_L)$ is represented by the line segment with endpoints $(W_0, W_0)$ and $(R_H W_0, R_L W_0)$. If the investor puts all of his wealth in the safe asset $\theta = 0$, then his future consumption in each state will be $C_H = C_L = W_0$. If he puts all his wealth in the risky asset, then his future consumption with be $R_H W_0$ in the high state and $R_L W_0$ in the low state. If he puts a fraction $\theta$ of his wealth in the risky asset, his consumption bundle $(C_H, C_L)$ is just a convex combination of these two endpoints with weights $1 - \theta$ and $\theta$ respectively. In other words, we can trace out the line joining these two endpoints just by varying the proportion of the risky asset between 0 and 1.

The optimal portfolio choice occurs where the investor's indifference curve is tangent to the consumption curve. The tangency condition is just a geometric version of the first-order condition above.

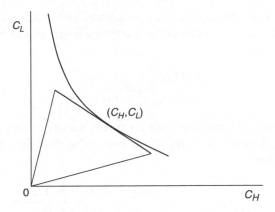

**Figure 2.10.** Optimal choice of portfolio with two assets.

Depending on the investor's risk preferences and the rates of return, the optimal portfolio may consist entirely of the safe asset, entirely of the risky asset, or a mixture of the two. It is interesting to see under which conditions each of these possibilities arises. To investigate this question, we need to find out more about the slopes of the indifference curves and the feasible set.

The slope of the feasible set is easily calculated. Compare the portfolio in which all income is invested in the safe asset with the portfolio in which income is all invested in the risky asset. The change in $C_H$ is $\Delta C_H = W_0 - W_0 R_H$ and the change in $C_L$ is $\Delta C_L = W_0 - W_0 R_L$. So the slope is

$$\frac{\Delta C_L}{\Delta C_H} = \frac{W_0 - W_0 R_L}{W_0 - W_0 R_H} = \frac{1 - R_L}{1 - R_H}.$$

The slope is negative if $R_L < 1 < R_H$.

An indifference curve is a set of points like $(C_H, C_L)$ that satisfy an equation like

$$\pi_H U(C_H) + \pi_L U(C_L) = \text{constant}.$$

Consider a "small" movement $(dC_H, dC_L)$ along the indifference curve: it must satisfy the equation

$$\pi_H U'(C_H) dC_H + \pi_L U'(C_L) dC_L = 0.$$

We can "solve" this equation to obtain the slope of the indifference curve:

$$\frac{dC_L}{dC_H} = -\frac{\pi_H U'(C_H)}{\pi_L U'(C_L)}.$$

Now we are ready to characterize the different possibilities. For an interior solution, $0 < \theta^* < 1$, the slope of the indifference curve must equal the slope of the feasible set, or

$$\frac{\pi_H U'(C_H)}{\pi_L U'(C_L)} = \frac{1 - R_L}{R_H - 1}.$$

A necessary and sufficient condition for this is that the indifference curve is flatter than the feasible set at $(R_H W_0, R_L W_0)$ and steeper than the feasible set at $(W_0, W_0)$. That is,

$$\frac{\pi_H U'(W_0)}{\pi_L U'(W_0)} > \frac{1 - R_L}{R_H - 1} > \frac{\pi_H U'(R_H W_0)}{\pi_L U'(R_L W_0)}.$$

The left hand inequality can be simplified to

$$\frac{\pi_H}{\pi_L} > \frac{1 - R_L}{R_H - 1}$$

or $\pi_H R_H + \pi_L R_L > 1$. In other words, the investor will hold a positive amount of the risky asset if and only if the expected return of the risky asset is greater than the return to the safe asset. This makes sense because there is no reward for bearing risk otherwise. The right hand inequality implies that

$$\frac{1 - R_L}{R_H - 1} > 0,$$

or $R_L < 1 < R_H$. In other words, the investor will hold the safe asset only if the risky asset produces a capital loss in the low state. Otherwise, the risky asset dominates (always pays a higher return than) the safe asset. Notice that even if the risky asset sometimes yields a loss, the investor may choose to invest all his wealth in the risky asset. It just depends on his attitude toward risk and the risk–return trade-off.

## 2.3 LIQUIDITY

The word liquidity is used in two senses here. First, we describe assets as liquid if they can be easily converted into consumption without loss of value. Second, we describe individuals as having a preference for liquidity if they are uncertain about the timing of their consumption and hence desire to hold liquid assets.

*Liquid assets*

Once again, we illustrate the essential ideas using a simple example. Time is divided into three periods or **dates** indexed by $t = 0, 1, 2$. At each date, there is a single all-purpose good which can be used for consumption or investment.

There are two assets that consumers can use to provide for future consumption, a short-term, liquid asset and a long-term, illiquid asset. In what follows, we refer to these as the **short** and **long** assets, respectively. Each asset is represented by a constant-returns-to-scale investment technology. The short asset is represented by a storage technology that allows one unit of the good at date $t$ to be converted into one unit of the good at date $t + 1$, for $t = 0, 1$. The long asset is represented by an investment technology that allows one unit of the good at date 0 to be converted into $R > 1$ units of the good at date 2. We assume the return of the long asset is known with certainty. This assumption simplifies the analysis and allows us to focus attention on the other source of uncertainty, that is, uncertainty about individual time preferences.

There is a trade-off between an asset's time to maturity and its return. The long asset takes two periods to mature, but pays a high return. The short asset matures after one period but yields a lower return. This trade-off is characteristic of the yield curve for bonds of different maturities, where we see that bonds with short maturities typically have lower returns than bonds with long maturities. The higher returns on the longer-dated assets can be interpreted both as a reward for the inconvenience of holding illiquid assets and as a reflection of the greater productivity of roundabout methods of production.

*Liquidity preference*

We model preference for liquidity as the result of uncertainty about time preference. Imagine a consumer who has an endowment of one unit of the good at date 0 and nothing at the future dates. All consumption takes place in the future, at dates 1 and 2, but the consumer is uncertain about the precise date at which he wants to consume. More precisely, we assume there are two types of consumers, **early consumers** who only want to consume at date 1 and **late consumers** who only want to consume at date 2. Initially, the consumer does not know his type. He only knows the probability of being an early or a late consumer. Let $\lambda$ denote the probability of being an early consumer and $1 - \lambda$ the probability of being a late consumer. The consumer learns whether he is an early or late consumer at the beginning of date 1.

Uncertainty about time preferences is a simple way of modeling what economists call a "liquidity shock," that is, an unanticipated need for liquidity resulting from an event that changes one's preferences. This could be an accident that requires an immediate expenditure, the arrival of an unexpected investment opportunity, or an unexpected increase in the cost of an expenditure that was previously planned. We can think of $\lambda$ as measuring the degree of a consumer's liquidity preference. Other things being equal, he will want to earn the highest return possible on his investments. But if he is uncertain about the timing of his consumption, we will also care about liquidity, the possibility of realizing the value of this asset at short notice. If $\lambda$ is one, the consumer's liquidity preference will be high, since he cannot wait until date 2 to earn the higher return on the long asset. If $\lambda$ is zero, he will have no preference for liquidity, since he can hold the long asset without inconvenience. For $\lambda$ between zero and one, the consumer's uncertainty about the timing of his consumption poses a problem. If the consumer knew that he was a late consumer, he would invest in the long asset because it gives a higher return. If he knew that he was an early consumer, he would hold only the short asset in spite of its lower return. Since the consumer is uncertain about his type, he will regret holding the short asset if he turns out to be a late consumer and he will regret holding the long asset if he turns out to be an early consumer. The optimal portfolio for the consumer to hold will depend on both his risk aversion and his liquidity preference and on the return to the long asset (the slope of the yield curve).

### Investment under autarky

Suppose the consumer has a period utility function $U(C)$ and let $C_1$ and $C_2$ denote his consumption at date 1 (if he is an early consumer) and date 2 (if he is a late consumer). Then his expected utility from the consumption stream $(C_1, C_2)$ is

$$\lambda U(C_1) + (1 - \lambda) U(C_2).$$

His consumption at each date will be determined by his portfolio choice at date 0. Let $\theta$ denote the proportion of his wealth invested in the short asset. Recall that he has an initial endowment of one unit of the good at date 0 so he invests $\theta$ in the short asset and $1 - \theta$ in the long asset. Then his consumption at date 1 is given by

$$C_1 = \theta,$$

since he cannot consume the returns to the long asset, whereas his consumption at date 2 is given by

$$C_2 = \theta + (1 - \theta)R,$$

since the returns to the short asset can be re-invested at date 1 and consumed at date 2. Note that $C_1 < C_2$ except in the case where $\theta = 1$, so the consumer faces some risk and if he is risk averse this will impose some loss of expected utility compared to a situation in which he can consume the expected value $\bar{C} = \lambda C_1 + (1 - \lambda) C_2$ for sure. Of course, he can choose $\theta = 1$ if he wants to avoid uncertainty altogether, but there is a cost to doing so: his average consumption will be lower.

The consumer's decision problem is to choose $\theta$ to maximize

$$\lambda U(\theta) + (1 - \lambda) U(\theta + (1 - \theta)R).$$

At an interior solution, the optimal value of $\theta$ satisfies

$$\lambda U'(\theta) + (1 - \lambda) U'(\theta + (1 - \theta)R)(1 - R) = 0.$$

For example, if $U(C) = \ln C$, then the first-order condition becomes

$$\frac{\lambda}{\theta} + \frac{(1 - \lambda)}{\theta + (1 - \theta)R}(1 - R) = 0,$$

or

$$\theta = \frac{\lambda R}{R - 1}.$$

So the fraction of wealth held in the short asset is greater if $\lambda$ is greater and lower if $R$ is greater. Note that $\theta = 0$ for any value of $\lambda$ greater than $1 - 1/R$.

### Risk pooling

As we have seen already, the consumer's attempt to provide for his future consumption needs is bound to lead to regret as long as he cannot perfectly foresee his type. If he could ensure against his liquidity shock, he could do better. Suppose that there is a large number of consumers, all of whom are ex ante identical and subject to the same shock, that is, they all have a probability $\lambda$ of being early consumers. If we assume further that their liquidity shocks are independent, then the law of large numbers assures us that there will be no aggregate uncertainty. Whatever happens to the individual consumer, the fraction of the total population who become early consumers will be $\lambda$ for certain. This suggests the potential for pooling risks and providing a better combination of returns and liquidity.

To see how this would work, suppose a financial institution were to take charge of the problem of investing the endowments of a large number of consumers and providing for their consumption. The financial institution would take the endowments at date 0 and invest a fraction $\theta$ in the short asset and a fraction $1 - \theta$ in the long asset. At date 1 it would provide consumption equal to $C_1$ units of the good to early consumers and at date 2 it would provide $C_2$ units of the good to late consumers. The important difference between the financial institution and the individual consumers is that the company faces no uncertainty: it knows for sure that a fraction $\lambda$ of its clients will be early consumers. Consequently, it knows for sure what the demand for the consumption good will be at date 1 and date 2. At date 1 it needs to provide $\lambda C_1$ per capita and at date 2 it needs to provide $(1 - \lambda)C_2$ per capita. Because the return to the short asset is lower than the return to the long asset, the financial institution will hold the minimum amount of the short asset it needs to provide for the early consumers' consumption at date 1, that is, $\theta = \lambda C_1$ and it will hold the rest of the portfolio in the long asset. Then the company's plans are feasible if

$$\lambda C_1 = \theta$$

and

$$(1 - \lambda)C_2 = (1 - \theta)R.$$

The company's decision problem is

$$\max \quad \lambda U(C_1) + (1 - \lambda)U(C_2)$$
$$\text{s.t.} \quad \lambda C_1 = \theta$$
$$(1 - \lambda)C_2 = (1 - \theta)R.$$

If we substitute for the $C_1$ and $C_2$ in the objective function, we get

$$\lambda U\left(\frac{\theta}{\lambda}\right) + (1 - \lambda)U\left(\frac{(1 - \theta)R}{1 - \lambda}\right)$$

and the first-order condition for maximizing this expression with respect to $\theta$ is

$$U'(C_1) - U'(C_2)R = 0.$$

Notice that the terms involving $\lambda$ have cancelled out. In terms of the earlier example, where the period utility function is $U(C) = \ln C$, the first-order condition implies that $C_2 = C_1 R$, or

$$\theta = \lambda.$$

## 2.4 CONCLUDING REMARKS

This chapter has provided a foundation in terms of the basic finance and economics that will be needed to understand this book. Those wishing to pursue these topics further can consult a textbook such as Mas-Collel et al. (1995).

## REFERENCE

Mas-Collel, A., M. Whinston, and J. Green (1995). *Microeconomic Theory*, Oxford: Oxford University Press.

# 3

## Intermediation and crises

With the exception of the Bretton Woods period from 1945 to 1971, banking crises have occurred fairly frequently in the past 150 years, as we saw in Chapter 1. There are two traditional ways of understanding crises. The first asserts that crises result from panics; the second asserts that crises arise from fundamental causes that are part of the business cycle. Both have a long history. For example, Friedman and Schwartz (1963) and Kindleberger (1978) argued that many banking crises resulted from unwarranted panics and that most of the banks that were forced to close in such episodes were illiquid rather than insolvent. The alternative view, put by Mitchell (1941) and others, is that financial crises occur when depositors have reason to believe that economic fundamentals in the near future look poor. In that case depositors, anticipating that future loan defaults will make it impossible for the bank to repay their deposits, withdraw their money now. The depositors in this case are anticipating insolvency rather than illiquidity. In this chapter, we consider both approaches.

Although the economic theory of banking goes back over 200 years, it was not until recently that a model of banking, in the contemporary sense, was provided in the seminal papers of Bryant (1980) and Diamond and Dybvig (1983). The publication of these papers marked an important advance in the theory of banking. Although the objective of the papers was to provide an explanation of bank runs, an equally important contribution was to provide a microeconomic account of banking activity that was distinct from other financial institutions. In fact, the papers contributed four separate elements to the theory of banking:

- a **maturity structure** of bank assets, in which less liquid assets earn higher returns;
- a theory of **liquidity preference**, modeled as uncertainty about the timing of consumption;
- the representation of a bank as an intermediary that provides **insurance** to depositors against liquidity (preference) shocks;
- an explanation of bank runs by depositors. In the case of Diamond and Dybvig (1983), the bank runs are modeled as the result of **self-fulfilling prophecies or panics**; in the case of Bryant (1980), they are modeled as the result of **fundamentals**.

In Sections 3.1–3.4 of this chapter, we describe a model of banking, loosely based on the Bryant (1980) and Diamond–Dybvig (1983) models, that shows how all these pieces fit together (see Chapter 2 for an introductory development of some of these ideas). Sections 3.5 and 3.6 develop a model based on the view that crises arise from panics while Section 3.7 develops a model based on the view that crises result from fundamentals. Section 3.8 contains a literature review and Section 3.9 concluding remarks.

## 3.1 THE LIQUIDITY PROBLEM

It is a truism that banks have liquid liabilities and illiquid assets. In other words, they borrow short and lend long. This makes banks vulnerable to sudden demands for liquidity (bank runs), but more on this later. This maturity mismatch reflects the underlying structure of the economy: individuals have a preference for liquidity but the most profitable investment opportunities take a long time to pay off. Banks are an efficient way of bridging the gap between the maturity structure embedded in the technology and liquidity preference.

We adopt the period structure introduced in Chapter 2. There are three dates indexed by $t = 0, 1, 2$. At each date there is a single good that can be used for consumption and investment and serves as a numeraire. There are two types of assets:

- The liquid asset (also called the *short asset*) is a constant returns to scale technology that takes one unit of the good at date $t$ and converts it into one unit of the good at date $t + 1$, where $t = 0, 1$.
- The illiquid asset (also called the *long asset*) is a constant returns to scale technology that takes one unit of the good at date 0 and transforms it into $R > 1$ units of the good at date 2; if the long asset is liquidated prematurely at date 1 then it pays $0 < r < 1$ units of the good for each unit invested.

At the first date there is a large number, strictly speaking a continuum, of ex ante identical economic agents (consumers, depositors).[1] Each consumer has an endowment of one unit of the good at date 0 and nothing at the later dates. In order to provide for future consumption, agents will have to invest, directly or indirectly, in the long and short assets.

---

[1] We represent the set of agents by the unit interval [0, 1], where each point in the interval is a different agent. We normalize the measure of the entire set of agents to be equal to one and measure the fraction of agents in any subset by its Lebesgue measure. The assumption of a large number of individually insignificant agents ensures perfect competition, that is, no one has enough market power to affect the equilibrium terms of trade.

The agents' time preferences are subject to a random shock at the beginning of date 1. With probability $\lambda$ an agent is an early consumer, who only values consumption at date 1; with probability $(1 - \lambda)$ he is a late consumer who only values consumption at date 2. The agent's (random) utility function $u(c_1, c_2)$ is defined by

$$u(c_1, c_2) = \begin{cases} U(c_1) & \text{w.pr. } \lambda \\ U(c_2) & \text{w.pr. } 1 - \lambda, \end{cases}$$

where $c_t \geq 0$ denotes consumption at date $t = 1, 2$ and $U(\cdot)$ is a neoclassical utility function (increasing, strictly concave, twice continuously differentiable). Because there is a large number of agents and their preference shocks are independent, the 'law of large numbers' holds and we assume that the fraction of early consumers is constant and equal to the probability of being an early consumer. Then, although each agent is uncertain about his type, early or late, there is no uncertainty about the proportion of each type in the population. With probability one there is a fraction $\lambda$ of early consumers and a fraction $1 - \lambda$ of late consumers.

This simple example illustrates the problem of liquidity preference. If an agent knew his type at date 0, he could invest in the asset that would provide him with consumption exactly when he needed it. For example, if he were an early consumer, he could invest his endowment in the short asset and it would produce a return of one unit at date 1, exactly when he wanted to consume it. If he were a late consumer, he could invest his endowment in the long asset, which yields a higher rate of return, and it would produce $R$ units at date 2 exactly when he wanted to consume it. The problem is precisely that he does not know his preferences regarding the timing of consumption when he has to make the investment decision. If he invests in the short asset and turns out to be a late consumer, he will regret not having invested in the higher-yielding long asset. If he invests in the long asset and turns out to be an early consumer, he will have nothing to consume and will clearly regret not having invested in the short asset. Even if he invests in a mixture of the two assets, he will still have some regrets with positive probability. It is this problem – the mismatch between asset maturity and time preferences – that financial intermediation is designed to solve.

## 3.2 MARKET EQUILIBRIUM

Before we consider the use of intermediaries to solve the liquidity problem, we consider a market solution. When we laid out the problem of matching investment maturities and time preferences in Chapter 2, we assumed that the agent existed in a state of autarky, that is, he was unable to trade assets and had to consume the returns generated by his own portfolio. The assumption of autarky is unrealistic. An agent often has the option of selling assets in order to realize their value in a liquid form. In fact, one of the main purposes of asset markets is to provide liquidity to agents who may be holding otherwise illiquid assets. So it is interesting to consider what would happen if long-term assets could be sold (liquidated) on markets and see whether this solves the problem of matching maturities to time preferences.

In this section, we assume that there exists a market on which an agent can sell his holding of the long asset at date 1 after he discovers his true type. Then, if he discovers that he is an early consumer, he can sell his holding of the long asset at the prevailing price and consume the proceeds. The existence of an asset market transforms the illiquid long asset into a liquid asset, in the sense that it can be sold for a predictable and sure price if necessary.

The possibility of selling the long asset at date 1 provides some insurance against liquidity shocks. Certainly, the agent must be at least as well off as he is in autarky and he may be better off. However, the asset market at date 1 cannot do as well as a complete set of contingent claims markets. For example, an agent might want to insure himself by trading goods for delivery at date 1 contingent on the event that he is an early or late consumer. As we shall see, if an agent can trade this sort of contingent claims at date 0, before his type is known, he can synthesize an optimal risk contract. The absence of markets for contingent claims in the present set up explains the agent's failure to achieve the first best.

At date 0, an investor has an endowment of one unit of the good which can be invested in the short asset or the long asset to provide for future consumption. Suppose he invests in a portfolio $(x, y)$ consisting of $x$ units of the long asset and $y$ units of the short asset. His budget constraint at date 0 is

$$x + y \leq 1.$$

At date 1 he discovers whether he is an early or late consumer. If he is an early consumer, he will liquidate his portfolio and consume the proceeds. The price of the long asset is denoted by $P$. The agent's holding of the short asset provides him with $y$ units of the good and his holding of the long asset can be sold for $Px$ units of the good. Then his consumption at date 1 is given by the budget constraint

$$c_1 = y + Px.$$

If the agent is a late consumer, he will want to rebalance his portfolio. In calculating the optimal consumption for a late consumer, there is no essential loss of generality in assuming that he always chooses to invest all of his wealth in the long asset at date 1. This is because the return on the short asset (between dates 1 and 2) is weakly dominated by the return on the long asset. To see this, note that if, contrary to our claim, the return on the short asset were greater than the return on the long asset, no one would be willing to hold the long asset at date 1 and the asset market could not clear. Thus, in equilibrium, either the two rates of return are equal or the long asset dominates the short asset (and no one holds the short asset at date 1). This ordering of rates of return implies that $P \leq R$ in equilibrium and that it is weakly optimal for the late consumer to hold only the long asset at date 1. Then the quantity of the long asset held by the late consumer is $x + y/P$ since he initially held $x$ units of the long asset and he exchanges the return on the short asset for $y/P$ units of the long asset. His consumption at date 2 will be given by the budget constraint

$$c_2 = \left(x + \frac{y}{P}\right) R.$$

From the point of view of an investor at date 0, the objective is to choose a portfolio $(x, y)$ to maximize the investor's expected utility

$$\lambda U \left(y + Px\right) + (1 - \lambda) U \left[\left(x + \frac{y}{P}\right) R\right].$$

The investor's decision at date 0 can be simplified if we note that, in equilibrium, the price of the long asset must be $P = 1$. To see this, note that if $P > 1$ then the long asset dominates the short asset and no one will hold the short asset at date 0. In that case, early consumers will be offering the long asset for sale but there will be no buyers at date 1. Then the price must fall to $P = 0$, a contradiction. On the other hand, if $P < 1$, then the short asset dominates the long asset and no one will hold the long asset at date 0. Early consumers will consume the returns on the short asset at date 1, realizing a return of $1 > P$; late consumers will try to buy the long asset to earn a return of $R/P > R$. Since no one has any of the long asset, the price will be bid up to $P = R$, another contradiction. Thus, $P = 1$ in equilibrium. At this price, the two assets have the same returns and are perfect substitutes. The agent's portfolio choice becomes immaterial. The agent's consumption is

$$c_1 = x + Py = x + y = 1$$

at date 1 and

$$c_2 = \left(x + \frac{y}{P}\right) R = (x + y)R = R$$

at date 2. Then the equilibrium expected utility is

$$\lambda U(1) + (1 - \lambda)U(R).$$

This level of welfare serves as a benchmark against which to measure the value of having a banking system that can provide insurance against liquidity (preference) shocks.

### The value of the market

It is obvious that the investor is at least as well off when he has access to the asset market as he is in autarky. Typically, he will be better off. To show this, we have to compare the market equilibrium allocation $(c_1, c_2) = (1, R)$ with the set of allocations that are feasible in autarky.

As we saw in Chapter 2, if the consumer does not have access to the asset market and is forced to remain in autarky, his consumption as an early consumer would be equal to his investment $y$ in the safe asset, and his consumption as a late consumer would be equal to the return $Rx = R(1 - y)$ on his investment in the long asset plus his investment in the safe asset $y$ which can be re-invested at the second date. Thus, the feasible consumption bundles have the form

$$c_1 = y$$
$$c_2 = y + R(1 - y)$$

for some feasible value of $y$ between 0 and 1. The set of such consumption bundles is illustrated in Figure 3.1.

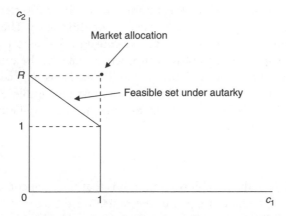

**Figure 3.1.** Comparison of the market allocation with the feasible set under autarky.

As the figure illustrates, the maximum value of early consumption is attained when $y = 1$ and $c_1 = 1$ and the maximum value of late consumption is attained when $y = 0$ and $c_2 = R$. The market allocation $(c_1, c_2) = (1, R)$ dominates every feasible autarkic allocation, that is, it gives strictly greater consumption at one date and typically gives greater consumption at both. Thus, access to the asset market does increase expected utility.

## 3.3 THE EFFICIENT SOLUTION

The market provides liquidity by allowing the investor to convert his holding of the long asset into consumption at the price $P = 1$ at the second date. Because the asset market is perfectly competitive, the investor can buy and sell any amount of the asset at the equilibrium price. This means that the market is **perfectly liquid** in the sense that the price is insensitive to the quantity of the asset that is traded. However, it turns out that the provision of liquidity is inefficient. We will discuss the reasons for this in greater detail later, but the short explanation for this inefficiency is that the set of markets in the economy described above is **incomplete**. In particular, there is no market at date 0 in which an investor can purchase **the good for delivery at date 1 contingent on his type**. If such a market existed, the equilibrium would be quite different.

We take as our definition of the efficient provision of liquidity, the level of welfare that could be achieved by a central planner who had command of all the allocation decisions in the economy. To begin with, we assume that the planner has complete information about the economy, including the ability to tell who is an early consumer and who is a late consumer. This important assumption will later be relaxed.

The central planner chooses the amount per capita $x$ invested in the long asset and the amount per capita $y$ invested in the short asset. Then he chooses the consumption per capita $c_1$ of the early consumers at date 1 and the consumption per capita $c_2$ of the late consumers at date 2. The central planner is not bound to satisfy any equilibrium conditions. He is only constrained by the condition that the allocation he chooses must be feasible. At date 0 the feasibility condition is simply that the total invested per capita must be equal to the per capita endowment:

$$x + y = 1. \tag{3.1}$$

At the second date, the feasibility condition is that the total consumption per capita must be less than or equal to the return on the short asset. Since the fraction of early consumers is $\lambda$ and each one is promised $c_1$ the consumption per capita (i.e. per head of the entire population) is $\lambda c_1$. Then the feasibility condition is

$$\lambda c_1 \leq y. \tag{3.2}$$

If this inequality is strict, some of the good can be re-invested in the short asset and consumed at date 2. Thus, the total available at date 2 (expressed in per capita terms) is $Rx + (y - \lambda c_1)$. The total consumption per capita (i.e. per head of the entire population) at date 2 is $(1 - \lambda)c_2$ since the fraction of late consumers is $1 - \lambda$ and each of them is promised $c_2$. So the feasibility condition is

$$(1 - \lambda)c_2 \leq Rx + (y - \lambda c_1),$$

which can also be written as

$$\lambda c_1 + (1 - \lambda)c_2 \leq Rx + y. \tag{3.3}$$

The planner's objective is to choose the investment portfolio $(x, y)$ and the consumption allocation $(c_1, c_2)$ to maximize the typical investor's expected utility

$$\lambda U(c_1) + (1 - \lambda)\, U(c_2),$$

subject to the various feasibility conditions (3.1)–(3.3).

This looks like a moderately complicated problem, but it can be simplified if we use a little common sense. The first thing to note is that it will never be optimal to carry over any of the short asset from date 1 to date 2. To see this, suppose that $y > \lambda c_1$ so that some of the good is left over at date 1. Then we could reduce the amount invested in the short asset at date 0 by $\varepsilon > 0$ say and invest it in the long asset instead. At date 2, there would be $\varepsilon$ less of the short asset but $\varepsilon$ more of the long asset. The net change in the amount of goods available would be $R\varepsilon - \varepsilon = (R - 1)\varepsilon > 0$, so it would be possible to increase the consumption of the late consumers without affecting the consumption of the early consumers. This cannot happen in an optimal plan, so it follows that in any optimal plan we must have $\lambda c_1 = y$ and $(1 - \lambda)c_2 = Rx$. Thus, once $x$ and $y$ are determined, the optimal consumption allocation is also determined by the relations

$$c_1 = \frac{y}{\lambda};$$

$$c_2 = \frac{Rx}{1 - \lambda}.$$

(Recall that $y$ is the return on the short asset *per head of the entire population*, whereas $c_1$ is the consumption of a typical early consumer, so $c_1$ is greater than $y$. Similarly, the consumption $c_2$ of a typical late consumer is greater than the return on the long asset *per head of the entire population*.) If we substitute these expressions for consumption into the objective function and use the date-0 feasibility condition to write $x = 1 - y$, we can see that the planner's problem boils down to choosing $y$ in the interval $[0, 1]$ to maximize

$$\lambda U\left(\frac{y}{\lambda}\right) + (1 - \lambda)\, U\left(\frac{R(1 - y)}{1 - \lambda}\right). \tag{3.4}$$

Ignoring the possibility of a boundary solution, where $y = 0$ or $y = 1$, a necessary condition for an optimal choice of $y$ is that the derivative of the function in (3.4) be zero. Differentiating this function and setting the derivative equal to zero yields

$$U'\left(\frac{y}{\lambda}\right) - U'\left(\frac{R(1 - y)}{1 - \lambda}\right) R = 0,$$

or, substituting in the consumption levels,

$$U'(c_1) = U'(c_2)\, R. \tag{3.5}$$

There are several interesting observations to be made about this first-order condition. First, the value of $\lambda$ does not appear in this equation: $\lambda$ drops out when we differentiate the objective function. The intuition for this result is that $\lambda$ appears symmetrically in the objective function and in the feasibility conditions. An increase in $\lambda$ means that early consumers get more weight in the objective function but it also means that they cost more per capita to feed. These two effects cancel out and leave the optimal level of consumption unchanged.

## The inefficiency of the market solution

The second point to note concerns the (in)efficiency of the market solution. The set of feasible consumption allocations for the planner's problem is illustrated in Figure 3.2. For each choice of $y$ in the interval between 0 and 1, the consumption allocation is defined by the equations

$$c_1 = \frac{y}{\lambda};$$

$$c_2 = \frac{R(1 - y)}{(1 - \lambda)}.$$

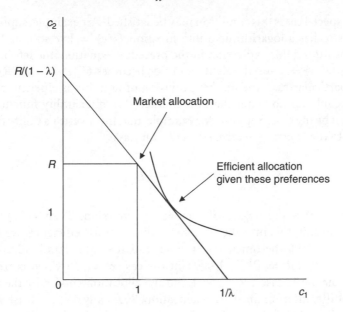

**Figure 3.2.** Comparison of the market allocation with the efficient allocation.

The consumption of the early consumers is maximized by putting $y = 1$, in which case $(c_1, c_2) = (1/\lambda, 0)$. Similarly, the consumption of the late consumers is maximized by putting $y = 0$, in which case $(c_1, c_2) = (0, R/(1 - \lambda))$. Since the equations for consumption are linear in $y$, we can attain any point on the line segment joining $(1/\lambda, 0)$ and $(0, R/(1 - \lambda))$. This feasible frontier is described in the figure. The efficient point is determined by the tangency of the consumers' indifference curve with the feasible frontier. Depending on the consumers' preferences, the point of tangency could occur anywhere along the feasible frontier.

The market allocation occurs on the feasible frontier. Simply put $y = \lambda$ and we get

$$(c_1, c_2) = \left( \frac{y}{\lambda}, \frac{R(1 - y)}{(1 - \lambda)} \right) = (1, R) \,.$$

This allocation could be efficient but typically it will not be. To see this, suppose that by some chance the market equilibrium resulted in the same allocation as the planner's problem. Then the first-order condition (3.5) becomes

$$U'(1) = U'(R)R \,.$$

In some special cases this condition may be satisfied. For example, suppose that the investor has a logarithmic utility function $U(c) = \ln c$ so that $U'(c) = 1/c$. Substituting this expression in the preceding equation, the left hand side becomes $U'(1) = 1$ and the right hand side becomes $U'(R)R = (1/R)R = 1$. In this particular case, the market provision of liquidity is efficient: a central planner could do no better than the market. For other utility functions, this would not be the case. Suppose, for example, that the investor's utility function belongs to the constant relative risk aversion class

$$U(c) = \frac{1}{1-\sigma}c^{1-\sigma}$$

where $\sigma > 0$ is the degree of relative risk aversion. Then $U'(c) = c^{-\sigma}$ and substituting this into the necessary condition for efficiency, we see that the left hand side becomes $U'(1) = 1$ and the right hand side becomes $U'(R)R = R^{-\sigma}R = R^{1-\sigma}$. Except in the case $\sigma = 1$ (which corresponds to the logarithmic case), $R^{1-\sigma} \neq 1$ and the allocation chosen by the planner must be different from the market allocation. So for any degree of risk aversion different from 1 the planner achieves a strictly better level of expected utility than the market.

### Liquidity insurance

A third insight that can be derived from the first-order condition (3.5) concerns the provision of insurance against liquidity shocks, that is, the event of being an early consumer. Even in the efficient allocation the individual faces uncertainty about consumption. The first-order condition $U'(c_1) = RU'(c_2)$ implies that $c_1 < c_2$ so the individual's consumption will be higher or lower depending on whether he is a late or an early consumer.

In the market allocation, the early consumers get 1 and the late consumers get $R > 1$ so it is clearly worse to be an early consumer than a late consumer. A risk averse investor would like to have more consumption as an early consumer and less as a late consumer, *assuming that the expected value of his consumption remains the same.* An interesting question is whether the planner provides insurance against the liquidity shock by reducing the volatility of consumption, that is, increasing consumption of early consumers and reducing consumption of late consumers *relative to the market solution.* In Figure 3.2, the consumption allocations that lie to the right of the market allocation all satisfy $c_1 > 1$ and $c_2 < R$, that is, they have less uncertainty about consumption than the market allocation. On the other hand, they also have lower expected consumption.

It is interesting to see under what conditions the optimal deposit contract gives the consumer more consumption at date 1 than the market solution, that is, when are the higher returns from the long asset shared between the early and late consumers. Substituting from the budget constraints into the first-order condition we get the equation

$$U'\left(\frac{y}{\lambda}\right) = RU'\left(\frac{(1-y)}{(1-\lambda)}R\right).$$

If $y = \lambda$ this condition reduces to $U'(1) = RU'(R)$, so a necessary and sufficient condition for $c_1 = y/\lambda > 1$ and $c_2 = R(1-y)/(1-\lambda) < R$ is that

$$U'(1) > RU'(R).$$

A sufficient condition is that $cU'(c)$ be decreasing in $c$, which is equivalent to saying that the relative risk aversion is greater than one:

$$\eta(c) \equiv -\frac{cU''(c)}{U'(c)} > 1.$$

If this inequality is reversed and $\eta(c) < 1$, early consumers get less and late consumers get more than in the benchmark case, that is,

$$c_1 = y/\lambda < 1,$$
$$c_2 = R(1-y)/(1-\lambda) > R.$$

These results have an intuitive explanation. The logarithmic utility function, which has a degree of relative risk aversion equal to unity, marks the boundary between two different cases. If relative risk aversion equals one, as in the natural log case, the market outcome is efficient and, in particular, the market's provision of liquidity is optimal. If relative risk aversion is greater than one, the market provision of liquidity is inefficient. An efficient allocation should provide more insurance by increasing the consumption of the early consumers and reducing the consumption of the late consumers. If relative risk aversion is less than one, there is paradoxically too much liquidity in the sense that efficiency requires a reduction in the consumption of the early consumers and an increase in the consumption of the late consumers.

This last result alerts us to the fact that insurance is costly. In order to provide more consumption to the early consumers, it is necessary to hold more of the short asset and, hence, less of the long asset. Since the long asset's return is greater than the short asset's, the increase in the amount of the short asset in the planner's portfolio must reduce average consumption across the two dates. As long as relative risk aversion is greater than one, the benefit from insurance is greater than the cost, at least to start with. If the relative risk aversion is less than one, the benefits of greater insurance are not worth the cost and, indeed, the efficient allocation requires the planner to increase the risk borne by the investors in order to capture the increased returns from holding the long asset.

Why do the investors hold the wrong portfolio in the market solution? Their portfolio decision is dependent upon the market price for the long asset $P = 1$. This price is determined by the condition that investors at date 0 must be willing to hold both assets. The market does not reveal how much investors would be willing to pay for the asset contingent on knowing their type. Consequently, the price does not reflect the value of being able to sell the long asset as an early consumer or being able to buy it as a late consumer.

## Complete markets

We mentioned earlier (in Section 3.2) the possibility of introducing markets that would allow individual agents to trade at date 0 claims on date-1 consumption contingent on their type, early or late. The existence of such markets would achieve the same allocation of risk and the same portfolio investment as the central planner. Unlike the model economy in which there are no contingent markets, an economy with markets for individual contingencies would signal the correct value of each asset to the market, in particular the value of liquidity, and ensure that the efficient allocation was achieved. To see this, suppose that an individual can purchase date-1 consumption at a price $q_1$ if he is early and $q_2$ if he is late. Note that these prices are measured in terms of the good at date 0. The implicit price of goods at date 2 in terms of goods at date 1 is $p = P/R$, as usual. Then the budget constraint for an individual at date 0 is

$$q_1 \lambda C_1 + q_2 p (1 - \lambda) C_2 \leq 1. \tag{3.6}$$

The left hand side represents the present value (at date 0) of expected consumption (since there is no aggregate uncertainty, each individual only pays for the expected value of his demand for goods at each date). With probability $\lambda$ he demands $C_1$ units of date-1 consumption and the present value of $\lambda C_1$ is $q_1 \lambda C_1$. Similarly, with probability $1 - \lambda$ he demands $C_2$ units of date-2 consumption and the present value of $(1 - \lambda) C_2$ is $q_2 p (1 - \lambda) C_2$.

The individual chooses $(C_1, C_2)$ to maximize $\lambda U (C_1) + (1 - \lambda) U (C_2)$ subject to (3.6) and the solution must satisfy the first-order conditions

$$\lambda U' (C_1) = \mu q_1 \lambda$$

and

$$(1 - \lambda) U' (C_2) = \mu q_2 p (1 - \lambda)$$

where $\mu > 0$ is the Lagrange multiplier associated with the constraint. Then

$$\frac{U'(C_1)}{U'(C_2)} = \frac{q_1}{q_2 p}.$$

Since the investment technology exhibits constant returns to scale, the equilibrium prices must satisfy two no-arbitrage conditions. To provide one unit of the good at date 1, it is necessary to invest 1 unit in the short asset at date 0. Thus, there are zero profits from investing in the short asset if and only if $q_1 = 1$. Similarly, to provide one unit of the good at date 2, it is necessary to invest $1/R$ units in the long asset at date 0. Thus, there are zero profits from investing in the long asset if and only if $pq_2 = 1/R$. This implies that

$$\frac{U'(C_1)}{U'(C_2)} = R,$$

the condition required for efficient risk sharing.

### Private information and incentive compatibility

So far we have assumed that the central planner knows everything, including whether an investor is an early or late consumer. This allows the planner to assign different levels of consumption to early and late consumers. Since an investor's time preferences are likely to be private information, the assumption that the planner knows the investor's type is restrictive. If we relax this assumption, we run into a problem: if time preferences are private information, how can the planner find out who is an early consumer and who is a late consumer? The planner can rely on the individual truthfully revealing his type if and only if the individual has no incentive to lie. In other words, the allocation chosen by the planner must be **incentive-compatible**.

In the present case, it is quite easy to show that the optimal allocation is incentive compatible. First, the early consumers have no opportunity to misrepresent themselves as late consumers. A late consumer is given $c_2$ at date 2 and since the early consumer only values consumption at date 1 he would certainly be worse off if he waited until date 2 to receive $c_2$. The late consumer poses more of a problem. He could pretend to be an early consumer, receive $c_1$ at date 1 and store it until date 2 using the short asset. To avoid giving the late consumer an incentive to misrepresent his preferences, he must receive at least as much consumption as the early consumer. This means that the allocation is incentive compatible if and only if

$$c_1 \leq c_2. \tag{3.7}$$

Fortunately for us, if we consult the first-order condition for the planner's problem, equation (3.5), we find that it implies that $c_1 < c_2$ since $R > 1$ and $U''(c) < 0$ so that the optimal allocation is automatically incentive-compatible.

The allocation that optimizes the typical investor's welfare subject to the incentive constraint (3.7) is called **incentive-efficient**. In this case, because the incentive constraint is not binding at the optimum, the incentive-efficient allocation is the same as the first-best allocation.

Although the incentive-compatibility condition does not have any effect on the optimal risk-sharing allocation, private information plays an important role in the account of banking that we give in the sequel. In particular, the fact that a bank cannot distinguish early and late consumers means that all consumers can withdraw from the bank at date 1 and this is a crucial feature of the model of bank runs.

## 3.4 THE BANKING SOLUTION

A bank, by pooling the depositors' investments, can provide insurance against the preference shock and allow early consumers to share the higher returns of the long asset. The bank takes one unit of the good from each agent at date 0 and invests it in a portfolio $(x, y)$ consisting of $x$ units of the long asset and $y$ units of the short asset. Because there is no aggregate uncertainty, the bank can offer each consumer a non-stochastic consumption profile $(c_1, c_2)$, where $c_1$ is the consumption of an early consumer and $c_2$ is the consumption of a late consumer. We can interpret $(c_1, c_2)$ as a deposit contract under which the depositor has the right to withdraw either $c_1$ at date 1 or $c_2$ at date 2, but not both.

There is assumed to be free entry into the banking sector. Competition among the banks forces them to maximize the ex ante expected utility of the typical depositor subject to a zero-profit (feasibility) constraint. In fact, the bank is in exactly the same position as the central planner discussed in the previous section. At date 0 the bank faces a budget constraint

$$x + y \leq 1. \tag{3.8}$$

At date 1, the bank faces a budget constraint

$$\lambda c_1 \leq y. \tag{3.9}$$

Recalling that it is never optimal to carry consumption over from date 1 to date 2 by holding the short asset, we can write the budget constraint for the bank at the third date as

$$(1 - \lambda) c_2 \leq Rx. \tag{3.10}$$

Formally, the bank's problem is to maximize the expected utility of the typical depositor

$$\lambda U(c_1) + (1 - \lambda) U(c_2)$$

subject to the budget constraints (3.8)–(3.10).

We do not explicitly impose the incentive-compatibility constraint because, as we saw previously, the solution to the unconstrained optimization problem will automatically satisfy the incentive constraint

$$c_1 \leq c_2.$$

So the bank is able to achieve the first-best allocation on behalf of its customers.

It is worth pausing to note how this account of bank behavior implements three of the four elements of banking theory mentioned at the beginning of this chapter.

- It provides a model of the **maturity structure** of bank assets, in which less liquid assets earn higher returns. In this case, there are two bank assets, the liquid short asset, which yields a return of 1, and the illiquid long asset, which yields a return of $R > 1$.
- It provides a theory of **liquidity preference**, modeled as uncertainty about the timing of consumption. The maturity mismatch arises because an investor is uncertain of his preferences over the timing of consumption at the moment when an investment decision has to be made.
- It represents the bank as an intermediary that provides **insurance** to depositors against liquidity (preference) shocks. By pooling his resources with the bank's and accepting an insurance contract in the form of promises of consumption contingent on the date of withdrawal, the investor is able to achieve a better combination of liquidity services and returns on investment than he could achieve in autarky or in the asset market.

The properties of the efficient allocation, derived in the preceding section, of course apply to the banking allocation, so we will not repeat them here. Instead, we want to focus on the peculiar fragility of the arrangement that the bank has instituted in order to achieve optimal risk sharing.

## 3.5 BANK RUNS

At the beginning of this chapter, we mentioned four contributions to banking theory made by the seminal papers of Bryant (1980) and Diamond and Dybvig (1983). We have discussed the first three and now we turn to the fourth, namely, the explanation of bank runs. In this section, we develop a model of bank runs as panics or self-fulfilling prophecies. Later we shall consider bank runs as the result of fundamental forces arising in the course of the business cycle.

Suppose that $(c_1, c_2)$ is the optimal deposit contract and $(x, y)$ is the optimal portfolio for the bank. In the absence of aggregate uncertainty, the portfolio $(x, y)$ provides just the right amount of liquidity at each date assuming that the early consumers are the only ones to withdraw at date 1 and the late consumers all withdraw at date 2. This is an equilibrium in the sense that the bank is maximizing its objective, the welfare of the typical depositor, and the early and late consumers are timing their withdrawals to maximize their consumption.

So far, we have treated the long asset as completely illiquid: there is no way that it can be converted into consumption at date 1. Suppose, instead, that there exists a **liquidation technology** that allows the long-term investment to be terminated prematurely at date 1. More precisely, we assume that

- if the long asset is liquidated prematurely at date 1, one unit of the long asset yields $r \leq 1$ units of the good.

Under the assumption that the long asset can be prematurely liquidated, with a loss of $R - r$ per unit, there exists another equilibrium if we also assume that the bank is required to liquidate whatever assets it has in order to meet the demands of the consumers who withdraw at date 1. To see this, suppose that all depositors, whether they are early or late consumers, decide to withdraw at date 1. The liquidated value of the bank's assets at date 1 is

$$rx + y \leq x + y = 1$$

so the bank cannot possibly pay all of its depositors more than one unit at date 1. In the event that $c_1 > rx + y$, the bank is insolvent and will be able to pay only a fraction of the promised amount. More importantly, all the bank's assets will be used up at date 1 in the attempt to meet the demands of the early withdrawers. Anyone who waits until the last period will get nothing. Thus, given that a late consumer thinks everyone else will withdraw at date 1 it is optimal for a late consumer to withdraw at date 1 and save the proceeds until date 2. Thus, bank runs are an equilibrium phenomenon. The following payoff matrix illustrates the two equilibria of this coordination game. The rows correspond to the decision of an individual late consumer and the columns to the decision of all the other late consumers. (Note: this is **not** a $2 \times 2$ game; the choice of column represents the actions of all but one late consumer.) The ordered pairs are the payoffs for the distinguished late consumer (the first element) and the typical late consumer (the second element).

|  | Run | No Run |
|---|---|---|
| Run | $(rx + y, rx + y)$ | $(c_1, c_2)$ |
| No Run | $(0, rx + y)$ | $(c_2, c_2)$ |

It is clear that if

$$0 < rx + y < c_1 < c_2$$

then (Run, Run) is an equilibrium and (No Run, No Run) is also an equilibrium.

The preceding analysis (of a bank run) is predicated on the assumption that the bank liquidates all of its assets in order to meet the demand for liquidity at date 1. This may be the result of legal restrictions. For example, bankruptcy law or regulations imposed by the banking authority may require that if any claim is not met, the bank must wind up its business and distribute the liquidated value of its assets to its creditors. Some critics of the Diamond–Dybvig model have argued that bank runs can be prevented by suspension of convertibility. If banks commit to suspend convertibility (i.e. they refuse to allow depositors to withdraw), once the proportion of withdrawals is equal to the proportion of early consumers, then late consumers will not have an incentive to withdraw. A late consumer knows that the bank will not have to liquidate the long asset and will have enough funds to pay him the higher promised amount in the second period. If such an agent were to join the run on the bank in the middle period, he would be strictly worse off than if he waited to withdraw at the last date.

To answer the criticism that suspension of convertibility solves the bank-run problem, Diamond and Dybvig (1983) proposed a *sequential service constraint*. Under this assumption, depositors reach the bank's teller one after another and withdraw $c_1$ until the bank is unable to meet any further demand. The sequential service constraint has two effects. It forces the bank to deplete its resources and it gives depositors an incentive to run early in hopes of being at the front of the queue. The bank cannot use suspension of convertibility to prevent runs since it does not find out a run is in progress until it is too late to stop it.

Another point to note about the suspension of convertibility is that it solves the bank-run problem only if the bank knows the proportion of early consumers. If the proportion of early consumers is random and the realization is not known by banks, the bank cannot in general implement the optimal allocation by using suspension of convertibility.

## 3.6 EQUILIBRIUM BANK RUNS

The analysis offered by Diamond and Dybvig pinpoints the fragility of banking arrangements based on liquid liabilities and illiquid assets, but it does not provide a complete account of equilibrium in the banking sector. Instead, it assumes that the bank's portfolio $(x, y)$ and deposit contract $(c_1, c_2)$ are chosen at date 0 in the expectation that the first-best allocation *will* be achieved. In other words, the bank run at date 1, if it occurs, is entirely unexpected at date 0. Taking the decisions at date 0 as given, we can define an equilibrium at date 1 in which a bank run occurs; but this is not the same thing as showing that there exists an equilibrium *beginning at date* 0 in which a bank run is expected to occur. If banks anticipated the possibility of a bank run, their decisions at date 0 would be different and that in turn might affect the probability or even the possibility of a bank run at date 1. What we need is an equilibrium account of bank runs that describes consistent decisions at all three dates. In this section, we provide a coherent account of bank runs as part of an equilibrium that includes the decisions made at date 0. We proceed by establishing a number of facts or properties of equilibrium bank runs before describing the overall picture.

### The impossibility of predicting bank runs

The first thing we need to notice in constructing an equilibrium account of bank runs is that a bank run cannot occur with probability one. If a bank run is certain at date 0, the bank knows that each unit of the good invested in the long asset will be worth $r$ units at date 1. If $r < 1$, the long asset is dominated by the short asset and the bank will not invest in the long asset at all. If $r = 1$, the two assets are for all intents and purposes identical. In either case, the optimal deposit contract is $(c_1, c_2) = (1, 1)$ and there is no motive for a bank run: a late consumer will get the same consumption whether he joins the run or not. So, the best we can hope for is a bank run that occurs *with positive probability*.

### The role of sunspots

The uncertainty of the bank run introduces a new element in our theory. In the current model, there is no uncertainty about aggregate fundamentals, such as asset returns, the proportion of early consumers, and so on. The kind of uncertainty we are contemplating here is *endogenous*, in the sense that it is not explained by shocks to the fundamentals of the model. How can we explain such uncertainty? Traditional accounts of bank runs often referred to "mob psychology." Modern accounts explain it as the result of coordination among individuals that is facilitated by extraneous variables called "sunspots." We shall have more to say about the distinction between these different types of uncertainty in Chapter 5. For the moment, it is enough to note that the uncertainty is not explained by exogenous shocks, but is completely consistent with the requirements of equilibrium, namely, that every individual is maximizing his expected utility and that markets clear.

We begin by hypothesizing that a bank run occurs at date 1 with probability $0 < \pi < 1$. To be more concrete, we can assume there is some random variable (sunspot) that takes two values, say, high and low, with probabilities $\pi$ and $1 - \pi$, respectively. When the realization of the random variable is high, depositors run on the bank and when it is low, they do not. Note that the random variable has no direct effect on preferences or asset returns. It is merely a device for coordinating the decisions of the depositors. It is rational for the depositors to change their behavior depending on the value of the sunspot merely because they expect everyone else to do so.

### The bank's behavior when bank runs are uncertain

The expectation of a bank run at date 1 changes the bank's behavior at date 0. As usual, the bank must choose a portfolio $(x, y)$ and propose a deposit contract $(c_1, c_2)$, but it does so in the expectation that the consumption stream $(c_1, c_2)$ will be achieved only if the bank is solvent. In the event of a bank run, on the other hand, the typical depositor will receive the value of the liquidated portfolio $rx + y$ at date 1. This means that

- with probability $\pi$ there is a bank run and the depositor's consumption is $rx + y$, regardless of his type;
- with probability $(1 - \pi)\lambda$ there is no run, the depositor is an early consumer, and his consumption at date 1 is $c_1$;
- and with probability $(1 - \pi)(1 - \lambda)$ there is no run, the depositor is a late consumer, and his consumption at date 2 is $c_2$.

The outcomes of the bank's decisions when runs are anticipated are illustrated in Figure 3.3.

### The optimal portfolio

If $c_1$ denotes the payment to early consumers when the bank is solvent and $(x, y)$ denotes the portfolio, then the expected utility of the representative

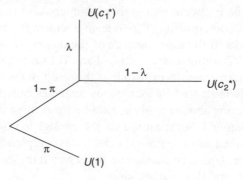

**Figure 3.3.** Equilibrium outcome when runs are anticipated with probability $\pi > 0$.

depositor can be written

$$\pi U(y + rx) + (1 - \pi) \{\lambda U(c_1) + (1 - \lambda) U(c_2)\}.$$

Now suppose that we increase $y$ by a small amount $\varepsilon > 0$ and decrease $x$ by the same amount. We increase $\lambda c_1$ by $\varepsilon$ and reduce $(1 - \lambda) c_2$ by $R\varepsilon$. This insures the feasibility constraints are satisfied at each date. Then the change in expected utility is

$$\pi U'(y + rx)(1 - r)\varepsilon + (1 - \pi) \{U'(c_1) - U'(c_2) R\} \varepsilon + o(\varepsilon).$$

The optimal portfolio must therefore satisfy the first-order condition

$$\pi U'(y + rx)(1 - r) + (1 - \pi) U'(c_1) = (1 - \pi) U'(c_2) R.$$

If $\pi = 0$ then this reduces to the familiar condition $U'(c_1) = U'(c_2) R$. These relations are graphed in Figure 3.4. The latter condition holds at $y^*$ while the former holds at $y^{**}$. Thus, the possibility of a run increases the marginal value of an increase in $y$ (the short asset has a higher return than the long asset in the bankruptcy state if $r < 1$) and hence increases the amount of the short asset held in the portfolio.

## The optimal deposit contract

Our next task is to show that a bank run is possible when the deposit contract is chosen to solve the bank's decision problem. To maximize expected utility, the bank must choose the deposit contract $(c_1{}^*, c_2{}^*)$ to satisfy the first-order condition

$$U'(c_1{}^*) = RU'(c_2{}^*). \tag{3.11}$$

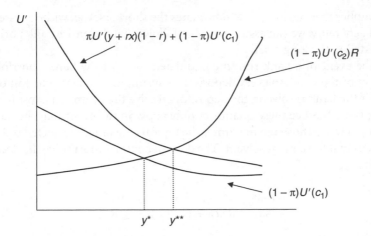

**Figure 3.4.** The determination of the optimal portfolio when bank runs are possible.

This condition, which is familiar from our characterization of the first best, plays a crucial role in determining whether the bank is susceptible to runs.

As we saw earlier, if relative risk aversion is greater than one, then the solution of the first-order condition (3.11) must satisfy the inequality

$$c_1 > 1.$$

This condition implies there exists the possibility of a run. If all the depositors try to withdraw at date 1, the total demand for consumption is $c_1^* > 1$ but the maximum that can be provided by liquidating all of the long asset is 1. However, there will be nothing left at date 2 so the depositors are better off joining the run than waiting until date 2 to withdraw.

In what follows, we assume that the agent's preferences satisfy the condition that

- relative risk aversion is greater than one, that is,

$$-\frac{U''(c)c}{U'(c)} > 1, \ \forall c > 0.$$

To simplify the characterization of the equilibrium, we only consider the special case in which the long asset, when liquidated prematurely, yields as much as the short asset. In other words,

- the liquidation value of the long asset is $r = 1$.

This implies that the long asset dominates the short asset so, without essential loss of generality, we can assume in what follows that the entire bank portfolio is invested in the long asset.

In the event of a bank run, the liquidated value of the bank's portfolio is one unit of the good, so every depositor's consumption is also one unit of the good. If the bank is solvent, the depositors receive the promised consumption profile $(c_1, c_2)$. Since these quantities only apply in the event that the bank is solvent, they are chosen to maximize the typical consumer's expected utility in the event that the bank is solvent. The deposit contract must solve the decision problem

$$\text{max} \quad \lambda U(c_1) + (1 - \lambda) U(c_2)$$
$$\text{s.t.} \quad R \lambda c_1 + (1 - \lambda) c_2 \leq R.$$

To see why the budget constraint takes this form, note that the bank has promised a total of $\lambda c_1$ units to the early consumers and this requires the bank to liquidate $\lambda c_1$ units of the long asset at date 1. The amount of the long asset left is $(1 - \lambda c_1)$ and this produces $R(1 - \lambda c_1)$ units of consumption at date 2. Thus, the maximum amount that can be promised to late consumers $(1 - \lambda) c_2$ must be less than or equal to $R(1 - \lambda c_1)$. In effect, one unit of consumption at date 1 is worth $R$ units of consumption at date 2.

## Equilibrium without runs

So far we have assumed that a run occurs with probability $\pi$ and that the bank takes this possibility as given in choosing an optimal deposit contract; however, the bank can avoid a run by choosing a sufficiently "safe" contract. Remember that our argument for the existence of a run equilibrium at date 1 was based on the assumption that $c_1 > 1$. Thus, if all the late consumers join the run on the bank at date 1 there is no way that the bank can provide everyone with $c_1$. In fact, the bank will have to liquidate all its assets and even then can only give each withdrawer 1, the liquidated value of its portfolio. More importantly, since the bank's assets are exhausted at date 1, anyone waiting until date 2 to withdraw will receive nothing.

In order to remove this incentive to join the run, the bank must choose a deposit contract that satisfies the additional constraint $c_1 \leq 1$. If we solve the problem

$$\text{max} \quad \lambda U(c_1) + (1 - \lambda) U(c_2)$$
$$\text{s.t.} \quad R \lambda c_1 + (1 - \lambda) c_2 \leq R$$
$$c_1 \leq 1$$

we find the solution $(c_1^{**}, c_2^{**}) = (1, R)$. In this case, the bank will be able to give everyone the promised payment $c_1$ at date 1 and if any late consumers wait until date 2 to withdraw there will be enough left over to pay them at least $R > 1$. More precisely, if $1 - \varepsilon$ of the depositors withdraw at date 1, the bank has to liquidate $1 - \varepsilon$ units of the long asset, leaving $\varepsilon$ units of the long asset to pay to the remaining late consumers. Then each consumer who withdraws at date 2 will receive $\varepsilon R / \varepsilon = R > 1$.

## A characterization of regimes with and without runs

If the bank anticipates a run with probability $\pi$, then with probability $\pi$ the depositor's consumption is 1, regardless of his type. With probability $1 - \pi$ there is no run and with probability $\lambda$ the depositor is an early consumer and his consumption is $c_1^*$ and with probability $1 - \lambda$ he is a late consumer and his consumption is $c_2^*$. The possible outcomes are illustrated in Figure 3.3 (above). The expected utility of the typical depositor will be

$$\pi U(1) + (1 - \pi) \left\{ \lambda U(c_1^*) + (1 - \lambda) U(c_2^*) \right\},$$

and we have shown that the bank's choice of portfolio $(x, y) = (1, 0)$ and deposit contract $(c_1^*, c_2^*)$ will maximize this objective, taking the probability $\pi$ of a run as given.

Alternatively, if the bank chooses a deposit contract that avoids all runs, the expected utility of the typical depositor is

$$\lambda U(c_1^{**}) + (1 - \lambda) U(c_1^{**}) = \lambda U(1) + (1 - \lambda) U(R).$$

Whether it is better for the bank to avoid runs or accept the risk of a run with probability $\pi$ depends on a comparison of the expected utilities in each case. Precisely, it will be better to avoid runs if

$$\pi U(1) + (1 - \pi) \left\{ \lambda U(c_1^*) + (1 - \lambda) U(c_2^*) \right\} > \lambda U(1) + (1 - \lambda) U(R).$$

Notice that the left hand side is a convex combination of the depositors' utility $U(1)$ when the bank defaults and their expected utility $\lambda U(c_1^*) + (1 - \lambda) U(c_2^*)$ when the bank is solvent. Now, the expected utility from the safe strategy $\lambda U(1) + (1 - \lambda) U(R)$ lies between these two values:

$$U(1) < \lambda U(1) + (1 - \lambda) U(R)$$
$$< \lambda U(c_1^*) + (1 - \lambda) U(c_2^*).$$

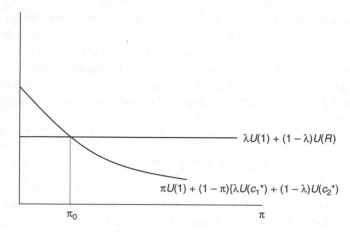

$$\lambda U(1) + (1 - \lambda)U(R)$$

$$\pi U(1) + (1 - \pi)\{\lambda U(c_1^*) + (1 - \lambda)U(c_2^*)\}$$

$$\pi_0 \qquad\qquad\qquad\qquad \pi$$

**Figure 3.5.** Determination of the regions of $\pi$ supporting (respectively not supporting) runs.

So there exists a unique value $0 < \pi_0 < 1$ such that

$$\pi_0 U(1) + (1 - \pi_0)\left\{\lambda U(c_1^*) + (1 - \lambda)\, U\left(c_2^*\right)\right\} = \lambda U(1) + (1 - \lambda)\, U(R)$$

and the bank will be indifferent between the two strategies if $\pi = \pi_0$. Obviously, the bank will prefer runs if $\pi < \pi_0$ and will prefer no runs if $\pi > \pi_0$. These two regions are illustrated in Figure 3.5.

We have shown that as long as the probability of a bank run is sufficiently small, there will exist an equilibrium in which the bank is willing to risk a run because the cost of avoiding the run outweighs the benefit. In that case, there will be a run if the sunspot takes the high value and not otherwise. There is an upper bound (less than one) to the probability of a run, however. If the probability of a run is too high, the bank will take action to discourage a run and the depositors will find it optimal to withdraw at the correct date.

Note that we have not specified what the sunspot is. It could be any publicly observed random variable that takes on a particular value with probability $\pi < \pi_0$. If such a variable exists, then depositors can in principle coordinate on this variable to support an equilibrium bank run.

## 3.7 THE BUSINESS CYCLE VIEW OF BANK RUNS

The previous sections have outlined a Diamond–Dybvig style account of bank runs in which extrinsic uncertainty plays a crucial role. Runs occur in this framework because of late consumers' beliefs. If all the late consumers believe there will be a run, they will all withdraw their money in the middle period. If they do not believe a run will occur, they will wait until the last period to withdraw. In both cases, beliefs are self-fulfilling. In the last section we used the terminology of sunspots to explain how coordination occurs. Traditional accounts of bank runs often referred to "mob psychology" as the motive for the bank run or "panic." This view of bank runs as panics has a long history but it is not the only view. An alternative view of bank runs is that they are a natural outgrowth of weak fundamentals arising in the course of the *business cycle*. An economic downturn will reduce the value of bank assets, raising the possibility that banks will be unable to meet their commitments in the future. If depositors receive information about an impending downturn in the cycle, they will anticipate financial difficulties in the banking sector and try to withdraw their funds. This attempt will precipitate the crisis. According to this interpretation, crises are not random events, but a rational response to unfolding economic circumstances. In other words, they are an integral part of the business cycle.

In Chapter 1 we briefly discussed financial crises in the US during the National Banking Era from 1865 to 1914. Gorton (1988) conducted an empirical study to differentiate between the sunspot view and the business cycle view of banking crises using data from this period. He found evidence consistent with the view that banking panics are predicted by the business cycle. It is difficult to reconcile this finding with the notion of crises as "random" events. Table 3.1 shows the recessions and crises that occurred in the US during the National Banking Era. It also shows the corresponding percentage changes in the currency/deposit ratio and the change in aggregate GDP, as proxied by the change in pig iron production during these periods. The five worst recessions, as measured by the change in pig iron production, were accompanied by crises. In all, crises occurred in seven of the eleven cycles. Using the liabilities of failed businesses as a leading economic indicator, Gorton finds that crises were predictable events: whenever this leading economic indicator reached a certain threshold, a panic ensued. The stylized facts uncovered by Gorton thus suggest that, at least during the US National Banking Era, banking crises were intimately related to the business cycle rather than some extraneous random variable. Calomiris and Gorton (1991) consider a broad range of evidence from this period and conclude that the data do not support the "sunspot" view that banking panics are random events. Among other things, they find that for the five episodes they focus on, stock prices fell by the largest amount by far during the pre-panic periods.

In this section, we adapt our model to allow us to consider the fundamental or business cycle view of banking crises. In particular, instead of assuming the

**Table 3.1.** National Banking Era panics.

| NBER Cycle Peak–Trough | Panic date | %$\Delta$(Currency/deposit)* | %$\Delta$ Pig iron[†] |
|---|---|---|---|
| Oct. 1873–Mar. 1879 | Sep. 1873 | 14.53 | −51.0 |
| Mar. 1882–May 1885 | Jun. 1884 | 8.80 | −14.0 |
| Mar. 1887–Apr. 1888 | No Panic | 3.00 | −9.0 |
| Jul. 1890–May 1891 | Nov. 1890 | 9.00 | −34.0 |
| Jan. 1893–Jun. 1894 | May 1893 | 16.00 | −29.0 |
| Dec. 1895–Jun. 1897 | Oct. 1896 | 14.30 | −4.0 |
| Jun. 1899–Dec. 1900 | No Panic | 2.78 | −6.7 |
| Sep. 1902–Aug. 1904 | No Panic | −4.13 | −8.7 |
| May 1907–Jun. 1908 | Oct. 1907 | 11.45 | −46.5 |
| Jan. 1910–Jan. 1912 | No Panic | −2.64 | −21.7 |
| Jan. 1913–Dec. 1914 | Aug. 1914 | 10.39 | −47.1 |

\* Percentage change of ratio at panic date to previous year's average.
† Measured from peak to trough.
(Adapted from Table 1, Gorton 1988, p. 233).

long asset has a certain return, we assume that the return is risky. Here we are following the approach developed in Allen and Gale (1998) (cf. also Bryant 1980).

- The *long asset* is a constant returns to scale technology that takes one unit of the good at date 0 and transforms it into $R_H$ units of the good at date 2 with probability $\pi_H$ and $R_L$ units with probability $\pi_L$. If the long asset is prematurely liquidated, one unit of the asset yields $r$ units of the good at date 1. We assume that

$$R_H > R_L > r > 0.$$

An intermediary takes a deposit of one unit from the typical consumer and invests it in a portfolio consisting of $y$ units of the safe, short asset and $x$ units of the risky, long asset, subject to the budget constraint

$$x + y \leq 1.$$

In exchange, the intermediary offers the consumer a contract promising $c_1$ units of consumption if he withdraws at date 1 and $c_2$ units of consumption if he withdraws at date 2. As before we assume that the intermediary cannot observe the consumer's type (i.e. early or late) and so cannot make the contract contingent on that. A more stringent requirement is that the intermediary cannot make the deposit contract contingent on the state of nature or, equivalently, the return to the risky asset.

Free entry and competition among the intermediaries leads them to maximize the expected utility of their customers. This implies that the intermediaries will receive zero profits in equilibrium. In particular, this requires that the consumers receive the entire value of the remaining assets at date 2. Because the terminal value of the assets is uncertain, the intermediary will promise a large amount that will certainly exhaust the value of the assets at date 2. Without loss of generality we put $c_2 = \infty$ and, in what follows, we can characterize the deposit contract by the single parameter $c_1 = d$, where $d$ stands for the face value of the deposit at date 1.

Introducing risk in the form of random asset returns does not eliminate the Diamond–Dybvig phenomenon of bank runs based on self-fulfilling expectations or coordination on sunspots. In fact, the Diamond–Dybvig model is just a special case of the current model with $R_H = R_L$. In order to distinguish this account of bank runs, we simply rule out the Diamond–Dybvig phenomenon by assumption and consider only **essential** bank runs, that is, runs that cannot be avoided. Loosely speaking, we assume that if there exists an equilibrium in which there is no bank run as well as one or more that have bank runs, then the equilibrium we observe is the one without a bank run rather than the one with a bank run.

Suppose that the bank has chosen a portfolio $(x, y)$ and a deposit contract $d$ at date 0. At date 1 the budget constraint requires

$$\lambda d \leq y$$

and we can assume, without loss of generality, that the intermediary always chooses $(x, y)$ and $d$ to satisfy this constraint. Otherwise, the intermediary will always have to default and the value of $d$ becomes irrelevant. Consequently, the consumption of the late consumers, conditional on no run, will be given by

$$(1 - \lambda)c_{2s} = R_s(1 - y) + y - \lambda d.$$

This is consistent with no run if and only if $c_{2s} \geq d$ or

$$d \leq R_s(1 - y) + y.$$

This last inequality is called the *incentive constraint*. If this inequality is satisfied, there is an equilibrium in which late consumers wait until date 2 to withdraw. Since we only admit essential runs, the necessary and sufficient condition for a bank run is that the incentive constraint is violated, that is,

$$d > R_s(1 - y) + y.$$

Since $R_H > R_L$, this condition tells us that there can never be an essential run in state $H$ unless there is also one in state $L$. There is no point choosing $d$ so large that a run always occurs, so we can restrict attention to cases in which a run occurs in state $L$ if it occurs at all. There are then three different cases that need to be considered. In the first, the incentive constraint is never binding and bankruptcy is not a possibility. In the second case, bankruptcy is a possibility but the bank finds it optimal to choose a deposit contract and portfolio so that the incentive constraint is (just) satisfied and there is no bankruptcy in equilibrium. In the third case, the costs of distorting the choice of deposit contract and portfolio are so great that the bank finds it optimal to allow bankruptcy in the low asset-return state.

## Case I: The incentive constraint is not binding in equilibrium

In this case, we solve the intermediary's decision problem without the incentive constraint and then check whether the constraint is binding or not. The intermediary chooses two variables, the portfolio $y$ and the deposit contract $d$ to maximize the depositor's expected utility, assuming that there is no bank run. With probability $\lambda$ the depositor is an early consumer and receives $d$ regardless of the state. With probability $1 - \lambda$, the depositor is a late consumer and then his consumption depends on the return to the risky asset. The total consumption in state $s$ is equal to the return to the risky asset plus the remainder of the returns from the safe asset after the early consumers have received their share, that is, $R_s(1 - y) + y - \lambda d$. The consumption of a typical late consumer is just this amount divided by the number of late consumers $1 - \lambda$. Thus, the expected utility is

$$\lambda U(d) + (1 - \lambda) \left\{ \pi_H U \left( \frac{R_H(1 - y) + y - \lambda d}{1 - \lambda} \right) \right.$$
$$\left. + \pi_L U \left( \frac{R_L(1 - y) + y - \lambda d}{1 - \lambda} \right) \right\}.$$

This expression is maximized subject to the feasibility constraints $0 \le y \le 1$ and $\lambda d \le y$.

Assuming that the optimal portfolio requires investment in both assets, i.e. $0 < y < 1$, the optimal choice of $(y, d)$ is characterized by the necessary and sufficient first-order conditions. Differentiating the objective function with respect to $d$ and taking account of the constraint $\lambda d \le y$, the first-order condition for the deposit contract is

$$U'(d) - \left\{ \pi_H U' \left( \frac{R_H(1-y) + y - \lambda d}{1-\lambda} \right) + \pi_L U' \left( \frac{R_L(1-y) + y - \lambda d}{1-\lambda} \right) \right\} \ge 0,$$

with equality if $\lambda d < y$. Differentiating with respect to $y$ and taking account of the constraint $\lambda d \leq y$, the first-order condition for the portfolio is

$$\pi_H U' \left( \frac{R_H(1-y) + y - \lambda d}{1-\lambda} \right) (1 - R_H)$$

$$+ \pi_L U' \left( \frac{R_L(1-y) + y - \lambda d}{1-\lambda} \right) (1 - R_L) \leq 0,$$

with equality if $\lambda d < y$. If $(y^*, d^*)$ denotes the solution to these inequalities, then $(y^*, d^*)$ represents an equilibrium if the incentive constraint is satisfied in state $L$:

$$d^* \leq R_L(1 - y^*) + y^*.$$

Let $U^*$ denote the maximized value of expected utility corresponding to $(y^*, d^*)$.

The consumption profile offered by the bank is illustrated in Figure 3.6, which shows the consumption at each date and in each state as a function of the return on the long asset. If the low state return $R_L$ is sufficiently high, say $R_L = R_L^*$, then the incentive constraint is never binding. The early consumers receive $c_{1s} = d = y/\lambda$ and the late consumers receive $c_{2s} = R_s (1 - y) / (1 - \lambda)$ in each state $s = H, L$.

If the solution to the relaxed problem above does not satisfy the incentive constraint, there are two remaining possibilities: either the intermediary chooses a contract that satisfies the incentive constraint, i.e. one that is constrained by it, or the intermediary chooses a contract that violates the

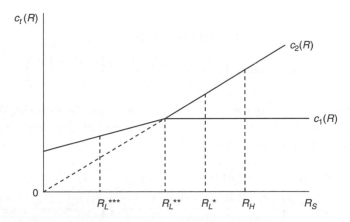

**Figure 3.6.** Illustration of consumption in each period and state as a function of the long asset's return $R_s$ for $s = H, L$.

incentive constraint in the low state, in which case there is default in the low state.

## Case II: The incentive constraint is binding in equilibrium

Suppose that $(y^*, d^*)$ does not satisfy the incentive constraint. If the intermediary chooses not to default, the decision problem is to choose $(y, d)$ to maximize

$$\lambda U(d) + (1 - \lambda) \{\pi_H U(c_H) + \pi_L U(c_L)\}$$

subject to the feasibility constraints $0 \leq y \leq 1$ and $\lambda d \leq y$ and subject to the incentive constraints

$$c_{2s} = \frac{R_s(1 - y) + y - \lambda d}{1 - \lambda} \geq d, \text{ for } s = H, L.$$

The incentive constraint will only bind in the low states $s = L$. Substituting for $c_{2L} = d$, the expression for expected utility can be written as

$$\lambda U(d) + (1 - \lambda) \left\{ \pi_H U \left( \frac{R_H(1 - y) + y - \lambda d}{1 - \lambda} \right) + \pi_L U(d) \right\},$$

where the assumption of a binding incentive constraint implies that

$$d \equiv R_L(1 - y) + y.$$

Since $d$ is determined by the choice of $y$, the optimal contract is entirely determined by a single first-order condition. Substituting for $d$ in the objective function we obtain

$$\{\lambda + (1 - \lambda)\pi_L\} U(R_L(1 - y) + y)$$

$$+ (1 - \lambda)\pi_H U \left( \frac{(R_H - \lambda R_L)(1 - y) + (1 - \lambda)y}{1 - \lambda} \right)$$

Note that the feasibility condition $\lambda d \leq y$ must also be satisfied. We treat this as a constraint while maximizing the objective function above. Then the first-order condition for $y$ takes the form

$$\{\lambda + (1 - \lambda)\pi_L\} U'(d)(1 - R_L)$$

$$+ (1 - \lambda)\pi_H U' \left( \frac{(R_H - \lambda R_L)(1 - y) + (1 - \lambda)y}{1 - \lambda} \right) \left( \frac{-R_H + \lambda R_L + 1 - \lambda}{1 - \lambda} \right) \leq 0$$

or

$$(\lambda + (1 - \lambda)\pi_L) U'(d)(1 - R_L)$$
$$+ \pi_H U' \left( \frac{R_H(1 - y) + y - \lambda d}{1 - \lambda} \right) (-R_H + \lambda R_L + 1 - \lambda) \leq 0,$$

with equality if $\lambda d < y$.

Let $(y^{**}, d^{**})$ denote the solution to this problem and let $U^{**}$ denote the corresponding maximized expected utility.

This case is also illustrated in Figure 3.6. If $R_L = R_L^{**}$ then the incentive constraint is binding and consumption is the same for early and late consumers in the low state: $c_{1L} = c_{2L} = d = y + R_L (1 - y)$. In the high state, $c_{1H} = d$ and $c_{2H} = R_H (1 - y) / (1 - \lambda)$ as usual.

### Case III: The incentive constraint is violated in equilibrium

Again, suppose that $(y^*, d^*)$ does not satisfy the incentive constraint. If there is default in the low state, the expected utility of the depositors is

$$\pi_H \left\{ \lambda U(d) + (1 - \lambda) U \left( \frac{R_H(1 - y) + y - \lambda d}{1 - \lambda} \right) \right\} + \pi_L U \left( r(1 - y) + y \right).$$

In this case, the first-order conditions that characterize the choice of $d$ and $y$ take the form

$$\pi_H \left\{ \lambda U'(d) - \lambda U' \left( \frac{R_H(1 - y) + y - \lambda d}{1 - \lambda} \right) \right\} \geq 0,$$

with equality if $\lambda d < y$ and

$$\pi_H U' \left( \frac{R_H(1 - y) + y - \lambda d}{1 - \lambda} \right) (1 - R_H) + \pi_L U' \left( r(1 - y) + y \right) (1 - R_L) \leq 0,$$

with equality if $\lambda d < y$. Let $(d^{***}, y^{***})$ denote the solution to this problem and $U^{***}$ the corresponding maximized expected utility.

This case is illustrated in Figure 3.6. If $R_L = R_L^{***}$ then bankruptcy occurs in the low state and both early and late consumers receive the same consumption: $c_{1L} = c_{2L} = y + R_L (1 - y) < d$. In the high state, $c_{1H} = d$ and $c_{2H} = R_H (1 - y) / (1 - \lambda)$ as usual. This is an equilibrium solution only if

$$d^{***} > R_L(1 - y) + y,$$

and

$$U^{***} > U^{**}.$$

The first condition guarantees that the incentive constraint is violated, so that the intermediary must default in state $L$, and the second condition guarantees that default is preferred to solvency. Otherwise the bank prefers $(d^{**}, y^{**})$ and there is no default.


## 3.8 THE GLOBAL GAMES APPROACH TO FINDING A UNIQUE EQUILIBRIUM

Section 3.6 demonstrated how the sunspot approach allowed a complete description of an equilibrium with bank runs. The weakness of this approach is that it does not explain why the sunspot should be used as a coordination device. There is no real account of what triggers a crisis. This is particularly a problem if there is a desire to use the theory for policy analysis.

Carlsson and van Damme (1993) showed how the introduction of a small amount of asymmetric information could eliminate the multiplicity of equilibria in coordination games. They called the games with asymmetric information about fundamentals *global games*. Their work showed that the existence of multiple equilibria depends on the players having common knowledge about the fundamentals of the game. Introducing noise ensures that the fundamentals are no long common knowledge and thus prevents the coordination that is essential to multiplicity. Morris and Shin (1998) applied this approach to models of currency crises. Rochet and Vives (2004) and Goldstein and Pauzner (2005) have applied the same technique to banking crises. In this section we present a simple example of the global games approach provided by Allen and Morris (2001).

There are two depositors in a bank. Depositor $i$'s type is $\ell_i$. If $\ell_i$ is less than 1, then depositor $i$ is an early consumer and needs to withdraw his funds from the bank. If $\ell_i$ is greater than or equal to 1, he is a late consumer and has no liquidity needs. In this case he acts to maximize his expected return. If a depositor withdraws his money from the bank, he obtains a guaranteed payoff of $\omega > 0$. If both depositors keep their money in the bank then both obtain $\rho$ where

$$\omega < \rho < 2\omega.$$

If a depositor keeps his money in the bank and the other depositor withdraws, he gets a payoff of 0.

Note that there are four states of liquidity demand: both are early consumers and have liquidity needs, depositor 1 only is an early consumer and has liquidity needs, depositor 2 only is an early consumer and has liquidity needs, and both are late consumers and have no liquidity needs. If there is common knowledge of fundamentals, and at least one depositor is an early consumer, the unique equilibrium has both depositors withdrawing. But if it is common knowledge that both depositors are late consumers, they are playing a coordination game with the following payoffs. (The first element represents the payoff to the player choosing the row strategy and the second element is the payoff to the player choosing the column strategy.)

|  | Remain | Withdraw |
|---|---|---|
| Remain | $(\rho, \rho)$ | $(0, \omega)$ |
| Withdraw | $(\omega, 0)$ | $(\omega, \omega)$ |

An important feature of this coordination game is that the total payoffs when only one person withdraws early are less than when both people withdraw early. One set of circumstances where this would arise, for example, is when the bank can close down after everybody has withdrawn, but when anybody keeps their money in the bank then extra costs are incurred to stay open and the bank's assets are dissipated more.

With common knowledge that neither investor is an early consumer, this game has two equilibria: both remain and both withdraw. We will next consider a scenario where neither depositor is an early consumer, both know that no one is an early consumer, both know that both know this, and so on up to any large number of levels, but nonetheless it is not common knowledge that no one is an early consumer. We will show that in this scenario, the unique equilibrium has both depositors withdrawing. In other words, beliefs about others' beliefs, or higher-order beliefs as they are called, in addition to fundamentals, determine the outcome.

Here is the scenario. The depositors' types, $\ell_1$ and $\ell_2$, are highly correlated; in particular suppose that a random variable $T$ is drawn from a smooth distribution on the non-negative numbers and each $\ell_i$ is distributed uniformly on the interval $[T - \varepsilon, T + \varepsilon]$, for some small $\varepsilon > 0$. Given this probability distribution over types, types differ not only in fundamentals, but also in beliefs about the other depositor's fundamentals, and so on.

To see why, recall that a depositor is an early consumer if $\ell_i$ is less than 1. But when do both depositors know that both $\ell_i$ are greater than or equal to 1 so they are late consumers? Only if both $\ell_i$ are greater than $1 + 2\varepsilon$. This is because both players knows that the other's $\ell_i$ is within $2\varepsilon$ of their own. For

example, suppose $\varepsilon = 0.1$ and depositor 1 has $\ell_1 = 1.1$. She can deduce that
$T$ is within the range $1.0-1.2$ and hence that $\ell_2$ is within the range $0.9-1.3$.
Only if $\ell_1 \geq 1.2$ does depositor 1 know that depositor 2 is a late consumer.

When do both investors know that both investors know that both $\ell_i$ are
greater than or equal to 1? Only if both $\ell_i$ are greater than $1 + 4\varepsilon$. To see this,
suppose that $\varepsilon = 0.1$ and depositor 1 receives $\ell_1 = 1.3$. She can deduce that
$T$ is within the range $1.2-1.4$ and hence that depositor 2's signal is within the
range $1.1-1.5$. However, if depositor 2 receives $\ell_2 = 1.1$, then he sets a positive
probability of depositor 1 having $\ell_1$ within the range $0.9-1.3$ as above. Only
if depositor 1's signal is greater or equal to $1 + 4\varepsilon$ would this possibility be
avoided and both would know that both know that both are late consumers.

As we go up an order of beliefs the range goes on increasing. Hence it can
never be common knowledge that both depositors are late consumers and have
no liquidity needs.

What do these higher-order beliefs imply? It is simplest to consider what
happens when $\varepsilon$ is very small. In this case, since $T$ is smoothly distributed the
probability of the other depositor having an $\ell_i$ above or below approaches 0.5
in each case as $\varepsilon \to 0$ (see Figure 3.7). We will take it as 0.5 in what follows. (An
alternative approach is to assume $T$ is uniformly distributed in which case it is
exactly 0.5 even away from the limit of $\varepsilon \to 0$ – see Morris and Shin (2003).)

How do depositors behave in equilibrium? Observe first that each depositor
will withdraw if $\ell_i < 1$ so the depositor is an early consumer. What about if
$\ell_i \geq 1$? Given the structure of the model with a person being an early consumer
when $\ell_i < 1$ and a late consumer when $\ell_i \geq 1$, the most natural strategy for
a depositor to follow is to choose a strategy of remaining only when $\ell_i > k$

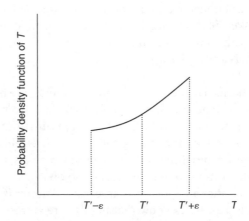

**Figure 3.7.** The probability of the other depositor's $\ell_i$ being above or below 0.5 as
$\varepsilon \longrightarrow 0$.

for some $k \geq 1$ and withdrawing otherwise. Suppose depositor 1 follows this strategy. Consider what happens when $\ell_2 = k$. Given our assumptions about $\varepsilon$ being small and $T$ being drawn from a smooth distribution, depositor 2 deduces that there is a 0.5 probability that $\ell_1 < k$ and depositor 1 will withdraw and a 0.5 probability that $\ell_1 \geq 1$ and that she will remain. The payoff of depositor 2 from **remaining** is

$$= 0.5 \times \rho + 0.5 \times 0 = 0.5\rho,$$

and the payoff from **withdrawing** is

$$= 0.5 \times \omega + 0.5 \times \omega = \omega.$$

Since it is assumed that $\rho < 2\omega$ or equivalently that $0.5\rho < \omega$ it follows that depositor 2 will also withdraw. In fact his unique best response is to withdraw if $\ell_2$ is less than some cutoff point $k^*$ strictly larger than $k$ where at $k^*$ the expected payoffs from remaining and withdrawing are equated. Since the two depositors are in symmetric positions, we can use the same argument to show that depositor 1 will have a cutoff point higher than $k^*$. There is a contradiction and both remaining cannot be an equilibrium. In fact the equilibrium for small $\varepsilon$ is unique, with both agents always withdrawing. Given the other is withdrawing, it is always optimal to withdraw.

The argument ruling out the equilibrium with both remaining depends on the assumption $\rho < 2\omega$. If this inequality is reversed then the same logic as above can be used to show that the unique equilibrium has both remaining. Again the multiplicity is eliminated.

The arguments used above to eliminate an equilibrium rely on depositors using a switching strategy where below some level they withdraw and above some level they remain. Note that other types of equilibria have not been ruled out here. For a full analysis of global games, see Morris and Shin (2003).

Using a global games approach to ensure the uniqueness of equilibrium is theoretically appealing. It specifies precisely the parameter values for which a crisis occurs and allows a comparative static analysis of the factors that influence this set. This is the essential analytical tool for policy analysis. However, what is really needed in addition to logical consistency is empirical evidence that such an approach is valid. Currently there is a very limited empirical literature. This is in the context of currency crises and is broadly consistent with the global games approach (see Prati and Sbracia 2002; Tillman 2004; and Bannier 2005).

## 3.9 LITERATURE REVIEW

There is a large literature on banking crises. Excellent surveys are provided by Bhattacharya and Thakor (1993), Freixas and Rochet (1997), and Gorton and Winton (2003). This review will therefore be brief.

Bryant (1980) and Diamond and Dybvig (1983) developed the first models of banking crises. Both papers had consumers with random liquidity demands and showed that deposit contracts allowed this risk to be insured. In Diamond and Dybvig (1983) bank runs were generated by sunspots while in Bryant (1980) they were the result of aggregate loan risk and asymmetric information about loan payoffs. Both papers were concerned with justifying deposit insurance. Diamond and Dybvig argue deposit insurance eliminates the bad equilibrium without cost because it removes the incentives of late consumers to withdraw early so in equilibrium there are no costs to providing the insurance. In Bryant's model, deposit insurance is desirable because it eliminates incentives to gather costly information that is not socially useful.

Following Diamond and Dybvig, much of the literature on panic-based runs was focused on the assumptions underlying their model. Cone (1983) and Jacklin (1987) pointed out that it was necessary for depositors to have restricted trading opportunities, otherwise banks would have to compete with financial markets and this would eliminate the insurance they could offer.

As we have seen, the possibility of panic-based bank runs depends in an important way on the sequential service (or "first come-first served") constraint. Without this, runs could be prevented by suspending convertibility. A number of papers sought to justify the existence of the sequential service constraint endogenously rather than appealing to legal restrictions. Wallace (1988) assumes that the fraction of the population requiring liquidity is random. He also assumes that agents are spatially separated from each other but are always in contact with the bank. These factors imply that a sequential service constraint is optimal. Whereas Diamond and Dybvig were able to show that deposit insurance was optimal, in Wallace's model it is not. Building on Wallace's model, Chari (1989) shows that if the interbank market does not work well, because of regulatory restrictions of the type in place during the National Banking Era in the US, then banking panics can occur. With a well functioning interbank market, however, runs do not occur. Calomiris and Kahn (1991) argue that the deposit contract, together with a sequential service constraint, can be optimal because it provides an incentive for depositors to monitor bank managers. Diamond and Rajan (2001) show that the possibility of runs arising from demand deposits and a sequential service constraint can be desirable if it ensures that banks will not renegotiate to extract more rents from entrepreneurs that have borrowed from the bank.

The second category of crises involves aggregate risk arising from the business cycle. Bryant's (1980) model falls in this category since he assumes aggregate loan risk and asymmetric information about the outcome of this risk to produce an incentive for some depositors to run. In Gorton's (1985) model, depositors receive a noisy signal about the value of bank assets and if this suggests the value is low there is a panic. Banks that are solvent suspend convertibility and pay a verification cost to demonstrate this to investors. Chari and Jagannathan (1988) focus on a signal extraction problem where part of the population observes a signal about future returns. Others must then try to deduce from observed withdrawals whether an unfavorable signal was received by this group or whether liquidity needs happen to be high. Chari and Jagannathan are able to show panics occur not only when the outlook is poor but also when liquidity needs turn out to be high. Jacklin and Bhattacharya (1988) also consider a model where some depositors receive an interim signal about risk. They show that the optimality of bank deposits compared to equities depends on the characteristics of the risky investment. Hellwig (1994) considers a model where the reinvestment rate is random and shows that the risk should be borne both by early and late withdrawers. Alonso (1996) demonstrates using numerical examples that contracts where runs occur may be better than contracts which ensure runs do not occur because they improve risk sharing. As discussed above, Allen and Gale (1998) develop a model of business cycle risk with symmetric information where future prospects can be observed by everybody but are not contractible. Runs occur when future prospects are poor.

As Section 3.6 illustrated, one of the key issues in the bank-run literature is that of equilibrium selection. Diamond and Dybvig appealed (among other things) to sunspots to act as the coordination device but did not model this fully. Postlewaite and Vives (1987) developed a model that does not rely on sunspots and that generates a unique equilibrium. In the context of currency crises, Morris and Shin (1998) showed how the global games approach of Carlsson and van Damme (1993) could be used to ensure equilibrium is unique. Their approach links the panic-based and fundamental-based approaches by showing how the probability of a crisis depends on the fundamentals. Morris and Shin (2003) provide an excellent overview of global games. Allen and Morris (2001) develop a simple example to show how these ideas can be applied to banking crises. Rochet and Vives (2004) use the unique equilibrium resulting from their global games approach to undertake policy analysis. They consider the role of ex ante regulation of solvency and liquidity ratios and ex post provision of liquidity by the central bank. Goldstein and

Pauzner (2005) use the global games approach to show how the probability of panic-based runs can be made endogenous and related to the parameters of the banking contract.

There is a large empirical literature on banking crises, which will only be briefly touched on here. Sprague (1910) is the classic study of crises in the National Banking Era. It was commissioned by the National Monetary Commission after the severe crisis of 1907 as part of an investigation of the desirability of establishing a central bank in the US. Friedman and Schwartz (1963) have written a comprehensive monetary history of the US from 1867 to 1960. Among other things, they argue that banking panics can have severe effects on the real economy. In the banking panics of the early 1930's, banking distress developed quickly and had a large effect on output. Friedman and Schwartz argued that the crises were panic-based and offered as evidence the absence of downturns in the relevant macroeconomic time series prior to the crises. Gorton (1988) showed that banking crises in the National Banking Era were predicted by a leading indicator based on liabilities of failed businesses. This evidence suggests banking crises are fundamental or business cycle related rather than panic-based. Calomiris and Gorton (1991) provide a wider range of evidence that crises are fundamental-based rather than panic-based. Wicker (1980, 1996) shows that, despite the absence of collapses in US national macroeconomic time series, in the first two of the four crises identified by Friedman and Schwartz in the early 1930's there were large regional shocks and attributes the crises to these shocks. Calomiris and Mason (2003) undertake a detailed econometric study of the four crises using a broad range of data and conclude that the first three crises were fundamental-based while the fourth was panic-based.

## 3.10  CONCLUDING REMARKS

Banking crises have been an important phenomenon in many countries in many historical periods. In this chapter we have developed a framework based on Bryant (1980) and Diamond and Dybvig (1983) for analyzing these crises. There are two approaches that can be captured by the framework. The first is crises that are based on panics. The second is crises that are based on poor fundamentals arising from the business cycle. There has been a significant debate in the literature on which of these is the "correct" approach to take to crises. As we have seen, there is evidence that both are empirically relevant. There is no need to confine attention to one or the other as is done in much of the literature. Both are important.

# REFERENCES

Allen, F. and D. Gale (1998). "Optimal Financial Crises," *Journal of Finance* 53, 1245–1284.

Allen, F. and S. Morris (2001). "Finance Applications of Game Theory," in K. Chatterjee and W. Samuelson (eds), *Advances in Business Applications of Game Theory,* Boston: Kluwer Academic Publishers, 17–48.

Alonso, I. (1996). "On Avoiding Bank Runs," *Journal of Monetary Economics* 37, 73–87.

Bannier, C. (2005). "The Role of Information Disclosure and Uncertainty in the 1994/95 Mexican Peso Crisis: Empirical Evidence," *Review of International Economics,* forthcoming.

Bhattacharya, S. and A. Thakor (1993). "Contemporary Banking Theory," *Journal of Financial Intermediation* 3, 2–50.

Bryant, J. (1980). "A Model of Reserves, Bank Runs, and Deposit Insurance," *Journal of Banking and Finance* 4, 335–344.

Calomiris, C. and G. Gorton (1991). "The Origins of Banking Panics, Models, Facts, and Bank Regulation," in R. Hubbard (ed), *Financial Markets and Financial Crises,* Chicago, IL: University of Chicago Press.

Calomiris, C. and C. Kahn (1991). "The Role of Demandable Debt in Structuring Optimal Banking Arrangements," *American Economic Review* 81, 497–513.

Calomiris, C. and J. Mason (2003). "Fundamentals, Panics, and Bank Distress During the Depression," *American Economic Review* 93, 1615–1647.

Carlsson, H. and E. van Damme (1993). "Global Games and Equilibrium Selection," *Econometrica* 61, 989–1018.

Chari, V. (1989). "Banking Without Deposit Insurance or Bank Panics: Lessons From a Model of the U.S. National Banking System," *Federal Reserve Bank of Minneapolis Quarterly Review* 13 (Summer), 3–19.

Chari, V. and R. Jagannathan (1988). "Banking Panics, Information, and Rational Expectations Equilibrium," *Journal of Finance* 43, 749–60.

Cone, K. (1983). *Regulation of Depository Institutions,* PhD Dissertation, Stanford University.

Diamond, D. and P. Dybvig (1983). "Bank Runs, Deposit Insurance, and Liquidity," *Journal of Political Economy* 91, 401–419.

Diamond, D. and R. Rajan (2001). Liquidity Risk, Liquidity Creation and Financial Fragility: A Theory of Banking," *Journal of Political Economy* 109, 2431–2465.

Freixas, X. and J. Rochet (1997). *Microeconomics of Banking.* Cambridge: MIT Press.

Friedman, M. and A. Schwartz (1963). *A Monetary History of the United States, 1867–1960,* Princeton, NJ: Princeton University Press.

Goldstein, I. and A. Pauzner (2005). "Demand-Deposit Contracts and the Probability of Bank Runs," *Journal of Finance* 60, 1293–1327.

Gorton, G. (1985). "Bank Suspension of Convertibility," *Journal of Monetary Economics* 15, 177–193.

Gorton, G. (1988). "Banking Panics and Business Cycles," *Oxford Economic Papers* 40, 751–781.

Gorton, G. and A. Winton (2003). "Financial Intermediation," in G. Constantinides, M. Harris, and R. Stulz (eds), *Handbook of the Economics of Finance*, Volume 1A, Chapter 8, Amsterdam: North Holland, 431–552.

Hellwig, M. (1994). "Liquidity Provision, Banking, and the Allocation of Interest Rate Risk," *European Economic Review* 38, 1363–1389.

Jacklin, C. (1987). "Demand Deposits, Trading Restrictions, and Risk Sharing," in E. Prescott and N. Wallace (eds), *Contractual Arrangements for Intertemporal Trade*, Minneapolis, MN: University of Minnesota Press, 26–47.

Jacklin, C. and S. Bhattacharya (1988). "Distinguishing Panics and Information-Based Bank Runs: Welfare and Policy Implications," *Journal of Political Economy* 96, 568–592.

Kindleberger, C. (1978). *Manias, Panics, and Crashes: A History of Financial Crises*, New York: Basic Books.

Mitchell, W. (1941). *Business Cycles and Their Causes*, Berkeley: University of California Press.

Morris, S. and H. Shin (1998). "Unique Equilibrium in a Model of Self-Fulfilling Currency Attacks," *American Economic Review* 88, 587–597.

Morris, S. and H. Shin (2003). "Global Games: Theory and Applications," in M. Dewatripont, L. Hansen and S. Turnovsky (eds), *Advances in Economics and Econometrics: Theory and Applications, Eighth World Congress* Volume I, 56–114.

Postlewaite, A. and X. Vives (1987). "Bank Runs as an Equilibrium Phenomenon," *Journal of Political Economy* 95, 485–491.

Prati, A. and M. Sbracia (2002). "Currency Crises and Uncertainty About Fundamentals," IMF Working Paper 02/3.

Rochet, J. and X. Vives (2004). "Coordination Failures and the Lender of Last Resort: Was Bagehot Right after All?" *Journal of the European Economic Association* 2, 1116–1147.

Sprague, O. (1910). *A History of Crises Under the National Banking System*, National Monetary Commission, Washington DC, US Government Printing Office.

Tillman, P. (2004). "Disparate Information and the Probability of Currency Crises: Empirical Evidence," *Economics Letters* 84, 61–68.

Wallace, N. (1988). "Another Attempt to Explain an Illiquid Banking System: The Diamond and Dybvig Model with Sequential Service Taken Seriously," *Federal Reserve Bank of Minneapolis Quarterly Review* 12 (Fall), 3–16.

Wicker, E. (1980). "A Reconsideration of the Causes of the Banking Panic of 1930," *Journal of Economic History* 40, 571–583.

Wicker, E. (1996). *The Banking Panics of the Great Depression*, Cambridge: Cambridge University Press.

# 4

## Asset markets

In the last chapter, we examined the role of intermediaries as providers of liquidity and risk sharing. We did so under the assumption that intermediaries operated in isolation. There were no other financial institutions and no financial markets. In the present chapter, by contrast, we restrict our attention to asset markets and assume that there are no financial institutions. In the chapters that follow, we use the building blocks developed in these two chapters to study economies in which financial intermediaries and financial markets coexist and interact with each other. Financial markets allow intermediaries to hedge risks and to obtain liquidity by selling assets, but this can be a mixed blessing. In some contexts, markets allow intermediaries to achieve superior risk sharing, but in others they lead to increased instability. To understand how markets can destabilize financial intermediaries, we first need to understand the relationship between market liquidity and asset-price volatility. This is an interesting topic in its own right. Its implications for the stability of the financial system will become clear in the next chapter.

### 4.1 MARKET PARTICIPATION

One of the most striking things about stock markets is the degree of price volatility. On any given day it is common for the largest movement of an individual stock to be around 25 percent. The total market often moves by one or two percent. In October 1987 the market fell by around a third in a single day. These large changes in prices can trigger financial instability. This is particularly true in modern financial systems where many institutions undertake complex risk management programs. Understanding asset price volatility is thus an important component of understanding financial crises. In this chapter we focus on asset markets alone. In the next chapter we will look at the interaction of markets and financial institutions and see how the effects investigated here can lead to fragility.

Why are stock prices so volatile? The traditional explanation is that price volatility is due to the arrival of new information about payoff streams and discount rates. There is a large body of evidence that suggests that information is an important determinant of asset-price volatility (see, e.g. Fama 1970 and Merton 1987) but whether it is the only determinant is hotly debated. The Crash of 1987 is an interesting example because stock prices fell by a large amount despite the apparent absence of new information that day. Leroy and Porter (1981) and Shiller (1981) have argued that stock prices are characterized by *excess volatility*: they are more volatile than the changes in payoff streams and discount rates would predict. A number of authors have suggested that the degree of excess volatility found by these studies can be attributed to the use of inappropriate econometric techniques (see Merton 1987 and West 1998 for surveys of the literature); however, subsequent work that avoids these problems still finds that there is excess volatility (see Campbell and Shiller 1988a,b and Leroy and Parke 1992).

So-called liquidity trading is another possible explanation for asset-price volatility. For a variety of reasons, financial institutions, firms, and individuals have sudden needs for cash and sell securities to meet such needs. If liquidity needs are uncorrelated, one would expect them to cancel out in a large market, thus reducing their impact. Similarly, in a large market one might expect that the other traders would absorb a substantial amount of liquidity. In Sections 4.1–4.2 we develop a simple model of asset-price volatility in which small amounts of liquidity trading can cause significant price volatility because the supply of liquidity in the market is also small.

The model in Sections 4.1–4.2 is based on *complete participation*, that is, every potential trader has unrestricted access to the market and participates actively in it. There is extensive empirical evidence, however, that the assumption of complete participation is not justified. In Section 4.3 we examine the implications of *limited market participation*. The fact is that most investors do not diversify across different classes of assets. For example, King and Leape (1984) analyze data from a 1978 survey of 6,010 US households with average wealth of almost $250,000. They categorize assets into 36 classes and find that the median number owned is eight. Mankiw and Zeldes (1991) find that only a small proportion of consumers hold stocks. More surprisingly, perhaps even among those with large liquid wealth, only a fairly small proportion own stocks; of those with other liquid assets in excess of $100,000, only 47.7 percent hold stocks. Guiso et al. (2002) document the direct and indirect holdings of stocks in a number of countries. Table 4.1 summarizes the results. It can be seen that equity holdings are increasing, particularly indirect holdings, in all the countries. However, holdings of equity are low, particularly in Germany and Italy, where the numbers of publically traded companies are small.

**Table 4.1.** Proportion of households investing in risky assets.

| Year | United States | United Kingdom | Netherlands | Germany | Italy |
|------|------|------|------|------|------|
| 1983 | 19.1 | 8.9 | *n.a.* | 9.7 | *n.a.* |
| 1989 | 16.8 | 22.6 | *n.a.* | 10.3 | 4.5 |
| 1995 | 15.2 | 23.4 | 11.5 | 10.5 | 4.0 |
| 1998 | 19.2 | 21.6 | 15.4 | *n.a.* | 7.3 |
| *Direct and indirect stockholding* | | | | | |
| 1983 | *n.a.* | *n.a.* | *n.a.* | 11.2 | *n.a.* |
| 1989 | 31.6 | *n.a.* | *n.a.* | 12.4 | 10.5 |
| 1995 | 40.4 | *n.a.* | 29.4 | 15.6 | 14.0 |
| 1998 | 48.9 | 31.4 | 35.1 | *n.a.* | 18.7 |

*Source:* Guiso et al. (2002), Table I.4, p. 9.

Other studies have found that investors' diversification within equity portfolios is also limited. Blume et al. (1974) develop a measure of portfolio diversification which takes into account the proportion of stocks held in individuals' portfolios. Using this measure, they find that the average amount of diversification is equivalent to having an equally weighted portfolio with two stocks. Blume and Friend (1978) provide more detailed evidence of this lack of diversification. They find that a large proportion of investors have only one or two stocks in their portfolios, and very few have more than 10. This observation cannot be explained by the argument that investors are mainly holding mutual funds. The reason is that in King and Leape's (1984) study, only one percent of investors' wealth was in mutual funds compared to 22.3 percent held directly in equities. The Blume et al. (1974) and Blume and Friend (1978) studies are from an earlier period when it is likely that the ownership of mutual funds was an even smaller proportion of wealth, given the growth in mutual funds that has occurred.

One plausible explanation of limited market participation is the fixed setup cost of participating in a market. In order to be active in a market, an investor must initially devote resources to learning about the basic features of the market such as the distribution of asset returns and so forth and how to monitor changes through time. Brennan (1975) has shown that with fixed setup costs of this kind, it is only worth investing in a limited number of assets. King and Leape (1984) find evidence that is consistent with this type of model. Haliassos and Bertaut (1995), Bertaut (1998), and Vissing-Jorgensen (2002) present theoretical and empirical evidence that a fixed participation cost is consistent with patterns of stock ownership.

Of course, it is not just individuals that we are interested in. Institutions are responsible for investing a significant fraction of total wealth. Portfolio managers also face fixed costs of entering markets. The knowledge required to operate successfully in markets suggests that a manager who tries to operate in a large number of markets will not perform as well as one who specializes. In addition, agency problems limit wide participation in markets. Investors are concerned that institutions will take undesirable risks with their money and so impose limits on the amount they can invest in particular classes of assets. Limited capital means that the amount that institutions trade within any market they participate in is also limited. For simplicity, we will treat all investors, whether individual and institutional, as if they were individual investors investing their own money.

Limited participation by itself does not explain excess volatility. By definition, a market is *liquid* if it can absorb liquidity trades without large changes in price. For asset-price volatility, what is needed is market illiquidity. In our model, the liquidity of the market does not depend on the number of investors who participate, that is, on the thickness or thinness of the market. On the contrary, we assume that the market is always "thick;" in other words, it always has a large number of traders. Instead, liquidity depends on the amount of cash held by the market participants: this is the amount of cash that is available at short notice to buy stocks from liquidity traders, investors who have experienced a sudden need for liquidity. If there is a lot of "cash in the market," liquidity trades are easily absorbed and have little effect on prices. If there is very little cash in the market, on the other hand, relatively small shocks can have a large effect on prices.

The impact of market liquidity on asset pricing is seen most strikingly in the equilibrium pricing kernel. In equilibrium, the price of the risky asset is equal to the lesser of two amounts. The first amount is the standard discounted value of future dividends. The efficient markets hypothesis claims that the price of a security is equal to the expected present value of the stream of future dividends. This is true in our model as long as there is no shortage of liquidity in the market. When there is a shortage of liquidity, however, the asset price is determined by the amount of cash in the market. More precisely, the asset price is equal to the ratio of available liquidity to the amount of the asset supplied. In this case assets, we have cash-in-the-market pricing. Assets are "underpriced" and returns are excessive relative to the standard efficient markets formula.

The amount of cash in the market will depend on the second important feature of our theory, which is the participants' *liquidity preference*. The higher the average liquidity preference of investors in the market, the greater is the average level of the short asset in portfolios and the greater the market's ability to absorb liquidity trading without large price changes. Building on this relationship between liquidity preference and asset-price volatility, we can see how market participation helps determine the degree of volatility in the market. The amount of cash in the market and the amount of liquidity trading both depend on who decides to participate. Thus the participation decision is one avenue by which large endogenous changes in volatility can be effected, as we shall see.

The main result in Section 4.3 is the existence of multiple Pareto-ranked equilibria. In one equilibrium, with limited participation, asset prices are highly volatile. In another (Pareto-preferred) equilibrium, participation is complete and asset prices are much less volatile.

## 4.2 THE MODEL

We make the usual assumptions of three **dates**, indexed by $t = 0, 1, 2$, and a single good at each date. There are the usual two assets, a short asset and a long asset.

- The **short asset** is represented by a storage technology: one unit of the good invested in the short asset at date $t$ is transformed into one unit of the good at date $t + 1$, where $t = 0, 1$.

- The **long asset** is represented by a productive investment technology with a two-period lag: one unit of the good invested in the long asset at date 0 is transformed into $R > 1$ units of the good at date 2.

The returns to both assets are assumed to be certain. The model can easily be extended to allow for uncertainty about asset returns (see Allen and Gale 1994), but here we want to focus on other sources of uncertainty.

The asset market contains a large number, strictly, a continuum,[1] of ex ante identical consumers. Each consumer is endowed with one unit of the good at date 0 and nothing at dates 1 and 2. There is no consumption at date 0 and consumers invest their endowment in a portfolio of long and short assets to provide for future consumption at dates 1 and 2.

Each consumer learns at date 1 whether he is an **early consumer** who only values consumption at date 1 or a **late consumer** who only values consumption at date 2. If a consumer expects $c_1$ units of consumption at date 1 when he

---

[1] We represent the set of agents by the unit interval $[0, 1]$, where each point in the interval is a different agent. We normalize the measure of the entire set of agents to be equal to one and measure the fraction of agents in any subset by its Lebesgue measure. The assumption of a large number of individually insignificant agents ensures perfect competition, that is, no one has enough market power to affect the equilibrium terms of trade.

is an early consumer and $c_2$ units of consumption at date 2 when he is a late consumer, his utility will be a random variable

$$u(c_1, c_2) = \begin{cases} U(c_1) & \text{with probability } \lambda, \\ U(c_2) & \text{with probability } 1 - \lambda \end{cases}$$

where the utility function $U(c)$ has the usual neoclassical properties with $U'(c) > 0$ and $U''(c) \leq 0$. The probability of being an early consumer is denoted by $\lambda > 0$. The only **aggregate** uncertainty concerns the demand for liquidity. We assume that $\lambda$ is a random variable. For simplicity, suppose $\lambda$ takes two values:

$$\lambda = \begin{cases} \lambda_H & \text{with probability } \pi \\ \lambda_L & \text{with probability } 1 - \pi \end{cases}$$

where $0 < \lambda_L < \lambda_H < 1$.

At date 0, individuals know the model and the prior distribution of $\lambda$. At date 1, they observe the realized value of $\lambda$ and discover whether they are early or late consumers.

## 4.3 EQUILIBRIUM

When a typical consumer makes his plans at date 0, he does not know whether state $H$ or state $L$ will occur and he does not know whether he will be an early or a late consumer; but he does know the probability of each of these events and rationally takes them into account in making his plans. More precisely, he knows that there are essentially four outcomes: he is either an early consumer in state $H$, a late consumer in state $H$, an early consumer in state $L$, or a late consumer in state $L$. Each state $s = H, L$ occurs with probability $1/2$ and then, conditional on the state, the consumer becomes an early consumer with probability $\lambda_s$ and a late consumer with probability $1 - \lambda_s$. The probabilities of the four outcomes are given in Table 4.2.

**Table 4.2.** Probability distribution of individual outcomes.

|          | Early              | Late                          |
|----------|--------------------|-------------------------------|
| State $H$ | $\frac{1}{2}\lambda_H$ | $\frac{1}{2}(1 - \lambda_H)$ |
| State $L$ | $\frac{1}{2}\lambda_L$ | $\frac{1}{2}(1 - \lambda_L)$ |

Although there is only a single good, we distinguish goods by the date and state in which they are delivered. Since all consumption occurs at dates 1 and 2 and there are two states of nature, $H$ and $L$, there are four contingent commodities, one for each ordered pair $(t, s)$ consisting of a date $t = 1, 2$ and a state $s = H, L$. A consumer will have a consumption bundle that consists of different quantities of all four contingent commodities. Let $c = (c_{1H}, c_{2H}, c_{1L}, c_{2L})$ denote the consumption bundle obtained in equilibrium, where $c_{ts}$ denotes consumption at date $t$ in state $s$, that is, consumption of the contingent commodity $(t, s)$. Figure 4.1 illustrates the outcomes for the individual consumer and the consumption associated with each outcome.

The expected utility associated with a consumption bundle $c = (c_{1H}, c_{2H}, c_{1L}, c_{2L})$ is given by

$$\frac{1}{2}\left\{\lambda_H U(c_{1H}) + (1 - \lambda_H) U(c_{2H})\right\} + \frac{1}{2}\left\{\lambda_L U(c_{1L}) + (1 - \lambda_L) U(c_{2L})\right\}.$$

If an individual is an early consumer and the state is $H$ then he consumes $c_{1H}$ and gets utility $U(c_{1H})$. The probability of this happening is $\frac{1}{2}\lambda_H$. The first term is the expected utility from being an early consumer in state $H$. The other terms are derived similarly. All of the consumer's decisions are assumed to maximize the value of his expected utility.

The consumption bundle obtained by a typical consumer depends on his portfolio decision at date 0 and the asset prices observed at future dates. Suppose the consumer invests $x \geq 0$ units in the long asset and $y \geq 0$ units in the short asset, where $x + y = 1$. The consumer's portfolio will produce $y$ units of the good at date 1 and $(1 - y)R$ units of the good at date 2. An early consumer

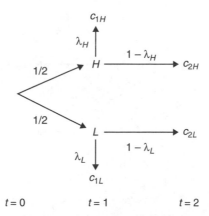

Figure 4.1. Information structure of the asset market model.

will want to consume as much as possible at date 1 and a late consumer will want to consume as much as possible at date 2. We assume there is an asset market at date 1. The price of the long asset, measured in terms of that good at date 1, is denoted by $P_s$ in state $s = H, L$. The present value of the investor's portfolio at date 1 in state $s$ will be

$$w_{1s} = y + P_s x. \tag{4.1}$$

Note that if the price of the long asset is $P_s$, then the implicit price of future consumption in terms of present consumption is $p_s \equiv P_s/R$. The investor's wealth in terms of consumption at date 2 is

$$\frac{w_{1s}}{p_s} = \left( \frac{y}{P_s} + x \right) R. \tag{4.2}$$

Figure 4.2 illustrates the determination of a typical profile of consumption at each date and state. Note that consumption is determined by the portfolio decision at date 0, that is, the choice of $x$ and $y$, and the asset prices in each state. Since consumers take prices as given, the consumer has determined his consumption (contingent on the state) once he has chosen the portfolio $(x, y)$.

The determination of equilibrium for the asset market model can be broken down into two steps. First, we can determine the asset prices in each state at date 1 taking as given the portfolio decisions made at date 0. Then, for any pair of prices $(P_H, P_L)$, we can determine the optimal portfolio at date 0, that is, the portfolio $(x, y)$ that maximizes expected utility. To be certain that we have found an equilibrium, we have to check that these two steps are consistent, that

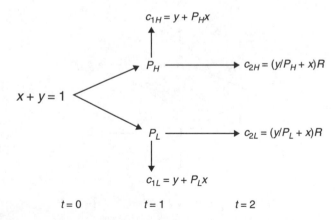

**Figure 4.2.** Asset returns in the asset market model.

is, that the portfolios chosen at date 0 will lead to the expected prices at date 1 and that the expectation of those prices will lead to the choice of the same portfolios at date 0. We begin with the analysis of market-clearing at date 1.

### 4.3.1 Market-clearing at date 1

Suppose that all the consumers have chosen the same portfolio $(x, y)$ at date 0. The budget constraint ensures that $x + y = 1$ so in what follows we let $1 - y$ denote the investment in the long asset. Also, because the true state is known and the analysis applies equally to both states, we can suppress the reference to the state and let $P$ denote the price of the long asset and $\lambda$ the fraction of early consumers.

The price $P$ is determined by demand and supply. The supply of the long asset comes from the early consumers. An early consumer wants to liquidate all his assets in order to consume as much as possible at date 1. In particular, the early consumers will inelastically supply their holdings of the short asset, whatever the price. So there is a vertical supply curve and the quantity supplied is

$$S = \lambda(1 - y)$$

because there are $\lambda$ early consumers and each of them has $1 - y$ units of the long asset.

The demand for the long asset comes from the late consumers, but the determination of demand is a little more subtle than the determination of supply. Because the late consumers do not want to consume until date 2, they have a non-trivial decision about which assets to hold between date 1 and date 2. Because the true state is known at date 1 there is no uncertainty and, in particular, the returns of the two assets are known for certain. One unit of the good invested in the short asset at date 1 will produce one unit at date 2. One unit of the good will purchase $1/P$ units of the long asset at date 0 and this will produce $R/P$ units of the good at date 2. Consumers will hold whichever asset has the highest returns. There are three cases to be considered.

1. If $R/P < 1$, the return on the long asset is less than the return on the short asset, and no one will want to hold the long asset between dates 1 and 2.

2. If $R/P = 1$, the one-period holding returns on the short and long assets are equalized at date 1. Then late consumers should be indifferent between holding the two assets at date 1.

3. If $R/P > 1$, the one-period holding return on the long asset is greater than the return on the short asset and no one will want to hold the short asset between date 1 and date 2.

In Case 1, the demand for the long asset is zero. In Case 2, the demand for the long asset is perfectly elastic, at least, up to the maximum amount that the late consumers could buy. In Case 3, the late consumers will want to hold only the long asset, and they will supply their holdings of the short asset inelastically in exchange for the long asset. Since there are $1 - \lambda$ late consumers and each holds $y$ units of the short asset, the total supply of the short asset is $(1 - \lambda)y$. If the price of the long asset is $P$ then the net demand for the long asset will be

$$D^*(P) = \frac{(1 - \lambda)y}{P}.$$

Thus the demand curve will have the form

$$D(P) = \begin{cases} 0 & \text{if } P > R, \\ [0, D^*(R)] & \text{if } P = R, \\ D^*(P) & \text{if } P < R. \end{cases}$$

Figure 4.3 illustrates the demand and supply curves for the long asset. There are two cases that are relevant. If $S \leq D^*(R)$, then the intersection of demand and supply occurs where the demand curve is perfectly elastic and the equilibrium price is $P = R$. If $S > D^*(R)$ then the intersection occurs at the downward-sloping section of the demand curve and the price satisfies $S = D^*(P)$. Substituting for the values of $S$ and $D^*(P)$ we see that $P$ is determined by the equation

$$\lambda(1 - y) = \frac{(1 - \lambda)y}{P}$$

or

$$P = \frac{(1 - \lambda)y}{\lambda(1 - y)}.$$

Putting together these two cases, we can see that

$$P = \min\left\{R, \frac{(1 - \lambda)y}{\lambda(1 - y)}\right\}. \tag{4.3}$$

This pricing formula illustrates the impact of liquidity on asset pricing. When liquidity is plentiful then the price of the long asset is simply the discounted payoff where the discount rate is the opportunity cost given by the return on the short asset. When liquidity is scarce the price of the long asset is determined by the cash in the market. The early consumers exchange all of their holdings of the long asset in exchange for the consumption goods given by the late consumers holdings of the short asset.

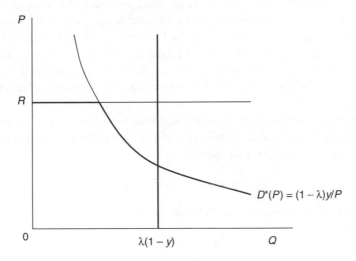

**Figure 4.3.** Demand for and supply of the long asset at date 1.

### 4.3.2 Portfolio choice

Now consider the investment decision of the consumers at date 0. Taking as given the asset prices $P_H$ and $P_L$ in each state at date 1, the investors will choose the portfolio $(y, 1 - y)$ to maximize their expected utility,

$$E\left[\lambda_s U\left(w_s\right) + (1 - \lambda_s) U\left(\frac{w_s}{p_s}\right)\right], \tag{4.4}$$

where $w_s = y + P_s(1 - y)$ and $p_s \equiv P_s/R$.

An equilibrium consists of a pair of asset prices $(P_H, P_L)$ and a portfolio choice $y$ such that prices are given by the equation (4.3) and the portfolio maximizes (4.4) at the given prices.

## 4.4 CASH-IN-THE-MARKET PRICING

Using the model described above, we can show how liquidity preference affects the prices of assets.

### No aggregate uncertainty

Consider first the case where there is no aggregate uncertainty, so $\lambda_H = \lambda_L$. Since the two states are identical we can reasonably assume that the asset price is the same in each state, say, $P_H = P_L = P$. As we saw in the previous chapter, when there is no uncertainty about the asset price $P$, the only possible equilibrium value is $P = 1$. At any other price, one of the two assets is dominated and will not be held at date 0, which implies that the asset market cannot clear at date 1.

When $P = 1$, the two assets have the same return at date 0 and the investor's wealth at date 1 is independent of his portfolio choice at date 0. If he is an early consumer, his consumption at date 1 is

$$c_1 = 1 - y + Py = 1$$

and, if he is a late consumer, his consumption at date 2 is

$$c_2 = \left(1 - y + \frac{y}{P}\right) R = R.$$

This consumption allocation is feasible for the economy if the average investment in the short asset satisfies $y = \lambda$. Then

$$\lambda c_1 = \lambda = y$$

and

$$(1 - \lambda) c_2 = (1 - y) R$$

as required.

### Aggregate uncertainty

Now suppose that there is aggregate uncertainty about the total demand for liquidity, as represented by fluctuations in $\lambda_s$. This implies non-zero asset-price volatility in the sense that

$$P_H < P_L.$$

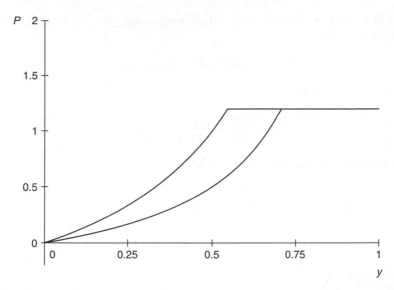

**Figure 4.4.** Prices as functions of $y$ for parameters $R = 1.2, \lambda_L = 0.5, \lambda_H = 0.67$.

From the formula for prices (4.3) and the fact that $\lambda_H > \lambda_L$, we can see that $P_H < P_L$ unless $P_H = P_L = R$. This fact is illustrated in Figure 4.4.

$P_H = P_L = R$ implies that no one will ever hold the short asset at date 0, because it is dominated by the long asset (one unit invested in the long asset is worth $R > 1$ units of the good at date 1). But if none of the short asset is held at date 0, the price of the asset at date 1 will be zero. This contradiction implies that the market-clearing prices must satisfy $P_H < P_L$. In fact, the short is undominated only if $P_H < 1$.

### Comparative statics

Suppose that we have cash-in-the-market pricing in both states, that is,

$$P_s = \frac{(1 - \lambda_s)y}{\lambda_s(1 - y)}$$

for states $s = H, L$. Then

$$\frac{P_H}{P_L} = \frac{(1 - \lambda_H)\lambda_L}{\lambda_H(1 - \lambda_L)}. \tag{4.5}$$

From this formula, we can derive a number of comparative static properties about the effect of liquidity shocks on asset-price volatility.

To illustrate the possibilities it is helpful to consider a single parameter family of liquidity shocks:

$$\lambda_H - 0.5 = 0.5 - \lambda_L = \varepsilon.$$

Then

$$\frac{P_H}{P_L} = \frac{(0.5 - \varepsilon)^2}{(0.5 + \varepsilon)^2}.$$

The solution is illustrated in Figure 4.5.

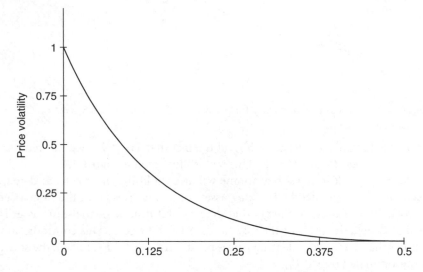

**Figure 4.5.** Price volatility $P_H/P_L$ as a function of liquidity shock parameter $\varepsilon$.

Interpreting this diagram, we have to remember that it is based on the assumption that cash-in-the-market pricing holds in both states. As the difference $\lambda_H - \lambda_L$ increases, however, the ratio $P_H/P_L$ converges to zero and it is more likely that $P_L = R$ will hold. Nonetheless, this gives a nice example of how the liquidity shocks can lead to very large fluctuations in asset prices.

To check these conclusions, we have calculated the complete equilibrium for the special case in which consumers have logarithmic utility functions $U(c) = \ln c$. Table 4.3 shows the equilibrium values of prices and the portfolio when $R = 1.2$ and the two states are equiprobable.

When $\lambda_H$ and $\lambda_L$ are not too far apart ($\varepsilon$ is small) we have cash-in-the-market pricing in both states. However, when the difference $\lambda_H - \lambda_L$ becomes

Table 4.3. The effect of aggregate uncertainty on prices; $\pi = 0.5; R = 1.2; U(c) = \ln(c)$.

| $\lambda_H$ | $\lambda_L$ | $P_H$ | $P_L$ | $y$ |
|---|---|---|---|---|
| 0.5 | 0.5 | 1 | 1 | 0.5 |
| 0.51 | 0.49 | 0.961 | 1.041 | 0.5 |
| 0.53 | 0.47 | 0.887 | 1.128 | 0.5 |
| 0.545 | 0.455 | 0.834 | 1.200 | 0.5 |
| 0.6 | 0.4 | 0.830 | 1.2 | 0.555 |
| 0.9 | 0.1 | 0.810 | 1.2 | 0.879 |

large enough ($\varepsilon = 0.1$), the price in the low state hits its upper bound $P_L = R$. Investors increase the amount in the short asset and this increase in liquidity means that increases in price volatility are damped relative to the case where there is cash in the market pricing in both states.

The effect of changes in the demand for aggregate liquidity on price volatility is determined by the the amount of cash in the market. If the amount of cash $y$ held by market participants is large relative to the variation in liquidity needs then prices will not be very volatile. In the example described in Table 4.3, large amounts of the short asset were held and this is why large changes in aggregate liquidity needs were needed to cause significant price volatility. If the amount of cash held by participants is small then even small changes in absolute liquidity needs can have a significant effect on prices. The example in Table 4.4 illustrates this phenomenon.

Table 4.4. The effect of aggregate uncertainty on prices with limited cash in the market; $\pi = 0.1; R = 1.2; U(c) = \ln(c)$.

| $\lambda_H$ | $\lambda_L$ | $P_H$ | $P_L$ | $y$ |
|---|---|---|---|---|
| 0.05 | 0.05 | 1 | 1 | 0.05 |
| 0.055 | 0.045 | 0.828 | 1.023 | 0.046 |
| 0.06 | 0.04 | 0.687 | 1.052 | 0.042 |
| 0.075 | 0.025 | 0.388 | 1.200 | 0.030 |
| 0.09 | 0.01 | 0.384 | 1.2 | 0.037 |

In this example, we have assumed that the high state is much less likely than the low state. The effect of this change is to significantly lower the amount of liquidity in the markets for similar values of $\varepsilon$. As a result, the effect of a given absolute change in liquidity demand on price volatility is much higher. Notice, however, that once we get to the point where $P_L = R$ then changes in aggregate uncertainty no longer affect price volatility very much.

Another interesting question is what happens when both $\lambda_H$ and $\lambda_L$ become small. If the probability of being an early consumer is small in both states, we should expect that consumers will tend to invest much more in the long asset and very little in the short asset. This raises the possibility that even very small changes in liquidity demand $\lambda_H - \lambda_L$ can have a large effect on prices. Once again it is helpful to consider a one-parameter family of shocks

$$\lambda_s = \begin{cases} k\varepsilon & \text{if } s = H \\ \varepsilon & \text{if } s = L \end{cases}$$

for some $k \geq 1$. Substituting these values in (4.5) we get

$$\frac{P_H}{P_L} = \frac{(1 - k\varepsilon)\varepsilon}{k\varepsilon(1 - \varepsilon)} = \frac{(1 - k\varepsilon)}{k(1 - \varepsilon)}.$$

Then

$$\lim_{\varepsilon \to 0} \frac{P_H}{P_L} = \frac{1}{k}.$$

Again, if $k$ becomes very large, then the upper bound $P_L = R$ may be binding, but even so we see that the variation in prices can be very large even if the variation in liquidity demand as measured by $\lambda_H - \lambda_L = (k - 1)\varepsilon$ is very small.

## 4.5　LIMITED PARTICIPATION

We have shown in the previous section that what matters for price volatility is not absolute changes in liquidity demand, but rather changes in liquidity demand relative to the supply of liquidity. If a liquidity shock is large relative to the supply of liquidity there is significant price volatility. This can be true even if the liquidity shock is arbitrarily small. In this section we develop these ideas one step further. We introduce a fixed cost of participating in a market. In order to be active in a market, an investor must initially devote resources to learning about the basic features of the market such as the trading rules, the distribution of asset returns, and how to monitor changes through time. When there are costs of participating in the market, asset price volatility is determined by the supply of liquidity from *the market participants* rather than from investors as a whole. If the market participants do not choose to supply much liquidity, the market will be characterized by high asset-price volatility, even if there is a willingness to supply liquidity elsewhere in the economy. This leads to the possibility of multiple equilibria, which differ in the extent of market participation and market liquidity.

We assume there are two types of investor in the economy. Type-A investors are aggressive, that is, they are more likely to participate in the market. They have a low probability of being early consumers, hence a low preference for liquidity, and they also have low risk aversion compared to the second type. Type-B investors are bashful, that is, they are less likely to participate in the market. They have a higher probability of being early consumers, hence a higher preference for liquidity, and a higher degree of risk aversion.

When the cost of entering the market is sufficiently small, we can show that there is always *full participation*. All investors enter the market, the average amount of liquidity is high, and asset prices are not excessively volatile. As the cost of participation increases, new types of equilibria emerge. For high entry costs there is no participation. For intermediate entry costs there exists a *limited-participation equilibrium*, in which only the aggressive investors are willing to enter the market. Because the market is dominated by investors with low liquidity preference, holding small reserves of the short asset, even small variations in the proportion of liquidity traders can cause a significant variation in prices. There are highly liquid investors in the economy, holding large reserves of liquidity which could potentially dampen this volatility, but they have chosen not to participate in this market, at least in the short run.

The two types of equilibria react quite differently to small liquidity shocks. In the limited-participation equilibrium, with just one type of investor in the market, there can be considerable price volatility even when shocks are small as shown in the previous section. In the full-participation equilibrium, the liquidity provided by the investors with high liquidity preference absorbs small liquidity trades, so a small amount of aggregate uncertainty implies a small amount of price volatility. Comparing the two equilibria, limited market participation has the effect of amplifying price volatility relative to the full-participation equilibrium.

We can also generate multiple equilibria: for a non-negligible set of entry costs, equilibria with full participation and with limited participation coexist. If asset prices are expected to be highly volatile, type-B investors will not participate. As a result, the market will be dominated by type-A investors who hold illiquid portfolios, which ensures that the market is illiquid and generates the expected volatility. In this way beliefs become self-confirming. On the other hand, if asset prices are expected to be stable, they will all participate, the market will be liquid because the average investor is holding a more liquid portfolio, and the expectation of stability becomes self-confirming.

The existence of multiple equilibria gives rise to the possibility of coordination failure. Comparing equilibria, we see that one has lower volatility than the other. For some parameter values, these differences ensure that we can Pareto-rank the two types of equilibria. Type-B investors are clearly better off when there is full participation, because they could have stayed out but chose to enter. Except when there are perverse income effects, the reduction in volatility also benefits the type-A aggressive investors. In general, the fact that the prices of financial assets are more volatile than other prices may or may not be socially undesirable. However, if there exists a Pareto-preferred equilibrium with lower volatility, we can say that high volatility represents a market failure.

### 4.5.1 The model

We start with a brief description of the model. As before there are three dates $t = 0, 1, 2$.

- There are two types of consumers/investors $i = A, B$ and a continuum of each type. The total number of agents of type $i$ is denoted $N_i > 0$.
- Consumers have the usual Diamond–Dybvig preferences, that is, they are early consumers with probability $\lambda_i$ or late consumers with probability $1 - \lambda_i$:

$$u_i(c_1, c_2) = \begin{cases} U_i(c_1) & \text{w. pr. } \lambda_i \\ U_i(c_2) & \text{w. pr. } 1 - \lambda_i \end{cases}$$

where $0 < \lambda_i < 1$ for $i = A, B$. They learn whether they are early or late consumers at date 1.
- Type $A$ is assumed to be less risk averse than type $B$.
- Each investor has an initial endowment of one unit of the good at date 0 and nothing at future dates.
- There is a single consumption good at each date and there are two assets:
  - the *short asset* produces one unit of consumption at date $t + 1$ for each unit invested at date $t$ and the amount chosen by each investor is denoted $y_i$;
  - the *long asset* produces $R > 1$ units of consumption at date 2 for each unit invested at date 0 and the amount chosen by investors of type $i$ is denoted $x_i$.
- Investors can hold the short asset without cost. However, the long asset can only be traded if an investor pays a fixed cost of $e \geq 0$ utils and enters the market for the long asset.

## 4.5.2 Equilibrium

*Individual decisions*

The decision tree faced by a typical investor is illustrated in Figure 4.6. Since the decisions are essentially the same for both types, we suppress the *i* subscript in this section.

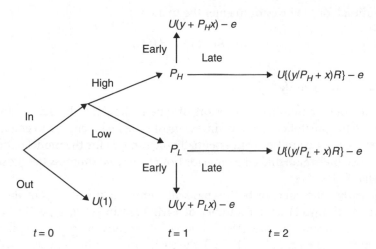

**Figure 4.6.** Consumer's decision tree with participation decision.

At date 0, an investor first decides whether or not to enter the asset market. If he decides not to enter, he can only invest in the short asset. Since the return on the short asset is one, his consumption will be equal to his initial endowment, i.e. $c = 1$, and his utility will be $U(1)$, whether he is an early or late consumer. If he decides to enter the asset market, he must pay the entry fee $e$ (in utils) and then divides his endowment between an investment of $x$ units in the long asset and $y$ units in the short asset.

At date 1, the investor learns the true state of nature and whether he is an early or late consumer. If he is an early consumer, he liquidates his portfolio and consumes the liquidated value. If the price of the long asset is $P_s$ in state $s = H, L$ then the early consumer's net utility will be $U(y + P_s x) - e$. Otherwise, he is a late consumer and he rolls over his assets until the final period when he consumes the liquidated value and receives a net utility $U\left(\left(\frac{y}{P_s} + x\right) R\right) - e$.

Given that the investor decides to enter the market, he chooses his portfolio $(x, y)$ to maximize his expected utility, taking as given the prices $P_H$ and $P_L$ that will prevail in each state. Using $x = 1 - y$, we can write his decision problem as

$$U^*(P_H, P_L) = \max_{0 \leq y \leq 1} E \left\{ \lambda_s U(y + P_s(1 - y)) - e \right.$$

$$\left. + (1 - \lambda_s) U \left( \left( \frac{y}{P_s} + (1 - y) \right) R \right) \right\}.$$

It is optimal for the investor to enter the market if

$$U^*(P_H, P_L) \geq U(1).$$

### Market clearing at date 1

Let $n_i$ denote the number of investors of type $i$ who enter the market and let $y_i$ denote the portfolio chosen by investors of type $i$ who choose to enter. The market-clearing conditions are essentially the same as for the model with one type. Since the argument is the same for both states, we suppress the subscript $s$ in what follows.

The early consumers of both types will supply their holdings of the long asset inelastically. The total number of early consumers of type $i$ is $n_i$, the number of entrants, times $\lambda_i$, the fraction of early consumers. Since each early consumer of type $i$ supplies $(1 - y_i)$, the total supply of the long asset will be

$$S = n_A \lambda_A (1 - y_A) + n_B \lambda_B (1 - y_B).$$

If $P = R$ then the late consumers are indifferent between holding the short and the long asset between date 1 and date 2. If $P < R$ then the long asset dominates the short asset and the late consumers will supply their holdings of the short asset inelastically in exchange for the long asset. The total demand for the long asset will be

$$D^*(P) = \frac{n_A (1 - \lambda_A) y_A + n_B (1 - \lambda_B) y_B}{P}$$

since there are $n_i(1 - \lambda_i)$ late consumers of type $i$ and each can purchase $y_i/P$ units of the long asset.

The price that satisfies $S = D^*(P)$ is given by the ratio $Y/S$, where

$$Y = n_A (1 - \lambda_A) y_A + n_B (1 - \lambda_B) y_B$$

is the supply of the short asset by early consumers and $S$ is the supply of the long asset by late consumers. By the usual argument, the price of the long asset is the minimum of $R$ and $Y/S$, that is,

$$P = \min\left\{R, \frac{Y}{S}\right\}.$$

This formula holds in each state. The difference in prices between the two states is due to the different demands for liquidity, that is, the different values of $\lambda_{is}$ for each type in each state.

## Equilibrium conditions

To describe an equilibrium we need to specify the following elements:

- the entry decisions of the investors, represented by the numbers $n_A$ and $n_B$;
- the portfolio choices of the investors, represented by the numbers $y_A$ and $y_B$;
- and the equilibrium prices $P_H$ and $P_L$.

As shown above, the equilibrium prices must satisfy the equation

$$P_s = \min\left\{R, \frac{Y_s}{X_s}\right\}$$

where

$$X_s = n_A \lambda_{As}\left(1 - y_A\right) + n_B \lambda_{Bs}\left(1 - y_B\right)$$

and

$$Y_s = n_A\left(1 - \lambda_{As}\right) y_A + n_B\left(1 - \lambda_{Bs}\right) y_B$$

for each $s = H, L$; the portfolio choice $y_i$ must solve

$$U^*(P_H, P_L) = \max_{0 \le y \le 1} E\left\{\lambda_{is} U(y + P_s(1 - y)) - e\right.$$

$$\left. + (1 - \lambda_{is}) U\left(\left(\frac{y}{P_s} + (1 - y)\right) R\right)\right\},$$

for each type $i$; and the entry decisions must be optimal in the sense that

$$U_i^*(P_H, P_L) > U_i(1) \implies n_i = N_i$$

and

$$U_i^*(P_H, P_L) < U_i(1) \implies n_i = 0.$$

### 4.5.3 Equilibrium with full participation

An equilibrium with full participation is one in which every investor chooses to enter the asset market, that is, $n_A = N_A$ and $n_B = N_B$.

Suppose that entry into the asset market is free, that is, $e = 0$. Then full participation is optimal. In fact, it is strictly optimal. To see this, consider the following strategy. At date 0 the investor invests everything in the short asset $y = 1$. At date 1 he consumes the returns to the short asset if he is an early consumer; otherwise, he invests in the long asset at date 1 and consumes the returns at date 2. The expected utility from this strategy is

$$\frac{1}{2}\left\{\lambda_{iH}U_1(1) + (1 - \lambda_{iH})U_i\left(\frac{R}{P_H}\right)\right\} + \frac{1}{2}\left\{\lambda_{iL}U_i(1) + (1 - \lambda_{iL})U_i\left(\frac{R}{P_L}\right)\right\}.$$

Since we know that $P_s \leq R$ for $s = H, L$ the expected utility must be at least $U(1)$. However, we cannot have $P_s = R$ for both states $s = H, L$, for then the short asset would be dominated at date 0, no one would hold the short asset, and the price of the long asset would be zero at date 1. Thus, in any equilibrium $P_s < R$ for at least one state $s = H, L$. But this means that consumption is strictly greater than one for the late consumers in some state. Thus, $U_i^*(P_H, P_L) > U_i(1)$.

If it is strictly optimal to enter the market when the entry cost is zero then it must also be strictly optimal to enter the market for all sufficiently small entry costs $e > 0$. Thus, we have proved the following proposition.

**Proposition 1** For all $e > 0$, sufficiently small, an equilibrium $\{(n_A, y_A), (n_B, y_B), (P_H, P_L)\}$ must entail full participation, that is,

$$n_A = N_A \text{ and } n_B = N_B.$$

### 4.5.4 Full participation and asset-price volatility

To illustrate further the properties of the full-participation equilibrium, we use an example in which the investors of type $A$ have a random liquidity shock and investors of type $B$ have a non-random liquidity shock:

$$\lambda_{As} = \begin{cases} k > 0 & \text{if } s = H \\ 0 & \text{if } s = L \end{cases}$$

and

$$\lambda_{BH} = \lambda_{BL} = \lambda_B.$$

When there is full participation the pricing formula requires $P_s = \min\{R, Y_s/S_s\}$. Now as $k \to 0$, so $\lambda_{AH} \to 0$, and type-$A$ investors become more and more certain of being late consumers $y_A \to 0$ so

$$\frac{Y_s}{S_s} \to \frac{(1 - \lambda_B)y_B}{\lambda_B x_B} = \bar{Q},$$

say, where $\bar{Q}$ is a constant since $\lambda_B$ is a constant. In the limit, $P_s = \min\{R, \bar{Q}\}$. Recall that $R > 1$ for all $s$. Then $\bar{Q} > 1$ implies $P_s > 1$ for all $s$. This implies that the short asset is dominated by the long asset at date 0 so no one will hold the short asset; but this is not consistent with equilibrium. On the other hand, if $\bar{Q} < 1$ then $P_s < 1$ for all $s$. This means that the short asset dominates the long asset at date 0, which is also inconsistent with equilibrium. Therefore,

$$P_s = \bar{Q} = 1 \text{ for } s = H, L.$$

Thus, as liquidity shocks among the type $A$s become small, the type $B$s are able to absorb the shocks, which have no effect on prices.

Along the same lines, it can be seen that as $N_B \to \infty$, holding $N_A$ constant, $P_s$ tends to the same limit, and a similar result holds. As the number of type $B$s goes up, the amount of liquidity in the market becomes large relative to the fluctuations in liquidity trading, and this dampens volatility.

### 4.5.5 Limited participation and asset-price volatility

Continuing with the special case considered in the preceding section, suppose that there exists an equilibrium in which only type $A$ investors enter the market. That is, $n_A = N_A$ and $n_B = 0$. With only type $A$ in the market at date 1, there will be no demand for the short asset in state $L$ and $P_L = R$. The price in state $P_H$ must satisfy the first-order condition that makes investors willing to hold both assets at the margin in date 0. In the limit, as $k \to 0$, investors of type $A$ are late consumers with probability one and invest all of their wealth in the long asset. So, in the limit, a late consumer receives utility $U_A(R)$ regardless of the state. The marginal utility of income is also constant across states, so the investor behaves as if he is risk neutral. Then in order to be willing to hold both assets, the expected returns must be equal over two periods, that is,

$$R = \frac{1}{2}\frac{R}{P_H} + \frac{1}{2}.$$

The left hand side is the return to one unit invested in the long asset. The right hand side is the expected return to one unit invested in the short asset at date 0.

To see this, suppose that the investor holds his wealth in the form of the short asset at date 0 and invests in the long asset at date 1 (this is always weakly optimal and will be strictly optimal if $P_s < R$). With probability $\pi$ he is in state $H$ at date 1 and can buy $1/P_H$ units of the long asset at date 1, which will yield $R/P_H$ at date 2. With probability $\frac{1}{2}$ he is in state $L$ at date 1 and can buy $1/P_L = 1/R$ units of the long asset at date 1, which will yield $R/R = 1$ at date 2. Taking the expected value of these returns gives us the right hand side of the equation. We can solve this equation for the asset price in the high state:

$$P_H = \frac{R}{2R - 1} < 1.$$

In this equilibrium, unlike the full-participation equilibrium, there is substantial asset price volatility even in the limit as $k \to 0$. If the asset-price volatility is sufficiently high and the type-$B$ investors are sufficiently risk averse, it may be optimal and hence an equilibrium phenomenon, for the type-$B$ investors to stay out of the market. This situation is illustrated in Figure 4.7.

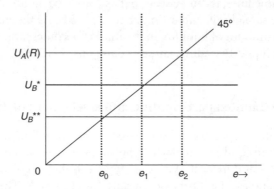

**Figure 4.7.** Investors' entry decisions for different entry costs.

On the horizontal axis we measure the entry cost $e$ and on the vertical axis the expected utility of entering the asset market. Without loss of generality, we normalize utilities so that $U_A(1) = U_B(1) = 0$. We have already seen that, in the limit as $k \to 0$, the expected utility of type $A$ is $U_A(R)$. Let $U_B^{**}$ denote the expected utility of type $B$, *before taking account of the entry cost*, in the limited participation equilibrium as $k \to 0$. Under the assumption that the utility from staying out of the market is zero, an investor will enter the market if the gross expected utility $U_B^{**}$ is greater than the entry cost $e$. In other words, he will enter if his payoff is above the 45° line. As long as $U_B^{**} < U_A(R)$ as drawn, there will be a range of entry costs in which the type-$A$ investors find it worth while to enter and the type-$B$ investors do not. For any $e < e_2$, it is worthwhile for the type-$A$ investors to enter and, for any $e > e_0$, it is not worthwhile for the type-$B$ investors to enter *if they anticipate the high degree of volatility associated with the limited participation equilibrium.* Thus, for any entry cost $e_1 < e < e_2$ there will be an equilibrium with limited participation.

### 4.5.6 Multiple Pareto-ranked equilibria

Figure 4.7 also illustrates the possibility of multiple equilibria. Let $U_B^*$ denote the expected utility of the type $B$ investors in the full participation equilibrium where asset-price volatility is extremely low. Again, $U_B^*$ is the gross expected utility before the entry cost is substracted. If $U_B^* < U_A(R)$, as shown in the diagram, then for any $e < e_1$ it is worthwhile for both types to enter if they anticipate the low asset-price volatility associated with the full-participation equilibrium. So there is a full-participation equilibrium corresponding to entry costs $e < e_1$.

If type-$B$'s (gross) expected utility in the limited participation equilibrium $U_B^{**}$ is less than the (gross) expected utility in the full-participation equilibrium $U_B^*$, as shown in the diagram, then $e_0 < e_1$ and there will be an interval $e_0 < e < e_1$ where both kinds of equilibria, those with full participation and those with limited participation, exist.

In fact, we can show that in the limit these equilibria are Pareto-ranked. The type-$B$ investors always prefer the full-participation equilibrium. They have the option of just holding the short asset, as they do in the limited participation equilibrium, but choose not to do so. The reason the full-participation equilibrium is better for them is that it allows them to obtain the benefits of the long asset's high return. As for the type-$A$ investors, in the limit as $k \to 0$, they obtain $U_A(R) - e$ in both equilibria and so are indifferent.

A general comparison of the type-$A$ investors outside the limit as $k \to 0$ is more complex for the simple reason that there are both *risk* and *income* effects. The risk effect arises from the fact that prices are more variable in the limited-participation equilibrium than in the full-participation equilibrium. This tends to make the type-$A$ investors prefer the full-participation equilibrium. However, in addition, there is an income effect which can more than offset the risk effect.

In the limited-participation equilibrium, the type-$A$ investors who are early consumers trade with the type-$A$ investors who are late consumers. Their initial expected utility is an average over these two states. There are no transfers between the type-$A$ investors and the type-$B$ investors. In the full-participation equilibrium, however, $\lambda_{As} < \lambda_B$ so there are proportionately fewer type-$A$

investors than type-$B$ investors who are early consumers, and more who are late consumers. On average, the type-$A$ investors buy more of the long-term asset from the type-$B$ investors than they sell to them. The price of the long-term asset determines whether there is a transfer from the type-$A$ investors to the type-$B$ investors or vice versa. It is possible that the transfer of income between the type-$A$ investors and the type-$B$ investors in the full-participation equilibrium outweighs the risk effect and the type-$A$ investors prefer the limited-participation equilibrium. Thus, the equilibria cannot be Pareto-ranked in general.

## 4.6 SUMMARY

The results in this chapter have been demonstrated for quite special examples. However, they hold for a fairly wide range of cases. Allen and Gale (1994) documents how the results hold if the return on the long asset $R$ is random and there is a continuous range of values concerning the uncertainty associated with the proportion of early consumers.

The first major result is to show that price volatility is bounded away from zero as aggregate uncertainty about liquidity demands tends to zero. When liquidity is scarce, asset prices are not determined by discounted cash flows, but rather by the amount of liquidity in the market. It is the relative variation in the amount of the long asset and the liquidity supplied to the market that is important for price volatility. The absolute amounts of both fall as aggregate uncertainty becomes negligible, but the relative variation remains the same.

There is considerable empirical evidence suggesting that investors participate in a limited number of markets because of transaction costs. We studied the interaction between liquidity preference and limited market participation and the effect of limited market participation on asset-price volatility. For a range of entry costs, there exist multiple equilibria with very different welfare properties. Asset-price volatility can be excessive in the sense of being Pareto-inferior as well as in the sense of being unexplained by the arrival of new information.

## REFERENCES

Allen, F. and D. Gale (1994). "Limited Market Participation and Volatility of Asset Prices," *American Economic Review* 84, 933–955.

Bertaut, C. (1998). "Stockholding Behavior of U.S. Households: Evidence from the 1983–1989 Survey of Consumer Finances," *Review of Economics and Statistics* 80, 263–275.

Blume, M., J. Crockett, and I. Friend (1974). "Stock Ownership in the United States: Characteristics and Trends," *Survey of Current Business* 54, 16–40.

Blume, M. and I. Friend (1978). *The Changing Role of the Individual Investor: A Twentieth Century Fund Report*, New York: Wiley.

Brennan, M. (1975). "The Optimal Number of Securities in a Risky Asset Portfolio when there are Fixed Costs of Transacting: Theory and Some Empirical Results," *Journal of Financial and Quantitative Analysis* 10, 483–496.

Campbell, J. and R. Shiller (1988a). "Stock Prices, Earnings and Expected Dividends," *Journal of Finance* 43, 661–676.

Campbell, J. and R. Shiller (1988b). "The Dividend-Price Ratio, Expectations of Future Dividends and Discount Factors," *Review of Financial Studies* 1, 195–228.

Fama, E. (1970). "Efficient Capital Markets: A Review of Theory and Empirical Work," *Journal of Finance* 25, 383–417.

Guiso, L., M. Haliassos, and T. Jappelli (2002). *Household Portfolios*. Cambridge, MA: MIT Press.

Haliassos, M. and C. Bertaut (1995). "Why Do So Few Hold Stocks?" *Economic Journal* 105, 1110–1129.

King, M. and J. Leape (1984). "Wealth and Portfolio Composition: Theory and Evidence," National Bureau of Economic Research (Cambridge, MA), Working Paper No. 1468.

LeRoy, S. and W. Parke (1992). "Stock Price Volatility: Tests Based on the Geometric Random Walk," *American Economic Review* 82, 981–992.

LeRoy, S. and R. Porter (1981)."The Present Value Relation: Tests Based on Implied Variance Bounds," *Econometrica* 49, 555–574.

Mankiw, N. G. and S. P. Zeldes (1991). "The Consumption of Stockholders and Non-Stockholders," *Journal of Financial Economics* 29, 97–112.

Merton, R. (1987). "On the Current State of the Stock Market Rationality Hypothesis," in R. Dornbusch, S. Fisher, and J. Bossons (eds), *Macroeconomics and Finance: Essays in Honor of Franco Modigliani*. Cambridge, MA: MIT Press, 99–124.

Shiller, R. (1981). "Do Stock Prices Move too Much to be Justified by Subsequent Changes in Dividends?" *American Economic Review* 71, 421–436.

Vissing-Jorgensen, A. (2002). "Towards an Explanation of Household Portfolio Choice Heterogeneity: Nonfinancial Income and Participation Cost Structures," working paper, University of Chicago.

West, K. (1988). "Dividend Innovations and Stock Price Volatility," *Econometrica* 56, 37–61.

# 5

## Financial fragility

In the preceding two chapters, we separately considered the operation of asset markets and intermediaries, such as banks. In the present chapter, we combine these elements and begin the study of their interaction. From this we will gain important insight into the phenomenon of *financial fragility*. We use the phrase "financial fragility" to describe situations in which small shocks have a significant impact on the financial system. One source of financial fragility is the crucial role of liquidity in the determination of asset prices. There are many historical illustrations of this phenomenon. For example, Kindleberger (1978, pp. 107–108) argues that the immediate cause of a financial crisis

may be trivial, a bankruptcy, a suicide, a flight, a revelation, a refusal of credit to some borrower, some change of view which leads a significant actor to unload. Prices fall. Expectations are reversed. The movement picks up speed. To the extent that speculators are leveraged with borrowed money, the decline in prices leads to further calls on them for margin or cash, and to further liquidation. As prices fall further, bank loans turn sour, and one or more mercantile houses, banks, discount houses, or brokerages fail. The credit system itself appears shaky and the race for liquidity is on.

A particularly interesting historical example is the financial crisis of 1763 documented by Schnabel and Shin (2004). The banks in those days were different from modern commercial banks. They did not take in deposits and make loans. Instead the "bankers" were merchants involved in the trade of goods such as wheat (this is where the term "merchant banker" comes from). Their primary financial role was to facilitate payments between parties using bills of exchange. A bill was like an IOU in which one party acknowledged that he had received a delivery of wheat, say, and promised payment at a specified future date. Sometimes reputable bankers could make their creditworthiness available to others, by allowing people known to them to draw bills on them in exchange for a fee. These bills could then be used as a means of payment or to raise capital by selling the bill in the capital market. The widespread use of these bills in financial centers, such as Amsterdam and Hamburg, led to interlocking claims among bankers.

The de Neufville brothers' banking house in Amsterdam was one of the most famous in Europe at the time. The end of the Seven Years War led to an economic downturn that triggered the bankruptcy of their banking house in Amsterdam. This forced them to sell their stocks of commodities. In the short run, the liquidity of the market was limited and the commodity sales resulted in lower prices. The fall in prices in turn put other intermediaries under strain and forced them to sell. A collapse in commodity prices and a financial crisis followed with many merchant bankers forced out of business.

Recent examples provide a stark illustration of how small events can cause large problems. As discussed in Chapter 1, in August 1998 the Russian government announced a moratorium on about 281 billion roubles ($13.5 billion) of government debt. Despite the small scale of the default, it triggered a global crisis and caused extreme volatility in many financial markets. The hedge fund Long Term Capital Management came under extreme pressure. Despite LTCM's small size in relation to the global financial system, the Federal Reserve Bank of New York was sufficiently worried about the potential for a crisis if LTCM went bankrupt that it helped arrange for a group of private banks to purchase the hedge fund and liquidate its positions in an orderly way. The Fed's concern was that, if LTCM went bankrupt, it would be forced to liquidate all its assets quickly. LTCM held many large positions in fairly illiquid markets. In such circumstances, prices might fall a long way if large amounts were sold quickly. This could put strain on other institutions, which would be forced to sell in turn, and this would further exacerbate the problem, as Kindleberger describes in the passage above.

In this chapter we will show how the interaction of financial intermediaries and markets can lead to financial fragility. In particular we will show that:

- Small events, such as minor liquidity shocks, can have a large impact on the financial system because of the **interaction** of banks and markets.
- The role of **liquidity** is crucial. In order for financial intermediaries to have an incentive to provide liquidity to a market, asset prices must be volatile.
- Intermediaries that are initially similar may pursue radically different strategies, both with respect to the types of asset they invest in and their risk of **default**.
- The interaction of banks and markets provides an explanation for **systemic** or economy-wide crises, as distinct from models, such as Bryant (1980) and Diamond and Dybvig (1983), that explain individual bank runs.

The central idea developed in the rest of this chapter is that, when markets are incomplete, financial institutions are forced to sell assets in order to obtain liquidity. Because the supply of and demand for liquidity are likely to be inelastic in the short run, a small degree of aggregate uncertainty can cause large fluctuations in asset prices. Holding liquidity involves an opportunity cost and the suppliers of liquidity can only recoup this cost by buying assets at firesale prices in some states of the world; so, the private provision of liquidity by arbitrageurs will always be inadequate to ensure complete asset-price stability. As a result, small shocks can cause significant asset-price volatility. If the asset-price volatility is severe enough, banks may find it impossible to meet their fixed commitments and a full-blown crisis will occur.

## 5.1 MARKETS, BANKS, AND CONSUMERS

The model used in this chapter combines intermediation and asset markets and is based on that in Allen and Gale (2004). Individual investors deposit their endowments in banks in exchange for a standard deposit contract, promising them a fixed amount of consumption at dates 1 and 2. The banks use the asset market at date 1 to obtain additional liquidity or get rid of excess liquidity as needed. As we shall see, there are also a number of small additional changes compared to the models of the preceding chapters.

There are three dates, $t = 0, 1, 2$; contracts are drawn up at date 0, and all consumption occurs at dates 1 and 2. There is a single good at each date. The good can be used for consumption or investment.

- Investment in the short or liquid asset can take place at date 1 or date 2. One unit of the good invested in the short asset at date $t$ yields one unit at date $t + 1$ for $t = 0, 1$.
- The long asset takes two periods to mature and is more productive than the short asset. Investment in the long asset can take place only at date 0. One unit invested at date 0 produces a certain return $R > 1$ units at date 2. Claims on the long asset can be traded at date 1.

There is the usual trade-off between liquidity and returns: long-term investments have higher returns but take longer to mature (are less liquid). By contrast, there is no risk–return trade-off: we assume that asset returns are non-stochastic in order to emphasize that, in the present model, financial crises are not driven by shocks to asset returns.

There is a continuum of ex ante identical consumers, whose measure is normalized to unity. Each consumer has an endowment $(1, 0, 0)$ consisting of one unit of the good at date 0 and nothing at subsequent dates. There are two (ex post) types of consumers at date 1: *early consumers*, who value consumption only at date 1; and *late consumers*, who value consumption only at date 2. If $\lambda$ denotes the probability of being an early consumer and $c_t$ denotes consumption at date $t = 1, 2$, then the consumer's ex ante utility is

$$E[u(c_1, c_2)] = \lambda U(c_1) + (1 - \lambda) U(c_2).$$

$U(\cdot)$ is a neoclassical utility function (increasing, strictly concave, twice continuously differentiable).

It is important in what follows to distinguish between two kinds of uncertainty. *Intrinsic* uncertainty is caused by stochastic fluctuations in the primitives or fundamentals of the economy. An example would be exogenous shocks that affect liquidity preferences. *Extrinsic* uncertainty by definition has no effect on the fundamentals of the economy. An equilibrium with no extrinsic uncertainty is called a *fundamental* equilibrium, because the endogenous variables are functions of the exogenous primitives or fundamentals of the model (endowments, preferences, technologies). An equilibrium with extrinsic uncertainty is called a *sunspot* equilibrium, because endogenous variables may be influenced by extraneous variables (sunspots) that have no direct impact on fundamentals. A crisis cannot occur in a fundamental equilibrium in the absence of exogenous shocks to fundamentals, such as asset returns or liquidity demands. In a sunspot equilibrium, by contrast, asset prices fluctuate in the absence of aggregate exogenous shocks, and crises appear to occur spontaneously.

There are three sources of intrinsic uncertainty in the model. First, each individual consumer faces idiosyncratic uncertainty about her preference type (early or late consumer). Second, each bank faces idiosyncratic uncertainty about the number of early consumers among the bank's depositors. For example, different banks could be located in regions subject to independent liquidity shocks. Third, there is aggregate uncertainty about the fraction of early consumers in the economy. To begin with, we ignore the banks' idiosyncratic uncertainty and focus on individual idiosyncratic uncertainty and aggregate uncertainty. Aggregate uncertainty is represented by a state of nature $s$ that takes on two values, $H$ and $L$, with probability $\pi$ and $1 - \pi$ respectively. The probability of being an early consumer in state $s$ is denoted by $\lambda_s$ where

$$0 < \lambda_L \leq \lambda_H < 1.$$

We adopt the usual "law of large numbers" convention and assume that the fraction of early consumers in state $s$ is identically equal to the probability $\lambda_s$. Note that there is aggregate intrinsic uncertainty only if $\lambda_L < \lambda_H$. If $\lambda_L = \lambda_H = \lambda$ then there is no aggregate (intrinsic) uncertainty and the state of nature $s$ represents extrinsic uncertainty.

All uncertainty is resolved at date 1. The true state $s$ is publicly observed and each consumer learns his type, that is, whether he is an early or a late consumer. An individual's type, early or late, is private information that only the individual can observe directly.

There are no asset markets for hedging against aggregate uncertainty at date 0; for example, there are no securities that are contingent on the state of nature $s$. At date 1, there is a market in which future (date-2) consumption can be exchanged for present (date-1) consumption. If $p_s$ denotes the price of date 2 consumption in terms of present consumption at date 1, then one unit of the long asset is worth $P_s = p_s R$ at date 1 in state $s$.

Markets are incomplete at date 0, because of the inability to hedge uncertainty about the state $s$. At date 1 markets are complete because all uncertainty has been resolved.

We assume that market participation is incomplete: financial institutions such as banks can participate in the asset market at date 1, but individual consumers cannot. Banks are financial institutions that provide investment and liquidity services to consumers. They do this by pooling the consumers' resources, investing them in a portfolio of short- and long-term assets, and offering consumers future consumption streams with a better combination of asset returns and liquidity than individual consumers could achieve by themselves.

Banks compete by offering deposit contracts to consumers in exchange for their endowments and consumers respond by choosing the most attractive of the contracts offered. Free entry ensures that banks earn zero profits in equilibrium. The deposit contracts offered in equilibrium must maximize consumers' welfare subject to the zero-profit constraint. Otherwise, a bank could enter and make a positive profit by offering a more attractive contract.

Anything a consumer can do, the bank can do. So there is no loss of generality in assuming that consumers deposit their entire endowment in a bank at date 0. Consumers cannot diversify by spreading their money across more than one bank. The bank invests $y$ units per capita in the short asset and $1 - y$ units per capita in the long asset and offers each consumer a deposit contract, which allows the consumer to withdraw either $d_1$ units at date 1 or $d_2$ units at date 2. Without loss of generality, we set $d_2 = \infty$. This ensures that consumers receive the residue of the bank's assets at date 2. Without this assumption the depositors' expected utility would not be maximized. The deposit contract is characterized by the promised payment at date 1. In what follows we write $d$ instead of $d_1$.

If $p_s$ denotes the price of future consumption at date 1 in state $\theta$, then the value of the bank's assets at date 1 is $y + p_s R(1 - y)$. Note that, unlike the Diamond–Dybvig model, the value of these assets does not depend on whether the bank is in default or not. Because there is a competitive market on which assets can be sold, the bank's portfolio is always marked-to-market.

In what follows, we assume that bank runs occur only if they are unavoidable. In other words, late consumers will withdraw at date 2 as long as the bank can offer them as much at date 2 as the early consumers receive at date 1. In the event of bankruptcy, the bank is *required* to liquidate its assets in an attempt to provide the promised amount $d$ to the consumers who withdraw at date 1. If the bank does not have enough resources to pay all of the early withdrawers an amount $d$, then there will be nothing left at date 2 for late consumers who do not join the run. Hence, in equilibrium, all consumers must withdraw at date 1 and each consumer will receive the liquidated value of the portfolio $y + p_s R(1 - y)$.

Under what conditions will a bank be forced to default on its date 1 promises and liquidate its assets? At date 1, all uncertainty is resolved. People find out their individual types and the aggregate state $s$ is realized. Early consumers will withdraw their deposits from the bank for sure. Late consumers have the option of leaving their money in the bank, but they could also pretend to be early consumers, withdraw their funds at date 1, and carry them forward to date 2 using the short asset. Late consumers will be willing to wait until date 2 to withdraw if they are confident that they will receive at least $d$ units of the good at date 2. Otherwise, they will run on the bank and withdraw $d$ at date 1. The cheapest way to satisfy the late consumers, so that they wait until date 2 to withdraw, is to give them $d$ at date 2. If the late consumers receive exactly $d$ at date 2, the present value of the claims on the bank is $\lambda d + (1 - \lambda)p_s d$. If

$$\lambda d + (1 - \lambda)p_s d \leq y + p_s R(1 - y), \tag{5.1}$$

it is possible to pay the late consumers at least $d$ so that they will be willing to wait until date 2 to withdraw. Otherwise, the bank cannot possibly honor its promise to give each early consumer $d$ and, at the same time, give late consumers at least $d$. A run on the bank at date 1 is inevitable.

If condition (5.1) is satisfied, the deposit contract is said to be *incentive-compatible*, in the sense that it is optimal for the late consumers to withdraw at date 2. We often refer to the inequality in (5.1) as the *incentive constraint*, although it also assumes that the bank's budget constraint is satisfied.

If the bank chooses $(d, y)$ at date 0, the depositor's consumption at date $t$ in state $s$ is denoted by $c_{ts}(d, y)$ and defined by

$$c_{1s}(d, y) = \begin{cases} d & \text{if (5.1) is satisfied} \\ y + p_s R(1 - y) & \text{otherwise,} \end{cases}$$

$$c_{2s}(d, y) = \begin{cases} \dfrac{y + p_s R(1 - y) - \lambda_s d}{(1 - \lambda_s)p_s} & \text{if (5.1) is satisfied} \\ y + p_s R(1 - y) & \text{otherwise.} \end{cases}$$

If (5.1) is satisfied then $c_{1s}$ is simply the promised amount $d$. Understanding $c_{2s}$ is a little more complex. The present value of the firm's assets at date 1 is $y + p_s R(1 - y)$. Of this, $\lambda_s d$ is paid out to early consumers so the remainder $y + p_s R(1 - y) - \lambda_s d$ is available to pay for the late consumers' consumption. Since the price of future consumption is $p_s$, we divide by $p_s$ to find the total amount of consumption available at date 2. There are $1 - \lambda_s$ late consumers, so we have to divide by $1 - \lambda_s$ to find the consumption of an individual late consumer. Thus, each late consumer receives $[y+p_s R(1-y)-\lambda_s d]/[(1-\lambda_s)p_s]$ at date 2.

If (5.1) is not satisfied, then there is a crisis and all consumers, both early and late, try to withdraw. The bank goes bankrupt and is liquidated for $y + p_s R(1 - y)$. The early consumers consume their share at date 1 while the late consumers carry over their share to date 2 using the short asset. Since they do not have access to the asset market, we do not divide by $p_s$.

Using this notation, the bank's decision problem can be written as

$$\max \quad E[\lambda U(c_{1s}) + (1 - \lambda) U(c_{2s})]$$
$$\text{s.t.} \quad 0 \le d, 0 \le y \le 1. \tag{5.2}$$

A bank's choice of deposit contract and portfolio $(d, y)$ is *optimal* for the given price vector $p = (p_H, p_L)$ if it solves (5.2).

As we saw in the preceding chapter, the asset market at date 1 can only clear if the price of future consumption is less than or equal to 1. If $p_s > 1$, the asset price is $P_s = p_s R > R$ and the banks would only be willing to hold the short asset. Then the market for the long asset cannot clear. If $p_s = 1$ then banks will be indifferent between holding the short asset and the long asset between dates 1 and 2, since in both cases the return on one unit of the good invested at date 1 is one unit of the good at date 2. On the other hand, if $p_s < 1$ then no one is willing to invest in the short asset at date 1 and everything is invested in the long asset. This is consistent with market clearing, because there is no stock of the short asset unless someone chooses to invest in it at date 1.

**Proposition 1**    For any state $s$, the asset market at date 1 clears only if $p_s \le 1$. If $p_s = 1$, banks are willing to hold both assets at date 1. If $p_s < 1$, then only the long asset is held by banks at date 1.

## 5.2 TYPES OF EQUILIBRIUM

In order to understand the different forms that equilibrium can take, it is helpful to consider some simple examples.

Example 1

$$U(c) = \ln(c);$$

$$R = 1.5;$$

$$\lambda_s = \begin{cases} 0.8 & \text{if } s = L \\ 0.8 + \varepsilon & \text{if } s = H; \end{cases}$$

$$(\pi, 1 - \pi) = (0.35, 0.65).$$

## 5.2.1 Fundamental equilibrium with no aggregate uncertainty

We start by considering the case where $\varepsilon = 0$, so $\lambda_H = \lambda_L = 0.8$ and $s$ represents extrinsic uncertainty, and look at the fundamental equilibrium, where $s$ plays no role. If there is no uncertainty, the bank can promise the depositors any consumption allocation that satisfies the budget constraint and the incentive constraint by putting the early consumers' promised consumption $c_1$ equal to $d$ and putting the late consumers' consumption $c_2$ equal to the residual value of the portfolio. Hence, in the fundamental equilibrium we do not need to concern ourselves with the form of the deposit contract. We can assume, without essential loss of generality, that the bank offers the depositors a consumption bundle $(c_1, c_2)$.

Since there is no aggregate uncertainty, banks use the short asset to provide consumption for the early consumers at date 1 and will use the long asset to provide consumption for the late consumers at date 2. Since the fraction of early consumers is 0.8, the amount of the short asset in the portfolio must satisfy $(0.8)\, c_1 = y$ or $c_1 = y/(0.8)$. Similarly, the amount of the long asset must satisfy $(0.2)\, c_2 = R(1 - y)$ or $c_2 = R(1 - y)/(0.2)$, where $1 - y$ is the amount invested in the long asset and $R = 1.5$ is the return on the long asset. The banks' decision problem then is

$$\begin{aligned} \max \quad & 0.8U(c_1) + 0.2U(c_2) \\ \text{s.t.} \quad & 0 \le y \le 1 \\ & c_1 = y/(0.8) \\ & c_2 = R(1 - y)/(0.2). \end{aligned}$$

Substituting the expressions for $c_1$ and $c_2$ from the budget constraints into the objective function and using $U(c) = \ln(c)$, the problem reduces to

$$\max \quad 0.8 \ln\left(\frac{y}{0.8}\right) + 0.2 \ln\left(\frac{R(1 - y)}{0.2}\right).$$

Assuming an interior solution with regard to $y$, the necessary and sufficient first-order condition for a solution to this problem is

$$\frac{0.8}{y} = \frac{0.2}{1-y},$$

which can be solved for

$$y = 0.8.$$

It follows that,

$$c_1 = \frac{y}{0.8} = 1;$$

$$c_2 = 1.5\frac{(1-y)}{0.2} = 1.5;$$

and

$$E\left[u(c_1, c_2)\right] = 0.8\ln(1) + 0.2\ln(1.5) = 0.081.$$

As we have seen before, when there is no uncertainty about the future, the asset markets at date 0 can only clear if the asset price at date 1 satisfies $P_H = P_L = 1$. This is the only price at which banks are willing to hold both assets at date 0 because it is the only price that equalizes the holding returns of the two assets between date 0 and date 1.

In each state $s$, the asset price $P_s = 1$ implies that one unit invested in the long asset at date 1 has a return of $R = 1.5$. Thus, the return on the long asset dominates the return on the short asset between date 1 and date 2 and banks will only hold the long asset at date 1.

The equilibrium that we have described for Example 1 is autarkic. Each bank can provide the required consumption for its depositors at each date without making use of the asset market at date 1. This is not the only fundamental equilibrium, in fact there are many, but they differ only in the investments made by banks and not with respect to the aggregate investment, consumption, and expected utility of the depositors. We have argued that banks are indifferent between holding the two assets at date 0, which yield the same return at date 1, in any fundamental equilibrium. So any portfolio is optimal for them. As long as the aggregate or average portfolio satisfies $y = 0.8$, there is no reason for banks not to hold different individual portfolios. For example, suppose that a fraction 0.8 of the banks hold only the short asset and a fraction 0.2 hold only the long asset. At date 1, a bank holding only the short asset will use 80% of its portfolio satisfying the early consumers who want to withdraw and with the remainder will buy 0.2 units of the long asset to provide the late consumers with consumption of 1.5 at date 2. Banks that have only held the long asset will liquidate 80% of their portfolio in order to obtain consumption for their early consumers and will hold onto the remaining 20% to provide for consumption of the late consumers at date 2.

Although the asset market is used in this example, it is not essential. A bank can still achieve the first best without using the market. If banks receive idiosyncratic liquidity shocks, on the other hand, they will have different liquidity needs at date 1. Some banks will have surplus liquidity and other banks will have a liquidity deficit. These surpluses and deficits can only be removed by using the market. At the end of this chapter, we will consider a case where the asset market plays an essential role, but for the moment we continue to ignore idiosyncratic shocks.

### 5.2.2 Aggregate uncertainty

Now suppose that $\varepsilon = 0.01$, so that $\lambda_L = 0.8$ and $\lambda_H = 0.81$. Uncertainty about the state $s$ gives rise to aggregate intrinsic uncertainty. Although the amount of aggregate uncertainty is small, the equilibrium we find for the economy with aggregate uncertainty is quite different from the fundamental equilibrium discussed above. We can easily identify some reasons for the dramatic effect of a small degree of aggregate uncertainty in the inelastic supply of and demand for liquidity. Suppose that all banks make identical choices at date 0. We shall later see that this assumption is not plausible, but it will serve to illustrate some important points. If the investment in the short asset is $y$ units, then the total amount of the good available for consumption in the economy at date 1 is $y$ units per capita, independently of the aggregate state and the prevailing asset prices. In this sense, the aggregate supply of liquidity is inelastic. We denote the aggregate supply of liquidity at date 1 by $S(P)$ and define it by putting

$$S_s(P) = y$$

for all price levels $P$ and states $s$.

Suppose that each bank also chooses a deposit contract that promises $d$ units of the good to any depositor who withdraws at date 1. Assuming there are no bank runs and, hence, no defaults, the only demand for liquidity at date 1 is to provide goods to the early consumers. Since the fraction of early consumers is 0.8 in state $s = L$ and 0.81 in state $s = H$, the aggregate amount of the good needed by banks is $(0.8)d$ with probability 0.65 and $(0.81)d$ with probability

0.35. Let $D_s(P)$ denote the aggregate demand for liquidity when the asset price is $P$ and the state is $s$. Then

$$D_s(P) = \begin{cases} (0.8)\,d & \text{if } s = L, \\ (0.81)\,d & \text{if } s = H. \end{cases}$$

The demand is price inelastic, because the promised payment $d$ is inelastic, but the aggregate demand varies with the state.

Market clearing requires that the demand for liquidity does not exceed the supply, that is,

$$D_s(P_s) \leq S_s(P_s)$$

for each state $s = H, L$. If the market clears in the high state $s = H$, however, there will be an excess of liquidity in the low state $s = L$, because

$$(0.8)\,d < (0.81)\,d \leq y.$$

As we have seen in our earlier discussions of equilibrium in the asset market, when there is excess liquidity at date 1 the price of the long asset will rise to $P_L = R = 1.5$. Only at this price will the returns on the short and long asset be equalized, so that banks are willing to hold the short asset until date 2. But banks must also hold both assets at date 0 and they will not do that if the short asset is dominated by the long asset. If $P_L = 1.5$ the short asset is undominated only if the asset price is lower in the high state. In fact, we must have $P_H \ll 1$. So the inelasticity of demand and supply means that even small aggregate liquidity shocks will cause large fluctuations in asset prices.

We have shown that, even in the absence of default, the equilibrium with a small amount of aggregate uncertainty $\varepsilon = 0.01$ will be quite different from the fundamental equilibrium in the limit economy where $\varepsilon = 0$. If we allow for the possibility of default, we discover another difference: banks that start out looking very similar will adopt quite different investment and risk-sharing strategies. To see this, suppose to the contrary that all the banks continue to make the same choices at the first date. As we assumed above, each bank invests $y$ units of the good in the short asset and offers a deposit contract promising $d$ units of consumption to depositors who withdraw at date 1. We have argued that a bank will default if and only if it fails to satisfy the incentive constraint (5.1) at date 1. But if every bank has made the same choices at date 1, either they will all violate the incentive constraint or none will. If every bank defaults, there will be no one to buy the long assets that must be liquidated at date 1 and the asset price will fall to zero. This cannot be an equilibrium, however. At a price of zero, someone would be tempted to deviate, choose $y$ and $d$ so that bankruptcy is avoided, and make a large capital gain by purchasing the long assets when their price falls to zero. So, in order to have default in equilibrium, equilibrium will have to be *mixed* in the sense that there are two types of banks, call them *safe banks* and *risky banks*, that make very different choices at date 0.

Safe banks hold a lot of the short asset and offer deposit contracts promising low payments at date 1. Risky banks hold a lot of the long asset and offer deposit contracts promising high payments at date 1. When liquidity demands are low ($s = L$) the safe banks have excess liquidity which they supply to the market by buying the long asset. Risky banks obtain the liquidity they need to honor their deposit contracts by selling the long asset. When liquidity demands are high ($s = H$) the market for the long asset is less liquid because the safe banks must devote more of their liquidity to satisfying the needs of their own customers. This liquidity shortage leads to a drop in the price of the long asset, which forces the risky banks to go bankrupt and liquidate their stocks of the long asset. The increase in the supply of the long asset can lead to a sharp drop in prices. In this case there is "cash-in-the-market" pricing. The safe banks hold just enough liquidity in excess of their customers' needs to enable them to buy up the long asset at a firesale price. The low price compensates them for the cost of holding the extra liquidity when liquidity demands are low and prices are high.

To see how such an equilibrium operates in detail, consider the following example in which the parameter values are the same as in Example 1 except that now $\varepsilon = 0.01$ rather than $\varepsilon = 0$. This variant with aggregate uncertainty is referred to as Example 1A.

**Example 1A**

$$U(c) = \ln(c);$$
$$R = 1.5;$$
$$\alpha = 0.8;$$
$$\pi = 0.35;$$
$$\varepsilon = 0.01.$$

Then

$$\lambda_s = \begin{cases} 0.8 \text{ with probability } 0.65; \\ 0.81 \text{ with probability } 0.35. \end{cases}$$

The asset price $P_s$ is random and takes the values

$$P_s = \begin{cases} p_H R = (0.430)\,(1.5) = 0.645 & \text{if } s = H; \\ p_L R = (0.940)\,(1.5) = 1.410 & \text{if } s = L. \end{cases}$$

Next we describe the behavior of the safe and risky banks. A proportion $\rho = 0.979$ of the banks adopt the safe strategy of avoiding bankruptcy and default. Specifically, they choose to invest a large amount $y^S$ in the short asset and promise a low amount $d^S$ to depositors who withdraw early.

$$y^S = 0.822; \quad d^S = 0.998.$$

Both choices make it easier for the bank to satisfy the incentive constraint. Once these choices are made, the prices and budget constraints determine the depositors' consumption at each date and in each state:

$$c_s^S = \begin{cases} \left(c_{1H}^S, c_{2H}^S\right) = (0.998, 1.572) & \text{if } s = H; \\ \left(c_{1L}^S, c_{2L}^S\right) = (0.998, 1.461) & \text{if } s = L. \end{cases}$$

Note that early consumers receive the same level of consumption ($d^S$) in each state. The late consumers have different levels of consumption in each state because they receive the residual value of the portfolio and this depends on the asset price $P_s$. Note that the late consumers are better off in the high state: the low asset price allows the bank to purchase future consumption cheaply. Alternatively, one can think of the bank as making capital gains from buying up long assets cheaply at date 1 and selling them more dearly at date 2.

A proportion $1 - \rho = 0.021$ of the banks adopt the risky strategy that will lead to default and bankruptcy when prices fall in state $s = H$. Unlike the safe banks, they choose a low level of $y^R$ and promise a high level of consumption to early withdrawers.

$$y^R = 0.016; \quad d^R = 1.405.$$

Both of these choices make it harder to satisfy the incentive constraint. The consumption levels determined by these choices and by the budget constraints are

$$c_s^R = \begin{cases} \left(c_{1H}^R, c_{2H}^R\right) = (0.651, 0.651) & \text{if } s = H; \\ \left(c_{1L}^R, c_{2L}^R\right) = (1.405, 1.486) & \text{if } s = L. \end{cases}$$

In the low state, the bank is solvent and can give both early and late consumers what was promised. In the high state, by contrast, the bank goes bankrupt and defaults on its promises and the early and late consumers both receive the liquidated value of the bank's portfolio.

In equilibrium, individuals must be indifferent between depositing their money in a safe or risky bank. Otherwise, one type of bank will attract no customers. If we compute the expected utility of consumption for depositors in the safe and risky banks, we find that both are equal to 0.078.

To check that these choices are consistent with equilibrium, the first thing we need to show is that markets clear at date 1. Consider what happens in state $s = L$. The safe banks can satisfy the liquidity demand of their depositors from their own holdings of the safe asset. A fraction $\lambda_L = 0.8$ of their customers are early consumers, so the demand for liquidity is $\lambda_L d^S = 0.8 \times 0.998 = 0.798$. Then the safe banks will each have $y^S - \lambda_L d^S = 0.822 - 0.798 = 0.024$ units of the good left over. Since the proportion of safe banks is $\rho = 0.979$, the total amount of excess liquidity is $\rho(y^S - \lambda_L d^S) = 0.979 \times 0.024 = 0.023$. Since $P_L = 0.940 < 1$ the short asset is dominated between date 1 and date 2, so the safe banks will only want to hold the long asset. Accordingly, they supply the entire 0.023 units of the good in exchange for the long asset.

Next consider the risky banks. Since they hold none of the short asset, they must sell part of their holdings of the long asset in order to provide the promised liquidity to their early consumers. The demand for liquidity from their customers is $\lambda_L d^R = 0.8 \times 1.405 = 1.124$. They have 0.016 from their holding of the short asset so they need $1.124 - 0.016 = 1.108$. Since the proportion of risky banks is $1 - \rho = 0.021$ the total demand for liquidity is $(1 - \rho)\lambda_L d^R = 0.021 \times 1.108 = 0.023$. Thus demand for liquidity equals supply when the state $s = L$.

In state $s = H$, the safe banks' supply of liquidity can be calculated in the same way, simply taking note that the proportion of early consumers is now $\lambda_H = 0.81$. The supply of liquidity is

$$\rho\left(y^S - \lambda_H d^S\right) = (0.979)\,(0.822 - 0.81 \times 0.998)$$
$$= 0.013.$$

The risky banks have $(1 - y^R) = 0.987$ units of the long asset. Because they are bankrupt, they must liquidate all their assets and this means they must supply the whole amount of the long asset at date 1. Implicitly, they are demanding $P_H = 0.645$ units of liquidity in exchange. Since there are $(1 - \rho) = 0.021$ risky banks, the total demand for liquidity is

$$(1 - \rho)\,P_H\left(1 - y^R\right) = 0.021 \times 0.645 \times 0.987 = 0.013.$$

Thus, the asset market clears in state $s = H$ too.

To show that markets clear at date 0, it is necessary to show that the portfolio held by each bank is optimal. This requires us to check the first-order conditions that show the effect of a small change in the portfolio on consumption in each state and on expected utility. This is a rather complicated exercise that we will not pursue here.

The example has shown that a small increase in $\varepsilon = \lambda_H - \lambda_L$ leads to very different price behavior compared to the fundamental equilibrium. It also leads to the possibility of banks defaulting in equilibrium. As we have argued above, substantial asset price volatility is a general property of equilibria with intrinsic uncertainty, however small that uncertainty may be. This leads us to ask two questions. First, what sort of equilibrium would we observe if we let $\varepsilon > 0$ converge to zero? Second, would the limit of this sequence of equilibria be an equilibrium of the limit economy where $\varepsilon = 0$? The answer to both questions is that the equilibrium with intrinsic uncertainty converges to a sunspot equilibrium of the limit economy. In this sunspot equilibrium, prices fluctuate even though there is no intrinsic aggregate uncertainty in the economy.

### 5.2.3 Sunspot equilibria

To describe the limit of the equilibria with intrinsic uncertainty, we return to Example 1. The parameters are identical but another equilibrium is found. To distinguish this case we refer to it as Example 1S.

**Example 1S** The asset price is random

$$P_s = \begin{cases} p_H R = (0.432)(1.5) = 0.648 & \text{if } s = H; \\ p_L R = (0.943)(1.5) = 1.415 & \text{if } s = L. \end{cases}$$

The proportion of safe banks is $\rho = 1$ and their choices are

$$y^S = 0.8; \ d^S = 1.$$

These choices and the equilibrium prices determine the consumption in each state at each date:

$$c_s^S = \begin{cases} \left(c_{1H}^S, c_{2H}^S\right) = (1.0, 1.5) & \text{if } s = H; \\ \left(c_{1L}^S, c_{2L}^S\right) = (1.0, 1.5) & \text{if } s = L. \end{cases} \tag{5.3}$$

Note that consumption is exactly the same as in the fundamental equilibrium. The expected utility obtained from this consumption is, as we claimed earlier, 0.081.

Risky banks on the other hand, continue to choose a low investment in the short asset $y^R$ and promise high consumption to early withdrawers $d^R$:

$$y^R = 0; \ d^R = 1.414$$

and the corresponding consumption is

$$c_s^R = \begin{cases} \left(c_{1H}^R, c_{2H}^R\right) = (0.648, 0.648) & \text{if } s = H; \\ \left(c_{1L}^R, c_{2L}^R\right) = (1.414, 1.500) & \text{if } s = L. \end{cases}$$

Now the risky banks invest nothing in the short asset and enter bankruptcy in the high state $s = H$. If we were to calculate the expected utility of this consumption plan, we would find that it equals the expected utility of the safe banks, 0.081. Thus, consumers are indifferent between the two types of banks, even though in equilibrium there are no risky banks since $\rho = 1$.

It may seem odd that it is optimal for banks to adopt a risky strategy even though none attempt to do so. In fact, this is a necessary requirement for any equilibrium that is the limit of equilibria as $\varepsilon$ converges to zero from above. In the equilibria with $\varepsilon > 0$, a positive fraction of the banks were risky, implying that it must be optimal for risky banks to operate. As $\varepsilon$ becomes vanishingly small, so does the fraction of risky banks, but it remains optimal in the limit for risky banks to operate, even though none choose to do so. The absence of default in the limit equilibrium results from the fact that, as we saw in the fundamental equilibrium, banks can achieve the first best without using the asset market. The only way for everyone to get the first best expected utility is for all banks to choose the safe strategy. Even though it is optimal for a single bank (of negligible size) to adopt the risky strategy, if a positive measure of banks were to do so, the depositors' welfare would be reduced below the first-best level. Thus, in the limit economy with $\varepsilon = 0$, equilibrium requires $\rho = 1$.

At the allocation given in (5.3), depositors bear no risk and so are approximately risk neutral in the face of small risks. They will be indifferent between holding a bit more or less of each asset if and only if the following condition is satisfied:

$$\pi \frac{R}{P_H} + (1 - \pi) \frac{R}{P_L} = R. \tag{5.4}$$

The right hand size is just the expected return at date 2 to an investment of one unit in the long asset at date 0. The left hand side is the expected return to the following strategy: invest one unit in the short asset at date 0 and use the returns at date 1 to buy as much of the long asset as possible. With probability $\pi$ the high state occurs, the price is $P_H$, and the strategy results in the purchase of $1/P_H$ units of the long asset; with probability $1 - \pi$ the low state occurs, the price is $P_L$, and one obtains $1/P_L$ units of the long asset. Each unit of the long asset yields $R$ at date 2 so the expected return from the investment strategy is equal to the left hand side of (5.4). In other words, the expected return from holding the short asset is the same as the expected return from holding the long asset if and only if (5.4) holds. It can easily be checked that

$$\frac{0.65 \times 1.5}{1.415} + \frac{0.35 \times 1.5}{0.648} = 1.5,$$

so the asset market does clear at date 1 in the limiting sunspot equilibrium.

There are many other sunspot equilibria. In fact, any pair of prices between 0 and 1.5 corresponds to a sunspot equilibrium if it satisfies (5.4). Such a large set of price vectors can clear the market and support an equilibrium precisely because the market is not needed when there is no aggregate uncertainty. The only function of the prices is to make sure (a) that banks are willing to hold the appropriate amounts of both assets at date 0 and (b) that none of them want to use the asset market. Condition (a) is guaranteed by the first-order condition (5.4) and condition (b) is guaranteed by the fact that banks have just enough liquidity to pay off their early withdrawers at date 1 and so have nothing to trade at date 1. The fact that $P_s < R$ for each state $s$ implies that banks only want to hold the long asset between dates 1 and 2 anyway.

The solutions to the variants of Example 1 are shown in Table 5.1. Panel 1F shows the fundamental equilibrium, Panel 1A shows the equilibrium with aggregate uncertainty, and Panel 1S shows the sunspot equilibrium.

### 5.2.4 Idiosyncratic liquidity shocks for banks

So far we have assumed that banks do not receive idiosyncratic liquidity shocks, that is, all banks have the same proportion of early and late consumers. Suppose next that banks can receive different proportions of early consumers. In this case all banks must use the markets to trade. If a bank has a high liquidity shock it needs to acquire liquidity; if it has a low liquidity shock it supplies

**Table 5.1.** Equilibria for Example 1.

| ♯ | $\varepsilon$ | $\begin{bmatrix} E[U^S] \\ E[U^R] \end{bmatrix}$ | $\begin{bmatrix} y^S \\ y^R \end{bmatrix}$ | $\begin{bmatrix} (c_{1H}^S, c_{2H}^S) \\ (c_{1L}^S, c_{2L}^S) \\ (c_{1H}^R, c_{2H}^R) \\ (c_{1L}^R, c_{2L}^R) \end{bmatrix}$ | $\begin{bmatrix} pH \\ pL \end{bmatrix}$ |
|---|---|---|---|---|---|
| 1F | 0 | 0.081 | 0.800 | $(1.000, 1.500)$ | 0.667 |
| 1A | 0.010 | $\begin{bmatrix} 0.078 \\ 0.078 \end{bmatrix}$ | $\begin{bmatrix} 0.822 \\ 0.016 \end{bmatrix}$ | $\begin{bmatrix} (0.998, 1.572) \\ (0.998, 1.461) \\ (0.651, 0.651) \\ (1.405, 1.486) \end{bmatrix}$ | $\begin{bmatrix} 0.430 \\ 0.940 \end{bmatrix}$ |
| 1S | 0 | $\begin{bmatrix} 0.081 \\ 0.081 \end{bmatrix}$ | $\begin{bmatrix} 0.800 \\ 0 \end{bmatrix}$ | $\begin{bmatrix} (1.000, 1.500) \\ (1.000, 1.500) \\ (0.648, 0.648) \\ (1.414, 1.500) \end{bmatrix}$ | $\begin{bmatrix} 0.432 \\ 0.943 \end{bmatrix}$ |

**Table 5.2.** Equilibria for Example 2.

| ♯ | $\varepsilon$ | $\begin{bmatrix} E[U^S] \\ E[U^R] \end{bmatrix}$ | $\begin{bmatrix} y^S \\ y^R \end{bmatrix}$ | $\begin{bmatrix} (c_{1H}^S, c_{2HL}^S, c_{2HH}^S) \\ (c_{1L}^S, c_{2LL}^S, c_{2LH}^S) \\ (c_{1H}^R, c_{2HL}^R, c_{2HH}^R) \\ (c_{1L}^R, c_{2LL}^R, c_{2LH}^R) \end{bmatrix}$ | $\begin{bmatrix} pH \\ pL \end{bmatrix}$ |
|---|---|---|---|---|---|
| 2F | 0 | 0.081 | 0.800 | $(1.000, 1.500)$ | 0.667 |
| 2A | 0.010 | $\begin{bmatrix} 0.077 \\ 0.077 \end{bmatrix}$ | $\begin{bmatrix} 0.814 \\ 0 \end{bmatrix}$ | $\begin{bmatrix} (0.995, 1.715, 1.392) \\ (0.995, 1.415, 1.627) \\ (0.678, 0.678, 0.678) \\ (1.360, 1.502, 1.503) \end{bmatrix}$ | $\begin{bmatrix} 0.452 \\ 0.907 \end{bmatrix}$ |
| 2S | 0 | $\begin{bmatrix} 0.080 \\ 0.080 \end{bmatrix}$ | $\begin{bmatrix} 0.798 \\ 0 \end{bmatrix}$ | $\begin{bmatrix} (0.998, 1.648, 1.281) \\ (0.998, 1.430, 1.652) \\ (0.681, 0.681, 0.681) \\ (1.364, 1.502, 1.503) \end{bmatrix}$ | $\begin{bmatrix} 0.454 \\ 0.910 \end{bmatrix}$ |

liquidity to the market. The main effect of the idiosyncratic shocks is that they lower the expected utility by forcing banks to trade at volatile prices.

To see the effect of introducing idiosyncratic liquidity shocks for banks we consider the following a variation on Example 1. Instead of assuming that $\lambda_s$ is purely a function of the state of nature, we assume that it is a random variable $\tilde{\lambda}_s$ in each state $s$.

**Example 2**

$$U(c_t) = \ln(c_t);$$

$$R = 1.5;$$

$$\tilde{\lambda}_H = \left\{ \begin{array}{ll} 0.75 + \varepsilon & \text{w. pr. } 0.5; \\ 0.85 + \varepsilon & \text{w. pr. } 0.5. \end{array} \right.$$

$$\tilde{\lambda}_L = \left\{ \begin{array}{ll} 0.75 & \text{w. pr. } 0.5; \\ 0.85 & \text{w. pr. } 0.5. \end{array} \right.$$

$$\pi = 0.35.$$

The equilibria of this example are shown in Table 5.2. The fundamental equilibrium shown in Panel 2F is unchanged from Panel 1F in Table 5.1. Since $P_H = P_L = 1$ it is possible to trade the long asset at date 1 and acquire the needed liquidity without any effect on depositor welfare. The sunspot equilibria in Panel 1S in Table 5.1 and Panel 2S in Table 5.2 are different, however. Trade occurs at the low price and this adversely affects the welfare of the safe banks as well as the risky banks. To mitigate the effects of trading at this low price, the safe banks lower $d^S$, from 1 in Panel 1S to 0.995 in Panel 2S. Similarly, $y^S$ is reduced to 0.798 from 0.800. Expected utility is lowered from 0.081 in Panel 1S to 0.080 in Panel 2S. As in the autarkic equilibria with no idiosyncratic risk, introducing a small amount of aggregate uncertainty eliminates equilibria with a non-stochastic price. Only the sunspot equilibrium is robust. Panel 2A shows the equilibrium with intrinsic uncertainty ($\varepsilon = 0.010$) is very close to the sunspot equilibrium. In this case $\rho = 0.989$ and $1 - \rho = 0.011$, so there is entry by both safe and risky banks.

### 5.2.5 Equilibrium without bankruptcy

In the examples considered above, bankruptcy is always optimal, even if it was not always observed in equilibrium. There are also equilibria in which bankruptcy is not optimal. In other words, we have a financial crisis that involves extreme price volatility but no bankruptcy. We next consider an example of this type. For simplicity, we return to the case where there is no idiosyncratic risk for banks.

**Table 5.3.** Equilibria for Example 3.

| ♯ | $\varepsilon$ | $\begin{bmatrix} E[U^S] \\ E[U^R] \end{bmatrix}$ | $\begin{bmatrix} y^S \\ y^R \end{bmatrix}$ | $\begin{bmatrix} (c_{2H}^S, c_{2H}^S) \\ (c_{2L}^S, c_{2L}^S) \\ (c_{2H}^R, c_{2H}^R) \\ (c_{2L}^R, c_{2L}^R) \end{bmatrix}$ | $\begin{bmatrix} pH \\ pL \end{bmatrix}$ |
|---|---|---|---|---|---|
| 3F | 0 | 0.203 | 0.500 | (1.000, 1.500) | 0.667 |
| 3A | 0.010 | $\begin{bmatrix} 0.199 \\ 0.110 \end{bmatrix}$ | $\begin{bmatrix} 0.508 \\ 0 \end{bmatrix}$ | $\begin{bmatrix} (0.996, 1.507) \\ (0.996, 1.497) \\ (0.561, 0.561) \\ (1.500, 1.500) \end{bmatrix}$ | $\begin{bmatrix} 0.374 \\ 1 \end{bmatrix}$ |
| 3S | 0 | $\begin{bmatrix} 0.203 \\ 0.111 \end{bmatrix}$ | $\begin{bmatrix} 0.500 \\ 0 \end{bmatrix}$ | $\begin{bmatrix} (1.000, 1.500) \\ (1.000, 1.500) \\ (0.563, 0.563) \\ (1.500, 1.500) \end{bmatrix}$ | $\begin{bmatrix} 0.375 \\ 1 \end{bmatrix}$ |

## Example 3

$$U(c) = \ln(c);$$
$$R = 1.5;$$
$$\lambda_s = \begin{cases} 0.5 \text{ if } s = L; \\ 0.5 + \varepsilon \text{ if } s = H. \end{cases}$$
$$\pi = 0.3.$$

The equilibria of this example are shown in Table 5.3. The fundamental equilibrium, where $\varepsilon = 0$, is shown in Panel 3F. It can straightforwardly be shown, as in Examples 1 and 2, that $c_1 = 1$, $c_2 = R = 1.5$ and $pH = pL = 0.667$, so $P_H = P_L = 1$. The expected utility is $0.5 \ln(1) + 0.5 \ln(1.5) = 0.203$.

Next consider the equilibrium with aggregate uncertainty, where $\varepsilon = 0.01$. This is shown in Panel 3A. The key feature of this equilibrium is that only the safe banks enter. Their holdings of the short asset, $y^S = 0.508$, are enough to cover their liquidity needs when $s = H$, i.e. liquidity demand is high. The safe banks need $\lambda_H d^S = 0.51 \times 0.996 = 0.508$ units of the good in the high state. This means that there is excess liquidity in the low state $s = L$. As we have seen, the only possible equilibrium price is $p_L = 1$, so $P_L = p_L R = 1.5$. Given this price in state $s = L$ it follows that $pH \ll 1$ is necessary in order for the banks to hold both the short and long assets between dates 0 and 1 (see Section 5.2.2).

In this example, $p_H = 0.374$. The safe banks offer the consumption plan

$$c_s^S = \begin{cases} \left(c_{1H}^S, c_{2H}^S\right) = (0.996, 1.507) & \text{if } s = H; \\ \left(c_{1L}^S, c_{2L}^S\right) = (0.996, 1.497) & \text{if } s = L. \end{cases}$$

The expected utility provided to depositors by the safe banks is 0.199.

If a risky bank were to enter, the best that it could do is to choose

$$y^R = 0; \quad d^R = 1.5$$

and offer depositors the consumption plan

$$c_s^R = \begin{cases} \left(c_{1H}^R, c_{2H}^R\right) = (0.561, 0.561) & \text{if } s = H; \\ \left(c_{1L}^R, c_{2L}^R\right) = (1.500, 1.500) & \text{if } s = L. \end{cases}$$

The expected utility a depositor would receive from the contract offered by the risky banks is 0.110, which is strictly worse than that offered by the safe banks. Thus, there will be no risky banks operating in equilibrium.

Panel 3S shows the sunspot equilibrium which is the limit of fundamental equilibria for economies with aggregate intrinsic uncertainty as $\varepsilon \searrow 0$. The allocation provided by the safe bank is the same as in the fundamental equilibrium and so is the expected utility, 0.203. We have $p_L = 1$, as in the case with aggregate uncertainty. Here, using equation (5.4), we can show that $p_H = 0.375$. At these prices, the best a risky bank can do is provide customers with expected utility 0.111, so again there is no entry.

Note that whether we have bankruptcy or not, there is price volatility in every equilibrium except the fundamental equilibrium.

### 5.2.6 Complete versus incomplete markets

The key feature of the market structure in this chapter is that there are no Arrow securities so markets are incomplete. When these securities are introduced the analysis is changed significantly. Rather than the sunspot equilibrium considered in the examples being the robust equilibrium, it is the fundamental equilibrium that becomes robust. This now becomes the limit equilibrium as $\varepsilon \searrow 0$. For small $\varepsilon$ the equilibria are very close to the fundamental equilibrium. When $\varepsilon = 0$ the sunspot equilibria are ruled out because of the trading in Arrow securities. The crucial determinant of the form of equilibrium is thus whether markets are complete or incomplete. We consider the complete markets case in the next chapter.

## 5.3 RELATION TO THE LITERATURE

The model presented in this chapter is related to the wider literature on sunspots and general equilibrium with incomplete (GEI) markets. The theoretical analysis of sunspot equilibria began with the seminal work of Azariadis (1981) and Cass and Shell (1983), which gave rise to two streams of literature. The Cass–Shell paper is most closely related to work in a Walrasian, general equilibrium framework; the Azariadis paper is most closely related to the macroeconomic dynamics literature. For a useful survey of applications in macroeconomics, see Farmer (1999); for an example of the current literature in the general equilibrium framework, see Gottardi and Kajii (1995, 1999).

It can be shown that sunspots do not matter when markets are complete (for a precise statement, see Shell and Goenka 1997). The incompleteness in our model reveals itself in two ways. First, sunspots are assumed to be noncontractible – that is, the deposit contract is not explicitly contingent on the sunspot variable. In this respect the model simply follows the incomplete contracts literature (see, e.g., Hart 1995). Second, there are no markets for Arrow securities contingent on the sunspot variable, so financial institutions cannot insure themselves against asset-price fluctuations associated with the sunspot variable. This is the standard assumption of the GEI literature (see, e.g., Geanakoplos 1990 or Magill and Quinzii 1996).

The results of this chapter help us understand the relationship between two traditional views of financial crises discussed in Chapter 3. One view is that they are spontaneous events, unrelated to changes in the real economy. Historically, banking panics were attributed to "mob psychology" or "mass hysteria" (see, e.g. Kindleberger 1978). The modern version of this theory explains banking panics as equilibrium coordination failures (Bryant 1980; Diamond and Dybvig 1983). An alternative view is that financial crises are a natural outgrowth of the business cycle (Gorton 1988; Calomiris and Gorton 1991; Calomiris and Mason 2000; Allen and Gale 1998, 2000a–c). The model of this chapter combines the most attractive features of both traditional approaches. Like the sunspot approach, it produces large effects from small shocks. Like the real business cycle approach, it makes a firm prediction about the conditions under which crises will occur.

There is a small but growing literature related to financial fragility in the sense that the term is used in this chapter. Financial multipliers were introduced by Bernanke and Gertler (1989). In the model of Kiyotaki and Moore (1997), the impact of illiquidity at one link in the credit chain has a large impact further down the chain. Chari and Kehoe (2000) show that herding behavior can cause a small information shock to have a large effect on capital flows.

Lagunoff and Schreft (2001) show how overlapping claims on firms can cause small shocks to lead to widespread bankruptcy. Bernardo and Welch (2004) develop a model of runs on financial markets and asset-price collapses based on the anticipation of liquidity needs.

Postlewaite et al. (2003) study a model in which transactions in a competitive market are preceded by fixed investments. They show that, in the absence of forward contracts, equilibrium spot prices are highly volatile even when the degree of uncertainty is very small.

## 5.4 DISCUSSION

At the beginning of the chapter we stressed four points. The first was that small shocks could have large effects because of the interaction of banks and markets. We have investigated *endogenous* crises, where small or negligible shocks set off self-reinforcing and self-amplifying price changes. In the limit, when the shocks become vanishingly small, there is no aggregate exogenous uncertainty, but this does not mean that there is no endogenous uncertainty. We distinguished two kinds of uncertainty. *Intrinsic* uncertainty is caused by stochastic fluctuations in the primitives or fundamentals of the economy. Examples would be exogenous shocks that effect liquidity preferences or asset returns. *Extrinsic* uncertainty by definition has no effect on the fundamentals of the economy. An equilibrium with no extrinsic uncertainty is called a *fundamental* equilibrium, because the endogenous variables are functions of the exogenous primitives or fundamentals of the model (endowments, preferences, technologies). An equilibrium with extrinsic uncertainty is called a *sunspot* equilibrium, because endogenous variables may be influenced by extraneous variables (sunspots) that have no direct impact on fundamentals. A crisis cannot occur in a fundamental equilibrium in the absence of exogenous shocks to fundamentals, such as asset returns or liquidity demands. In a sunspot equilibrium, by contrast, asset prices fluctuate in the absence of aggregate exogenous shocks, and crises appear to occur spontaneously.

Our second point was the key role of liquidity in determining asset prices. The supply of liquidity is determined by the banks' initial portfolio choices. Subsequently, small shocks to the demand for liquidity, interacting with the fixed supply, cause a collapse in asset prices. Once the supply of liquidity is fixed by the banks' portfolio decisions, shocks to the demand for liquidity can cause substantial asset-price volatility and/or default. The supply of liquidity is fixed in the short run by the banks' portfolio decisions at date 0. In the absence of default, the demand for liquidity is perfectly inelastic in the short run. If the banks' supply of liquidity is sufficient to meet the depositors' demand when liquidity preference is high, there must be an excess supply of liquidity when liquidity preference is low. The banks will be willing to hold this excess liquidity between dates 1 and 2 only if the interest rate is zero (the price of date-2 consumption in terms of date-1 consumption is 1). A low interest rate implies that asset prices are correspondingly high. However, asset prices cannot be high in all states for then the short asset would be dominated at date 0 and no one would be willing to hold it. So, in the absence of default, there will be substantial price volatility. This argument does not require large shocks to liquidity demand.

Our third point was the role of mixed equilibria, in which ex ante identical banks must choose different strategies. For some parameter specifications, we show that one group of banks follows a risky strategy by investing almost all of their funds in the long asset. They meet their demands for liquidity by selling the asset in the market. Another group of banks follows a safe strategy and hold a large amount of the short asset. The safe banks provide liquidity to the risky banks by purchasing the risky banks' long-term assets. Safe banks also provide liquidity to each other: because there are idiosyncratic shocks to liquidity demand, the safe banks with a high demand for liquidity sell long-term assets to those with a low demand.

Finally, our fourth point concerned the difference between systemic risk and economy-wide crises. There are important differences between the present model of systemic or economy-wide *crises* and models of individual bank runs or *panics* of Bryant (1980) and Diamond and Dybvig (1983) discussed in Chapter 3. In the model of this chapter a crisis is a *systemic event*. It occurs only if the number of defaulting banks is large enough to affect the equilibrium asset price. In the panic model, by contrast, bank runs are an idiosyncratic phenomenon. Whether a run occurs at a particular bank depends on the decisions taken by the bank's depositors, independently of what happens at other banks. It is only by coincidence that runs are experienced by several banks at the same time.

Another difference between panics and crises concerns the reasons for the default. In the Bryant–Diamond–Dybvig story, bank runs are spontaneous events that depend on the decisions of late consumers to withdraw early. Given that almost all agents withdraw at date 1, early withdrawal is a best response for every agent; but if late consumers were to withdraw at date 2, then late withdrawal is a best response for every late consumer. So there are two "equilibria" of the coordination game played by agents at date 1, one with a bank run and one without. This kind of coordination failure plays no role in the present model. In fact, coordination failure is explicitly ruled out: a bank run occurs only if the bank cannot simultaneously satisfy its budget constraint and its incentive constraint. From the point of view of a single, price-taking bank, default results from an exogenous shock. When bankruptcy does occur, it is the result of low asset prices. Asset prices are endogenous, of course, and there is a "self-fulfilling" element in the relationship between asset prices and crises. Banks are forced to default and liquidate assets because asset prices are low, and asset prices are low as a result of mass bankruptcy and the associated liquidation of bank assets.

Several features of the model are special and deserve further consideration. First, we have noted the importance of inelastic demand for liquidity in generating large fluctuations in asset prices from small demand shocks. The inelasticity of demand follows from two assumptions. The first is the assumption that banks use demand deposits, which do not allow the payment at date 1 to be contingent on demand (or anything else). The second is the assumption of Diamond–Dybvig preferences, which rule out intertemporal substitution of consumption. We see both the Diamond–Dybvig preferences and the use of demand deposits as a counterpart to the empirical fact that financial contracts are typically written in a "hard" way that requires strict performance of precisely defined acts, independently of many apparently relevant contingencies. These hard contracts may be motivated by enforcement and incentive problems, but it would be too difficult to include them explicitly in the model. There seems little doubt that such factors are relevant in real markets and should be taken into account here.

Second, an alternative justification for incomplete contracts is that they provide a way of modeling – within the standard, Walrasian, auction-market framework – some realistic features of alternative market-clearing mechanisms. In an auction market, prices and quantities adjust simultaneously in a tatônnement process until a full equilibrium is achieved. An alternative mechanism is one in which quantities are chosen before prices are allowed to adjust. An example is the use of market orders in markets for company stocks. In the banking context, if depositors were required to make a withdrawal decision before the asset price was determined in the interbank market, then the same inelasticity of demand would be observed even if depositors had preferences that allowed for intertemporal substitution. There may be other institutional structures that have the qualitative features of the model of this chapter.

Finally, pecuniary externalities "matter" in the model because markets are incomplete: if banks could trade Arrow securities contingent on the states $\theta$, they would be able to insure themselves against changes in asset values. With a complete set of Arrow securities, risk sharing must be efficient, so in the absence of intrinsic uncertainty ($\varepsilon = 0$) the only possible equilibrium is the one we have called the fundamental equilibrium. The equilibrium allocation is incentive-efficient, sunspots have no real impact, and there are no crises. Note that, although the existence of the markets for Arrow securities has an effect (by eliminating the other equilibria), there is no trade in Arrow securities in the fundamental equilibrium. When intrinsic uncertainty is introduced ($\varepsilon > 0$) the fundamental equilibrium is now robust. It is the limit equilibrium as $\varepsilon \searrow 0$. We consider the case with complete markets and contrast it with the incomplete markets case in the next chapter.

## REFERENCES

Allen, F. and D. Gale (1998). "Optimal Financial Crises," *Journal of Finance* 53, 1245–1284.

Allen, F. and D. Gale (2000a). "Financial Contagion," *Journal of Political Economy* 108, 1–33.

Allen, F. and D. Gale (2000b). "Optimal Currency Crises," *Carnegie Rochester Series on Public Policy* 53, 177–230.

Allen, F. and D. Gale (2000c). "Bubbles and Crises," *The Economic Journal* 110, 236–256.

Allen, F. and D. Gale (2004). "Financial Fragility, Liquidity, and Asset Prices," *Journal of the European Economic Association* 2, 1015–1048.

Azariadis, C. (1981). "Self-Fulfilling Prophecies," *Journal of Economic Theory* 25, 380–396.

Bernanke, B. and M. Gertler (1989). "Agency Costs, Net Worth, and Business Fluctuations," *American Economic Review* 79, 14–31.

Bernardo, A. and I. Welch (2004). "Financial Market Runs," *Quarterly Journal of Economics* 119, 135–158.

Bryant, J. (1980). "A Model of Reserves, Bank Runs, and Deposit Insurance," *Journal of Banking and Finance* 4, 335–344.

Calomiris, C. and G. Gorton (1991). "The Origins of Banking Panics, Models, Facts, and Bank Regulation." In *Financial Markets and Financial Crises*, edited by R. Hubbard. Chicago, IL: University of Chicago Press.

Calomiris, C. and J. Mason (2000). "Causes of U.S. Bank Distress During the Depression." NBER Working Paper W7919.

Cass, D. and K. Shell (1983). "Do Sunspots Matter?" *Journal of Political Economy* 91, 193–227.

Chari, V. and P. Kehoe (2000). "Financial Crises as Herds." Federal Reserve Bank of Minneapolis Working Paper.

Diamond, D. and P. Dybvig (1983). "Bank Runs, Deposit Insurance, and Liquidity," *Journal of Political Economy* 91, 401–419.

Farmer, R. (1999). *The Macroeconomics of Self-Fulfilling Prophecies.* Cambridge and London: MIT Press.

Geanakoplos, J. (1990). "An Introduction to General Equilibrium with Incomplete Asset Markets," *Journal of Mathematical Economics* 19, 1–38.

Gorton, G. (1988). "Banking Panics and Business Cycles," *Oxford Economic Papers* 40, 751–781.

Gottardi, P. and A. Kajii (1995). "Generic Existence of Sunspot Equilibria: The Real Asset Case," University of Pennsylvania, CARESS Working Paper 95/12.

Gottardi, P. and A. Kajii (1999). "The Structure of Sunspot Equilibria: The Role of Multiplicity," *Review of Economic Studies* 66, 713–732.

Hart, O. (1995). *Firms, Contracts and Financial Structure.* Oxford: Oxford University Press.

Kindleberger, C. (1978). *Manias, Panics, and Crashes: A History of Financial Crises.* New York, NY: Basic Books.

Kiyotaki, N. and J. Moore (1997). "Credit Chains," *Journal of Political Economy* 99, 220–264.

Lagunoff, R. and S. Schreft (2001). "A Model of Financial Fragility," *Journal of Economic Theory* 99, 220–264.

Magill, M. and M. Quinzii (1996). *Theory of Incomplete Markets, Volume I.* Cambridge and London: MIT Press.

Postlewaite, A., G. Mailath and L. Samuelson (2003). "Sunk Investments Lead to Unpredictable Prices." University of Pennsylvania: http://www.ssc.upenn.edu/~apostlew/.

Schnabel, I. and H. Shin (2004). "Liquidity and Contagion: The Crisis of 1763," *Journal of the European Economic Association* 2, 929–968.

Shell, K. and A. Goenka (1997). "When Sunspots Don't Matter," *Economic Theory* 9, 169–178.

# 6

## Intermediation and markets

In the preceding chapter we studied financial fragility from the point of view of *positive* economics, that is, trying to understand the factors that give rise to financial crises and the reasons why a financial system might be sensitive to small shocks. We noted in passing that financial crises might be inefficient, but this was not the focus of our analysis. Now it is time to turn to *normative* questions and try to understand why financial crises are a "bad thing."

To understand why financial crises are a "bad thing," we begin by asking a different question "Under what circumstances are financial crises efficient?" We take this indirect approach for several reasons.

- First, we want to challenge the conventional wisdom that financial crises are always and everywhere a "bad thing." It may well be true that financial crises impose substantial costs on the economy. Certainly there have been many historical episodes in many countries that suggest the costs of financial crises can be very substantial. At the same time, any regulation of the financial system involves costs. The most important of these costs are the distortions imposed on the financial system by a regulatory regime that restricts what financial institutions may and may not do. To measure the costs and benefits of any policy, we need to have a clear understanding of the conditions for efficiency in the financial system, including the conditions for efficient financial crises.

- A second reason for studying the conditions under which crises are efficient is that knowledge of these conditions may suggest techniques for managing crises and reducing their costs. Casual observation suggests that the central banking techniques developed over the past two centuries are mainly the result of trial and error, without much rigorous theory behind them. The first step in developing an optimal financial stability policy is to carry out a thorough welfare analysis of financial crises, including the conditions for efficient financial crises.

- A third reason for adopting the proposed approach is that economists have a well developed set of tools for studying optimal economic systems. So it is somewhat easier to address normative questions by characterizing the conditions for efficiency rather than the reverse.

One of the lessons of this chapter is the important role of missing markets. Although it may not have been obvious at the time, the properties of the model studied in Chapter 5 depend crucially on the absence of certain financial markets, specifically, markets for Arrow securities.[1] As we saw, deposit contracts commit intermediaries to provide each depositor who withdraws at date 1 a fixed amount of consumption, independently of the state of nature. If the demand for liquidity is high, the only way for the intermediary to obtain enough liquidity to meet its commitments is through asset sales. From the point of view of the intermediary, selling assets is unfortunate for two reasons. First, the intermediary may be forced to dispose of assets at "fire-sale" prices. Depositors receive lower payouts as a result. Second, if a large number of intermediaries sell at the same time, the selling pressure will drive prices down further, forcing the intermediaries to unload even more assets, and worsening the crisis. These two effects together explain the inefficiency and severity of the financial crisis.

There are two types of incompleteness in the preceding chapter's analysis of financial fragility. We say that a contract is complete if the outcome is (in principle) contingent on all states of nature. Deposit contracts are not complete in this sense because the amount of consumption promised to withdrawers at date 1 is fixed, i.e. not contingent on the state of nature. We say that markets are complete if there are markets on which intermediaries can trade Arrow securities for each state of nature. These markets allow intermediaries to purchase liquidity contingent on the state of nature. If there are no markets for Arrow securities, then markets are incomplete. Of the two types of incompleteness, it is the incompleteness of markets that accounts for the inefficiency of financial crises.

To see the importance of missing markets, suppose that markets for Arrow securities were introduced to the model of financial fragility. If an intermediary anticipated a shortage of liquidity in a particular state of nature, it would be possible to purchase Arrow securities that pay off in that state in order to provide extra liquidity and avoid the need for asset sales. This would cut the link between the demand for liquidity and the sale of assets. As a result, the pricing of assets would be insulated from liquidity shocks and the destabilizing effects of incomplete contracts would be reduced if not avoided altogether.

---

[1] An Arrow security is a promise to deliver one unit of account (one "dollar" ) if a specified state of nature occurs and nothing otherwise. The concepts of Arrow securities and complete markets are reviewed in Chapter 2.

Another benefit of markets for Arrow securities is improved risk sharing. They allow the intermediary to pay for liquidity in the state where it is needed by selling liquidity in the other state. In effect, the intermediary is transferring wealth from a state where the marginal utility of consumption is low to a state where it is high. This is what efficient risk sharing requires. Asset sales, by contrast, force the intermediary to reduce consumption in the state where marginal utility is already high, increasing the variation in consumption across states and resulting in inefficient risk sharing.

In the rest of this chapter, we explore the implications of complete markets for the efficiency of the incidence of financial crises. Under certain additional assumptions, which are analogous to the assumptions of the fundamental theorems of welfare economics, we shall show that complete markets guarantee the efficiency of laisser-faire equilibrium. In this context at least, a financial crisis does not represent a market failure and, hence, does not provide a reason for government intervention or regulation.

## 6.1 COMPLETE MARKETS

Since the time of Adam Smith, economists have been fascinated with the properties of a decentralized market system. Over the last two centuries, they have refined their theoretical understanding of the conditions that must be satisfied if the market allocation is to be efficient. The conditions are not innocuous:

- markets must be perfectly competitive;
- there must be no externalities;
- there must be no asymmetric information (moral hazard or adverse selection);
- there must be no transaction costs;
- and markets must be complete.

From our perspective, the critical condition is the completeness of markets. Technically, we say that markets are *complete* if it is possible to trade, at a single point in time, all the commodities that will ever exist. In defining commodities, we distinguish goods that are delivered at different dates or in different places as different commodities. We also distinguish contingent commodities, that is, goods whose delivery is contingent on the occurrence of an uncertain event. In order for markets to be complete, it must be possible to trade all the commodities, so-defined, at a single date.

It is both a strength and a weakness of the theory that the definition of commodities is very broad. On the one hand, the assumption of complete markets may seem like a "tall order." Most economists would not claim that markets are even approximately complete and this is a weakness of the theory.[2] On the other hand, the assumption of complete markets is crucial because it allows us to extend the theory to cover many new phenomena just by defining commodities appropriately. The economic principles that were developed originally to explain exchange of ordinary goods in spot markets can be used to study allocation decisions across space and time and in the face of uncertainty. Conversely, we can characterize many market failures as examples of "missing markets." Finally, the efficiency of economies with complete markets suggests that the invention of new markets may provide a remedy for certain market failures.

To get an idea of the role of the complete markets assumption in the analysis of efficient markets and lay the groundwork for our later analysis of financial crises, it is helpful to consider a simple example and ask what a complete set of markets would look like in this case.

## Commodities

As usual, we assume there are three dates, $t = 0, 1, 2$ and a single, all-purpose good at each date. There are two states of nature, denoted by $s = H, L$. At date 0 the state is unknown, although individuals know the true probability $\pi_s$ of each state $s$. The true state is revealed at the beginning of date 1. Since the state is unknown at date 0, we cannot make the delivery of the good contingent on the state at date 0; so there is a single commodity at date 0, the good delivered independent of the state at date 0. At dates $t = 1, 2$, the state is known with certainty so we can define contingent commodities corresponding to each state, the good delivered at date $t = 1, 2$ in state $s = H, L$. Thus, there are five commodities in all, the single noncontingent commodity at $t = 0$ and the four contingent commodities $(t, s) = (1, H), (2, H), (1, L), (2, L)$ at the subsequent dates. This commodity space is illustrated in Figure 6.1.

## Consumption

Suppose that a consumer has an endowment of one unit of the good at date 0 and nothing at dates 1 and 2. In terms of our definition of commodities, the

---

[2] Markets can be effectively complete even if there does not exist a complete set of markets for all possible contingent commodities. Dynamic trading strategies using a limited set of securities allow investors to synthesize a much larger set of derivatives. It is possible that in some circumstances such strategies can effectively complete the set of markets. Whether a good approximation to complete markets is achieved is ultimately an empirical issue which we are unable to resolve here; but we believe that incompleteness is an important issue even for financial institutions and sophisticated investors.

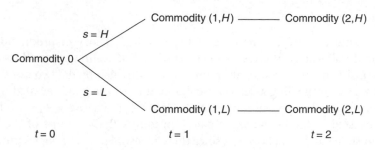

Figure 6.1. Commodity space with two states and three dates.

endowment consists of a vector $e = (1, 0, 0, 0, 0)$, indicating that the consumer has one unit of the single commodity at date 0 and none of the contingent commodities corresponding to dates 1 and 2 and the states $H$ and $L$. We suppose as usual that the consumer only values consumption at dates 1 and 2 and that his preferences are represented by a VNM utility function

$$U(c_1) + \beta U(c_2),$$

where $c_1$ denotes consumption at date 1 and $c_2$ denotes consumption at date 2. If we denote consumption at date $t$ in state $s$ by $c_{ts}$ then the consumer's consumption bundle is described by a vector $c = (0, c_{1H}, c_{2H}, c_{1L}, c_{2L})$ and the expected utility of this bundle is

$$\pi_H \{U(c_{1H}) + \beta U(c_{2H})\} + \pi_L \{U(c_{1L}) + \beta U(c_{2L})\},$$

where $\pi_s$ denotes the probability of state $s$ occurring.

Since markets are complete, the consumer can purchase any consumption bundle $c = (0, c_{1H}, c_{2H}, c_{1L}, c_{2L})$ that satisfies his budget constraint at date 0. Since only relative prices matter, there is no essential loss of generality in choosing the good at date 0 as the numeraire and setting its price $p_0$ equal to one. Letting $p_{ts}$ denote the price of one unit of the contingent commodity $(t, s)$, we can write the consumer's budget constraint as

$$p_{1H} c_{1H} + p_{2H} c_{2H} + p_{1L} c_{1L} + p_{2L} c_{2L} \leq p_0 1 = 1.$$

The right hand side is the value of the consumer's endowment and the left hand side is the value of his consumption bundle. This looks just like the standard budget constraint and that is one of the great strengths of the Arrow–Debreu model: by reinterpreting goods at different dates and in different states of nature as different commodities, we can extend the standard budget constraint and indeed the theory of competitive equilibrium to deal with uncertainty and time.

*Production*

In the same way, we can reinterpret the standard theory of production to explain the allocation of investment. The production technology for this economy consists of the investment opportunities provided by the two assets, the short asset and the long asset. As usual, one unit of the good invested in the short asset at date $t$ produces one unit at date $t + 1$, where $t = 0, 1$, and one unit invested in the long asset at date 0 produces $R_s > 1$ units of the long asset in state $s$ at date 2; however, since these investment technologies produce contingent commodities, some care is required in their interpretation.

Let's start with the short asset. A single unit invested at date 0 produces one unit of the good at date 1, independently of the state. In terms of our definition of commodities, one unit of the good at date 0 produces one unit of the contingent commodity $(1, H)$ and one unit of the contingent commodity $(1, L)$. We can represent this technology by the production vector

$$a_0 = (-1, 1, 0, 1, 0),$$

where the entry $-1$ denotes an input of one unit at date 0 and the other entries denote outputs of contingent commodities.

Investment in the short asset at date 1 is similar, except that the true state is already known, so both the input and the output are contingent on the state. For example, if one unit is invested at date 1 in state $H$, the input consists of one unit of $(1, H)$ and the output consists of one unit of $(2, H)$. Thus, we have two technologies at date 1, one for each state, represented by the production vectors

$$a_{1H} = (0, -1, 1, 0, 0)$$

and

$$a_{1L} = (0, 0, 0, -1, 1).$$

The long asset represents a technology that can only be used at date 0, so it is simpler to analyze. One unit invested at date 0 produces $R_s > 1$ units at date 2 in state $s$, so the output is a bundle of contingent commodities, namely, $R_H$ units of $(2, H)$ and $R_L$ units of $(2, L)$. This technology can be represented by the vector

$$a_2 = (-1, 0, R_H, 0, R_L).$$

Since each of these production technologies operates subject to constant returns to scale, in a competitive equilibrium the profits derived from each process will be zero. If profits were positive, a profit-maximizing firm would be tempted to operate at an infinite scale, which is inconsistent with market clearing. If the profits per unit were negative, the firm would shut down and earn zero profits. So the firm can only operate at a positive scale if the profit per unit is zero. Because equilibrium profits are zero, it does not matter who undertakes the different production activities. We can assume that a representative firm does this or we can assume that individual consumers do it. With complete markets there are many degrees of freedom. Here we will assume that a representative firm makes all production decisions.

The representative firm chooses a level of investment in each of the activities described above. Let $y_0$ denote investment in the short asset at date 0, let $y_{1s}$ denote investment in the short asset at date 1 in state $s = H, L$, and let $x$ denote investment in the long asset at date 0 . Each activity must yield non-positive profits, so

$$-1 + p_{1H} + p_{1L} \leq 0, \tag{6.1}$$

with equality if $y_0 > 0$,

$$-p_{1s} + p_{2s} \leq 0, \tag{6.2}$$

with equality if $y_{1s} > 0$ for $s = H, L$, and

$$-1 + p_{2H}R_H + p_{2L}R_L \leq 0, \tag{6.3}$$

with equality if $x > 0$. These conditions are necessary and sufficient for profit maximization.

One interesting point to note is that, even though the true state is unknown when all the decisions are made at date 0, the firm does not face any uncertainty. This is because the firm buys and sells contingent commodities at known prices at date 0. For example, in the case of investment in the short asset at date 0, the firm buys one unit of the good at date 0 as an input and sells one unit of each of the contingent commodities at date 1 . The cost of the input is 1 and the revenue from selling the outputs is $p_{1H} + p_{1L}$, so the profit is $p_{1H} + p_{1L} - 1$. This profit is "realized" at date 0, when the commodities are traded, rather than at date 1 when the outputs are produced.

## Equilibrium

The requirements for competitive equilibrium are that, at the given prices,

(a) each consumer chooses a consumption bundle that maximizes his expected utility, subject to his budget constraint;

(b) the representative firm chooses investments in the various activities to maximize profits; and

(c) the choices of the consumers and the firm are consistent with market clearing (i.e. demand equals supply).

For the purposes of illustration, let us assume there are two types of consumers, $A$ and $B$ with preferences described by VNM utility functions $U^A(c_1) + \beta U^A(c_2)$ and $U^B(c_1) + \beta U^B(c_2)$. Formally, a competitive equilibrium consists of a price vector $p^* = (1, p_{1H}^*, p_{2H}^*, p_{1L}^*, p_{2L}^*)$, a consumption bundle $c^{i*} = (0, c_{1H}^{i*}, c_{2H}^{i*}, c_{1L}^{i*}, c_{2L}^{i*})$ for consumers $i = A, B$ and a vector of investments $I^* = (y_0^*, y_{1H}^*, y_{1L}^*, x^*)$ such that

(a) $c^{i*}$ maximizes consumer $i$'s expected utility subject to his budget constraint, for each $i = A, B$;

(b) $I^*$ satisfies the zero profit conditions; and

(c) all markets clear.

Since all trading occurs at date 0, market clearing is achieved at date 0 as well. The actual delivery of goods takes place later, but the decisions have already been made at date 0 and they must be consistent. The market for the good at date 0 will clear if

$$x^* + y_0^* = 2;$$

the two consumers supply their one-unit endowments and the firm demands inputs $x^*$ and $y_0^*$ for investment in the long and short assets, respectively. At date 1, there are two contingent commodities, one for each state $s$. For the corresponding markets to clear at date 0 requires

$$c_{1s}^{A*} + c_{1s}^{B*} + y_{1s}^* = y_0^*,$$

for each $s = H, L$; here the firm supplies $y_0^*$ units of the good (the payoff from the investment in the short asset) and demands $y_{1s}^*$ units to invest in the short asset and the consumer demands $c_{1s}^*$ units to consume. At date 2, there are again two contingent commodities, one for each state $s$. For the corresponding markets to clear at date 0 requires

$$c_{2s}^{A*} + c_{2s}^{B*} = y_{1s}^* + R_s x^*,$$

for each $s = H, L$; the firm supplies $y_{1s}^* + R_s x^*$ units of the good (the return on investment in the long asset at date 0 and the short asset at date 1) and the consumers demand $c_{2s}^{A*} + c_{2s}^{B*}$ units of the good for consumption.

**Example 1** To illustrate the model in the simplest possible way, consider a Robinson Crusoe economy in which there is a single type of consumer with endowment $e = (1, 0, 0)$ and preferences given by the familiar Cobb–Douglas version of the VNM utility function

$$U(c_1) + \beta U(c_2) = \ln c_1 + \ln c_2.$$

Assume that the states are equiprobable

$$\pi_H = \pi_L = 0.5$$

and the returns on the long asset are

$$(R_H, R_L) = (3, 0).$$

Since there is a single representative consumer, there is a unique Pareto-efficient allocation for this economy, namely, the allocation that maximizes the representative consumer's expected utility. The first fundamental theorem of welfare economics ensures that a competitive equilibrium is Pareto efficient. Using this fact, we can solve for the competitive equilibrium in two stages. First, we solve for the unique efficient allocation. Second, we find the prices that support this allocation as an equilibrium.

Suppose that a planner chooses an attainable allocation that maximizes the expected utility of the representative consumer. He invests in $x$ units in the long asset and $y$ units in the short asset. A necessary condition for maximizing expected utility is that, in each state $s$, the consumption bundle $(c_{1s}, c_{2s})$ maximizes the consumer's utility $\ln c_1 + \ln c_2$ subject to the feasibility conditions

$$c_{1s} \leq y,$$

and

$$c_{1s} + c_{2s} \leq y + R_s x,$$

for $s = H, L$.

The allocation of consumption between dates 1 and 2 depends on the value of $R_s$, the return to the long asset. If $R_s$ is high ($R_s x > y$), it is optimal to put $c_1 = y$ and $c_2 = R_s x$. If $R_s$ is low ($R_s x < y$), it is optimal to equalize consumption between the two dates, so that $c_1 = c_2 = \frac{1}{2}(y + R_s x)$. The consumption functions are illustrated in Figure 6.2.

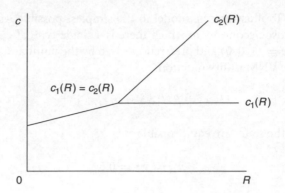

**Figure 6.2.** Consumption at dates 1 and 2 as a function of the return on the long asset.

In state $L$ the return to the long asset is zero, so the planner divides the return to the short asset evenly between consumption at date 1 and date 2:

$$c_{1L} = c_{2L} = \frac{y}{2}.$$

In state $H$, by contrast, the liquidity constraint will be binding at date 1:

$$c_{1H} = y, \quad c_{2H} = 3x.$$

Now that we have guessed the optimal consumption allocation as a function of the first period investments in the long and short assets, we need to determine the optimal portfolio $(x, y)$. The planner should choose $(x, y)$ so that an extra unit invested in either asset would increase expected utility by the same amount. So the first-order condition for maximizing expected utility is

$$\frac{1}{2} \left\{ \frac{1}{c_{1H}} + \frac{1}{c_{1L}} \right\} = \frac{1}{2} \left\{ \frac{3}{c_{2H}} + \frac{0}{c_{2L}} \right\}.$$

The left hand side is the increase in expected utility from increasing $y$. The right hand side is the increase in expected utility from increasing $x$. Substituting our hypothesized expressions for consumption into the first-order condition gives

$$\frac{1}{2} \left\{ \frac{1}{y} + \frac{2}{y} \right\} = \frac{1}{2} \frac{1}{x},$$

which is satisfied only if

$$(x, y) = \left( \frac{1}{4}, \frac{3}{4} \right).$$

Then we can use the consumption functions to deduce the efficient consumption allocation,

$$c = (c_{1H}, c_{2H}, c_{1L}, c_{2L}) = \left(y, 3x, \frac{y}{2}, \frac{y}{2}\right) = \left(\frac{3}{4}, \frac{3}{4}, \frac{3}{8}, \frac{3}{8}\right).$$

It remains to find prices that will support this allocation as an equilibrium. The consumer's equilibrium decision problem is to maximize his expected utility

$$\frac{1}{2}\{\ln c_{1H} + \ln c_{2H}\} + \frac{1}{2}\{\ln c_{1L} + \ln c_{2L}\}$$

subject to the budget constraint

$$p_{1H}c_{1H} + p_{2H}c_{2H} + p_{1L}c_{1L} + p_{2L}c_{2L} = 1.$$

From the properties of the Cobb–Douglas utility function, we know that the consumer will spend the same share of his wealth on each of the four contingent commodities. Thus,

$$p_{1H}c_{1H} = p_{2H}c_{2H} = p_{1L}c_{1L} = p_{2L}c_{2L} = \frac{1}{4}.$$

Using the efficient consumption bundle we can solve for the price vector that will support the consumer's choice of this consumption bundle

$$p = (p_{1H}, p_{2H}, p_{1L}, p_{2L}) = \left(\frac{1}{3}, \frac{1}{3}, \frac{2}{3}, \frac{2}{3}\right).$$

In the notation introduced earlier,

$$I = (y_0, y_{1H}, y_{1L}, x) = \left(\frac{3}{4}, 0, \frac{3}{8}, \frac{1}{4}\right).$$

As we have already shown, the firm invests $y_0 = \frac{3}{4}$ in the short asset and $x = \frac{1}{4}$ in the long asset at date 0. At date 1 there is no investment in the short asset in state $H$ because all the returns to the short asset are consumed. At date 1 in state $L$, by contrast, half of the return to the short asset is stored until date 2 because the return to the long asset is zero.

The zero-profit conditions (6.1)–(6.3) corresponding to $y_0$, $x$, and $y_{1L}$ hold as equations because investment is positive. The zero-profit condition (6.2) corresponding to $y_{1H}$ is an inequality because the investment is zero. In fact, we can show that all the zero-profit conditions are satisfied exactly. The zero-profit condition for the short asset at date 0, i.e. condition (6.1), is satisfied because

$$p_{1H} + p_{1L} = \frac{1}{3} + \frac{2}{3} = 1.$$

The zero-profit condition for the long asset at date 0, i.e. condition (6.3), is satisfied because

$$R_H p_{2H} + R_L p_{2L} = 3 \times \frac{1}{3} + 0 \times \frac{1}{4} = 1.$$

The zero-profit constraint for the short asset at date 1, i.e. condition (6.2), is satisfied in each state because

$$p_{1H} = p_{2H} = \frac{1}{3} \text{ and } p_{1L} = p_{2L} = \frac{2}{3}.$$

Thus, all the conditions for competitive equilibrium are satisfied.

## 6.2 INTERMEDIATION AND MARKETS

To study the role of financial markets in allowing intermediaries to hedge risks, we use a variant of the model used in the preceding chapters. There are three dates $t = 0, 1, 2$ and at each date an all-purpose good that can be used for consumption or investment. There are two assets, the short asset represented by a storage technology that yields one unit of the good at date $t + 1$ for every unit invested at date $t$, and a long asset represented by a constant returns to scale technology that yields $R > 1$ units of the good at date 2 for every unit invested at date 0.

As usual, there is a continuum of economic agents at date 0, each of whom has an endowment of one unit of the good at date 0 and nothing at future dates. At date 1, each agent learns whether he is an early consumer, who only values the good at date 1, or a late consumer, who only values the good at date 2. The probability of being an early consumer is $0 < \lambda < 1$. Ex post, the fraction of early consumers in the economy is assumed to be $\lambda$ as well.

The main difference between the current model and those used in the preceding chapters lies in the specification of uncertainty. We assume that the economy is divided into two regions, labeled $A$ and $B$. Ex ante the two regions are identical, with the same number of identical agents and the same assets.

There are two aggregate states of nature, denoted by $HL$ and $LH$. Each state is equally likely, that is, each occurs with probability 0.5. In state $HL$ the fraction of early consumers in region $A$ is $\lambda_H$ and the fraction of early consumers in region $B$ is $\lambda_L$, where $0 < \lambda_L < \lambda_H < 1$. In state $LH$ the fractions are reversed. We assume that

$$\lambda = \frac{1}{2}(\lambda_H + \lambda_L),$$

so that the fraction of early consumers in each state is $\lambda$. This also implies that the probability of any investor becoming an early consumer is also $\lambda$.

The investors' attitudes toward risk are represented by a common VNM utility function. If an investor consumes $c$ units of the good at the appropriate date, his utility is $U(c)$, where $U(\cdot)$ satisfies all the usual properties.

All uncertainty is resolved, as usual, at the beginning of date 1 when the true state $HL$ or $LH$ is revealed and each investor learns his type, early or late.

The uncertainty and information structure are illustrated in Figure 6.3.

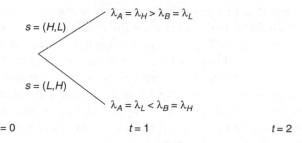

Figure 6.3. Liquidity shocks of groups A and B in states $(H, L)$ and $(L, H)$.

### 6.2.1 Efficient risk sharing

Suppose a central planner was responsible for making the decisions in this economy. Would the division of investors into two regions matter? Evidently not. The investors are ex ante identical and the number of early consumers is the same in each state, so there is no reason why the planner should pay any attention to the region to which an investor belongs. The planner will allocate a fraction $y$ of the endowment to the short asset and a fraction $1 - y$ to the long asset and offer $c_1$ units of the good at date 1 to the early consumers and $c_2$ units of the good at date 2 to the late consumers, *independently of the state*. These variables are chosen to maximize the expected utility of the representative investor

$$\lambda U(c_1) + (1 - \lambda)U(c_2),$$

subject to the usual feasibility conditions

$$\lambda c_1 = y$$

and

$$(1 - \lambda)c_2 = (1 - y)R.$$

As usual, the first best is characterized by the feasibility conditions and by the first-order condition $U'(c_1) = RU'(c_2)$. Since the first-order condition implies that $c_1 < c_2$, the incentive constraint is also satisfied, in case the planner does not directly observe the investor's type. The important point is that the optimal consumption allocation for each individual does not depend on the state. It only depends on whether the individual is an early or a late consumer.

Now suppose that an intermediary wanted to implement the first-best outcome. There would be no difficulty if the intermediary served a representative sample of investors from Region $A$ and Region $B$, for in that case the fraction of early consumers would be exactly $\lambda$ in each state and the first-best allocation would clearly be feasible for the intermediary. A more interesting case is one in which intermediaries are heterogeneous, that is, have different proportions of investors drawn from Region $A$ and Region $B$. In that case, the proportion of early consumers for a given intermediary may not be certain and equal to $\lambda$ and, as a result, the first best may not be attainable.

To illustrate the problem, consider the extreme case where an intermediary is allowed to operate in either region, but not both. Legal restrictions of this form were common in the United States in the past. Even in the present day, there are still many US banks that, because of their size, operate only within a small region. As usual, we assume that there is free entry and that competition forces intermediaries to maximize their depositors' expected utility.

The problem for the intermediary is that the fraction of early consumers among his depositors will now vary with the aggregate state. If the fraction of early consumers is high, then

$$\lambda_H c_1 > \lambda c_1 = y.$$

There is not enough liquidity at date 1 to provide the early consumers with the promised amount of consumption. Similarly, if the fraction of early consumers is low, then

$$(1 - \lambda_L)c_2 > (1 - \lambda)c_2 + (\lambda - \lambda_L)c_1$$
$$= (1 - y)R + (y - \lambda_L c_1).$$

The intermediary has too much liquidity at date 1 and not enough to distribute at date 2. So, clearly, the intermediary cannot achieve the first best in autarky.

## 6.2.2 Equilibrium with complete financial markets

The intermediary's problem is easily solved if we introduce markets in which the intermediary can insure against getting a high liquidity shock. Since there is no aggregate uncertainty, whenever some intermediaries get a high liquidity shock and hence have too little liquidity to give their depositors the first-best consumption $c_1$, there will be intermediaries in the other region with a low liquidity shock and too much liquidity at date 1. These intermediaries would be happy to lend to the liquidity-constrained intermediaries in order to get more consumption at date 2 when they will need it.

In order to implement the first best, we need complete markets. There are five contingent commodities, the good at date 0, the good at date 1 in states $HL$ and $LH$, and the good at date 2 in states $HL$ and $LH$. Taking the good at date 0 as the numeraire ($p_0 \equiv 1$), let $p_{ts}$ denote the price of the good at date $t$ in state $s$, where $t = 1, 2$ and $s = HL, LH$. The no-arbitrage condition for the short asset at date 0 implies that $p_{1HL} + p_{1LH} = 1$. The symmetry of the two states suggests that there exists a symmetric equilibrium in which $p_{1HL} = p_{1LH}$. Putting together these two conditions gives

$$p_{1HL} = p_{1LH} = \frac{1}{2}.$$

Similarly, we assume that $p_{2HL} = p_{2LH}$ and use the no-arbitrage condition for the long asset, $(p_{2HL} + p_{2LH}) R = 1$, to conclude that

$$p_{2HL} = p_{2LH} = \frac{1}{2R}.$$

Then without risk of confusion we can write $p_1$ for the price of the good at date 1 and $p_2$ for the price of the good at date 2 *in either state*. Suppose the intermediary in Region $A$ promises a consumption profile $(c_1, c_2)$ that is independent of the state. The intermediary's budget constraint is

$$p_{1HL}\lambda_H c_1 + p_{1LH}\lambda_L c_1 + p_{2HL}(1 - \lambda_H) c_2 + p_{2LH}(1 - \lambda_L) c_2 = 1$$
$$\Longleftrightarrow p_1(\lambda_H + \lambda_L) c_1 + p_2(1 - \lambda_H + 1 - \lambda_L) c_2 = 1$$
$$\Longleftrightarrow \lambda c_1 + \frac{1}{R}(1 - \lambda) c_2 = 1.$$

The analogous calculation for intermediaries in Region $B$ yields an identical budget constraint. Then each intermediary is choosing a profile $(c_1, c_2)$ to maximize the expected utility $\lambda U(c_1) + (1 - \lambda) U(c_2)$ subject to the budget constraint above and this requires that the first-order condition $U'(c_1) = RU'(c_2)$ be satisfied. In other words, the first-best consumption profile satisfies the intermediary's budget constraint and satisfies the first-order condition, hence is optimal. It is also easy to check that the zero-profit conditions are satisfied.

This allocation is feasible for the economy, as we have already seen in our analysis of the planner's problem. So markets will clear when each intermediary chooses the first-best consumption profile and the corresponding production plan. Thus, complete markets allow precisely the transfers between states that are necessary for first-best risk sharing.

**Example 2**    In the preceding sketch of the intermediary's problem we assumed that consumers received the same consumption independently of the state. We will obtain this condition as part of the solution to the intermediary's problem using the following parameters:

$$R = 3;$$
$$U(c) = -\frac{1}{5}c^{-5};$$
$$\lambda_H = 0.6, \lambda_L = 0.4;$$
$$\pi_{HL} = \pi_{LH} = 0.5.$$

Suppose that

$$p_{1HL} = p_{1LH} = p_1 = \frac{1}{2}$$

and

$$p_{2HL} = p_{2LH} = p_2 = \frac{1}{6}.$$

We look at the problem from the perspective of an intermediary in Region $A$ and let $(c_{1H}, c_{2H})$ (resp. $(c_{1L}, c_{2L})$) denote the consumption profile promised when the fraction of early consumers is $\lambda_H$ (resp. $\lambda_L$) for that intermediary. The intermediary needs to maximize the representative depositor's expected utility

$$\frac{1}{2} \{0.6U(c_{1H}) + 0.4U(c_{2H}) + 0.4U(c_{1L}) + 0.6U(c_{2L})\}$$

subject to the intermediary's budget constraint

$$p_1 (0.6c_{1H} + 0.4c_{1L}) + p_2 (0.4c_{2H} + 0.6c_{2L}) = 1.$$

The first-order conditions for this problem are

$$U'(c_{1H}) = U'(c_{1L}) = \mu p_1 = \frac{\mu}{2}$$

$$U'(c_{2H}) = U'(c_{2L}) = \mu p_2 = \frac{\mu}{6}$$

where $\mu$ is the Lagrange multiplier for the budget constraint. Substituting the formula for marginal utility into the first-order conditions we get

$$(c_{1H})^{-6} = (c_{1L})^{-6} = \mu p_1 = \frac{\mu}{2}$$

$$(c_{2H})^{-6} = (c_{2L})^{-6} = \mu p_2 = \frac{\mu}{6}.$$

Then $c_{1H} = c_{1L} = c_1$ and $c_{2H} = c_{2L} = c_2$, that is, consumption is independent of the state, as we should expect in an efficient allocation, and we can solve these first-order conditions for the optimal consumption ratio

$$\frac{c_2}{c_1} = \sqrt[6]{3} = 1.201.$$

Using the relationship between $c_1$ and $c_2$ and the budget constraint we can solve for

$$p_1 (0.6c_1 + 0.4c_1) + p_2 (0.4c_2 + 0.6c_2) = p_1 c_1 + p_2 c_2$$

$$= \frac{1}{2}c_1 + \frac{1}{6}c_2$$

$$= \frac{1}{2}c_1 + \frac{1}{6}(1.201) c_1 = 1.$$

This equation can be solved for $c_1$

$$c_1 = 1.428$$

and then we use the optimal ratio to find $c_2$

$$c_2 = 1.201c_1 = (1.201)(1.428) = 1.715.$$

### 6.2.3 An alternative formulation of complete markets

An alternative to assuming a complete set of markets for contingent commodities at date 0 is to allow trade to occur sequentially. As described in Section 6.1, markets are sequentially complete, in the simple, two-state, three-period model, if there are two Arrow securities at date 0 and spot and forward markets for the good at date 1. We first describe the spot and forward markets at date 1, after all uncertainty has been resolved, and then we describe the Arrow security markets at date 0.

At date 1 we assume there is a forward market in which intermediaries can trade the good at date 1 for promises to deliver the good at date 2. Let $p$ denote the value of one unit of the good at date 2 in terms of units of the good at date 1. In other words, $p$ is the present value of one unit of the good at date 2. Since one unit of the long asset yields $R$ units of the good at date 2, the value of one unit of the asset at date 1 will be $pR$.

Suppose that an intermediary has a portfolio, including trades in Arrow securities made at date 0, that is worth $w_s$ in the state where the liquidity shock is $\lambda_s$, $s = H, L$. The intermediary's budget constraint is

$$\lambda_s c_1 + p(1 - \lambda_s)c_2 = w_s$$

and the intermediary will choose $(c_1, c_2)$ to maximize

$$\lambda U(c_1) + (1 - \lambda_s)U(c_2)$$

subject to this budget constraint. Let $V(p, w_s; \lambda_s)$ denote the maximized value of this utility function.

In Section 6.1 we assumed that the forward price $p$ was state-dependent. Here the two states are different from the point of view of an individual intermediary but identical from a macroeconomic point of view. In other words, the proportions of early consumers in the intermediary vary from state to state but the proportion of early consumers in the economy as a whole is the same. Since the two states that can occur at date 1 are identical from an aggregate point of view, we consider a symmetric equilibrium in which the price

$p$ is independent of the state. This means that the returns to the two assets are certain at date 0. In order to persuade intermediaries to hold both assets, the one-period returns must be equal, which, as we have seen in Chapter 4, requires $p = 1/R$. Then the value of the intermediary's portfolio at date 1 is independent of the amount invested in the short and long assets.

Now consider the intermediary's problem at date 0. An Arrow security at date 0 promises delivery of one unit of the good in one state at date 1 and nothing in the other state. Since we are considering a symmetric equilibrium, the prices of the two securities should be equal, and without loss of generality we can normalize them to equal 1. Let $z_s$ be the amount of the Arrow security that pays off in the state where the intermediary's liquidity shock is $\lambda_s$. Note that $s$ refers to the intermediary's state, not the aggregate state, but since the two are perfectly correlated, this should not lead to any confusion. Without loss of generality, we can assume that the intermediary invests all of its deposits in the short and long assets, so the trades in Arrow securities must balance, that is,

$$z_H + z_L = 0.$$

In other words, the intermediary buys Arrow securities in one state and sells them in another. The value of the intermediary's portfolio at date 1 will be

$$w_s = y + p(1-y)R + z_s$$
$$= 1 + z_s$$

for $s = H, L$. Clearly, the intermediary can attain any pattern of date-1 payoffs $(w_H, w_L)$ that satisfy $w_H + w_L = 2$. So the intermediary should choose a portfolio of Arrow securities $(z_H, z_L)$ to maximize the expected value of the indirect utility function

$$\sum_s V(p, w_s; \lambda_s)$$

subject to the budget constraint

$$\frac{1}{2}(w_H + w_L) = 1.$$

The solution of this problem implies that the marginal utility of consumption must be the same in each state, that is, $w_H = w_L$, which in turn implies that the consumption allocation $(c_1, c_2)$ will be the same in each state.

The importance of this alternative approach using sequential trade is that it makes clear (a) that complete markets for contingent commodities are not strictly necessary for markets to be effectively complete and (b) one can achieve the same results with *fewer* markets. In general, if there are $S$ states and $T + 1$ periods and uncertainty is resolved at date 1, there are $ST + 1$ contingent commodities and hence $ST + 1$ markets in the Arrow–Debreu model. The sequential trade model, by contrast, requires $S$ Arrow securities and market for the $T + 1$ dated commodities in each state, so the number of markets is $S + T + 1$. When the number of states and dates is large (or there are many physical goods in each date and state), the difference between the two approaches becomes even greater.

### 6.2.4 The general case

The two-state model developed in Section 6.2 is quite special, not only because it is restricted to two states, $HL$ and $LH$, but especially as regards the lack of aggregate uncertainty. The argument based on this special case is quite general, however. Allen and Gale (2004) present a general model of an economy with financial markets for aggregate risks and intermediaries and establish similar results. It is beyond the scope of this chapter to do more than give some of the flavor of the Allen–Gale analysis. We can do this by extending the two-state model to a more general environment with aggregate uncertainty about both asset shocks and liquidity shocks. To simplify the notation, we continue to assume that there are two regions, $A$ and $B$, that the probability of being an early consumer may be different in each region, but that the asset returns are the same in each region.

There is assumed to be a finite number of states indexed by $s = 1, \ldots, S$ and each state $s$ occurs with probability $\pi_s > 0$. There are three dates, $t = 0, 1, 2$, the state is unknown at date 0 and the true state is revealed at the beginning of date 1. At date 1, each agent learns whether he is an early or late consumer. The utility of consumption is represented by a common VNM utility function $U(c)$. The probability of being an early consumer can depend on both the state $s$ and the region $i$. We let $\lambda_i(s)$ denote both the probability of being an early consumer and the proportion of early consumers in region $i$ in state $s$. There are two assets, short and long. The return to the short asset is always one, independently of the state, but the return to the long asset may depend on the state. We let $R(s)$ denote the return to one unit invested in the long asset if the state is $s$.

Markets play an essential role only if there is heterogeneity among intermediaries; otherwise there are no gains from trade. We focus on the extreme case where there are distinct intermediaries for regions $A$ and $B$. An intermediary of type $i$ draws all its depositors from region $i$. Since the proportion of early consumers can be different in each region, intermediaries can insure the risk of liquidity shortages by trading on markets for contingent commodities, buying liquidity in states where it expects high demand and selling it in states where it expects low demand for liquidity. The sharing of risk is intermediated by the markets, so the risk sharing across regions is not immediately apparent. What the intermediary appears to be doing is demanding an optimal consumption profile for its depositors, subject to a budget constraint; however, the effect is the same as if the intermediaries in different regions were writing optimal risk-sharing contracts with each other, promising to share the available liquidity in the way a central planner would.

The intermediary takes an endowment of one unit from each agent at date 0 and offers in exchange $c_1(s)$ units of the good in state $s$ to everyone who withdraws at date 1 and $c_2(s)$ units of the good in state $s$ to everyone who withdraws at date 2. Since the intermediary cannot tell whether the person withdrawing is an early or a late consumer, the intermediary has to ensure that late consumers have no incentive to pretend that they are early consumers and withdraw at date 1. So we assume that every consumption plan satisfies the incentive constraint

$$c_1(s) \leq c_2(s) \text{ for } s = 1, \ldots, S. \tag{6.4}$$

A consumption plan $c = \{(c_1(s), c_2(s))\}_{s=1}^{S}$ specifies a consumption profile $c(s) = (c_1(s), c_2(s))$ for every state $s$. The consumption plan is called **incentive-compatible** if it satisfies the incentive constraint (6.4).

There is a single commodity at date 0 and a contingent commodity for every state $s = 1, \ldots, S$ and date $t = 1, 2$. Let the commodity at date 0 be the numeraire and let $p_1(s)$ denote the price of the good in state $s$ at date 1 and $p_2(s)$ denote the price of the good in state $s$ at date 2. The intermediary is assumed to be able to trade all the contingent commodities at date 0. The intermediary receives one unit of the commodity at date 0 and uses this to purchase the contingent commodities that it has promised to the depositors. The intermediary's budget constraint can be written as

$$\sum_{s=1}^{S} \left\{ p_1(s)\lambda_i c_1(s) + p_2(s)(1 - \lambda_i(s)) c_2(s) \right\} \leq 1, \tag{6.5}$$

where the left hand side is the cost of the consumption plan and the right hand side is the value of a single agent's deposit.

Free entry and competition require the intermediary to maximize the expected utility of the representative depositor, so the intermediary's decision problem is to choose an incentive compatible consumption plan $c = \{c(s)\}$ to maximize the expected utility of the representative depositor

$$\sum_{s=1}^{S} \pi_s \{\lambda_i(s) U(c_1(s) + (1 - \lambda_i(s) U(c_2(s))\}$$

subject to the budget constraint (6.5).

As before, the existence of a complete set of markets makes the physical assets redundant in the sense that an intermediary does not need to hold them. Someone must hold them, however, to produce outputs of the goods at dates 1 and 2 but we can assume that a representative firm chooses to invest $y_0$ in the short asset at date 0, $x$ in the long asset at date 0 and $y_1(s)$ in the short asset at date 1 in state $s$. Since these investments earn zero profits in equilibrium, it really does not matter who makes the investments. Let $I = (y_0, \{y_1(s)\}, x)$ denote the vector of investments undertaken.

The zero-profit conditions are analogous to the ones we derived before. Since investment in the assets is subject to constant returns to scale, positive profits are inconsistent with equilibrium and positive investment will occur only if the profits are non-negative (i.e. zero). One unit invested in the short asset at date 0 yields one unit at date $s$ in each state, so the zero-profit condition is

$$\sum_{s=1}^{S} p_1(s) \leq 1, \tag{6.6}$$

with equality if $y_0 > 0$. The left hand side of (6.6) is the value of the outputs at date 1 and the right hand side is the value of the input at date 0. The inequality states that investing in the short asset at date 0 yields non-positive profits and the profits must be zero if investment is positive.

Similarly, one unit invested in the short asset at date 1 in state $s$ yields one unit at date 2 in state $s$, so the zero-profit condition is

$$p_2(s) \leq p_1(s), \tag{6.7}$$

with equality if $y_1(s) > 0$, for $s = 1, \ldots, S$. Again, the left hand side of (6.7) is the value of outputs and the right hand side is the value of inputs. Finally, one unit invested in the long asset at date 0 yields $R(s)$ units at date 2 in state $s$, so the zero-profit condition is

$$\sum_{s=1}^{S} p_2(s) R(s) \leq 1, \tag{6.8}$$

with equality if $x > 0$.

All contingent commodities are traded at date 0. Subsequently, intermediaries simply fulfill the commitments they entered into at date 0. If the markets clear at date 0, the subsequent execution of these trades must be feasible. First, consider the market for the commodity delivered at date 0. The supply of the commodity is equal to the endowment of the good. The demand for the commodity equals the investment in the short and long asset at date 0. Then market clearing requires

$$x + y_0 = 1. \tag{6.9}$$

There is a contingent commodity for each state $s$ at date 1. The demand for this commodity equals the total consumption of the early consumers in the two regions plus the investment in the short asset. The supply of this commodity equals the output from the investment in the short asset at date 0. Then market clearing requires

$$\frac{1}{2} \{\lambda_A(s) c_{A1}(s) + \lambda_B(s) c_{B1}(s)\} + y_1(s) = y_0, \tag{mc2}$$

for each $s = 1, \ldots, S$. Note that on the left hand side the total demand for consumption is the average of consumption in the two regions, because half the population is in each region.

There is a contingent commodity for each state $s$ at date 2. The demand for this commodity is equal to the total consumption of the late consumers from the two regions (there is no investment at date 2). The supply is the output from the investment in the short asset at date 1 plus the output from the investment in the long asset at date 0. Market clearing requires

$$\frac{1}{2} \{(1 - \lambda_A(s)) c_{A2}(s) + (1 - \lambda_B(s)) c_{B2}(s)\} = R(s)x + y_1(s), \tag{6.10}$$

for each $s = 1, \ldots, S$.

In the economy just described, the incentive constraint (6.4) may be binding. If it is binding, then the first-best allocation (the allocation a central planner would choose if he had complete information about the agents' types) may not be feasible. We take the view that a regulator or planner has no more information than the market and so the consumption plans implemented by the planner must also satisfy the incentive constraint. In that case, the first best is not the appropriate benchmark. We should instead ask: "What could a central planner achieve if he had the same information as the market and were subject to the same incentive constraint?" This sort of reasoning leads to the concept of incentive efficiency. An allocation consisting of the consumption plans

$c = (c_A, c_B)$ and the investment plan $I$ is **attainable** if it satisfies the market-clearing conditions (6.9)–(6.10). An attainable allocation $(c, I)$ is **incentive compatible** if the consumption plans satisfy the incentive constraint (6.4). An incentive-compatible allocation $(c, I)$ is **incentive efficient** if there does not exist an incentive-compatible allocation $(c', I')$ that makes both regions of investors better off ex ante. In other words, the planner cannot do better than the market when the planner has the same information as the market.

Allen and Gale (2004) show that any equilibrium allocation is incentive efficient as long as markets are complete and investors are restricted to using intermediaries to access the markets. We sketch the argument here. Suppose that $(c^*, I^*)$ is an equilibrium allocation and $p^*$ is the equilibrium price vector. If both regions can be made better off by choosing an incentive-compatible allocation $(c, I)$, then it must be the case that $c_A$ and $c_B$ are not within the intermediaries' budget sets, that is,

$$\sum_{s=1}^{S} \left\{ p_1^*(s) \lambda_i c_{i1}^*(s) + p_2^*(s) \left(1 - \lambda_i(s)\right) c_{i2}^*(s) \right\} > 1 \qquad (6.11)$$

for each $i = A, B$. For all the investment activities, either profits are zero or the investment level is zero. This implies that the sum of profits is zero:

$$\left( \sum_{s=1}^{S} p_1^*(s) - 1 \right) y_0 + \sum_{s=1}^{S} \left( p_2^*(s) - p_1^*(s) \right) y_1(s)$$

$$+ \left( \sum_{s=1}^{S} p_2^*(s) R(s) - 1 \right) x = 0. \qquad (6.12)$$

Rearranging this equation we get

$$\sum_{s=1}^{S} p_1^*(s) \left( y_0 - y_1(s) \right) + \sum_{s=1}^{S} p_2^*(s) \left( R(s)x + y_1(s) \right) = x + y_0, \qquad (6.13)$$

and substituting from the market-clearing conditions (6.9)–(6.10) into equation (6.13) we have

$$\sum_{s=1}^{S} p_1^*(s) \left( \frac{1}{2} \left\{ \lambda_A(s) c_{A1}(s) + \lambda_B(s) c_{B1}(s) \right\} \right)$$

$$+ \sum_{s=1}^{S} p_2^*(s) \left( \frac{1}{2} \left\{ (1 - \lambda_A(s)) c_{A2}(s) + (1 - \lambda_B(s)) c_{B2}(s) \right\} \right) = 1$$

or

$$\frac{1}{2} \sum_{i=A,B} \sum_{s=1}^{S} \left\{ p_1^*(s) \lambda_i(s) c_{i1}(s) + p_2^*(s) (1 - \lambda_i(s)) c_{i2}(s) \right\} = 1$$

contradicting the inequality (6.11).

## 6.2.5 Implementing the first best *without* complete markets

In very special cases, it may be possible to implement the first best without complete markets. To see this, we return to the special model with two regions, $A$ and $B$, and two states, $HL$ and $LH$, and suppose that there is an asset market at date 1. An intermediary could sell some of the long asset in order to get additional liquidity in the "high" state and buy the long asset with the excess liquidity in the "low" state. In the special case of logarithmic utility and no aggregate uncertainty, this is enough to achieve the first best. Suppose the VNM utility function is

$$U(c) = \ln(c)$$

and the planner's problem is to maximize

$$\lambda \ln(c_1) + (1 - \lambda) \ln(c_2)$$

subject to the constraints

$$\lambda c_1 = y$$
$$(1 - \lambda) c_2 = R(1 - y).$$

The solution to this problem is the allocation that gives early consumers $c_1^* = 1$ and late consumers $c_2^* = R$. To achieve this consumption profile, the investment in the short asset at date 0 must be $y^* = \lambda$. Then

$$\lambda c_1^* = \lambda = y^*$$

and

$$(1 - \lambda) c_2^* = (1 - \lambda) R = R(1 - y^*).$$

This is the allocation that a central planner, who could move goods between the regions, would implement. Can the intermediaries do the same by trading on the asset market at date 1?

In the absence of aggregate uncertainty (remember, intermediaries from both regions trade in the economy-wide asset market) the asset price at date 1 must be $P = 1$. Otherwise, intermediaries would not be willing to hold both assets at date 0. Suppose that the intermediaries invest $y = \lambda$ in the short asset and $1 - y$ in the long asset and promise the early consumers $c_1 = 1$ at date 1. Then at date 1, an intermediary in the high state will need $\lambda_H c_1 = \lambda_H$ units of the good but only has $y = \lambda$ units of the short asset. So it needs an additional $\lambda_H - \lambda$ units of the good. To get this, it must sell $\lambda_H - \lambda$ units of the long asset (remember the asset price is $P = 1$). An intermediary in the low state has $y = \lambda$ units of the short asset but only needs $\lambda_L c_1 = \lambda_L$ units of the good to pay the early consumers. Since $P < R$, the short asset is dominated at date 1 and no one wants to hold it between date 1 and date 2. All of the intermediary's excess liquidity $\lambda - \lambda_L$ will be supplied in exchange for the long asset. So the supply of the long asset is $\lambda_H - \lambda$, the demand is $\lambda - \lambda_L$, these two amounts are equal because $\lambda = \frac{1}{2}(\lambda_H + \lambda_L)$, and the market clears at date 1.

What happens at the last date? In the high state, the intermediary has

$$(1 - y) - (\lambda_H - \lambda) = (1 - \lambda) - (\lambda_H - \lambda) = 1 - \lambda_H$$

units of the long asset and so can provide $R$ units to each of the $1 - \lambda_H$ late consumers. Similarly, an intermediary in the low state has

$$(1 - y) + (\lambda - \lambda_L) = (1 - \lambda) + (\lambda - \lambda_L) = 1 - \lambda_L$$

units of the long asset, and so can provide $R$ units of the good to each of the $1 - \lambda_L$ late consumers. So the intermediaries can achieve the first-best allocation of risk sharing in each state and this is clearly the best that they can do.

For the economy as a whole there is no change in the proportion of early consumers and so efficient risk sharing requires that an individual's consumption should depend on whether he is an early or late consumer, but not on the proportion of early consumers in his region. This is only possible because the market allows liquidity to be reshuffled between regions. Regions with excess liquidity supply it to regions with insufficient liquidity in exchange for the long asset. A region with a high proportion of early consumers will have a low proportion of late consumers and so needs less of the long asset to provide consumption to late consumers. A region with a low proportion of early consumers has a high proportion of late consumers and needs more of the long asset. So these trades satisfy everyone's needs.

This result is special and relies both on the absence of aggregate uncertainty and the assumption of logarithmic utility. A couple of numerical examples will serve to show what is special about the case of logarithmic utility and what goes wrong when we have incomplete markets with other preferences.

**Example 3** To illustrate the implementation of the first best with logarithmic utility, suppose that

$$R = 3;$$

$$U(c) = \ln(c);$$

$$\lambda_H = 0.6, \lambda_L = 0.4.$$

Then the efficient allocation is given by $c_1^* = 1$, $c_2^* = 3$, and $y^* = \lambda = 0.5$.

At $t = 1$, an intermediary in the high state provides $\lambda_H c_1^* = 0.6$ units of consumption to early consumers, but only receives $y^* = 0.5$ units from the short asset. It therefore has to sell 0.1 units of the long asset to make up the difference. At $t = 2$, it now has

$$1 - y^* - 0.1 = 0.5 - 0.1 = 0.4$$

units of the long asset. The proportion of late consumers is

$$1 - \lambda_H = 1 - 0.6 = 0.4,$$

so each consumer gets

$$\frac{0.4R}{(1 - \lambda_H)} = \frac{0.4 \times 3}{0.4} = 3$$

units of consumption, as required.

At $t = 1$, an intermediary in the low state provides

$$\lambda_L c_1^* = 0.4 \times 1 = 0.4$$

units of consumption to early consumers, but receives $y^* = 0.5$ units from the short asset. It therefore has 0.1 units of the good to sell in exchange for the long asset. At $t = 2$, it now has

$$1 - y^* + 0.1 = 0.5 + 0.1 = 0.6$$

units of the long asset. The fraction of late consumers is $1 - \lambda_L = 1 - 0.4 = 0.6$, so each consumer gets

$$\frac{0.6R}{(1 - \lambda_L)} = \frac{0.6 \times 3}{0.6} = 3$$

units of consumption, as required.

**Example 4**   Now suppose that the parameters of the example are the same except that the utility function is assumed to be

$$U(c) = -\frac{1}{5}c^{-5}, \tag{6.14}$$

that is, the constant coefficient of relative risk aversion is six. The optimal consumption allocation (for a central planner) satisfies $U'(c_1^*) = RU'(c_2^*)$ and the feasibility condition $\lambda c_1^* + (1 - \lambda) c_2^*/R = 1$. These conditions can be solved to give us the optimal consumption allocation

$$c_1^* = 1.428$$

and

$$c_2^* = 1.715.$$

The central planner can implement this consumption allocation by choosing

$$y^* = \lambda c_1^* = (0.5)(1.428) = 0.714.$$

Note that at $t = 1$ the long asset will produce

$$R(1 - y^*) = (3)(0.286) = 0.858$$

and the late consumers receive a total of

$$(1 - \lambda) c_2^* = (0.5)(1.715) = 0.858.$$

If an intermediary tries to implement the same allocation, at $t = 1$ in the high state the intermediary needs to give the early consumers

$$\lambda_H c_1^* = (0.6)(1.424) = 0.854$$

but only has

$$y^* = 0.714$$

from the short asset. The intermediary will have to obtain the difference $0.854 - 0.714 = 0.140$ by selling $0.140$ units of the long asset. Then at $t = 1$, the intermediary will have

$$(1 - y^*) - 0.140 = 0.286 - 0.140 = 0.146$$

units of the long asset, which will yield a return of

$$(3)(0.146) = 0.437 < 0.858 = (1 - \lambda)c_2^*.$$

In other words, the intermediary in the high state will not be able to give the late consumers $c_2^*$ if it gives the early consumers $c_1^*$. The intermediary cannot implement the first best.

In Examples 3 and 4, the intermediary wealth at date 1 is always $w = 1$, regardless of the portfolio chosen, because $P = 1$. With logarithmic utility, the optimal consumption profile gives early and late consumers the same present value of consumption. If the proportion of early consumers changes, the budget is still balanced because in present value terms the cost of early and late consumers is the same. When relative risk aversion is greater than one, the optimal consumption profile gives early consumers a higher present value of consumption (but a lower level of actual consumption) than late consumers. So if the proportion of early consumers goes up, the cost of the consumption profile increases. So consumption at both dates must be reduced to balance the budget. Without markets to allow intermediaries to make trades contingent on the state, there is no way the intermediary can achieve the first best. The logarithmic case is the unique case (with constant relative risk aversion) in which complete markets are not required.

Another way to think of the problem is to argue that, although there are enough assets and goods in the economy to give everyone the first-best consumption allocation, *the price of liquidity is too high* (the price of the long asset is too low). The intermediary in the high state has to give up too much of the long asset in order to get the liquidity it needs at $t = 1$ and so finds itself short of goods at $t = 2$. The intermediary in the low state, by contrast, does very well out of this state of affairs. It gets a large amount of the long asset in exchange for its supply of liquidity at $t = 1$ and can give its customers more than $c_2^*$ at $t = 2$.

Although there are gainers and loses ex post, from the point of view of an intermediary at $t = 0$, uncertain whether it will be in the high or the low state, the gains in the low state do not compensate for the losses in the high state. The intermediary's depositors are unambiguously worse off than in the first best.

## 6.3 INCOMPLETE CONTRACTS

There is no aggregate uncertainty in the simple two-state economy discussed in Sections 6.2.1 and 6.2.2. As a result, the first-best allocation of consumption does not depend on the state of nature. This is a rather special case, however.

In general, we should expect the first-best allocation will depend on every state in a more or less complicated way. Then the first best can only be achieved by a risk-sharing contract that is contingent on every state of nature. We call such contracts **complete**. In the preceding sections, we have assumed that intermediaries can make consumption contingent on the state, even if they did not choose to do so. In this sense, we implicitly assumed that contracts were complete. In practice, we often observe intermediaries using much simpler contracts. An example is the familiar deposit contract, where an intermediary promises its depositors $d_1$ units of consumption if they withdraw at date 1 and $d_2$ units if they withdraw at date 2, independently of the state of nature. We call this contract **incomplete** because the promised amounts are *required* to be independent of the state.

Incomplete contracts place an additional constraint on the set of feasible allocations and may prevent the achievement of the first best. If the first best is not attainable, it is tempting to say that there is a market failure, but we should remember that there are reasons why contracts are incomplete. For example, transaction costs makes it costly to write and implement complete contracts. We take the view that these costs impose a constraint on the planner as well as on market participants. Then the appropriate benchmark is not the first best, but rather the best that a planner could do subject to the same costly contracting technology. We should ask: "What is the best that can be achieved using the available contracting technology?" We will see that as long as markets are complete, the use of incomplete contracts does not lead to market failure: the laisser-faire equilibrium is **constrained efficient**, in the sense that a planner cannot do better using the same contracting technology.

### 6.3.1 Complete markets and aggregate risk

To illustrate, we adapt the model of Sections 6.2.1 and 6.2.2 by assuming that there is a single type of investor ex ante and that, ex post, investors are early consumers with probability $\lambda$, independently of the state. We also assume that the returns to the long asset are stochastic. More precisely, there are two equiprobable states, $H$ and $L$, and the return is $R_H$ in state $H$ and $R_L$ in state $L$. Because there is a single type of investor ex ante, a single intermediary can act like a central planner and implement the optimal allocation without resorting to trade in markets. In other words, markets are trivially complete.

If the intermediary can offer a complete contingent contract $c = (c_{1H}, c_{2H}, c_{1L}, c_{2L})$ then it will achieve the first best. The intermediary chooses a portfolio $(x, y)$ and consumption allocation $c = (c_{1H}, c_{2H}, c_{1L}, c_{2L})$ to maximize the expected utility of the typical depositor

$$\frac{1}{2} \{\lambda U(c_{1H}) + (1 - \lambda) U(c_{2H})\} + \frac{1}{2} \{\lambda U(c_{1L}) + (1 - \lambda) U(c_{2L})\}$$

subject to the feasibility constraints

$$\lambda c_{1s} \leq y$$

and

$$\lambda c_{1s} + (1 - \lambda) c_{2s} \leq y + R_s x,$$

for $s = H, L$.

Now suppose that the intermediary is constrained to use an incomplete contract. For example, suppose that he offers a deposit contract $(d_1, d_2)$ to the investors who deposit their endowments. As usual, we assume that $d_2$ is chosen large enough that it always exhausts the value of the assets at date 2. In other words, the late consumers always receive the residual value of the intermediary's assets. Then we can forget about the value of $d_2$ and characterize the deposit contract by the single parameter $d_1 - d$.

In the absence of default, the intermediary must choose a portfolio $(x, y)$ and consumption bundle $c = (c_{1H}, c_{2H}, c_{1L}, c_{2L})$ such that $c_{1H} = c_{1L} = d$. The efficient incomplete contract must solve the problem of maximizing expected utility

$$\frac{1}{2} \{\lambda U(d) + (1 - \lambda) U(c_{2H})\} + \frac{1}{2} \{\lambda U(d) + (1 - \lambda) U(c_{2L})\}$$

subject to the feasibility constraints

$$\lambda d \leq y$$

and

$$\lambda d + (1 - \lambda) c_{2s} \leq y + R_s x,$$

for $s = H, L$.

The incompleteness of contracts imposes a welfare cost on investors, since their consumption is constrained to be the same in each state, independently of the costs and benefits of consumption. This raises the possibility that default might be optimal, since default allows for a greater degree of contingency in consumption. For example, suppose that the optimal consumption is higher in state $H$ than in state $L$. In the absence of default, a deposit contract implies a consumption allocation that is a compromise between the first-best consumption levels, being too low in state $H$ and too high in state $L$. It might be better for investors to offer the first-best consumption in state $H$, that is, to choose $(d_1, d_2) = (c_{1H}, c_{2H})$ and default in state $L$. If the intermediary defaults on the contract in state $L$, the portfolio is liquidated and the early and late investors share the liquidated value of the portfolio. Default allows the level of consumption to vary between the states but there is another constraint: in the default state, the level of consumption has to be equal at each date. Thus, the intermediary will choose $(x, y)$ and $c = (c_{1H}, c_{2H}, c_{1L}, c_{2L})$ to maximize

$$\frac{1}{2}U(y + R_L x) + \frac{1}{2}\{\lambda U(d) + (1 - \lambda)U(c_{2H})\}$$

subject to the constraint

$$\lambda d + (1 - \lambda)c_{2H} = y + R_H x.$$

Which of these provides the higher level of expected utility depends on all the parameters and prices. The crucial point for the current discussion is that, with complete markets, the intermediary makes the correct choice. Clearly, we cannot hope for the first best to be achieved, because the consumption plan is constrained by the incompleteness of the contract and by the bankruptcy code. However, subject to these constraints, a planner can do no better than the intermediary. More precisely, an equilibrium is defined to be **constrained efficient** if there does not exist a feasible allocation that can be implemented using a deposit contract and that makes some agents better off and no one worse off. The reason is essentially the same as in the case studied in Section 6.2: if there is a preferred choice for the intermediary it must be outside the budget set and if every intermediary violates its budget constraint the attainability condition cannot be satisfied. Thus, whether or not the intermediary chooses to default in equilibrium, there is no market failure. The incidence of financial crises is constrained efficient.

Allen and Gale (2004) have proved the constrained-efficiency of laisser-faire equilibrium under general conditions. The importance of this result is that it shows that financial crises do not necessarily constitute a market failure. There are welfare losses associated with the use of incomplete contracts, to be sure, but these losses are present whether there is a crisis or not. The crucial observation is that given the contracting technology, the market achieves the best possible welfare outcome. A planner subject to the same constraints could not do better.

**Example 5** We have argued that, as long as markets are complete, an intermediary will choose the optimal incidence of default. To illustrate the possibilities we use a numerical example. Suppose that each investor has an endowment $e = (1, 0, 0)$ and preferences are given by the VNM utility

$$U(c_1) + \beta U(c_2) = \ln c_1 + \ln c_2.$$

Assume that the states are equiprobable

$$\pi_H = \pi_L = 0.5,$$

the proportion of early consumers is

$$\lambda = 0.5,$$

and the returns on the long asset are

$$(R_H, R_L) = (3, 0).$$

With no default, the consumption allocation is

$$c = (c_{1H}, c_{2H}, c_{1L}, c_{2L}) = (d, c_{2H}, d, d),$$

where $d = y$ and $c_{2H} = 2(R_H x + y/2) = 6x + y$. The first-order condition that determines the optimal portfolio is

$$\frac{1}{2} \left\{ \frac{1}{y} + \frac{1}{y} \right\} = \frac{1}{2} \left\{ \frac{3}{6x + y} + \frac{0}{y} \right\},$$

which implies that $x = \frac{1}{12}$ and $y = \frac{11}{12}$. Then the consumption allocation is

$$c = (y, 6x + y, y, y) = \left( \frac{11}{12}, \frac{17}{12}, \frac{11}{12}, \frac{11}{12} \right)$$

and expected utility is

$$\frac{1}{4} \{ U(c_{1H}) + U(c_{2H}) + U(c_{1L}) + U(c_{2L}) \} = \frac{1}{4} \left\{ 3 \ln \frac{11}{12} + \ln \frac{17}{12} \right\}$$

$$= \frac{1}{4} \times 0.087.$$

Now suppose that we allow for default. Nothing changes in the low state, because the only asset that has value is the short asset and this is already being divided evenly between the early and late consumers. In the high state, by contrast, the first-best allocation can be achieved. This requires giving the early consumers $2y$ and the late consumers $2R_H x = 6x$. Then the first-order condition for the optimal portfolio is

$$\frac{1}{2}\left\{\frac{1}{2y} + \frac{1}{y}\right\} = \frac{1}{2}\left\{\frac{3}{6x} + \frac{0}{y}\right\},$$

which implies that $x = \frac{1}{4}$ and $y = \frac{3}{4}$. Then

$$c = (2y, 6x, y, y) = \left(\frac{3}{2}, \frac{3}{2}, \frac{3}{4}, \frac{3}{4}\right)$$

and the expected utility is

$$\frac{1}{4}\{U(c_{1H}) + U(c_{2H}) + U(c_{1L}) + U(c_{2L})\}$$

$$= \frac{1}{4}\left\{2\ln\frac{3}{2} + 2\ln\frac{3}{4}\right\} = \frac{1}{4} \times 0.236.$$

Clearly, default increases expected utility here because default relaxes the distortion of the deposit contract (the requirement that consumption at date 1 be the same in each state) without introducing an offsetting distortion (in the default state, consumption is equal at both dates, whether there is default or not) as in Zame (1993).

### 6.3.2 The intermediary's problem with incomplete markets

Example 3 showed us that the case of log utility is very special. It has the property that, at the first best, the present value of consumption is the same for early and late consumers, that is,

$$c_1^* = \frac{1}{R}c_2^*.$$

This is not true for most utility functions. If $c_1^* > c_2^*/R$, as in the case of the utility function (6.14) in Example 4, then the present value of consumption for the early consumers is greater than the present value of consumption for the late consumers. An increase in the proportion of early consumers will increase the present value of total consumption, so in order to satisfy the budget constraint the intermediary will have to reduce someone's consumption. Since early consumers are promised a fixed amount $d$, the intermediary will end up giving less to the late consumers, assuming it can do so without causing a run. Assuming that $c_1 = d$, the late consumers receive $c_{2s}$ in state $s = H, L$, where

$$c_{2s} = \frac{(1 - \lambda_s d) R}{1 - \lambda_s}.$$

With an asset price $P = 1$, the intermediary's wealth at date 1 is

$$y + P(1 - y) = y + (1 - y) = 1.$$

Because the intermediary's wealth at date 1 is independent of $y$, any choice of $y$ is optimal for the intermediary at date 0. If the intermediary gives $\lambda_s d$ to the early consumers it has $1 - \lambda_s d$ (in present value) for the late consumers. But one unit at $t = 1$ will buy $R$ units at $t = 2$, so the intermediary can buy $(1 - \lambda_s d) R$ units of consumption at $t = 2$ and since there are $1 - \lambda_s$ late consumers each of them will receive $(1 - \lambda_s d) R / (1 - \lambda_s)$. The late consumers receive the same amount in each state if and only if $d = 1$. In general, the late consumer's consumption varies with the state and the intermediary's problem is to choose $d$ and $y$ to maximize

$$\lambda U(d) + \frac{1}{2} \left\{ (1 - \lambda_H) U \left( \frac{(1 - \lambda_H d) R}{1 - \lambda_H} \right) + (1 - \lambda_L) U \left( \frac{(1 - \lambda_L d) R}{1 - \lambda_L} \right) \right\},$$

$$(6.15)$$

subject to the incentive constraint $c_{2s} \geq d$, which we shall assume is satisfied.

Since every choice of $y$ is optimal, the intermediary only has to optimize with respect to $d$. The first-order condition for a solution to this problem is

$$\lambda U'(d) + \frac{1}{2} \left\{ (1 - \lambda_H) U' \left( \frac{(1 - \lambda_H d) R}{1 - \lambda_H} \right) \frac{-\lambda_H R}{1 - \lambda_H} \right.$$

$$\left. + (1 - \lambda_L) U' \left( \frac{(1 - \lambda_L d) R}{1 - \lambda_L} \right) \frac{-\lambda_L R}{1 - \lambda_L} \right\}$$

$$= 0$$

which simplifies to

$$U'(d) = R \left\{ \frac{\lambda_H}{2\lambda} U' \left( \frac{(1 - \lambda_H d) R}{1 - \lambda_H} \right) + \frac{\lambda_L}{2\lambda} U' \left( \frac{(1 - \lambda_L d) R}{1 - \lambda_L} \right) \right\}. \quad (6.16)$$

This is analogous to the usual condition $U'(c_1) = RU'(c_2)$, except that the term in braces on the right hand side is a weighted average of the different marginal utilities in each state at date 2.

**Example 4 (Continued)**   If the intermediary cannot achieve the first best, what should it do? To illustrate, we go back to the parameters of Example 4 and calculate the explicit solution. The first-order condition (6.16) tells us that

$$d^{-6} = 3 \left\{ 0.6 \left( \frac{(1 - 0.6d)\,3}{0.4} \right)^{-6} + 0.4 \left( \frac{(1 - 0.4d)\,3}{0.6} \right)^{-6} \right\},$$

which can be solved for $d = 1.337$. This implies that the consumption of the late consumers is

$$c_{2H} = \frac{(1 - \lambda_H d)\,R}{(1 - \lambda_H)} = \frac{(1 - (0.6)\,(1.337))\,(3)}{0.4} = 1.485$$

in the high state and

$$c_{2L} = \frac{(1 - \lambda_L d)\,R}{(1 - \lambda_L)} = \frac{(1 - (0.4)\,(1.337))\,(3)}{0.6} = 2.327.$$

Notice that although the late consumers do quite well in the low state, this does not compensate for the low consumption in the high state. If we calculate the equilibrium expected utility (6.15) explicitly, we get

$$(0.5)\,\frac{-1}{5}\,(1.337)^{-5} + (0.5) \left\{ (0.4)\,\frac{-1}{5}\,(1.485)^{-5} + (0.6)\,\frac{-1}{5}\,(2.327)^{-5} \right\}$$

$$= -0.030,$$

whereas the first best is

$$(0.5)\,\frac{-1}{5}\,(1.428)^{-5} + (0.5)\,\frac{-1}{5}\,(1.715)^{-5} = -0.024.$$

Finally, notice that the incentive constraint $c_{2s} \geq d$ is satisfied in each state, even though we did not impose it on the solution. This justifies our assumption that the incentive constraint is satisfied. Moreover, it shows that it is optimal to have no default in equilibrium.

## 6.4 CONCLUSION

We can summarize the chapter's conclusions briefly as follows. As long as we have complete markets for hedging aggregate risk and intermediaries can use complete contingent risk-sharing contracts, the equilibrium in a laisser-faire economy will be incentive efficient. If intermediaries are forced by transaction costs to use incomplete contracts, the equilibrium will be constrained efficient. In either case, it is wrong to suggest that financial crises constitute a source of market failure. A central planner subject to the same informational constraints or the same transaction costs could not do better than the market. If contracts are complete, there is never any need to default. The intermediary can achieve the same ends by simply altering the terms of the contract. Incomplete contracts, on the other hand, distort the choices that an intermediary would otherwise make; relaxing these constraints by defaulting in some states of nature allows the intermediary to provide the depositor with superior risk sharing and/or higher returns. Whether the intermediary chooses to default or not, its choices maximize the welfare of its depositors. Since markets are complete, prices give the right signals to intermediaries and guide them to choose the efficient allocation of risk and investments. It is only when markets are incomplete that we encounter inefficiencies that could in principle be corrected by government regulation and lead to a potential improvement in welfare. We explore the scope for welfare-improving regulation and the form it takes in the next chapter.

## REFERENCES

Allen, F. and D. Gale (2004). "Financial Intermediaries and Markets," *Econometrica* 72, 1023–1061.

Zame, W. (1993). "Efficiency and the Role of Default when Security Markets are Incomplete," *American Economic Review* 83, 1142–1164.

# 7

## Optimal regulation

For the most part, the development of financial regulation has been an empirical process, a matter of trial and error, driven by the exigencies of history rather than by formal theory. An episode that illustrates the character of this process is the Great Depression in the US. The financial collapse in the US was widespread and deeply disruptive. It led to substantial changes in the laws regulating the financial system, many of which shape our current regulatory framework. The SEC was established to regulate financial markets. Investment and commercial banking were segregated by the Glass–Steagall Act (subsequently repealed and replaced by the Gramm–Leach–Bliley Act of 1999). The Federal Reserve Board revised its operating procedures in the light of its failure to prevent the financial collapse. The FDIC and FSLIC were set up to provide deposit insurance to banks and savings and loan institutions.

Looking back, there is no sign of formal theory guiding these changes. Everyone seems to have agreed the experience of the Great Depression was terrible; so terrible that it must never be allowed to happen again. According to this mind set, the financial system is fragile and the purpose of prudential regulation is to prevent financial crisis at all costs. Why does the mind set of the 1930's continue to influence thinking about policy? What does policy making continue to be an empirical exercise, with little attention to the role of theory? This empirical procedure is unusual. Indeed, the area of financial regulation is somewhat unique in the extent to which the empirical developments have so far outstripped theory. In most areas of economics, when regulation becomes an issue, economists have tried to identify some specific market failure that justifies the proposed intervention. Sometimes they have gone further and have derived the optimal form of regulation. This has not been the usual procedure with financial regulation, however.

The purpose of this chapter is to show how the framework developed in Chapter 6 can be used as the basis for analyzing optimal regulation. The widespread perception that financial systems are "fragile," together with many historical episodes of financial instability, has created a presumption that regulation is required to prevent costly financial crises. In the previous chapter we argued to the contrary that, under conditions analogous to the assumptions of the fundamental theorems of welfare economics, a laisser-faire equilibrium may be efficient. The occurrence of default and financial collapse in equilibrium does not necessarily indicate a market failure. If a planner using the same contracting technology can do no better, we say that equilibrium is **constrained efficient**. Unless the authorities have access to a superior technology, intervention is not justified when the incidence of financial instability is constrained efficient.

To provide a justification for regulation of the financial system, we first need to identify a source of market failure (constrained inefficiency). Then we need to identify a practical policy that can remedy or at least ameliorate that failure. In this chapter we undertake two policy exercises. First we look at the potential benefits of regulating capital structure. Then we look at the potential benefits of regulating liquidity. In each case, we are interested in determining whether a laisser-faire equilibrium is constrained efficient and, if not, what can be done about it. Our view is that it is not enough merely to show that there *exists* a welfare-improving policy. We also need to characterize the policy and show that it can be implemented. A badly designed intervention could make things worse. If the welfare-improving policy is too complicated or depends on information that is unlikely to be available to the policymaker, such mistakes are likely.

## 7.1 CAPITAL REGULATION

Capital adequacy requirements are rules that specify a minimum level of capital that a bank must maintain in relation to its assets. This rule may take the form of a simple fraction of the assets or a more complicated formula. Capital adequacy requirements are one of the most important instruments of bank regulation. The first Basel Accord imposed uniform capital adequacy requirements on the banks of all the signatory countries. A second Basel Accord introduces more sophisticated methods of determining the appropriate level of capital for banks, but the idea that banks must be compelled to hold the appropriate level of capital remains a basic principle of the regulatory system.

These accords provide an example of regulation that is empirically rather than theoretically motivated. Practitioners have become experts at the details of a highly complex system for which there is no widely agreed rationale based in economic theory. What is the optimal capital structure? What market failure necessitates the imposition of capital adequacy requirements? Why can't the market be left to determine the appropriate level of capital? We do not find good answers to these questions in the theoretical literature.

In the literature on capital adequacy, it is often argued that capital adequacy requirements are necessary to control the moral hazard problems generated by the existence of deposit insurance. Deposit insurance was introduced in the 1930's to prevent bank runs or, more generally, financial instability. Because banks issue insured debt-like obligations (e.g. bank deposits) they have an incentive to engage in risk-shifting behavior. In other words, the bank has an incentive to make excessively risky investments, because it knows that in the event of failure the loss is borne by the deposit insurance fund and in the event of success the bank's shareholders reap the rewards. The existence of bank capital reduces the incentive to take risks because, in the event of failure, the shareholders lose their capital. Thus, capital adequacy requirements are indirectly justified by the desire to prevent financial crises. A large literature investigates the effect of capital adequacy requirements on risk taking. While the effect of capital adequacy requirements is usually to decrease risk taking, the reverse is also possible (see, e.g. Kim and Santomero 1988; Furlong and Keeley 1989; Gennotte and Pyle 1991; Rochet 1992; and Besanko and Kanatas 1996).

The incentive to take risks may also be offset by the loss of charter value when a firm goes bankrupt (see, e.g. Bhattacharya 1982). This effect will be smaller the more competitive the structure of the banking market. Keeley (1990) has provided evidence that the sharp increase in bank failures in the US in the early 1980's was due to increased competition in the banking sector and the associated fall in charter values.

It appears from our review of the literature that the justification for capital adequacy requirements is found in the existence of deposit insurance. It could be argued that an important question is being begged here: one bad policy (deposit insurance) does not justify another (capital adequacy requirements). Even if it is assumed that deposit insurance prevents financial crises, it is not clear why we should want to reduce the incidence of financial crises, still less eliminate them altogether. As we demonstrated in Chapter 6, the incidence of financial crises may be socially optimal in a laisser-faire system. And if not, for example, if financial crises involve deadweight losses, it should be recognized that regulation also involves administrative costs and distorts economic decisions. Any analysis of optimal policy must weigh the costs and benefits of regulation. This can only be done in a model that explicitly models the possibility of crises.

Hellman et al. (2000) is an exception in the literature on capital adequacy requirements. Rather than simply taking the existence of deposit insurance as given, the authors also examine what happens in the absence of deposit insurance. In the rest of the literature, the rationale for deposit insurance and in particular its role in preventing financial crises is discussed but not explicitly modeled. In the absence of explicit modeling of the costs of financial crises, it is difficult to make a case for the optimality of inter-vention. As a corollary, it is difficult to make a case for capital adequacy requirements as a means of offsetting the risk taking generated by deposit insurance.

Allen and Gale (2003) argue that, in the absence of a welfare-relevant pecuniary externality, banks will choose the socially optimal capital struc-ture themselves, without government coercion. For a long time, policymakers have taken it as axiomatic that crises are best avoided. By contrast, in Allen and Gale's framework, a laisser-faire financial system with complete markets achieves a constrained-efficient allocation of risk and resources. When banks are restricted to using noncontingent deposit contracts, default introduces a degree of contingency that may be desirable from the point of view of opti-mal risk sharing. Far from being best avoided, financial crises can actually be *necessary* in order to achieve constrained efficiency. By contrast, avoiding default is costly. It requires either holding a very safe and liquid portfolio (and earning lower returns), or reducing the liquidity promised to the depositors at the intermediate date. In any case, the bank optimally weighs the costs and benefits and chooses the efficient level of default in equilibrium.

Our argument is that avoidance of crises should not be taken as axiomatic. If regulation is required to minimize or obviate the costs of financial crises, it needs to be justified by a microeconomic welfare analysis based on standard assumptions. Furthermore, the form of the intervention should be derived from microeconomic principles. After all, financial institutions and financial markets exist to facilitate the efficient allocation of risks and resources. A policy that aims to prevent financial crises has an impact on the normal functioning of the financial system. Any government intervention may impose deadweight costs by distorting the normal functioning of the financial system. One of the advantages of a microeconomic analysis of financial crises is that it clarifies the costs associated with these distortions.

In addition to the **incentive function**, discussed above, bank capital has another main function. This is the **risk-sharing function**. Capital acts as a buffer that offsets the losses of depositors in the event of a bank failure and allows an orderly liquidation of the bank's assets, thus avoiding the need to dispose of assets at "firesale" prices.

These functions of bank capital explain why shareholders and depositors should care about the bank's capital structure, but they do not explain why governments need to regulate capital structure. To the extent that capital struc-ture affects the efficiency of risk sharing or the bank's incentive to take risk, the costs and benefits should be internalized by the bank's objective function. In the absence of some sort of externality not taken into account by the banks, there is no obvious reason why the bank, left to its own devices, should not choose the (socially) optimal capital structure. In other words, we have not (yet) identified a source of market failure that gives rise to a need for intervention by the regulator.

Incomplete markets provide one possible justification for capital regulation, in the sense that pecuniary externalities have an impact on welfare when markets are incomplete, and in that case regulation of capital (or anything else) can potentially improve welfare. In the following sections, we adapt the model from the previous chapter to show that, when markets are incomplete, there is a role for bank capital to improve risk sharing and a role for government intervention to improve welfare.

### 7.1.1 Optimal capital structure

As usual there are three dates $t = 0, 1, 2$ and an all-purpose good that can be used for consumption or investment. There are two assets, a short asset represented by a storage technology that yields one unit at date $t + 1$ for each unit invested at date $t$, and a long asset represented by a constant returns to scale technology that yields $R > 1$ units of the good at date 2 for each unit invested at date 0.

There is a continuum of identical investors at date 0 each of whom has an endowment of one unit of the good at date 0 and nothing at future dates. At date 1 each consumer learns whether he is an early consumer, who only values consumption at date 1, or a late consumer, who only values consumption at date 2. The probability that an investor becomes an early consumer is $0 < \lambda < 1$. The investors' attitudes to risk are represented by a VNM utility function. If $c$ is the investor's consumption, his utility is $U(c)$, where the function $U(\cdot)$ satisfies the usual neoclassical properties.

There are two groups of consumers, group $A$ and group $B$, and exactly half of the consumers belong to each group. There are two aggregate states of nature, denoted by $(H, L)$ and $(L, H)$. Each state is equally likely, that is, each occurs with probability 0.5. In state $(H, L)$ the fraction of early consumers in group $A$ is $\lambda_H$ and the fraction of early consumers in group $B$ is $\lambda_L$, where $0 < \lambda_L < \lambda_H < 1$. In state $(L, H)$ the fractions are reversed. Then the fraction of early consumers in each state is given by

$$\lambda = \frac{1}{2}(\lambda_H + \lambda_L).$$

The investors' attitudes toward risk are represented by a VNM utility function. If an investor consumes $c$ units of the good at the appropriate date, his utility is $U(c)$, where $U(\cdot)$ satisfies all the usual properties.

All uncertainty is resolved at the beginning of date 1, when the true state is revealed and each investor learns his type.

In the previous chapter we assumed that markets were complete. Specifically, we assumed the existence of two Arrow securities at date 0, which allow the transfer of wealth between states $(H, L)$ and $(L, H)$, and an asset market on which the long asset can be traded at date 1. Here we assume that markets are *incomplete*. Specifically, we assume that there are no Arrow securities, but there is an asset market at date 1.

The incompleteness of markets would have no effect on the allocation of risk if intermediaries served a representative sample of the population. Instead, we assume that intermediaries draw their customers from either group $A$ or group $B$, but not both. One interpretation of this assumption is that groups $A$ and $B$ correspond to different regions and that intermediaries are restricted by law to operate in only one region. In any case, the heterogeneity of intermediaries gives rise to gains from risk sharing which cannot be realized because markets are incomplete.

Apart from the incompleteness of markets, we do not impose any frictions on the model. In particular, intermediaries are allowed to use complete risk-sharing contracts. An intermediary takes a deposit of one unit of the good from each consumer at date 0 and invests it in a portfolio $(x, y)$ consisting of $x$ units of the long asset and $y$ units of the short asset. In exchange, the consumer gets a consumption stream $(c_{1H}, c_{2H}, c_{1L}, c_{2L})$, where $c_{1H}$ is the consumption promised if he withdraws at date 1 when the proportion of early consumers is $\lambda_H$, $c_{2H}$ is the consumption promised if he withdraws at date 2 when the proportion of early consumers is $\lambda_H$, and so on.

In order to discuss capital structure, we introduce a class of risk neutral investors to provide capital to intermediaries (see Gale 2003, 2004). Each investor is assumed to have a large endowment of the good at date 0 and nothing at dates 1 and 2. The investors are risk neutral, but their consumption must be non-negative (otherwise, the investors could absorb all risk and the first best would be achieved). Capital is assumed to be expensive in the sense that investors demand a higher return than the intermediary's investment opportunities can provide. We model the opportunity cost of capital by assuming that investors are impatient: one unit of consumption at date 0 is worth $\rho > R$ units of future consumption. For every unit of capital invested in the intermediary at date 0 the investors will demand an expected return of $\rho$ units in the future. Since the intermediary's investments cannot yield a return higher than $R$, the intermediary has to transfer some of the depositors' returns to the investors to compensate them for the use of their capital. Even though capital is costly, it is optimal to raise a positive amount of capital because it allows for improved risk sharing.

The intermediary offers investors a contract $(e_0, e_H, e_L)$, where $e_0$ denotes the amount of capital provided by the investors at date 0 and $e_H$ and $e_L$ denote the returns paid to the investors when the fractions of early consumers are $\lambda_H$ and $\lambda_L$, respectively. Without loss of generality, we can assume that $e_H$ and $e_L$ are paid at date 2 because equilibrium requires that the date 1 price of date 2 consumption $p \leq 1$, so the good is always at least as cheap at date 2 as at date 1. Investors will supply capital to the bank only if the returns cover their opportunity cost, that is,

$$\frac{1}{2}(e_H + e_L) \geq \rho e_0. \tag{7.1}$$

Since there is a large number of investors, each of whom has a large endowment, competition among investors implies that they get no surplus in equilibrium, that is, the inequality (7.1) holds as an equation. So we can assume without loss of generality that the intermediary chooses a portfolio $(x, y)$, capital structure $(e_0, e_H, e_L)$, and consumption plan $(c_{1H}, c_{2H}, c_{1L}, c_{2L})$ to maximize the expected utility of the typical depositor subject to the investors' participation constraint (7.1) and the feasibility constraints. At date 0 the total investment is constrained by the depositor's endowment and the capital supplied by the investors:

$$x + y \leq e_0 + 1.$$

At date 1, the intermediary's budget constraint is

$$\lambda_s c_{1s} + (1 - \lambda_s)pc_{2s} + pe_s \leq y + Px$$

for $s = H, L$ where $P = Rp$ is the price of the asset at date 1.

Given there is no aggregate uncertainty the price $p$ will be determined in the usual way. In order for the banks to be willing to hold both assets between dates 0 and 1 they must be indifferent between them so

$$p = \frac{1}{R}; \quad P = 1.$$

Since groups $A$ and $B$ are symmetric, and in each state of nature one group has a high proportion and one has a low proportion of early consumers, the market-clearing conditions at date 1 and date 2 are

$$\frac{1}{2}(\lambda_H c_{1H} + \lambda_L c_{1L}) = y.$$

and

$$\frac{1}{2}((1 - \lambda_H)c_{2H} + e_H + (1 - \lambda_L)c_{2L} + e_L) = Rx.$$

From the second of the two budget constraints, we can see that if $e_H$ and $e_L$ are both positive, then the first-best risk sharing must be achieved, that is, $c_{2H} = c_{2L}$. Otherwise, one can increase expected utility by reducing $e_s$ in one state and increasing it in the other. For example, suppose that $c_{2H} < c_{2L}$. Then paying the investors $e_H - \varepsilon$ in state $H$ and $e_L + \varepsilon$ in state $L$ satisfies the investors' participation constraint (7.1) and makes consumers better off because consumption is raised by $\varepsilon/(1 - \lambda_H)$ in state $H$ and lowered by $\varepsilon/(1 - \lambda_L)$ in state $L$ so the change in expected utility is proportional to

$$(1 - \lambda_H)U'(c_{2H})\frac{\varepsilon}{1 - \lambda_H} - (1 - \lambda_L)U'(c_{2L})\frac{\varepsilon}{1 - \lambda_L} > 0.$$

The marginal value of insurance is zero when risk sharing is complete whereas the marginal cost of capital is positive. So it is never optimal to hold enough capital to achieve complete risk sharing. Consequently, $e_s$ must be zero in at least one state, the one in which consumption $c_{2s}$ is lower. For example, suppose that $\sigma > 1$. Then we know by the usual argument that $c_{1s} > pc_{2s}$ and average consumption is lower when the proportion of early consumers is high. Then the optimal capital structure should increase consumption in the high state and reduce it in the low state. So $e_H = 0$ and $\frac{1}{2}e_L = \rho e_0$.

**Proposition 1** Suppose consumers have a constant degree of relative risk aversion $\sigma$ and let $(e_0, e_H, e_L)$ be the optimal capital structure, where $e_0 > 0$. Then

$$e_H > e_L = 0$$

if $\sigma < 1$ and

$$e_L > e_H = 0$$

if $\sigma > 1$.

In the last chapter we saw that, when there is no aggregate uncertainty, a Pareto-efficient allocation gives every consumer a consumption allocation $(c_1, c_2)$ that is independent of the state of nature. Whether the efficient allocation can be achieved depends on the cost of capital $\rho$. If $\rho$ is very high, in relation to $R$, the optimal capital structure will entail a small infusion of capital $e_0$ at date 0, the intermediary's ability to smooth consumption between states will be limited, and the first best will not be attained. It is tempting to conclude in cases like this that the market has failed because the market outcome is not Pareto-efficient; but this assumes that the planner is not subject to the transaction costs and other frictions that prevent markets from being complete. Before we decide that the market has failed and that some intervention is required, we should ask whether the central planner could do better if he were constrained to use only the trading opportunities available to the market participants. For example, it is clear that a planner can improve on the laisser-faire allocation by transferring goods from intermediaries whose depositors have a low marginal utility of consumption to intermediaries whose depositors have a high marginal utility of consumption. In doing so, the planner is performing the function of the missing markets for Arrow securities that allow intermediaries to transfer wealth across states and achieve the first best. But if the market participants are prevented by transaction costs or other frictions from making these trades, perhaps the planner will be too. This suggests that the appropriate test for market failure is to ask whether a planner could improve on the laisser-faire allocation using the same technology available to the market participants.

It is not entirely clear what the technology available to the planner should be, but one approach would be to restrict the planner to altering decisions made at date 0 and requiring him to allow the market to determine the allocation at dates 1 and 2 in the usual way. This would ensure that we are not granting the planner a questionable technological advantage over the market. We will say that a laisser-faire allocation is **constrained efficient** if the planner cannot improve on it merely by changing the allocation at date 0 and leaving the market to determine the future allocation (Geanakoplos and Polemarchakis 1986).

Since the intermediary chooses an optimal capital structure and an optimal investment portfolio and consumption plan, the planner can do better than the intermediary only if he changes the equilibrium price. Without a change in price, the choice of the planner is identical to the choice set of the intermediaries. Then it is easy to see that forcing the intermediary to adopt a different capital structure cannot improve welfare because with no aggregate uncertainty the equilibrium asset price is determined by the condition that the rates of return on the two assets should be equalized in the usual way. In other words, the equilibrium price is independent of the capital structure. Since there is no pecuniary externality that can be exploited by the regulator, forcing the intermediary to raise more or less capital can only distort the optimal decision.

**Proposition 2**  Under the maintained assumptions, the laisser-faire equilibrium is constrained efficient and welfare cannot be improved by changing the equilibrium capital structure.

## 7.1.2 Models with aggregate uncertainty

The case we have examined is very special. Because the asset price $P$ is a constant at date 1, it is determined by the requirement that the returns on the short and long assets be equal. This means that no change in portfolios or capital structure at date 0 can have any effect on prices at date 1 and, as we have seen, price changes are the essential ingredient of any improvement in welfare. In models with aggregate uncertainty, the asset price fluctuates between states. Although there is a first-order condition that constrains the distribution of prices, capital adequacy requirements can have an effect on equilibrium prices and hence have some impact on welfare. Since equilibria with incomplete markets are typically *not* constrained efficient, these changes in asset prices can be manipulated to increase welfare. The crucial question, however, is what kind of capital regulation will lead to an improvement in welfare. It is not obvious that requiring intermediaries to hold more capital will be beneficial. In fact, simple examples with no pathological features can give rise to the surprising conclusion that increasing capital lowers welfare and reducing capital increases welfare.

To illustrate these results, we describe a model studied by Gale and Özgür (2005). The model is identical to the one described above except for the structure of liquidity shocks. All individuals and intermediaries are ex ante identical. Ex post there are intermediaries of two types. One type consists entirely of early consumers and the other type consists of late consumers. There are two (aggregate) states of nature, $H$ and $L$, which occur with probability 0.5. The proportion of early consumers in state $s$ is denoted by $\lambda_s$, where $1 > \lambda_H > \lambda_L > 0$. The proportion of intermediaries consisting of early consumers in state $s$ is $\lambda_s$ and the probability that any intermediary has only early consumers is $\lambda_s$ too. If $\lambda_i$ is the proportion of early consumers in intermediary $i$ then

$$\lambda_i = \begin{cases} 1 & \text{w. pr. } \lambda_s \text{ in state } s, \\ 0 & \text{w. pr. } 1 - \lambda_s \text{ in state } s, \end{cases}$$

for $s = H, L$.

The existence of aggregate uncertainty requires some additional complexity in the intermediaries' contracts with consumers and investors. Specifically, the payments made to both groups will depend, in general, on both the intermediary's state (1 or 0) and on the aggregate state ($H$ or $L$).

A consumer deposits his entire endowment with a single intermediary who offers him a consumption contract $c = \{(c_{1s}, c_{2s}) : s = H, L\}$ in exchange, where $c_{1s}$ is consumption offered to an early consumer at date 1 in state $s$ and $c_{2s}$ is the consumption offered to a late consumer at date 2 in state $s$.

The intermediary writes a contract $e = \{(e_0, e_{1s}, e_{2s}) : s = H, L\}$ with investors, where $e_0 \geq 0$ is the amount of capital invested at date 0, $e_{1s} \geq 0$ is the amount of the good promised to investors in state $s$ if all the depositors are early consumers and $e_{2s} \geq 0$ is the amount of the good promised in state $s$ at date 2 if all the depositors are late consumers.

In order to reduce the volatility of consumption, the capital structure $e$ should be chosen so that payments to investors occur when consumption is high and not when it is low. Since there are four possible payment opportunities, this leaves a lot of scope for designing the optimal risk sharing arrangements. As usual, because capital is costly, it is not optimal to eliminate the fluctuations in consumption altogether. This means that changes in prices will have income effects that can increase the ex ante expected utility of depositors.

Since the intermediaries are assumed to choose their capital structure optimally, taking as given the prices corresponding to each state of nature, it is clear that capital regulation can improve welfare only by changing the equilibrium prices. The impact of these income effects may be complex. For example, when an intermediary has only early consumers, it sells its holding of the long asset to meet its obligations to its depositors. An increase in asset prices will therefore raise their consumption. For an intermediary that has only late consumers, the effect will be reversed. If late consumers are doing better on average than early consumers, the net effect on ex ante utility may be beneficial. But then we need to consider the possibility that an increase in asset prices in one state may necessitate a reduction in another. Ultimately, the question is: what change in capital structure will effectively increase welfare?

The answer found by Gale and Özgür depends, not surprisingly, on the degree of relative risk aversion. They consider a model with constant relative risk aversion and solve for equilibrium numerically for various parametric assumptions. They find that, if the degree of risk aversion is high enough (greater than $\sigma \approx 2$), a *reduction* in bank capital reduces price volatility and increases welfare. For lower risk aversion (i.e. lower than $\sigma \approx 2$), an increase in bank capital increases volatility and welfare. The intuition behind these results appears to be that forcing banks to raise costly capital will raise both their investment in the short asset and in the long asset, but it raises investment in the short asset less than investment in the long asset. This is because the bank is trying to minimize the cost of capital by investing excess capital in the higher-yielding asset. As a result of this shift in portfolio composition, the asset market becomes less liquid and this reduces asset prices in the high state and increases volatility overall.

It is not known how robust these results are when the model specification is altered or generalized, but even if the results turn out to be special they reinforce the lesson that, when general-equilibrium effects are involved, it is very difficult to predict the macroeconomic effect of changes in capital structures across the financial system. Until we have a general theory to guide us, caution in policy making would seem to be advisable.

## 7.2 CAPITAL STRUCTURE WITH COMPLETE MARKETS

The function of bank capital in the preceding section is to allow risk sharing between risk neutral investors and risk averse depositors. The investors' returns are concentrated in those states where the demand for liquidity is low relative to the supply. By varying the investors' returns across states, it is possible to reduce the fluctuations in the depositors' consumption, in other words, it is possible to provide depositors with insurance against liquidity shocks or asset return shocks. An optimal capital structure is one way to provide this kind of insurance, but it is not the only way. If markets at date 0 were complete, insurance could be provided through the markets and the need for capital would be eliminated entirely.

Let the good at date 0 be the numeraire and let $p_{ts}$ denote the price of one unit of the good at date $t = 1, 2$ in state $s = H, L$. An intermediary will want liquidity at date 1 if its depositors are early consumers and at date 2 if they are late consumers. So what the intermediary wants is an option on the good at each date. What will this option cost? Since the probability of having depositors who are early consumers is $\lambda_s$ in state $s$, the cost of the option should be $\lambda_s p_{1s}$ for date 1 and $(1 - \lambda_s)p_{2s}$ for date 2. If the intermediary uses the complete markets to obtain an optimal risk-sharing contract for its depositors, it will offer a consumption plan $(c_{1H}, c_{2H}, c_{1L}, c_{2L})$ to maximize the expected utility

$$\frac{1}{2}\{\lambda_H U(c_{1H}) + (1 - \lambda_H)U(c_{2H})\} + \frac{1}{2}\{\lambda_L U(c_{1L}) + (1 - \lambda_L)U(c_{2L})\}$$

subject to the budget constraint

$$\lambda_H p_{1H} c_{1H} + (1 - \lambda_H)p_{2H} c_{2H} + \lambda_L p_{1L} c_{1L} + (1 - \lambda_L)p_{2L} c_{2L} \leq 1.$$

Similarly, investors can use markets to spread their consumption over the three dates. As usual, there is no loss of generality in assuming that they consume only in the first and last periods, so they will choose a bundle $(e_0, e_H, e_L)$ where $e_0$ is the amount of the good supplied at date 0 and $e_s$ is the consumption at date 2 in state $s$, to maximize

$$\frac{1}{2}\{e_H + e_L\} - \rho e_0 \tag{7.2}$$

subject to the budget constraint

$$p_{2H}e_H + p_{2L}e_L \leq e_0. \tag{7.3}$$

Because markets are complete, investments in the short and long assets yield zero profits. It does not matter who makes the investments, since they add nothing to wealth or the possibility of risk sharing, so we can, without loss of generality, assume that all investments are made by a representative firm. In equilibrium, the firm will buy the goods supplied by the intermediaries and the investors at date 0, that is, $1 + e_0$, invest them in the short and long assets, and use the returns from these assets to supply goods to the investors and the intermediary at dates 1 and 2. In addition to the zero-profit conditions, the usual market-clearing conditions must be satisfied (see Chapter 6).

Because the usual assumptions, including the assumption of complete markets, are satisfied, the fundamental theorems of welfare economics ensure that an equilibrium is Pareto-efficient (or incentive efficient if the incentive constraints are binding). Thus, with complete markets, we get **efficient risk sharing** between investors, on the one hand, and the intermediaries and their customers, on the other. Although it is intermediated by the market, the provision of insurance is similar to what happens in a model with capital structure. The investors supply "capital" at date 0 that must be invested in real assets in order to provide future consumption. They take their returns in the form of consumption at date 2. Because they are risk neutral, they will consume only in the state where the price $p_{2s}$ is a minimum, leaving more consumption for the depositors in other states. This bunching of consumption by the investors in a single state allows the depositors to smooth their consumption across states and, in particular, to consume more in the state with a high cost of consumption.

The existence of complete markets not only provides a perfect substitute for optimal capital structure, thus making capital redundant, it also makes the optimal capital structure indeterminate. This is because any capital structure can be undone by transactions in the market. Suppose that $(\hat{e}_0, \hat{e}_H, \hat{e}_L)$ is an action that maximizes (7.2) subject to (7.3). Because the objective function and the constraint are both linear in $(e_0, e_H, e_L)$, the optimal trade must satisfy

$$\frac{1}{2}\{\hat{e}_H + \hat{e}_L\} - \rho\hat{e}_0 = 0$$

and

$$p_{2H}\hat{e}_H + p_{2L}\hat{e}_L - \hat{e}_0 = 0.$$

Now suppose that the intermediary adopts $(\hat{e}_0, \hat{e}_H, \hat{e}_L)$ as its capital structure. Because the intermediary has access to complete markets, the only effect of capital structure is on the intermediaries budget constraint. This capital structure is optimal for the intermediary in the sense that it minimizes the cost subject to the investors' participation constraint. Because the cost is zero, it does not affect the set of consumption plans the intermediary can afford and the optimal plan $(c_{1H}, c_{2H}, c_{1L}, c_{2L})$ will satisfy the budget constraint

$$\lambda_H p_{1H} c_{1H} + (1 - \lambda_H) p_{2H} c_{2H} + \lambda_L p_{1L} c_{1L}$$
$$+ (1 - \lambda_L) p_{2L} c_{2L} + p_{2H}\hat{e}_H + p_{2L}\hat{e}_L - \hat{e}_0 \leq 1.$$

Finally, if both $(\hat{e}_0, \hat{e}_H, \hat{e}_L)$ and $(e_0, e_H, e_L)$ maximize the investors' objective function (7.2) subject to the budget constraint (7.3), then so does $(e_0, e_H, e_L) - (\hat{e}_0, \hat{e}_H, \hat{e}_L)$, so we can assume that the intermediaries choose to trade $(e_0, e_H, e_L) - (\hat{e}_0, \hat{e}_H, \hat{e}_L)$ in equilibrium. Then the combined effect of the optimal contract between the intermediaries and the investors $(\hat{e}_0, \hat{e}_H, \hat{e}_L)$ and the net trade in the markets $(e_0, e_H, e_L) - (\hat{e}_0, \hat{e}_H, \hat{e}_L)$ is precisely equivalent to the trade $(e_0, e_H, e_L)$ in the original equilibrium.

Thus, the optimal capital structure is indeterminate. This is simply a version of the Modigliani–Miller theorem.

In the analysis of the preceding section, there are two sources of liquidity for intermediaries that suffer a bad liquidity shock at date 1. One is the capital structure negotiated with investors, which allows payment to investors to be reduced in the event of a bad liquidity shock; the other is asset sales to other intermediaries. The capital structure is chosen optimally by the intermediaries, so this is not a source of inefficiency. Rather the incompleteness of markets forces banks to sell assets at prices that are determined ex post by the demand for and supply of liquidity in each state. As we have seen, the ex post provision of liquidity may be inefficient because intermediaries end up selling their assets at a low price in states where the marginal utility of their depositors is high, the opposite of what good insurance requires. By contrast, when markets are complete at date 0, the intermediary can transfer wealth across states at the prevailing prices and this ensures that the marginal rates of substitution across states are equalized for all depositors.

It is worth noting that the heterogeneity of intermediaries ex post is crucial for this result. If intermediaries were identical at date 1 there would be no gains from trade and hence no need for markets. To put it another way, markets are always effectively complete in a Robinson Crusoe economy. So markets can be incomplete without any effect on efficiency if each intermediary has a representative sample of consumers at each date. The indeterminacy of capital structure does not survive, however: if there are no markets for contingent commodities the capital structure is determinate because it is only through the capital structure that efficient risk sharing can be achieved.

## 7.3 REGULATING LIQUIDITY

Now we turn to the study of liquidity regulation, that is, the possibility of improving welfare by regulating the amount of the short asset held in equilibrium. To keep things simple, we eliminate the risk neutral investors, so there is no provision of capital. Otherwise, the assumptions are the same as in Section 7.1. The example is based on one in Allen and Gale (2004).

Apart from the incompleteness of markets, we do not impose any frictions on the model. In particular, intermediaries are allowed to use complete risk-sharing contracts. An intermediary takes a deposit of one unit of the good from each consumer at date 0 and invests it in a portfolio $(x, y)$ consisting of $x$ units of the long asset and $y$ units of the short asset. In exchange, the consumer gets a consumption stream $(c_{1H}, c_{2H}, c_{1L}, c_{2L})$, where $c_{1H}$ is the consumption promised if he withdraws at date 1 when the proportion of early consumers is $\lambda_H$, $c_{2H}$ is the consumption promised if he withdraws at date 2 when the proportion of early consumers is $\lambda_H$, and so on.

Because there is no aggregate uncertainty, we can assume the price of the asset at date 1 is independent of the state, that is,

$$P_{HL} = P_{LH} = P.$$

Since equilibrium requires that both assets are held at date 0, the one-period holding returns on both assets must also be the same at date 0. The return on the short asset is equal to one and the return on the long asset is equal to $P$, so the equilibrium price must be

$$P = 1.$$

If $P = 1$ is the price of $R$ units of the good at date 2, the price of one unit is $p = 1/R$.

Because of the symmetry of the model, we focus on a symmetric equilibrium and describe the behavior of a representative intermediary. Although intermediaries are heterogeneous, they solve essentially the same decision problem. Each has an equal probability of having a high or a low proportion of early consumers, and it is the number of early consumers, $\lambda_H$ or $\lambda_L$, that matters to the intermediary, not the state of nature $(H, L)$ or $(L, H)$. So we can describe the intermediaries' decision problem in terms of the intermediary's "state" $H$ or $L$, meaning the number of early consumers is $\lambda_H$ or $\lambda_L$.

At date 0, an intermediary takes in a deposit of one unit from each consumer and invests it in a portfolio $(x, y)$ and a contingent consumption plan $c = (c_{1H}, c_{2H}, c_{1L}, c_{2L})$. Since all intermediaries choose the same portfolio and consumption plan, we can describe an allocation by a triple $(x, y, c)$. An allocation $(x, y, c)$ is attainable if it satisfies the market-clearing conditions at each date. At date 0 this requires that total investment equal the endowment of goods:

$$x + y = 1.$$

At date 1, the supply of goods is $y$ (since $P < R$ no one will want to invest in the short asset at this date). The demand for goods will be $\frac{1}{2}(\lambda_H c_{1H} + \lambda_L c_{1L})$ since half the intermediaries are in state $H$ and half are in state $L$. Then market-clearing at date 1 requires

$$\frac{1}{2}(\lambda_H c_{1H} + \lambda_L c_{1L}) = y.$$

Similarly, market-clearing at date 2 requires

$$\frac{1}{2}[(1 - \lambda_H)c_{2H} + (1 - \lambda_L)c_{2L}] = Rx.$$

Each intermediary chooses the portfolio $(x, y)$ and the consumption plan $c$ to maximize the expected utility of the typical depositor. At the equilibrium asset price $P = 1$, all portfolios $(x, y)$ will have the same value at date 1:

$$Px + y = x + y = 1$$

so the intermediary is indifferent among all feasible portfolios. Moreover, since the value of the intermediary's portfolio is the same in each state, the intermediary can maximize expected utility in each state independently by choosing $(c_{1s}, c_{2s})$ to maximize

$$\lambda_s U(c_{1s}) + (1 - \lambda_s)U(c_{2s})$$

subject to the budget constraint

$$\lambda_s c_{1s} + (1 - \lambda_s)\frac{c_{2s}}{R} = 1.$$

So an equilibrium consists of the equilibrium asset price $P = 1$ and an attainable allocation $(x, y, c)$ such that, for each state $s = H, L$, the consumption plan $(c_{1s}, c_{2s})$ maximizes expected utility subject to the budget constraint in that state.

### 7.3.1 Comparative statics

Before we can begin the analysis of optimal regulation, we have to establish a number of comparative static properties. We begin by focusing on the behavior of an intermediary in a particular state. Since the two states are symmetric, we can suppress the reference to the state for the time being. If the fraction of early consumers is $\lambda$ at date 1 then the intermediary's budget constraint at date 1 is

$$\lambda c_1 + (1 - \lambda)\frac{c_2}{R} = 1. \tag{7.4}$$

Maximizing expected utility $\lambda U(c_1) + (1 - \lambda)U(c_2)$ subject to this budget constraint gives the usual first-order condition

$$U'(c_1) = RU'(c_2). \tag{7.5}$$

It is important to notice that, although the number of early consumers does not appear in the first-order condition, it does affect the optimal consumption allocation because it appears in the budget constraint. The first-order condition implies that $c_1$ and $c_2$ vary together, so a change in $\lambda$ will typically raise or lower consumption at both dates. In fact, an increase in $\lambda$ increases the left hand side of (7.4) if and only if $c_1 > c_2/R$. Intuitively, if the present value of early consumption is greater than the present value of late consumption, an increase in the proportion of late consumers will increase the present value of total consumption. In order to satisfy its budget constraint, the intermediary will have to reduce average consumption. If $c_1 < c_2/R$, an increase in $\lambda$ will have the opposite effect.

**Proposition 3** For each date $t = 1, 2$, consumption is lower in state $H$ than in state $L$ if $c_1 > Rc_2$ for all pairs $(c_1, c_2)$ satisfying the first-order condition (7.5). Conversely, consumption is higher in state $H$ than in state $L$ if $c_1 < Rc_2$ for all order pairs satisfying the first-order condition (7.5).

This effect turns out to be crucial for the comparative static properties of the equilibrium, so we investigate it in more detail. To do this, consider the special case where the VNM utility function exhibits constant relative risk aversion $\sigma$:

$$U(c) = \frac{1}{1-\sigma} c^{1-\sigma}.$$

The first-order condition (7.5) becomes

$$(c_1)^{-\sigma} = R(c_2)^{-\sigma},$$

which implies

$$c_1 = c_2 R^{\frac{-1}{\sigma}} = \left(\frac{c_2}{R}\right) R^{1-\frac{1}{\sigma}}.$$

Then it is easy to see that

$$c_1 > \frac{c_2}{R} \iff R^{1-\frac{1}{\sigma}} > 1 \iff \sigma > 1.$$

The present value of consumption is higher at date 1 than at date 2 if and only if the degree of relative risk aversion is greater than one.

**Proposition 4**   If the consumers' degree of relative risk aversion is a constant $\sigma$, then $c_1 > Rc_2$ for all pairs $(c_1, c_2)$ satisfying the first-order condition (7.5) if and only if $\sigma > 1$.

The role of risk aversion in determining the consumption allocation has an intuitive interpretation. The first-order condition implies that marginal utility is lower at date 2 than at date 1. In other words, $c_1$ is less than $c_2$. Other things being equal (i.e. holding constant the expected value of consumption) a risk averse consumer would prefer to reduce the uncertainty about his level of consumption. Other things are not equal, of course. In order to reduce consumption-risk it is necessary to hold more of the short asset and less of the long asset. A more liquid portfolio yields lower average returns and provides lower average consumption. Given this trade-off between consumption risk and average consumption levels, we should expect the degree of risk aversion to affect the intermediary's choice. The more risk averse the consumer, the more he values insurance and the lower the average level of consumption he is willing to accept in order to smooth consumption over the two periods. The critical value $\sigma = 1$ corresponds to the case in which it is optimal to equalize the present value of consumption between the two periods: $c_1 = c_2/R$. If risk aversion is less than one, the high returns from delaying consumption outweigh the value of insurance and the optimal consumption allocation gives early consumption a lower present value than late consumption. If risk aversion is greater than one, the value of insurance outweighs the return from delaying consumption and the optimal consumption allocation gives early consumption higher present value than late consumption.

Figure 7.1 illustrates the relationship between risk aversion and consumption risk. When the degree of relative risk aversion is very low, it is optimal to take a high risk of being an early consumer who gets very low consumption in order to have a chance of being a late consumer who gets a very high consumption. By contrast, when the degree of relative risk aversion is high, the difference between consumption at the two dates is reduced to the point where the present value of future consumption is lower than the value of present consumption.

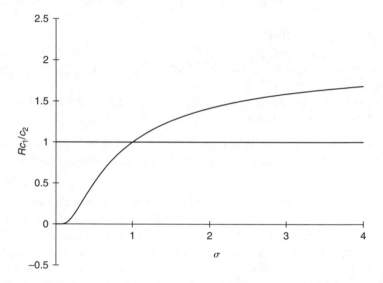

**Figure 7.1.** Illustration of relationship between $\sigma$ and the ratio of the present values $c_1$ and $c_2/R$ for $R = 2$.

The correspondence between risk aversion and the present value of consumption at the two dates translates immediately into a correspondence between risk aversion and the slope of the consumption functions relating the value of $\lambda$ and the level of consumption. If $\sigma$ is greater than one, both $c_1$ and $c_2$ decline as $\lambda$ increases. If $\sigma$ is less than one, $c_1$ and $c_2$ increase as $\lambda$ increases.

**Proposition 5** Suppose the consumers' degree of relative risk aversion is a constant $\sigma$ and let $c = (c_{1H}, c_{2H}, c_{1L}, c_{2L})$ be the optimal consumption allocation chosen by the representative intermediary. Then $c_{1H} < c_{1L}$ and $c_{2H} < c_{2L}$ if and only if $\sigma > 1$.

Figure 7.2 illustrates the optimal levels of consumption at date 1 and date 2 as a function of $\lambda$, the fraction of early consumers, when the degree of relative risk aversion is greater than one. For each value of $\lambda$, consumption at date 1 is less than consumption at date 2, but the ratio of $c_2$ to $c_1$ is less than $R = 2$, so the present value of consumption at date 1 is greater than the present value of consumption at date 2. Thus, as $\lambda$ increases, consumption at both dates falls.

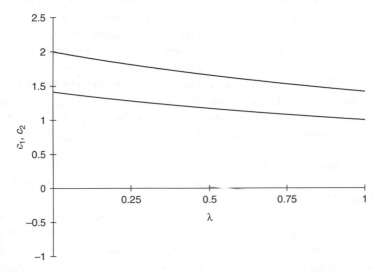

**Figure 7.2.** Illustration of relationship between $\lambda$ and $(c_1, c_2)$ for $\sigma = 2, R = 2$.

In terms of welfare, if $\sigma > 1$, consumers are better off when the number of early consumers is low and, if $\sigma < 1$, consumers are better off at both dates when the number of early consumers is high. This property of equilibrium is the key to understanding the welfare effects of any intervention in the market.

## 7.3.2 Too much or too little liquidity?

In the last chapter we saw that, when there is no aggregate uncertainty, a Pareto-efficient allocation gives every consumer a consumption allocation $(c_1, c_2)$ that is independent of the state of nature. The preceding analysis shows that, in the absence of Arrow securities that allow wealth to be transferred across states, the equilibrium consumption allocation will depend on the fraction of early consumers and hence on the state. So an unconstrained central planner can certainly achieve a higher level of welfare than the intermediaries can in the absence of Arrow securities; however, as we argued in Section 7.1, the relevant question is whether the equilibrium is constrained efficient.

It is well known that models with incomplete markets are typically *not* constrained efficient, so our presumption is that by manipulating decisions at date 0 the planner can potentially improve on the laisser-faire allocation. More precisely, there exists a welfare-improving intervention, but it is not obvious what it is. This is an important distinction for the policymaker: it is not sufficient to know that there exists some (possibly complex) policy that will improve welfare. The policymaker needs to know what to do; otherwise, he may make things worse. Our objective in this section is to characterize the welfare-improving policies. As we shall see, even in the context of this simple example, it is not easy to say what the right policy is.

In what follows, we assume that the planner's intervention is limited to controlling the portfolio choices of the intermediaries, specifically, the amount of the short asset they hold. The planner's ability to improve on the laisser-faire allocation depends upon the possibility of changing the equilibrium prices. In a laisser-faire equilibrium, the intermediaries choose portfolios and consumption plans optimally, taking as given the asset prices they face in the future. It is rational for intermediaries to treat prices as parameters beyond their control because the number of intermediaries is so large that no single intermediary can have a significant impact on the market-clearing asset price. A planner, on the other hand, does not take future prices as given. Although intermediaries will make future consumption decisions taking prices as given, the planner anticipates that his influence over the intermediaries' portfolio decisions will have some impact on prices. It is through the effect of portfolio choices on prices that the planner can potentially improve the welfare of the intermediaries' depositors.

Suppose that the planner requires intermediaries to hold more of the short asset in their portfolios. This action will have two immediate effects. First, it will have a direct effect on portfolios, increasing $y$ and reducing $x$. Second, it will change the market-clearing asset prices at date 1. Presumably, increasing the amount of liquidity and reducing the stock of the long asset will increase the asset price. The consumers' welfare depends only on consumption, so the effect of any change in portfolios and prices on welfare will be indirect. The change in the portfolio and the asset prices at date 1 will shift the intermediaries' budget constraints at date 1, causing them to choose different consumption plans. We know that all feasible portfolios $(x, y)$ have the same market value at date 1 because the long and short assets have equal returns. Thus, to a first approximation, a small change in the portfolio has no impact on the intermediary's budget constraint. A change in prices, on the other hand, will have an impact on the intermediary's budget constraint, in fact, it will have both substitution and income effects. In analyzing the impact of the policy intervention on consumers' welfare, we only need to pay attention to income effects. The envelope theorem assures us that, since the intermediary chooses the consumption plan to maximize the typical consumer's expected utility, a small movement along the budget constraint will have no impact on expected utility. So it is only the income effect of the price change that is relevant for welfare analysis.

Suppose that a change in $y$ increases $P$ (and $p$) in each state. What will be the income effect of this change? Consider the budget constraint of the intermediary in state $H$,

$$\lambda_H c_1 + (1 - \lambda_H)pc_{2H} = y + pRy.$$

An increase in $p$ increases the left hand because it increases the present value of the consumption provided at date 2. An increase in $p$ also increases the right hand side because it increases the present value of the return to the long asset. Thus, the income effect of an increase in $p$ is given by $Ry - (1 - \lambda_H)c_{2H}$. More precisely, this is the amount by which we could increase expenditure on the early consumers and still balance the budget in state $H$. Similarly, the income effect of the price change in state $L$ is given by $Ry - (1 - \lambda_L)c_{2L}$.

Now the market-clearing condition at date 2 requires that

$$\frac{1}{2}[(1 - \lambda_H)c_{2H} + (1 - \lambda_L)c_{2L}] = Ry,$$

so, in this case, the income effects in the two states sum to zero

$$Ry - (1 - \lambda_H)c_{2H} + Ry - (1 - \lambda_L)c_{2L} = 0.$$

The income effect of a price change raises consumption in one state and lowers consumption by an equal amount in the other state. When markets are complete, so that marginal utility of consumption is the same in each state, a transfer of consumption from one state to another has no effect. When markets are incomplete, by contrast, the marginal utility of consumption is typically higher in one state than in the other and this makes it possible for income effects to increase expected utility.

Suppose, for example, that the degree of relative risk aversion is greater than one, so that consumption at each date is higher in state $L$ than in state $H$. This implies that

$$Ry - (1 - \lambda_H)c_{2H} > 0 > Ry - (1 - \lambda_L)c_{2L},$$

so the income effect of an increase in $p$ is positive in state $H$ and negative in state $L$. Furthermore, the marginal utility of consumption for early consumers is higher in state $H$ than in state $L$. Thus, if we assume that the change in real income is reflected in the consumption of early consumers in each state, the gain to the early consumers in state $H$ will more than offset the loss to the early consumers in state $L$. Formally,

$$U'(c_{1H})\left\{Ry - (1 - \lambda_H)c_{2H}\right\} > -U'(c_{1L})\left\{Ry - (1 - \lambda_L)c_{2L}\right\}.$$

By a similar argument, we would get the opposite result if we started by assuming that the degree of relative risk aversion was less than one.

There is no loss of generality in assuming that only the consumption of the early consumers changes. By the envelope theorem, we cannot do better by dividing the change in consumption between early and late consumers. Thus, we have a necessary and sufficient condition for an improvement in welfare from an increase in $p$ which we state as the next proposition.

**Proposition 6** Starting at the laisser-faire equilibrium, an increase in $p$ (or $P$) is welfare improving (i.e. will increase depositors' expected utility) if and only if the degree of relative risk aversion is greater than one.

It remains to connect the change in price at date 1 to the change in portfolios at date 0. Intuitively, we expect an increase in $y$ to be associated with an increase in $P$ (or $p$) because it increases the supply of the good at date 1 and decreases the supply of the long asset. However, in the laisser-faire equilibrium intermediaries are indifferent between the two assets at date 0 and the quantity they hold in their portfolios is determined by the requirements for market clearing at date 1. If consumption at date 1 goes up, the amount of the short asset must increase to provide that consumption. So whether an increase in $p$ is associated with an increase in $y$ depends on the reaction of the intermediary's consumption plans. What we can say is that for any small change in $p$ there will be an equilibrium in which intermediaries' portfolio choices are constrained appropriately.

Irwin et al. (2006) have extended the simple example for considering the regulation of liquidity considered in Allen and Gale (2004) and this chapter. They show that while minimum liquidity controls can lead to Pareto improvements when intermediaries are homogeneous ex ante, this is not the case when they are heterogeneous ex ante. In this case other policies such as state-contingent tax and transfer schemes or state-contingent lender of last resort policies are necessary for improvements in efficiency.

What lessons can we draw from the kind of exercise conducted in this section? For starters, a policymaker who wishes to increase welfare needs to have detailed knowledge about the risk-sharing arrangements undertaken by the financial sector. More generally, the effects of increased liquidity in the market are indirect and work through the general-equilibrium determination of asset prices and consumption plans. So it takes a lot of information about the structure of the model and the equilibrium to predict the effect of policy on equilibrium. If this is true in a fairly trivial example, one would expect the problems facing a policymaker in the 'real' world to be quite challenging.

## 7.4 LITERATURE REVIEW

There have been a number of good surveys and overviews of banking regulation. These include Herring and Santomero (2000), Santos (2001), Freixas and Santomero (2004), Barth et al. (2006). For this reason, this section will be kept short.

There is widespread agreement that the most important rationale for banking regulation is the prevention of systemic risk. However, as discussed initially in this chapter there is not agreement about the nature of the market failure that leads to this systemic risk. The policies that have been used to try and limit systemic risk include capital adequacy ratios, liquidity requirements, reserve requirements, deposit insurance, and asset restrictions. Another important motivation for regulation is consumer protection. Conflict of interest rules and interest rate ceilings on loans are examples of policies aimed at protecting consumers. Other policies, such as competition policy, are directed at industry generally but enhance the efficiency of the banking system. The government also tries to implement broader social objectives, such as the prevention of money laundering through reporting requirements for large cash transactions. Dewatripont and Tirole (1994) have pointed to another category of rationale for justifying banking regulation. Bankers, like the managers of any other coporation, need to be monitored by investors. Bank depositors are particularly unsuited for this role because they typically have limited resources and limited experience. Regulation can be a substitute for monitoring to ensure the bank acts in the interests of the depositors.

## 7.5 CONCLUDING REMARKS

In this chapter, we have argued that the first step in finding optimal regulatory policies is the identification of market failure(s). The model considered in Chapter 6 provides conditions under which market forces lead to an efficient allocation of resources. Moreover, the optimal allocation can involve financial crises. So it is not the case that eliminating systemic risk is always optimal. A careful analysis of the costs and benefits of crises is necessary to understand when intervention is necessary. This analysis is typically missing from proposals for capital adequacy regulations such as the Basel Accords. Incomplete financial markets provide one plausible source of market failure and a possible justification for capital regulation. The form this regulation takes is complex and informationally intensive, however, so it is not clear that this provides the basis for a practical policy. One also needs to keep in mind the continuing financial innovation that allows banks to hedge risks in ever more sophisticated ways. Whether this makes the assumption of complete markets realistic is an open and important empirical question. Allen and Gale (2006) contains a further discussion of some of these issues.

Regulation is only one of the ways that governments intervene in the financial system. The other important way is through the actions of the central bank. The next chapter considers the role of monetary policy.

## REFERENCES

Allen, F. and D. Gale (2003). "Capital Adequacy Regulation: In Search of a Rationale," in *Economics for an Imperfect World: Essays in Honor of Joseph Stiglitz* edited by R. Arnott, B. Greenwald, R. Kanbur and B. Nalebuff, Cambridge, MA: MIT Press, 83–109.

Allen, F. and D. Gale (2004). "Financial Intermediaries and Markets," *Econometrica* 72, 1023–1061.

Allen, F. and D. Gale (2006). "Systemic Risk and Regulation," in R. Stulz and M. Carey (eds.), *Financial Risk and Regulation*. Cambridge, MA: NBER..

Barth, J., G. Caprio Jr. and R. Levine (2006). *Rethinking Banking Regulation: Till Angels Govern*, Cambridge, New York and Sydney: Cambridge University Press.

Besanko, D. and G. Kanatas (1996). "The Regulation of Bank Capital: Do Capital Standards Promote Bank Safety?" *Journal of Financial Intermediation* 5, 160–183.

Bhattacharya, S. (1982). "Aspects of Monetary and Banking Theory and Moral Hazard," *Journal of Finance* 37, 371–384.

Dewatripont, M. and J. Tirole (1994). *The Prudential Regulation of Banks*, Cambridge, MA: MIT Press.

Freixas, X. and A. Santomero (2004). "Regulation of Financial Intermediaries: A Discussion," in *Credit Intermediation and the Macroeconomy, Models and Perspectives*, edited by S. Bhattacharya, A. Boot and A. Thakor, Oxford and New York: Oxford University Press.

Furlong, F. and M. Keeley (1989). "Capital Regulation and Bank Risk-Taking: A Note," *Journal of Banking and Finance* 13, 883–891.

Gale, D. (2003). "Financial Regulation in a Changing Environment," in T. Courchene and E. Neave (eds.), *Framing Financial Structure in an Information Environment.* Kingston, Ontario: John Deutsch Institute for the Study of Economic Policy, Queen's University.

Gale, D. (2004). "Notes on Optimal Capital Regulation," in P. St-Amant and C. Wilkins (eds.), *The Evolving Financial System and Public Policy.* Ottawa: Bank of Canada.

Gale, D. and O. Özgür (2005). "Are Bank Capital Ratios Too High or Too Low: Risk Aversion, Incomplete Markets, and Optimal Capital Structures," *Journal of the European Economic Association* 3, 690–700.

Geanakoplos, J. and H. Polemarchakis (1986). "Existence, Regularity, and Constrained Suboptimality of Competitive Allocations When the Asset Market Is Incomplete," in W. Heller, R. Starr, and D. Starrett (eds.), *Essays in honor of Kenneth J. Arrow: Volume 3, Uncertainty, information, and communication.* Cambridge, New York and Sydney: Cambridge University Press, 65–95.

Gennotte, G. and D. Pyle (1991). "Capital Controls and Bank Risk," *Journal of Banking and Finance* 15, 805–824.

Hellmann, T., K. Murdock, and J. Stiglitz (2000). "Liberalization, Moral Hazard in Banking, and Prudential Regulation: Are Capital Requirements Enough?" *American Economic Review* 90, 147–165.

Herring, R. and A. Santomero (2000). "What is Optimal Financial Regulation?" *The New Financial Architecture, Banking Regulation in the 21st Century*, edited by B. Gup, Westport, Connecticut: Quorum Books, 51–84.

Irwin, G., V. Saporta, and M. Tanaka (2006). "Optimal Policies to Mitigate Financial Stability when Intermediaries are Heterogeneous," working paper, Bank of England.

Keeley, M. (1990). "Deposit Insurance, Risk, and Market Power in Banking," *American Economic Review* 80, 1183–1200.

Kim, D. and A. Santomero (1988). "Risk in Banking and Capital Regulation," *Journal of Finance* 43, 1219–1233.

Rochet, J-C. (1992). "Capital Requirements and the Behaviour of Commercial Banks," *European Economic Review* 36, 1137–1178.

Santos, J. (2001). "Bank Capital Regulation in Contemporary Banking Theory: A Review of the Literature," *Financial Markets, Institutions and Instruments* 14, 289–328.

# 8

## Money and prices

In the preceding chapters, we have assumed that intermediaries offer depositors "real" contracts, that is, contracts that are denominated in terms of goods. For example, an intermediary offers its depositors a **deposit contract** that promises $c_1$ units of the good if the depositor withdraws at date 1 and $c_2$ units of the good if the depositor withdraws at date 2. In practice, the terms of deposit contracts and debt contracts in general are written in "nominal" terms, that is, they specify payments in terms of money. Economists often justify the substitution of "real" for "nominal" contracts by claiming that money is a "veil" that hides the reality we are interested in, namely, the goods and services that firms produce and individuals consume; but the fact that contracts are written in terms of money has some important implications that are not captured by "real" models. The most important feature of nominal contracts is that changes in the **price level** (the general level of prices measured in terms of money) change the real value of the contract.

A. C. Pigou was one of the first to point out the impact of the price level on the real value of debt. More precisely, outside money, the part of the money supply that constitutes a claim on the government, represents part of the private sector's net wealth. A fall in the price level by definition increases the real value of outside money and, consequently, increases the private sector's **real** wealth, that is, its wealth measured in terms of goods and services. This "wealth effect" subsequently came to be known as the "Pigou effect." Pigou used it to criticize Keynes' argument that a general fall in prices would have no effect on demand for goods and services. Keynes relied on the familiar homogeneity property of demand functions: because demand and supply depend only on relative prices, an equal proportionate change in prices and wages should have no effect on demand and supply. Pigou argued to the contrary that a fall in the general level of prices would increase perceived wealth and that this might lead consumers to demand more goods and services.

An important element of Pigou's argument was the distinction between **inside** and **outside** money. Outside money consists of currency and deposits with the Federal Reserve System, sometimes called the monetary base or high-powered money. Inside money consists of bank deposits and other liabilities of the banking system. Inside money consists of obligations of the private sector to itself whereas outside money represents an obligation of the government to the private sector. A fall in the price level will increase the value of private debts, thus reducing the net wealth of the debtor; but there will be an equal and opposite effect on the wealth of the creditor. When aggregated over the entire private sector, these debts and credits will cancel out, thus leading to a zero effect on the net wealth of the private sector as a whole. This leaves the wealth effect of price changes on outside money but since the quantity of outside money is usually small this wealth effect is also small.

To a first approximation, this may be a reasonable approach in normal times, but in cases of financial crises where the change in the price level is large, as it was during the Great Depression of the 1930's, it can be misleading. The reason is that a very large fall in the price level may make it impossible for firms and individuals to pay their debts, in which case they may be forced to default and seek the protection of bankruptcy. If bankruptcy had no real effect on the value of the creditors' claims, it might not matter to Pigou's argument; but in practice bankruptcy often involves large deadweight costs. These include not only the legal costs of liquidation but also the loss of organizational capital that occurs when an enterprise ceases to be a going concern and the dislocation that can spread throughout the economy while productive activities are being reorganized. These deadweight losses, which can amount to a significant fraction of GDP, are one of the reasons why financial crises are regarded with such horror by policymakers.

Just as a fall in the general price level has the effect of increasing the level of real indebtedness in the economy, an increase in the price level has the effect of reducing the real level of indebtedness. Often governments burdened with a large national debt have resorted to the expedient of reducing it by creating inflation. This is often referred to as "monetizing" the debt, since the inflationary process begins with an increase in the money supply and the final effect is to reduce the real value of the debt and to increase the quantity of money balances held by individuals. It does not require hyperinflation to have a significant effect on the real value of the national debt. Steady but modest inflation had a very significant impact on the real value of the US national debt left at the end of the Second World War, for example, and many other countries had a similar experience.

More recent episodes also illustrate the importance of nominal debt contracts. A good example is the Asian crisis of 1997. Many of the countries affected by that crisis had large amounts of external debt denominated in terms of dollars. Foreign lenders were unwilling to accept debt issued in terms of the local currency because they did not trust the government to maintain its value. By contrast, the same lenders felt somewhat protected if their investment was denominated in dollars. One example of a country affected by the existence of foreign currency debt was Thailand. Many Thai firms had borrowed in dollars to make investments in the Thai economy. The value of the Thai currency, the baht, was pegged to the dollar, which may have made the loans seem less risky to the borrowers. However, when the dollar began to rise in terms of other currencies, the baht had to rise with it, thus making Thai exports more expensive and causing the balance of trade to deteriorate. Speculators anticipated that the government would have to devalue the baht and began to sell. The currency attack led to a balance of payments crisis and the baht was devalued. This left the Thai businesses that had borrowed large amounts of dollars in a tenuous position. Their revenues were denominated in baht and their debts in dollars. The debts had grown relative to their ability to pay and many had to default.

Another illustration of the importance of nominal contracts comes from Japan, which suffered from low investment and slow growth throughout the 1990's as a result of the bursting of an asset-price bubble in 1990. The government of Japan adopted Keynesian remedies (government expenditure on construction projects and low interest rates) with little effect. At one point, there was a considerable fear that **deflation** (a general fall in the prices of goods and services) might cause a serious problem. Since many Japanese firms were heavily indebted and many banks were saddled with non-performing loans, this fear of deflation was quite real. Fortunately, the deflation was not too severe and this episode passed without further mishap, but it provided an object lesson on the relevance of the price level when debt is denominated in terms of money.

In this chapter we want to focus on some of the more benign aspects of the price level when debt is denominated in nominal terms, in particular, we show how variations in the price level, by varying the real value of debt, can introduce a desirable level of contingency in risk-sharing contracts. Simple debt contracts promise fixed repayments, independently of the state of nature. An optimal risk-sharing contract, on the other hand, will typically make payments contingent on the state. By varying prices, a contract that is fixed in nominal terms can be made contingent in real terms. This increase in the contingency of the contract may improve risk sharing under certain conditions.


## 8.1 AN EXAMPLE

We illustrate the role of price level variability in supporting efficient risk sharing by presenting a simple example based on one in Allen and Gale (1998). As usual, we assume that time is divided into three periods or **dates**, indexed by

$t = 0, 1, 2$. There is a single good, which can be used for consumption or investment, at each date. There are two (real) assets, a **short asset**, represented by a storage technology which produces one unit of the good at date $t + 1$ for every unit invested at date $t$, and a **long asset**, represented by a long-term investment technology which produces $R > 1$ units of the good at date 2 for every unit invested at date 0. There is a large number of identical consumers at date 0, each with an endowment of one unit of the good at date 0 and nothing at date 1. The consumers are subject to liquidity preference shocks: they are either **early consumers** who only value consumption at date 1 or **late consumers** who only value consumption at date 2. There are two states of nature, $s = H, L$, with probabilities $\pi_H$ and $\pi_L$, respectively. The probability that an individual becomes an early consumer depends on the state. Let $\lambda_s$ denote the fraction of early consumers, which equals the probability of becoming an early consumer, in state $s = H, L$. We assumed that $0 < \lambda_L < \lambda_H < 1$. All uncertainty is resolved at the beginning date 1, when the true state of nature is revealed and each consumer learns whether he is an early or a late consumer.

We assume that free entry and competition force intermediaries to maximize the expected utility of the typical depositor, subject to a zero profit constraint. The intermediary takes a deposit of one unit from each depositor at date 0 and invests it in a portfolio $(x, y)$ consisting of $x$ units of the long asset and $y$ units of the short asset. In exchange, the intermediary offers a risk-sharing contract $c = (c_{1H}, c_{2H}, c_{1L}, c_{2L})$ that promises $c_{ts}$ units of consumption to a consumer who withdraws at date $t = 1, 2$ in state $s = H, L$. If $U(c)$ denotes a consumer's utility from consuming $c$ units of the good, the expected utility of this contract is

$$\sum_{t,s} \pi_s \{\lambda_s U(c_{1s}) + (1 - \lambda_s) U(c_{2s})\} \tag{8.1}$$

and a competitive intermediary will choose the portfolio $(x, y)$ and the consumption allocation $c$ to maximize (8.1) subject to the feasibility constraints

$$x + y \leq 1; \tag{8.2}$$

$$\lambda_s c_{1s} \leq y, \quad \forall s = H, L; \tag{8.3}$$

$$\lambda_s c_{1s} + (1 - \lambda_s) c_{2s} \leq y + Rx, \quad \forall s = H, L. \tag{8.4}$$

Suppose that the portfolio $(x, y)$ has been chosen and consider the optimal allocation of consumption in a given state $s$. The consumption allocation $(c_{1s}, c_{2s})$ has to maximize expected utility in that state, that is, maximize

$$\lambda_s U(c_{1s}) + (1 - \lambda_s) U(c_{2s})$$

subject to the feasibility conditions (8.3) and (8.4). We know that $c_{1s}$ must be less than or equal to $c_{2s}$; otherwise we could increase expected utility by using the short asset to shift consumption to date 2. We also know that if $\lambda_s c_{1s} < y$, so that the short asset is actually being used to transfer consumption between the dates, then $c_{1s}$ must equal $c_{2s}$; otherwise we could increase expected utility by reducing the investment in the short asset and shifting consumption to date 1. Thus, there are two situations to consider:

$$\lambda_s c_{1s} < y \quad \text{and} \quad c_{1s} = c_{2s} = y + Rx$$

or

$$c_{1s} = \frac{y}{\lambda_s} \leq c_{2s} = \frac{Rx}{1 - \lambda_s}.$$

For a given portfolio $(x, y)$ we can see that the consumption allocation $(x, y)$ is a function of $\lambda$ as illustrated in Figure 8.1.

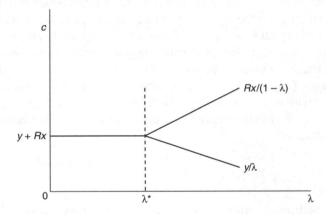

**Figure 8.1.** Consumption $c_1$ and $c_2$ at dates 1 and 2, respectively, as functions of the proportion $\lambda$ of early consumers.

What can we say about the equilibrium consumption allocation? Since $\lambda_L < \lambda_H$ we know that there are three possible situations, depending on where $\lambda_L$ and $\lambda_H$ stand in relation to $\lambda^*$. One of these possibilities is illustrated in Figure 8.2 and this case can be ruled out immediately.

If both $\lambda_H$ and $\lambda_L$ are to the left of $\lambda^*$ as illustrated in Figure 8.2, then the level of consumption is the same at both dates and in both states. But this is inconsistent with the first-order condition that can be derived in the usual way from the portfolio choice problem. By reducing the investment in the short asset and increasing the investment in the long asset, the intermediary can

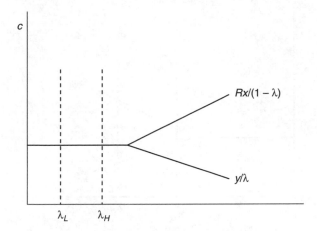

**Figure 8.2.** Consumption $c_1$ and $c_2$ at dates 1 and 2, respectively, as functions of the proportion $\lambda$ of early consumers.

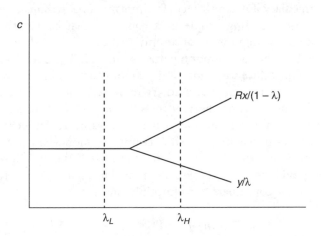

**Figure 8.3.** Consumption $c_1$ and $c_2$ at dates 1 and 2, respectively, as functions of the proportion $\lambda$ of early consumers.

reduce consumption by $1/\lambda_s$ at date 1 in both states and increase consumption by $R/(1-\lambda_s)$ at date 2 in both states. This will leave expected utility unchanged if and only if $U'(c_{1s}) = RU'(c_{2s})$, which is impossible if $c_{1s} = c_{2s}$. So the case illustrated in Figure 8.2 cannot arise. This leaves us with the case illustrated in Figure 8.3 or the case illustrated in Figure 8.4.

In either of the cases illustrated in Figures 8.3 and 8.4 the level of consumption depends on the state of nature at both date 1 and date 2. This is problematic

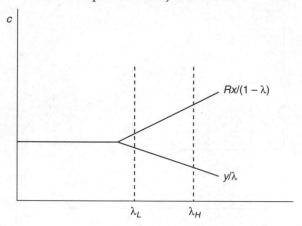

**Figure 8.4.** Consumption $c_1$ and $c_2$ at dates 1 and 2, respectively, as functions of the proportion $\lambda$ of early consumers.

for the intermediary if it is restricted, for informational reasons or because of transaction costs, to using simple debt contracts, that is, deposit contracts that promise a fixed amount of consumption at each date. A deposit contract cannot reproduce the consumption patterns shown in Figures 8.3 and 8.4.

Default can introduce some additional contingency, and under very special conditions it may allow the intermediary to achieve the first-best allocation, but it may also introduce deadweight costs that lead to a loss of welfare.

Here is where a nominal contract may have advantages. Suppose the intermediary promises to pay the depositor $D$ units of money either at date 1 or at date 2, depending when he chooses to withdraw. If the price level (i.e. the price of the good in terms of money) is denoted by $p_{ts}$ at date $t = 1, 2$ in state $s = H, L$, then the consumers' consumption must satisfy

$$p_{1H} c_{1H} = p_{2H} c_{2H} = p_{1L} c_{1L} = p_{2L} c_{2L} = D.$$

If the central bank can control the price level, it can ensure that the optimal consumption allocation is achieved simply by regulating the price level so that the real value of the deposit $D/p_{ts}$ equals the optimal consumption allocation in each state at each date.

Notice that the fact that $c_{1s} \leq c_{2s}$ implies that $p_{1s} \geq p_{2s}$ for each state $s$. Declining nominal prices simply implies a positive real interest rate. An alternative but equivalent approach would assume that the bank pays nominal interest on accounts, so that the early withdrawers receive $D$ and the late withdrawers receive $(1 + r)D$. This would be consistent with stable or rising prices, but would leave real values unchanged.

Given the right level of prices and a fixed nominal payment, the consumers must get the right level of consumption, but is this an equilibrium? What is going on behind these formulae? In order to pay its depositors at date 1, the intermediary has to borrow money from the central bank. It pays out this money to the depositors who demand repayment, and they in turn spend this money on goods. The banks supply goods in exchange for money and earn just enough to repay their loan to the central bank at the end of the period. The same procedure is followed at date 2. Again, we need to distinguish cases where the early consumers consume the entire returns to the short asset from the case where there is excess liquidity and some of the short asset is rolled over to the last date. In the first case, we have $c_{1s} < c_{2s}$ and $p_{1s} > p_{2s}$. The nominal return to holding the short asset until date 2 is $p_{2s} - p_{1s} < 0$, so the bank should be willing to sell all of the goods it produces from the short asset and this is what happens in equilibrium since $\lambda_s c_{1s} = y$. On the other hand, if $\lambda_s c_{1s} < y$, then $p_{1s} = p_{2s}$ and the return on the short asset is $p_{2s} - p_{1s} = 0$ and the intermediary is content to hold back some of the goods it has produced at date 1 and reinvest them in the short asset. In either case, the market clears and the banks are doing the best they can taking the prices as given. The circular flow of income is illustrated in Figure 8.5.

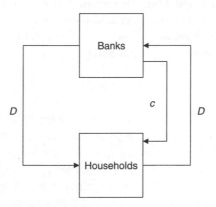

**Figure 8.5.** Banks pay deposits $D$ to households which use the money to purchase consumption $c$.

## 8.2 OPTIMAL CURRENCY CRISES

Just as a change in the domestic price level changes the real value of nominal contracts within a country, a change in the country's exchange rate changes the external value of debt denominated in the domestic currency. In this section we will develop a simple version of the model in Allen and Gale (2000) and show that appropriate adjustments in the exchange rate play a role in achieving optimal risk sharing by transferring risk from a small country to the rest of the world.

Imagine a country that is so small in relation to the rest of the world (ROW) that, for all practical purposes, we can assume that what happens in the small country has no impact on the ROW. The small country faces risk in the form of uncertainty about the size of its GDP. We assume that the rest of the world (ROW) is risk neutral and we normalize the gross return on a riskless asset to one. Optimal risk sharing between the small country and the ROW would require all risk to be borne by the risk neutral party, that is, the ROW. If the small country's output were sold on the world equity market, its value would be equal to the expected value $E[\tilde{Y}]$ of its GDP. Because of imperfections in capital markets, the ROW may not be willing to take an equity stake in the small country. If debt is used to finance investment in the small country and either (a) the debt is denominated in terms of foreign currency or (b) the exchange rate is fixed, the risk of fluctuations in GDP will be borne by the domestic investors. By contrast, if the country can issue debt denominated in the domestic currency and adjust its exchange rate appropriately, we shall see that most of the risk can be transferred to the ROW.

Domestic investors have an endowment $W$ which they want to invest. The country's output is given by a production function

$$Y = \theta F(K),$$

where $Y$ is output, $K$ is the domestic capital stock, $\theta$ (a random variable) is a productivity shock and $F(\cdot)$ is an increasing, concave function. Suppose it is possible for the domestic banking system to borrow from the ROW at the competitive rate of interest and lend to domestic entrepreneurs who invest in the domestic capital stock. In equilibrium, the marginal product of capital should equal the opportunity cost of funds, that is, the equilibrium capital stock $K^*$ should satisfy

$$E[\theta F'(K^*)] = 1.$$

The banking sector is assumed to invest in a portfolio consisting of riskless international bonds and loans to domestic producers. Domestic investors deposit their endowment $W$ in the banking sector. The banking sector buys $B$ international bonds and lends $K^*$ to domestic producers. The demand for foreign borrowing to finance investment in domestic loans and international

**Table 8.1.** Banking sector balance sheet.

| Assets | | Liabilities | |
| --- | --- | --- | --- |
| Loans | $K^*$ | Domestic deposits | $W$ |
| Securities | $B$ | Foreign deposits | $B + K^* - W$ |
| Total | $B + K^*$ | Total | $B + K^*$ |

bonds is $B + K^* - W$. Table 8.1 shows the banking sector's assets and liabilities in real terms.

We assume that the price level in the ROW is constant and equal to one, so the international currency (dollars) is equivalent to goods and the exchange rate $e$, which is the dollar price of one unit of the domestic currency, is equal to the real value of the domestic currency. Now suppose the domestic banks issue debt (deposits) equal to $D$ units of the domestic currency. Part of this is bought by domestic investors in exchange for their endowment $W$ and part by foreigners in exchange for dollars and international bonds $B$. The future exchange rate will adjust so that the real value of the debt is equal to the combined value of the country's output and the stock of foreign assets:

$$eD = \tilde{Y} + B.$$

Let $k$ be the fraction of the debt held by the ROW. Since the ROW is risk neutral, its expected return must equal the return on the safe asset, so its total expected return equals the investment it made in the small country. Thus,

$$kE[\tilde{Y} + B] = B + K^* - W,$$

or

$$k = \frac{B + K^* - W}{E[\tilde{Y} + B]}.$$

Then the residual amount held by domestic investors is given by

$$(1 - k)\left(\tilde{Y} + B\right) = \left(1 - \frac{B + K^* - W}{E[\tilde{Y} + B]}\right)\left(\tilde{Y} + B\right)$$

$$= \left(E\left[\tilde{Y}\right] - \left(K^* - W\right)\right)\frac{\tilde{Y} + B}{E[\tilde{Y} + B]}.$$

The term $\frac{\tilde{Y}+B}{E[\tilde{Y}+B]}$ is random, but as $B \to \infty$ this term converges in probability to 1 and this proves that the domestic investors share converges to a constant:

$$\lim_{B\to\infty} (1-k)\left(\tilde{Y}+B\right) = E\left[\tilde{Y}\right] - \left(K^* - W\right).$$

In other words, by borrowing a large amount and using it to form a large portfolio consisting of a small fraction of domestic loans and a large fraction of international bonds, the banking system can export most of the risk to the ROW, thus improving the welfare of risk averse domestic investors at no cost.

The role of exchange rate fluctuations in this exercise is limited to converting domestically denominated debt into an equity stake. Without this assumption, the risk would still be borne by domestic investors.

## 8.3 DOLLARIZATION AND INCENTIVES

In the preceding section we assumed that foreign investors were willing to accept debt denominated in the domestic currency and showed that this arrangement was consistent with optimal risk sharing. Two very important assumptions underlie this result. The first is that foreign investors correctly anticipate fluctuations in the future exchange rate and adjust the value of the debt accordingly. The second is that the domestic government can commit to an exchange rate policy. One of the reasons why foreign investors may be unwilling to accept debt denominated in the domestic currency is precisely the fear that the government will inflate the currency or reduce the exchange rate in order to expropriate the foreign investors. For this reason, foreign investors may insist that debt be denominated in an international currency such as the dollar. Alternatively, the government of the small country may take steps to ensure that the exchange rate will be maintained, for example, by establishing a **currency board** that pegs the exchange rate to a foreign currency and removes monetary policy from the control of the government.

By giving up control of the exchange rate and monetary policy, the government may be paying a high price to obtain foreign investment, but it has been argued that the discipline imposed by such arrangements may pay dividends to the country. A simple example based on Gale and Vives (2002) will illustrate the idea. Suppose that a representative entrepreneur wants to undertake a risky venture using foreign capital. The venture requires an investment of $K$ and produces a revenue of $Y_H$ if successful and $Y_L$ if unsuccessful, where

$$Y_H > K > Y_L > 0.$$

The probability of success depends on the effort taken by the entrepreneur. If the entrepreneur takes effort the probability of success is $\pi > 0$; otherwise it is zero. The cost of effort is $C$.

Suppose that the entrepreneur finances his project by issuing real or dollar bonds with face value $D$. Foreign investors are assumed to be risk neutral and the return on the safe asset is one, so the foreign investors are willing to lend $K$ if and only if the expected repayment is equal to $K$. If the entrepreneur takes no effort, the output will be $Y_L$ with probability one, so the most the investors will receive is $Y_L$ which is less than $K$. So the investors will not be willing to buy the bonds issued by the entrepreneur unless they are sure that he will make an effort.

Now suppose that the entrepreneur makes an effort. If the project is successful, he can repay $D < Y_H$ but if the project fails he can only repay $Y_L < D$. Thus, the total repayment is

$$\pi D + (1 - \pi)Y_L = K,$$

which implies that $\pi D = K - (1 - \pi)Y_L$. In the event of success, the entrepreneur receives a profit of $Y_H - D$; in the event of failure he receives nothing. Thus, his expected profit is

$$\pi(Y_H - D) = \pi Y_H + (1 - \pi)Y_L - K.$$

If effort is costly, the profit he receives may not be sufficient to encourage the entrepreneur to undertake the effort required to make the project successful with probability $\pi$. If the cost of effort is $C$ then

$$\pi Y_H + (1 - \pi)Y_L - K < C.$$

Suppose next that he gets a private benefit $B$ from the success of the project, for example, he develops a reputation as a successful entrepreneur that allows him to take advantage of future profitable opportunities. Then if

$$\pi Y_H + (1 - \pi)Y_L - K + \pi B > C$$

the entrepreneur is willing to undertake the project with costly effort and everyone is happy.

Now suppose that the entrepreneur borrows in the domestic currency and the exchange rate $e$ is controlled by the government. Ex ante, the government has an incentive to say that it will maintain the exchange rate in order to encourage foreign investment. Ex post, if the investment projects are unsuccessful, it has an incentive to reduce the exchange rate so that the face value of the debt is only $eD = Y_L$. This allows the entrepreneur to retain his private benefit $B$ from avoiding default and still allows the foreign investors to retain their claim to the output $Y_L$ in the low state. It might be thought that since the foreign investors receive the same payment in each state, they do not care whether the domestic currency is devalued or not. They should care because the entrepreneur's incentives have changed. Since he receives the private benefit $B$ in any event, it no longer affects his willingness to take effort. The net gain to taking effort is now

$$\pi Y_H + (1 - \pi) Y_L - K < C,$$

so the entrepreneur does not take effort, the outcome is $Y_L$ for sure, and the foreign investors are unwilling to finance the project.

## 8.4 LITERATURE REVIEW

### Money and banking crises

Most models of banking crises, such as those discussed in Chapter 3, do not consider the role of money. Banks contract with depositors in real terms. Allen and Gale (1998) showed how the use of nominal deposit contracts and the injection of money by a central bank could prevent crises. As discussed above, variations in the price level allowed risk to be shared and acted as a substitute for state contingent contracts.

Smith (2002) considers a model where spatial separation and limited communication introduces a role for money into a standard banking model with early and late consumers. He shows that the lower the inflation rate and nominal interest rate, the lower is the probability of a banking crisis. Reducing the inflation rate to zero in line with the Friedman rule eliminates banking crises. However, this is inefficient as it leads banks to hold excessive cash reserves at the expense of investment in higher yielding assets.

In addition to the literature on money and banking crises, there is also a literature on how the cost of bail-outs after banking crises should be funded. Should they be paid for using tax proceeds or by money creation? Boyd et al. (2004) show that, in a general equilibrium context where savings, deposits, bank reserves, and the inflation tax base are endogenous, monetizing at least part of the cost can be desirable.

Diamond and Rajan (2001) develop a model where banks have special skills to ensure that loans are repaid. By issuing real demand deposits, banks can precommit to recoup their loans. This allows long-term projects to be funded and depositors to consume when they have liquidity needs. However, this arrangement leads to the possibility of a liquidity shortage in which banks curtail credit when there is a real shock. Diamond and Rajan (2006) introduce money and nominal deposit contracts into the model to investigate whether monetary policy can help alleviate this problem. They assume there are two sources of value for money. The first arises from the fact that money can be used to pay taxes (the fiscal value). The second is that money facilitates transactions (the transactions demand). They show that the use of money can improve risk sharing since price adjustments introduce a form of state contingency to contracts. However, this is not the only possibility. In some cases variations in the transaction value of money can lead to bank failures. Monetary intervention can help ease this problem. If the central bank buys bonds with money, this changes liquidity conditions in the market and allows banks to fund more long-term projects than would be possible in the absence of intervention. The model thus provides a different perspective on the operation of monetary policy through bank lending.

## Currency crises and twin crises

There is a large literature on currency crises. Flood and Marion (1999) provide a survey. Krugman (2000) contains a number of analyses of historic and recent currency crises. Fourçans and Franck (2003) is an excellent book on the subject. Chui and Gai (2005) explains the global games approach to analyzing crises. This literature review will therefore be kept brief.

The first-generation currency crisis models were designed to explain the problems experienced by a number of Latin American countries in the 1970's and early 1980's. An important characteristic of these episodes was that they had their origins in macroeconomic imbalances. The classic references here are Krugman (1979) and Flood and Garber (1984). These papers show how a fixed exchange rate plus a government budget deficit leads to a currency crisis. In equilibrium, there cannot be a discontinuous change in the exchange rate as this would lead to an arbitrage opportunity. Instead, the exchange rate adjusts continuously so that the real rate of return on domestic currency is equated to the real rate of return on foreign currency. The fiscal deficit is covered by a combination of depletion of foreign reserves and an inflation tax on the domestic money stock. When the exchange rate hits the level that would occur without support there is a speculative attack and reserves are exhausted.

Although the first-generation models had many nice features, they had difficulty explaining episodes such as the Exchange Rate Mechanism (ERM) crisis of 1992, in which the pound and the lira dropped out of the mechanism. First, the timing of these currency crises is very unpredictable. Second, there are often "discontinuous" jumps in exchange rates. Finally, the models assume that no steps are taken by the government to eliminate deficits.

These problems led to the development of second generation models. For example, Obstfeld (1996) shows how a conditional government policy can lead to multiple equilibria – one without a speculative attack and one with a speculative attack. The existence of multiple equilibria and uncertainty about the timing of an attack permit a discontinuous jump in the exchange rate. The outcome of the attack depends on the resources the government is willing to commit to maintain the exchange rate.

Equilibrium selection is an important issue in this literature. Morris and Shin (1998) show how asymmetric information can lead to uniqueness of equilibrium in models of currency crises as coordination games. Chui and Gai (2005) provide an excellent account of the so-called *global games approach*.

The large movements in exchange rates that occurred in many East Asian countries in 1997 led to the development of a third generation of currency crisis models. In contrast to the first and second generation models, many of the countries that experienced problems in the recent East Asian crisis had pursued consistent and sustainable macroeconomic policies. This characteristic of the recent crises prompted a re-examination of theoretical models of currency crises.

Another characteristic of the South East Asian crises is the simultaneous crises that occurred in the banking systems of these countries. Kaminsky and Reinhart (1999) have investigated the relationship between banking crises and currency crises. They find that in the 1970's, when financial systems were highly regulated in many countries, currency crises were not accompanied by banking crises. However, after the financial liberalization that occurred during the 1980's, currency crises and banking crises became intertwined. The usual sequence of events is that problems in the banking sector are followed by a currency crisis and this in turn exacerbates and deepens the banking crisis. Although banking crises typically precede currency crises, the common cause of both is usually a fall in asset values due to a recession or a weak economy. Often the fall is part of a boom–bust cycle that follows financial liberalization. It appears to be rare that banking and currency crises occur when economic fundamentals are sound.

In recent episodes, despite the apparent inter-relationship between currency crises and banking crises, the literatures on these topics have for the most part developed separately. Important exceptions are Chang and Velasco (2000, 2001). The first paper develops a model of currency and banking crises based on the Diamond and Dybvig (1983) model of bank runs. Chang and Velasco introduce money as an argument in the utility function. A central bank controls the ratio of currency to consumption. Different exchange rate regimes correspond to different rules for regulating the currency-consumption ratio. There is no aggregate uncertainty in these models: banking and currency crises are "sunspot" phenomena. In other words, there are at least two equilibria, a "good" equilibrium in which early consumers receive the proceeds from short-term assets and late consumers receive the proceeds from long-term assets and a "bad" equilibrium in which everybody believes a crisis will occur and these beliefs are self-fulfilling. Chang and Velasco (2000) shows that the existence of the bad equilibrium depends on the exchange rate regime in force. In some regimes, only the good equilibrium exists; in other regimes there exists a bad equilibrium in addition to the good equilibrium. The selection of the good or the bad equilibrium is not modeled. In Chang and Velasco (2001) a similar model is used to analyze recent crises in emerging markets. Again, there is no aggregate uncertainty and crises are sunspot phenomena.

Corsetti et al. (1999) have developed a model of twin crises designed to explain the Asian meltdown in 1997. The basic reason that twin crises occur in their framework is because of moral hazard arising from government guarantees. Foreigners are willing to lend for unprofitable projects against the promise of future government bailouts. When the project payoffs turn out to be low there will be a banking crisis. The prospect of the government using seigniorage to finance the bailouts leads to the prospect of inflation and so the currency also collapses.

Kaminsky and Reinhart's (1999) finding that crises are related to economic fundamentals is consistent with work on US financial crises in the nineteenth and early twentieth centuries. Gorton (1988) and Calomiris and Gorton (1991) argue that the evidence is consistent with the hypothesis that banking crises are an essential part of the business cycle rather than a sunspot phenomenon. As discussed above, Allen and Gale (2000) extends the model of Allen and Gale (1998) to consider twin crises. A model is developed in which the "twin" crises result from low asset returns. Large movements in exchange rates are desirable to the extent that they allow better risk sharing between a country's bank depositors and the international bond market.

## Dollarization

De Nicoló et al. (2003) point out that the domestic use of foreign currency, in other words dollarization, has increased substantially in recent years. According to Galindo and Leiderman (2005), this has been particularly true in Latin America. Some countries have adopted the use of foreign currency entirely but most have adopted a mixed system where dollars (or euros) are used alongside the domestic currency.

What are the benefits of dollarization? Dollarization began in most countries as a reaction to high inflation rates and a way to protect the value of savings. De Nicoló et al. (2003) find that dollarization leads to more financial intermediation only if inflation rates are already high. The theory of Gale and Vives (2002), discussed above, suggests that another benefit of full dollarization is the disciplining of firms.

The potential problems associated with dollarization are more varied. Although it is often argued that dollarization limits the abilities of governments to act independently, Reinhart et al. (2003) do not find significant differences in the ability of governments in partially dollarized economies to control inflation or stabilize output. They also find that revenue from seigniorage is generally independent of the level of dollarization. Citing the example of Peru, Galindo and Leiderman (2005) argue that partial dollarization does not prevent countries from running an independent monetary policy. However, dollarization does appear to make countries more vulnerable to adverse shocks.

## 8.5 CONCLUDING REMARKS

Most of this book is concerned with theories of crises where contracts are in real terms. This chapter has considered the effect of allowing contracts to be in nominal terms and money to be introduced into the analysis. Three effects have been focused on. The first is that variations in the price level allow nominal debt to become effectively state contingent so that risk sharing is improved. The second is that fluctuations in the exchange rate, combined with foreign holdings of domestic debt and domestic holdings of foreign debt, allow risk to be transferred away from the domestic economy to diversified international investors. Finally, complete dollarization may provide good incentives to firms. This is only a small subset of the topics related to the interaction of monetary policy and financial crises. Much work remains to be done in this area. The next chapter considers a way in which expansive monetary policy can lead to financial crises through the creation of bubbles.

## REFERENCES

Allen, F. and D. Gale (1998). "Optimal Financial Crises," *Journal of Finance* 53, 1245–1284.

Allen, F. and D. Gale (2000). "Optimal Currency Crises," *Carnegie-Rochester Conference Series on Public Policy* 53, 177–230.

Boyd, J., C. Chang, and B. Smith (2004). "Deposit Insurance and Bank Regulation in a Monetary Economy: A General Equilibrium Exposition," *Economic Theory* 24, 741–767.

Calomiris, C. and G. Gorton (1991). "The Origins of Banking Panics, Models, Facts, and Bank Regulation," in R. Hubbard (ed.), *Financial Markets and Financial Crises*, Chicago, IL: University of Chicago Press.

Chang, R. and A. Velasco (2000). "Financial Fragility and the Exchange Rate Regime," *Journal of Economic Theory* 92, 1–34.

Chang, R. and A. Velasco (2001). "A Model of Financial Crises in Emerging Markets," *Quarterly Journal of Economics* 116, 489–517.

Chui, M. and P. Gai (2005). *Private Sector Involvement and International Financial Crises*, Oxford and NewYork: Oxford University Press.

Corsetti, G., P. Pesenti, and N. Roubini (1999). "Paper Tigers? A Model of the Asian Crisis," *European Economic Review* 43, 1211–1236.

De Nicoló, G., P. Honohan, and I. Ize (2003). "Dollarization of the Banking System: Good or Bad?" World Bank Policy Research Working Paper 3116, Washington, DC.

Diamond, D. and P. Dybvig (1983). "Bank Runs, Deposit Insurance, and Liquidity," *Journal of Political Economy* 91, 401–419.

Diamond, D. and R. Rajan (2001). "Liquidity Risk, Liquidity Creation and Financial Fragility: A Theory of Banking," *Journal of Political Economy* 109, 287–327.

Diamond, D. and R. Rajan (2006). "Money in a Theory of Banking," *American Economic Review* 96, 30–53.

Flood, R. and P. Garber (1984). "Gold Monetization and Gold Discipline," *Journal of Political Economy* 92, 90–107.

Flood, R. and N. Marion (1999). "Perspectives on the Recent Currency Crisis Literature," *International Journal of Finance & Economics* 4, 1–26.

Fourçans, A. and R. Franck (2003). *Currency Crises: A Theoretical and Empirical Perspective*, Cheltenham, UK; Northampton, MA, USA: Edward Elgar.

Gale, D. and X. Vives (2002). "Dollarization, Bailouts, and the Stability of the Banking System," *Quarterly Journal of Economics* 117, 467–502.

Galindo, A. and L. Leiderman (2005). "Living with Dollarization and the Route to Dedollarization," Inter-American Development Bank, Research Department, Working Paper #526.

Gorton, G. (1988). "Banking Panics and Business Cycles, *Oxford Economic Papers* 40, 751–781.

Kaminsky, G. and C. Reinhart (1999). "The Twin Crises: The Causes of Banking and Balance-of-Payments Problems," *American Economic Review* 89, 473–500.

Krugman, P. (1979). "A Model of Balance of Payments Crises," *Journal of Money, Credit and Banking* 11, 311–325.

Krugman, P. (ed.) (2000). *Currency Crises*, National Bureau of Economic Research, Chicago: The University of Chicago Press.

Morris, S. and H. Shin (1998). "Unique Equilibrium in a Model of Self-Fulfilling Currency Attacks," *American Economic Review* 88, 587–597.

Obstfeld, M. (1996). "Models of Currency Crises with Self-fulfilling Features," *European Economic Review* 40, 1037–1047.

Reinhart, C., K. Rogoff, and M. Savastano (2003) "Addicted to Dollars," NBER Working Paper 10015.

Smith, B. (2002). "Monetary Policy, Banking Crises, and the Friedman Rule," *American Economic Review* 92, 128–134.

# 9

## Bubbles and crises

In the previous chapter we considered the role of money and the price level in sharing risk. In this chapter we consider the role of money and credit in the determination of asset prices and the prevention of crises. The idea that the amount of money and credit available is an important factor in the determination of asset prices is not new. In his description of historic bubbles Kindleberger (1978, p. 54) emphasizes the role of this factor: "Speculative manias gather speed through expansion of money and credit or perhaps, in some cases, get started because of an initial expansion of money and credit."

In many recent cases where asset prices have risen and then collapsed dramatically an expansion in credit following financial liberalization appears to have been an important factor. Perhaps the best known example of this type of phenomenon is the dramatic rise in real estate and stock prices that occurred in Japan in the late 1980's and their subsequent collapse in 1990. Financial liberalization throughout the 1980's and the desire to support the US dollar in the latter part of the decade led to an expansion in credit. During most of the 1980's asset prices rose steadily, eventually reaching very high levels. For example, the Nikkei 225 index was around 10,000 in 1985. On December 19, 1989 it reached a peak of 38,916. A new Governor of the Bank of Japan, less concerned with supporting the US dollar and more concerned with fighting inflation, tightened monetary policy and this led to a sharp increase in interest rates in early 1990 (see Frankel 1993; Tschoegl 1993). The bubble burst. The Nikkei 225 fell sharply during the first part of the year and by October 1, 1990 it had sunk to 20,222. Real estate prices followed a similar pattern. The next few years were marked by defaults and retrenchment in the financial system. The real economy was adversely affected by the aftermath of the bubble and growth rates during the 1990's were typically slightly positive or negative, in contrast to most of the post-war period when they were much higher.

Similar events occurred in Norway, Finland, and Sweden in the 1980's (see Heiskanen 1993; Drees and Pazarbasioglu 1995; Englund and Vihriälä 2006). In Norway the ratio of bank loans to nominal GDP went from 40 percent in 1984 to 68 percent in 1988. Asset prices soared while investment and consumption also increased significantly. The collapse in oil prices helped burst the bubble and caused the most severe banking crisis and recession since the war. In Finland an expansionary budget in 1987 resulted in massive credit expansion. The ratio of bank loans to nominal GDP increased from 55 percent in 1984 to 90 percent in 1990. Housing prices rose by a total of 68 percent in 1987 and 1988. In 1989 the central bank increased interest rates and imposed reserve requirements to moderate credit expansion. In 1990 and 1991 the economic situation was exacerbated by a fall in trade with the Soviet Union. Asset prices collapsed, banks had to be supported by the government and GDP shrank by 7 percent. In Sweden a steady credit expansion through the late 1980's led to a property boom. In the fall of 1990 credit was tightened and interest rates rose. In 1991 a number of banks had severe difficulties because of lending based on inflated asset values. The government had to intervene and a severe recession followed.

Mexico provides a dramatic illustration of an emerging economy affected by this type of problem. In the early 1990's the banks were privatized and a financial liberalization occurred. Perhaps most significantly, reserve requirements were eliminated. Mishkin (1997) documents how bank credit to private non-financial enterprises went from a level of around 10 percent of GDP in the late 1980's to 40 percent of GDP in 1994. The stock market rose significantly during the early 1990's. In 1994 the Colosio assassination and the uprising in Chiapas triggered the collapse of the bubble. The prices of stocks and other assets fell and banking and foreign exchange crises occurred. These were followed by a severe recession.

These examples suggest a relationship between the occurrence of significant rises in asset prices or *positive* bubbles and monetary and credit policy. They also illustrate that the collapse in the bubble can lead to severe problems because the fall in asset prices leads to strains on the banking sector. Banks holding real estate and stocks with falling prices (or with loans to the owners of these assets) often come under severe pressure from withdrawals because their liabilities are fixed. This forces them to call in loans and liquidate their assets which in turn appears to exacerbate the problem of falling asset prices. In other words there may be *negative* asset price bubbles as well as positive ones. These negative bubbles where asset prices fall too far can be very damaging to the banking system. This can make the problems in the real economy more severe than they need have been. In addition to the role of monetary and credit policy in causing positive price bubbles there is also the question of whether monetary policy has a role to play in preventing asset prices from falling too far. In the Scandinavian and Mexican examples discussed above, asset prices quickly rebounded and the spillovers to the real economy were relatively short-lived. In Japan asset prices did not rebound for a long time and the real economy has been much less robust. It was only in 2005 that the economy started to grow strongly again.

Despite the apparent empirical importance of the relationship between monetary policy and asset price bubbles there is no widely agreed theory of what underlies these relationships. This chapter considers the relationship between asset price bubbles, financial crises and the role of the central bank. Section 9.1 looks at the relationship between credit expansion and positive bubbles. Allen and Gale (2000) provide a theory of this based on the existence of an agency problem. Many investors in real estate and stock markets obtain their investment funds from external sources. If the ultimate providers of funds are unable to observe the characteristics of the investment, there is a classic *risk-shifting* problem. Risk shifting increases the return to investment in risky assets and causes investors to bid up prices above their fundamental values. A crucial determinant of asset prices is thus the amount of credit that is provided. Financial liberalization, by expanding the volume of credit and creating uncertainty about the future path of credit expansion, can interact with the agency problem and lead to a bubble in asset prices.

When the bubble bursts either because returns are low or because the central bank tightens credit, banks are put under severe strain. Many of their liabilities are fixed while their assets fall in value. Depositors and other claimants may decide to withdraw their funds in anticipation of problems to come. This will force banks to liquidate some of their assets and this may result in a further fall in asset bubbles because of a lack of liquidity in the market. Section 9.2 considers how such negative bubbles arise. Rather than focusing on the relationship between the bank and borrowers who make investment decisions as in Section 9.1, the focus is on depositors and their decisions. It is shown that when there is a market for risky assets then their price is determined by "cash-in-the-market pricing" in some states and can fall below their fundamental value. This leads to an inefficient allocation of resources. The central bank can eliminate this inefficiency by an appropriate injection of liquidity into the market.

Finally, Section 9.3 contains concluding remarks.

## 9.1 AGENCY PROBLEMS AND POSITIVE BUBBLES

How can the positive bubbles and ensuing crashes in Japan, Scandinavia, and Mexico mentioned above be understood? The typical sequence of events in such crises is as follows.

There is initially a financial liberalization of some sort and this leads to a large expansion in credit. Bank lending increases by a significant amount. Some of this lending finances new investment but much of it is used to buy assets in fixed supply such as real estate and stocks. Since the supply of these assets is fixed the prices rise above their "fundamentals." Practical problems in short selling such assets prevent the prices from being bid down as standard theory suggests. The process continues until there is some real event that means returns on the assets will be low in the future. Another possibility is that the central bank is forced to restrict credit because of fears of "overheating" and inflation. The result of one or both of these events is that the prices of real estate and stocks collapse. A banking crisis results because assets valued at "bubble" prices were used as collateral. There may be a foreign exchange crisis as investors pull out their funds and the central bank chooses between trying to ease the banking crisis or protect the exchange rate. The crises spill over to the real economy and there is a recession.

In the popular press and academic papers, these bubbles and crises are often related to the particular features of the country involved. However, the fact that a similar sequence of events can occur in such widely differing countries as Japan, Norway, Finland, Sweden, and Mexico suggest such bubbles and crashes are a general phenomenon.

How can this phenomenon be understood? The crucial issues we will focus on below are:

   (i)  What initiates a bubble?

  (ii)  What is the role of the banking system?

 (iii)  What causes a bubble to burst?

## 9.1.1 The risk-shifting problem

A simple example from Allen and Gale (2004) is developed to illustrate the model in Allen and Gale (2000).[1] They develop a theory based on rational behavior to try and provide some insight into these issues. Standard models of asset pricing assume people invest with their own money. We identify the price of an asset in this benchmark case as the "fundamental." A bubble is said to occur when the price of an asset rises above this benchmark.[2] If the people making investment decisions borrow money then because of default they are only interested in the upper part of the distribution of returns of the risky asset. As a result there is a risk-shifting problem and the price of the risky asset is bid up above the benchmark so there is a bubble.

---

[1] For ease of exposition the example is slightly different from the model presented in the paper.
[2] See Allen et al. (1993) for a discussion of the definition of fundamental and bubble.

In the example the people who make investment decisions do so with borrowed money. If they default there is limited liability. Lenders cannot observe the riskiness of the projects invested in so there is an agency problem. For the case of real estate this representation of the agency problem is directly applicable. For the case of stocks there are margin limits that prevent people directly borrowing and investing in the asset. However, a more appropriate interpretation in this case is that it is institutional investors making the investment decisions. This group constitutes a large part of the market in many countries. The agency problem that occurs is similar to that with a debt contract. First, the people that supply the funds have little control over how they are invested. Second, the reward structure is similar to what happens with a debt contract. If the assets the fund managers invest in do well, the managers attract more funds in the future and receive higher payments as a result. If the assets do badly there is a limit to the penalty that is imposed on the managers. The worse that can happen is that they are fired. This is analogous to limited liability (see Allen and Gorton 1993).

Initially there are two dates $t = 1, 2$. There are two assets in the example. The first is a safe asset in variable supply. For each 1 unit invested in this asset at date 1 the output is 1.5 at date 2. The second is a risky asset in fixed supply that can be thought of as real estate or stocks. There is 1 unit of this risky asset. For each unit purchased at price $P$ at date 1 the output is 6 with probability 0.25 and 1 with probability 0.75 at date 2 so the expected payoff is 2.25. The details of the two assets are given in Table 9.1.

## The fundamental

Suppose each investor has wealth 1 initially and invests her own wealth directly. Since everybody is risk neutral the marginal returns on the two assets must be equated:

$$\frac{2.25}{P_F} = \frac{1.5}{1}$$

Table 9.1. All agents in the model are assumed to be risk neutral.

| Asset | Supply | Investment at date 1 | Payoff at date 2 |
|-------|--------|----------------------|------------------|
| Safe | Variable | 1 | 1.5 |
| Risky | 1 | $P$ | $R = \begin{cases} 6 \text{ with prob. } 0.25 \\ 1 \text{ with prob. } 0.75 \\ ER = 2.25 \end{cases}$ |

or

$$P_F = \frac{2.25}{1.5} = 1.5.$$

The value of the asset is simply the discounted present value of the payoff where the discount rate is the opportunity cost of the investor. This is the classic definition of the fundamental. The benchmark value of the asset is thus 1.5 and any price above this is termed a bubble.

### Intermediated case

Suppose next that investors have no wealth of their own. They can borrow to buy assets at a rate of $33\frac{1}{3}$ percent. The most they can borrow is 1. If they borrow 1 they repay 1.33 if they are able to. If they are unable to pay this much the lender can claim whatever they have. As explained above lenders can't observe how loans are invested and this leads to an agency problem.

The first issue is can $P = 1.5$ be the equilibrium price?

Consider what happens if an investor borrows 1 and invests in the safe asset.

$$\text{Marginal return safe asset} = 1.5 - 1.33$$

$$= 0.17.$$

Suppose instead that she borrows 1 and invests in the risky asset. She purchases 1/1.5 units. When the payoff is 6 she repays the principal and interest of 1.33 and keeps what remains. When it is 1 she defaults and the entire payoff goes to the lender so she receives 0.

$$\text{Marginal return risky asset} = 0.25 \left( \frac{1}{1.5} \times 6 - 1.33 \right) + 0.75 \times 0$$

$$= 0.25(4 - 1.33)$$

$$= 0.67.$$

The risky asset is clearly preferred when $P = 1.5$ since $0.67 > 0.17$. The expected payoff of 1.5 on the investment in 1 unit of the safe asset is the same as on the investment of 1/1.5 units of the risky asset. The risky asset is more attractive to the borrower though. With the safe asset the borrower obtains 0.17 and the lender obtains 1.33. With the risky asset the borrower obtains 0.67 while the lender obtains $0.25 \times 1.33 + 0.75 \times 1 \times (1/1.5) = 1.5 - 0.67 = 0.83$. The risk of default allows 0.5 in expected value to be shifted from the lender to the borrower. This is the risk shifting problem. If the lender could prevent the borrower from investing in the risky asset he would do so but he cannot since this is unobservable.

What is the equilibrium price of the risky asset given this agency problem?

In an equilibrium where the safe asset is used, the price of the risky asset, $P$, will be bid up since it is in fixed supply, until the expected profit of borrowers is the same for both the risky and the safe asset:

$$0.25 \left( \frac{1}{P} \times 6 - 1.33 \right) + 0.75 \times 0 = 1.5 - 1.33$$

so

$$P = 3.$$

There is a bubble with the price of the risky asset above the benchmark of 1.5.

The idea that there is a risk-shifting problem when the lender is unable to observe how the borrower invests the funds is not new (see, e.g. Jensen and Meckling 1976 and Stiglitz and Weiss 1981). However, it has not been widely applied in the asset pricing literature. Instead of the standard result in corporate finance textbooks that debt-financed firms are willing to accept negative net present value investments, the manifestation of the agency problem here is that the debt-financed investors are willing to invest in assets priced above their fundamental.

The amount of risk that is shifted depends on how risky the asset is. The greater the risk the greater the potential to shift risk and hence the higher the price will be. To illustrate this consider the previous example but suppose the return on the risky asset is a mean-preserving spread of the original returns, as shown in Table 9.2. Now the price of the risky asset is given by

$$0.25 \left( \frac{1}{P} \times 9 - 1.33 \right) + 0.75 \times 0 = 1.5 - 1.33$$

Table 9.2.

| Asset | Supply | Investment at date 1 | Payoff at date 2 |
|-------|--------|----------------------|------------------|
| Risky | 1 | $P$ | $R = \begin{cases} 9 \text{ with prob. } 0.25 \\ 0 \text{ with prob. } 0.75 \end{cases}$ <br> $ER = 2.25$ |

so

$$P = 4.5.$$

More risk is shifted and as a result the price of the risky asset is bid up to an even higher level.

It is interesting to note that in both the stock market boom of the 1920's and the one in the 1990's the stocks that did best were "high-tech" stocks. In the 1920's it was radio stocks and utilities that were the star performers (see White 1990). In the 1990's it was telecommunications, media and entertainment, and technology stocks that did the best. It is precisely these stocks which have the most uncertain payoffs because of the nature of the business they are in.

One of the crucial issues is why the banks are willing to lend to the investors given the chance of default. To see this consider again the case where the payoffs on the risky asset are those in Table 9.1 and $P = 3$. In this case the quantity of the risky asset purchased when somebody borrows 1 is $1/P = 1/3$. In the equilibria considered above the investors are indifferent between investing in the safe and risky asset. Suppose for the sake of illustration the fixed supply of the risky asset is 1. The amount of funds depositors have is 10 and the number of borrowers is 10. In the equilibrium where $P = 3$, 3 of the borrowers invest in the risky asset and 7 in the safe in order for the fixed supply of 1 unit of the risky asset to be taken up. In this case 30 percent of borrowers are in risky assets and 70 percent are in safe assets. A bank's expected payoff from lending one unit is then given by the following expression.

$$\text{Bank's expected payoff} = 0.3[0.25 \times 1.33 + 0.75 \times (1/3) \times 1] + 0.7[1.33]$$
$$= 1.11.$$

The first term is the payoff to the bank from the 30 percent of investors in the risky asset. If the payoff is 6, which occurs with probability 0.25, the loan and interest is repaid in full. If the payoff is 1, which occurs with probability 0.75, the borrower defaults and the bank receives the entire proceeds from the $1/3$ unit owned by the borrower. The payoff is thus $(1/3) \times 1$. The 70 percent of investors in the safe asset are able to pay off their loan and interest of 1.33 in full.

If the banking sector is competitive the receipts from lending, 1.11, will be paid out to depositors. In this case it is the depositors that bear the cost of the agency problem. In order for this allocation to be feasible markets must be segmented. The depositors and the banks must not have access to the assets that the investors who borrow invest in. Clearly if they did they would be better off to just invest in the safe asset rather than put their money in the bank.

## 9.1.2  Credit and interest rate determination

The quantity of credit and the interest rate have so far been taken as exogenous. These factors are incorporated in the example next to illustrate the relationship between the amount of credit and the level of interest rates. We start with the simplest case where the central bank determines the aggregate amount of credit $B$ available to banks. It does this by setting reserve requirements and determining the amount of assets available for use as reserves. For ease of exposition we do not fully model this process and simply assume the central bank sets $B$. The banking sector is competitive. The number of banks is normalized at 1 and the number of investors is also normalized to 1. Each investor will therefore be able to borrow $B$ from each bank.

The return on the safe asset is determined by the marginal product of capital in the economy. This in turn depends on the amount of the consumption good $x$ that is invested at date 1 in the economy's productive technology to produce $f(x)$ units at date 2. The total amount that can be invested is $B$ and the amount that is invested at date 1 in the risky asset since there is 1 unit is $P$. Hence the date 1 budget constraint implies that

$$x = B - P.$$

It is assumed

$$f(x) = 3(B - P)^{0.5}. \tag{9.1}$$

Provided the market for loans is competitive the interest rate $r$ on bank loans will be such that

$$r = f'(B - P) = 1.5(B - P)^{-0.5}. \tag{9.2}$$

At this level borrowing and investing in the safe asset will not yield any profits for investors. If $r$ was lower than this there would be an infinite demand for bank loans to buy the safe asset. If $r$ was higher than this there would be zero demand for loans and nobody would invest in the safe asset but this is a contradiction since $f'(0) = \infty$.

The amount the investors will be prepared to pay for the risky asset assuming its payoffs are as in Table 9.1 is then given by

$$0.25 \left( \frac{1}{P} \times 6 - r \right) + 0.75 \times 0 = 0.$$

Using (9.2) in this,

$$P = 4(B - P)^{0.5}.$$

Solving for $P$ gives

$$P = 8(-1 + \sqrt{1 + 0.25B}). \tag{9.3}$$

When $B = 5$ then $P = 4$ and $r = 1.5$. The relationship between $P$ and $B$ is shown by the solid line in Figure 9.1. By controlling the amount of credit the central bank controls the level of interest rates and the level of asset prices. Note that this relationship is different from that in the standard asset pricing model when the price of the risky asset is the discounted expected payoff.

$$P_F = \frac{2.25}{r}.$$

This case is illustrated by the dotted line in Figure 9.1. A comparison of the two cases shows that the fundamental is relatively insensitive to the amount of credit compared to the case where there is an agency problem. Changes in aggregate credit can cause relatively large changes in asset prices when there is an agency problem.

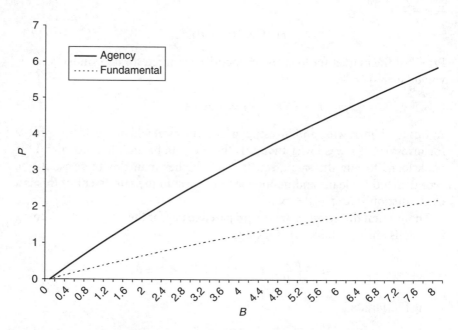

**Figure 9.1.** Credit and asset prices (from Figure 1 of Allen and Gale 2004).

### 9.1.3 Financial risk

The previous section assumed that the central bank could determine the amount of credit $B$. In practice the central bank has limited ability to control the amount of credit and this means $B$ is random. In addition there may be changes of policy preferences, changes of administration, and changes in the external environment which create further uncertainty about the level of $B$. This uncertainty is particularly great in countries undergoing financial liberalization. In order to investigate the effect of this uncertainty an extra period is added to the model. Between dates 1 and 2 everything is the same as before. Between dates 0 and 1 the only uncertainty that is resolved is about the level of $B$ at date 1. Thus between dates 0 and 1 there is *financial uncertainty*. The uncertainty about aggregate credit $B$ at date 1 causes uncertainty about prices at date 1. Given that investors are borrowing from banks at date 0 in the same way as before this price uncertainty again leads to an agency problem and risk shifting. The price of the risky asset at date 0 will reflect this price uncertainty and can lead the asset price to be even higher than at date 1.

Suppose that there is a 0.5 probability that $B = 5$ and a 0.5 probability that $B = 7$ at date 1. Then using (9.2) and (9.3) the prices and interest rates are as shown in Table 9.3.

Table 9.3.

| Probability | $B$ | $P$ | $r$ |
|---|---|---|---|
| 0.5 | 5 | 4 | 1.5 |
| 0.5 | 7 | 5.27 | 1.14 |

The pricing equation at date 0 is

$$0.5 \left( \frac{1}{P_0} \times 5.27 - r_0 \right) + 0.5 \times 0 = 0,$$

where $r_0$, the date 0 interest rate, is given by (9.2) with $B$ and $P$ replaced by $B_0$ and $P_0$. Substituting for $r_0$ and simplifying

$$P_0 = \frac{5.27}{1.5} (B_0 - P_0)^{0.5}.$$

Taking $B_0 = 6$ and solving for $r_0$ and $P_0$ gives

$$r_0 = 1.19$$

$$P_0 = 4.42.$$

As when the uncertainty is due to variations in asset returns, the greater the financial uncertainty the greater is $P_0$. Consider a mean preserving spread on the financial uncertainty so that Table 9.3 is replaced by Table 9.4.

**Table 9.4.**

| Probability | B | P | r |
|---|---|---|---|
| 0.5 | 4 | 3.14 | 1.81 |
| 0.5 | 8 | 5.86 | 1.03 |

In this case it can be shown

$$r_0 = 1.27$$
$$P_0 = 4.61.$$

The risk-shifting effect operates for financial risk in the same way as it does for real risk. Although the expected payoff at date 2 is only 2.25 the price of the risky asset at date 1 in the last case is 4.61. The possibility of credit expansion over a period of years may create a great deal of uncertainty about how high the bubble may go and when it may collapse. This is particularly true when economies are undergoing financial liberalization. As more periods are added it is possible for the bubble to become very large. The market price can be much greater than the fundamental.

### 9.1.4 Financial fragility

The examples in the previous section illustrated that what is important in determining the risky asset's price at date 0 is expectations about aggregate credit at date 1. If aggregate credit goes up then asset prices will be high and default will be avoided. However, if aggregate credit goes down then asset prices will be low and default will occur. The issue here is what is the dynamic path of aggregate credit. The point is that the expectation of credit expansion is already taken into account in the investors' decisions about how much to borrow and how much to pay for the risky asset. If credit expansion is less than expected, or perhaps simply falls short of the highest anticipated levels, the investors may not be able to repay their loans and default occurs. In Allen and Gale (2000) it is shown that even if credit is always expanded then there may still be default. In fact it is shown that there are situations where the amount of credit will be arbitrarily close to the upper bound of what is anticipated and widespread default is almost inevitable.

## 9.2 BANKING CRISES AND NEGATIVE BUBBLES

In the previous section we focused on how asset prices could get too high because of an agency problem between lenders and the people making investment decisions. In this section we consider what happens when asset prices are low relative to the fundamental. An important feature of many of the historic and recent banking crises is the collapse in asset prices that accompanies them. The purpose of this section is to consider this phenomenon using the model of Allen and Gale (1998, 2004). We start by developing a simple model and derive the optimal allocation of resources. If there is a market for risky assets that allows banks to sell their assets then the allocation is not efficient. The simultaneous liquidation of all banks' assets that accompanies a crisis leads to a negative bubble and inefficient risk sharing. However, by adopting an appropriate monetary policy a central bank can implement the optimal allocation.

### 9.2.1 The model

Time is divided into three periods $t = 0, 1, 2$. There are two types of assets, a safe asset and a risky asset, and a consumption good. The safe asset can be thought of as a storage technology, which transforms one unit of the consumption good at date $t$ into one unit of the consumption good at date $t + 1$. The risky asset is represented by a stochastic production technology that transforms one unit of the consumption good at date $t = 0$ into $R$ units of the consumption good at date $t = 2$, where $R$ is a non-negative random variable with

$$R = \begin{cases} R_H & \text{with probability } \pi \\ R_L & \text{with probability } 1 - \pi. \end{cases}$$

At date 1 depositors observe a signal, which can be thought of as a leading economic indicator, similarly to Gorton (1988). This signal predicts with perfect accuracy the value of $R$ that will be realized at date 2. Initially it is assumed that consumption can be made contingent on the leading economic indicator, and hence on $R$. Subsequently, we consider what happens when banks are restricted to offering depositors a standard deposit contract, that is, a contract which is not explicitly contingent on the leading economic indicator.

There is a continuum of ex ante identical depositors (consumers) who have an endowment of 1 of the consumption good at the first date and none at the second and third dates. Consumers are uncertain about their time preferences. Some will be *early consumers*, who only want to consume at date 1, and some will be *late consumers,* who only want to consume at date 2. At date 0 consumers know the probability of being an early or late consumer, but they do not know which group they belong to. All uncertainty is resolved at date 1 when each consumer learns whether he is an early or late consumer and what the return on the risky asset is going to be. For simplicity, we assume that there are equal numbers of early and late consumers and that each consumer has an equal chance of belonging to each group. Then a typical consumer's expected utility can be written as

$$\lambda U(c_1) + (1 - \lambda) U(c_2) \tag{9.4}$$

where $c_t$ denotes consumption at date $t = 1, 2$. The period utility functions $U(\cdot)$ are assumed to be twice continuously differentiable, increasing and strictly concave. A consumer's type is not observable, so late consumers can always imitate early consumers. Therefore, contracts explicitly contingent on this characteristic are not feasible.

The role of banks is to make investments on behalf of consumers. We assume that only banks can hold the risky asset. This gives the bank an advantage over consumers in two respects. First, the banks can hold a portfolio consisting of both types of assets, which will typically be preferred to a portfolio consisting of the safe asset alone. Second, by pooling the assets of a large number of consumers, the bank can offer insurance to consumers against their uncertain liquidity demands, giving the early consumers some of the benefits of the high-yielding risky asset without subjecting them to the volatility of the asset market.

Free entry into the banking industry forces banks to compete by offering deposit contracts that maximize the expected utility of the consumers. Thus, the behavior of the banking industry can be represented by an optimal risk-sharing problem. A variety of different risk-sharing problems can be used to represent different assumptions about the informational and regulatory environment.

### 9.2.2 Optimal risk sharing

Initially consider the case where banks can write contracts in which the amount that can be withdrawn at each date is contingent on $R$. This provides a benchmark for optimal risk sharing. Since the risky asset return is not known until the second date, the portfolio choice is independent of $R$, but the payments to early and late consumers, which occur after $R$ is revealed, will depend on it. Let $y$ and $x = 1 - y$ denote the representative bank's holding of the risky and safe assets, respectively. The deposit contract can be represented by a pair of functions, $c_1(R)$ and $c_2(R)$ which give the consumption of early and late consumers conditional on the return to the risky asset.

The optimal risk-sharing problem can be written as follows.

$$
\begin{aligned}
\max \quad & E[\lambda U(c_1(R)) + (1 - \lambda)U(c_2(R))] \\
\text{s.t.} \quad \text{(i)} \quad & y + x \leq 1; \\
\text{(ii)} \quad & \lambda c_1(R) \leq y; \\
\text{(iii)} \quad & \lambda c_1(R) + (1 - \lambda)c_2(R) \leq y + Rx; \\
\text{(iv)} \quad & c_1(R) \leq c_2(R).
\end{aligned}
\tag{9.5}
$$

The first constraint says that the total amount invested must be less than or equal to the amount deposited. There is no loss of generality in assuming that consumers deposit their entire wealth with the bank, since anything they can do the bank can do for them. The second constraint says that the holding of the safe asset must be sufficient to provide for the consumption of the early consumers at date 1. The bank may want to hold strictly more than this amount and roll it over to the final period, in order to reduce the uncertainty of the late consumers. The next constraint, together with the preceding one, says that the consumption of the late consumers cannot exceed the total value of the risky asset plus the amount of the safe asset left over after the early consumers are paid off, that is,

$$
(1 - \lambda)c_2(R) \leq (y - \lambda c_1(R)) + Rx.
\tag{9.6}
$$

The final constraint is the incentive compatibility constraint. It says that for every value of $R$, the late consumers must be at least as well off as the early consumers. Since late consumers are paid off at date 2, an early consumer cannot imitate a late consumer. However, a late consumer can imitate an early consumer, obtain $c_1(R)$ at date 1, and use the storage technology to provide himself with $c_1(R)$ units of consumption at date 2. It will be optimal to do this unless $c_1(R) \leq c_2(R)$ for every value of $R$.

The following assumptions are maintained throughout the section to ensure interior optima. The preferences and technology are assumed to satisfy the inequalities

$$
E[R] > 1
\tag{9.7}
$$

and

$$
U'(0) > E[U'(RE)R].
\tag{9.8}
$$

The first inequality ensures a positive amount of the risky asset is held while the second ensures a positive amount of the safe asset is held.

An examination of the optimal risk-sharing problem shows us that the incentive constraint (iv) can be dispensed with. To see this, suppose that we solve the problem subject to the first three constraints only. A necessary condition for an optimum is that the consumption of the two types be equal, unless the feasibility constraint $\lambda c_1(R) \leq y$ is binding, in which case it follows from the first-order conditions that $c_1(R) \leq c_2(R)$. Thus, the incentive constraint will always be satisfied if we optimize subject to the first three constraints only and the solution to (9.5) is the first-best allocation.

It can be shown that the solution to the problem is

$$c_1(R) = c_2(R) = y + Rx \text{ if } \frac{y}{\lambda} \geq \frac{Rx}{1-\lambda}, \tag{9.9}$$

$$c_1(R) = y/\lambda, \, c_2(R) = Rx/(1-\lambda) \text{ if } \frac{y}{\lambda} < \frac{Rx}{1-\lambda}, \tag{9.10}$$

$$y + x = 1 \tag{9.11}$$

$$E[U'(c_1(R))] = E[U'(c_2(R))R]. \tag{9.12}$$

(See Allen and Gale 1998 for a formal derivation of this.)

The optimal allocation is illustrated in Figure 9.2. When the signal at date 1 indicates that $R = 0$ at date 2, both the early and late consumers receive $y$ since $y$ is all that is available and it is efficient to equate consumption given the form of the objective function. The early consumers consume their share $\lambda y$ at date 1 with the remaining $(1 - \lambda)y$ carried over until date 2 for the late consumers. As $R$ increases both groups can consume more until $y/\lambda = \bar{R}x/(1-\lambda)$. Provided $R < (1-\lambda)y/\lambda x \equiv \bar{R}$ the optimal allocation involves carrying over some of

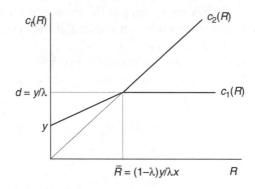

**Figure 9.2.** Optimal risk sharing.

the liquid asset to date 2 to supplement the low returns on the risky asset for late consumers. When the signal indicates that $R$ will be high at date 2 (i.e. $R \geq (1 - \lambda)y/\lambda x \equiv \bar{R}$), then early consumers should consume as much as possible at date 1 which is $y/\lambda$ since consumption at date 2 will be high in any case. Ideally, the high date 2 output would be shared with the early consumers at date 1, but this is not technologically feasible. It is only possible to carry forward consumption, not bring it back from the future.

To illustrate the operation of the optimal contract, we adopt the following numerical example:

$$U = \ln(c_t);$$

$$EU = 0.5 \ln(c_1) + 0.5 \ln(c_2); \tag{9.13}$$

$$R = \begin{cases} 2 & \text{with probability } 0.9; \\ 0.6 & \text{with probability } 0.1. \end{cases}$$

For these parameters, it can readily be shown that $(y, x) = (0.514, 0.486)$ and $\bar{R} = 1.058$. The levels of consumption are

$$c_1(2) = 1.028; c_2(2) = 1.944 \quad \text{with probability } 0.9;$$
$$c_1(0.6) = c_2(0.6) = 0.806 \quad \text{with probability } 0.1.$$

The level of expected utility achieved is $EU = 0.290$.

### 9.2.3 Optimal deposit contracts

Suppose next that contracts can't be explicitly conditioned on $R$. Let $d$ denote the fixed payment promised to the early consumers at date 1. Initially we assume there is no market for the long term asset. If the bank is unable to make the payment $d$ to all those requesting it at date 1 then the short-term asset that it does have is split up equally between them. Since the banking sector is competitive and the objective of the bank is to maximize the expected utility of depositors the late consumers will always be paid whatever is available at the last date. In that case, in equilibrium the early and late consumers will have the same consumption.

It can straightforwardly be seen in the example that the optimal allocation can be implemented using a deposit contract. To do this the bank chooses $(y, x) = (0.514, 0.486)$ and sets $d = 1.028$. Anything left over at date 2 is distributed equally among the remaining depositors. When $R = R_H = 2$ the bank uses all the short asset to pay out to its early consumers and they receive $c_1(2) = d = 0.514/0.5 = 1.028$. The late consumers receive $c_2(2) = 0.486 \times 2/0.5 = 1.944$.

When $R = R_L = 0.6$ the late consumers can calculate that if all the early consumers were to receive $d = 1.028$ and exhaust all the short asset then the amount remaining for each late consumer at date 2 would be

$$\frac{0.6 \times 0.486}{0.5} = 0.583 < 1.028.$$

Thus some of the late consumers will also withdraw at date 1. This means the bank will not be able to satisfy all those withdrawing. Since there is no market for the long asset, what happens is that the available proceeds are split equally among those asking to withdraw, as explained above. Suppose $\alpha(0.6)$ late consumers withdraw early, then the $\lambda + \alpha(0.6)$ withdrawing early and the $1 - \lambda - \alpha(0.6)$ withdrawing late will have the same expected utility when

$$\frac{y}{\lambda + \alpha(0.6)} = \frac{Rx}{1 - \lambda - \alpha(0.6)}.$$

Substituting

$$\frac{0.514}{0.5 + \alpha(0.6)} = \frac{0.6 \times 0.486}{1 - 0.5 - \alpha(0.6)}$$

and solving for $\alpha(0.6)$ gives

$$\alpha(0.6) = 0.138.$$

Hence the consumption of everybody is

$$c_1(0.6) = \frac{0.514}{0.5 + 0.138} = c_2(0.6) = \frac{0.6 \times 0.486}{1 - 0.5 - 0.138} = 0.806.$$

In Allen and Gale (1998) it is shown more generally that the optimal allocation can be implemented using a deposit contract.

### 9.2.4 An asset market

Suppose next that there is a competitive market for liquidating the long-term asset for price $P$. If the bank can make the payment $d$ to the depositors who request to withdraw at date 1 then it continues until date 2. But if the bank is unable to do this then it goes bankrupt and its assets are liquidated and distributed on a pro rata basis among its depositors. Then the standard deposit contract promises the early consumers either $d$ or, if that is infeasible, an equal share of the liquidated assets.

The participants in the long-term asset market are the banks, who use it to obtain liquidity, and a large number of wealthy, risk neutral speculators who hope to make a profit in case some bank has to sell off assets cheaply to get liquidity. The speculators hold some cash (the safe asset) in order to purchase the risky asset when its price at date 1 is sufficiently low. The return on the cash is low, but it is offset by the prospect of speculative profits when the price of the risky asset falls below its fundamental value. Suppose the risk neutral speculators hold some portfolio $(y_s, x_s)$. They cannot short sell or borrow. In equilibrium they will be indifferent between the portfolio $(y_s, x_s)$ and putting all their money in the risky asset.

The impact of introducing the asset market can be illustrated using Figure 9.3. The graphs in this figure represent the equilibrium consumption levels of early and late consumers, respectively, as a function of the risky asset return $R$. For high values of $R$ (i.e. $R \geq R^*$), there is no possibility of a bank run. The consumption of early consumers is fixed by the standard deposit contract at $c_1(R) = d$ and the consumption of late consumers is given by the budget constraint $c_2(R) = (y + Rx - d)/(1 - \lambda)$. For lower values of $R$ ($R < R^*$), it is impossible to pay the early consumers the fixed amount $d$ promised by the standard deposit contract without violating the late consumers' incentive constraint

$$\frac{y + Rx - \lambda d}{1 - \lambda} \geq d$$

and a bank run inevitably ensues. The terms of the standard deposit contract require the bank to liquidate all of its assets at the second date if it cannot pay

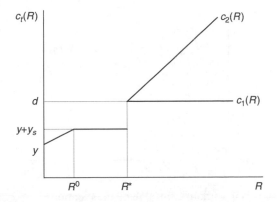

Figure 9.3. Consumption without Central Bank intervention.

*d* to every depositor who demands it. Since late withdrawers always receive as much as the early consumers by incentive compatibility, the bank has to liquidate all its assets unless it can give at least *d* to all consumers. The value of $R^*$ is determined by the condition that the bank can just afford to give everyone *d* so

$$(1 - \lambda)d = y + R^*x - \lambda d$$

or

$$R^* = \frac{d - y}{x}.$$

Below $R^*$ it is impossible for the bank to pay all the depositors *d*, and the only alternative is to liquidate all its assets at the first date and pay all consumers less than *d*. Since a late withdrawer will receive nothing, all consumers will choose to withdraw their deposits at the second date.

There is a discontinuity in the consumption profiles at the critical value of $R^*$ that marks the upper bound of the interval in which runs occur. The reason for this discontinuity is the effect of asset sales on the price of the risky asset. By selling the asset, the bank drives down the price, thus handing a windfall profit to the speculators and a windfall loss to the depositors. This windfall loss is experienced as a discontinuous drop in consumption.

The pricing of the risky asset at date 1 is shown in Figure 9.4. For $R > R^*$ the speculators continue to hold both assets and are indifferent between them. Since one unit of the safe asset is worth 1 in the last period, the fundamental value of each unit of the risky asset is $R/1 = R$. For $R < R^*$ the banks are forced to liquidate all of their assets. Now the speculators can use their cash to

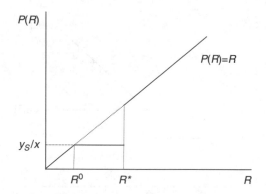

**Figure 9.4.** Asset pricing without Central Bank intervention.

buy the risky asset. Provided $R$ is such that $R_0 < R < R^*$ where

$$R_0 = \frac{y_S}{x},$$

the speculators will want to use all of their cash to buy the risky asset. The amount of cash in the market $y_S$ is insufficient to pay the fundamental value of the risky asset, so the price is determined by the ratio of the speculators' cash to the bank's holding of the risky asset

$$P(R) = \frac{y_S}{x}.$$

For $R_0 < R < R^*$ there is "cash-in-the-market pricing" and the price of the risky asset is below its fundamental value. In other words there is a negative bubble. For small values of $R$ ($R < R_0$) the fundamental value of the risky asset is less than the amount of cash in the market, so the asset price is equal to the fundamental value once again.

Since the price is independent of $R$ for $R_0 < R < R^*$ consumption is independent of $R$ in this interval as Figure 9.3 indicates. The consumption available at date 1 consists of the bank's holding of the safe asset, $y$, and the speculators' holding $y_s$. This is split among the early and late consumers so each receives $y + y_s$.

To sum up, introducing a market for the risky asset has a number of important implications. It allows the bank to liquidate all its assets to meet the demands of the early withdrawers, but this has the effect of making the situation worse. First, because a bank run exhausts the bank's assets at date 1, a late consumer who waits until date 2 to withdraw will be left with nothing, so whenever there is a bank run, it will involve all the late consumers and not just some of them. Second, if the market for the risky asset is illiquid, the sale of the representative bank's holding of the risky asset will drive down the price, thus making it harder to meet the depositors' demands.

The all-or-nothing character of bank runs is, of course, familiar from the work of Diamond and Dybvig (1983). The difference is that in the present model bank runs are not "sunspot" phenomena: they occur only when there is no other equilibrium outcome possible. Furthermore, the deadweight cost of a bank run in this case is endogenous. There is a cost resulting from suboptimal risk sharing. When the representative bank is forced to liquidate the risky asset, it sells the asset at a low price. This is a transfer of value to the purchasers of the risky asset, not an economic cost. The deadweight loss arises because the transfer occurs in bad states when the consumers' consumption is already low. In other words, the market is providing negative insurance.

The outcome with an asset market is in fact Pareto worse than the optimal allocation. The bank depositors are clearly worse off since they have lower consumption for $R_0 \leq R \leq R^*$ and the speculators are indifferent. This can be illustrated using a variant of the numerical example above. Suppose that the wealth of the speculators $W_s = 1$ and that the other parameters are as before. The optimal contract for depositors has $(y, x) = (0.545, 0.455)$, $R^0 = 0.070, R^* = 1.193$, with $P(R) = 0.070$ for $R^0 < R < R^*$ and $EU = 0.253$. For the speculators $(y_s, x_s) = (0.032, 0.968)$ and their expected utility is $EU_s = 1.86$. They receive the same level of expected utility as they would if they invested all their funds in the risky asset. Note that the depositors are significantly worse off in this equilibrium compared to the allocation corresponding to the solution to (9.5) where $EU = 0.290$.

### 9.2.5 Optimal monetary policy

The inefficiency in the allocation when there is an asset market arises from the negative bubble in asset prices. A central bank can prevent the collapse in asset prices and ensure that the allocation is the same as in Figure 9.2 by an appropriate intervention. The essential idea behind the policy that implements the solution to (9.5) is that the central bank enters into a repurchase agreement (or a collateralized loan) with the representative bank, whereby the bank sells some of its assets to the central bank at date 1 in exchange for money and buys them back for the same price at date 2. By providing liquidity in this way, the central bank ensures that the representative bank does not suffer a loss by liquidating its holdings of the risky asset prematurely.

We assume that the standard deposit contract is now written in nominal terms. The contract promises depositors a fixed amount of money $D$ in the middle period and pays out the remaining value of the assets in the last period. The price level at date $t$ in state $R$ is denoted by $p_t(R)$ and the *nominal* price of the risky asset at date 1 in state $R$ is denoted by $P(R)$. We want the risky asset to sell for its fundamental value, so we assume that $P(R) = p_1(R)R$. At this price, the safe and risky assets are perfect substitutes. Let $(y, x)$ be the portfolio corresponding to the solution of (9.5) and let $(c_1(R), c_2(R))$ be the corresponding consumption allocations. For large values of $R$, we have $c_1(R) = y/\lambda < c_2(R) = Rx/(1-\lambda)$; for smaller values we have $c_1(R) = c_2(R) = y+Rx$. Implementing this allocation requires introducing contingencies through price variation: $p_1(R)c_1(R) = D < p_2(R)c_2(R)$ for $R > \bar{R}$ and $p_1(R)c_1(R) = D = p_2(R)c_2(R)$ for $R < \bar{R}$. These equations determine the values of $p_1(R)$ and $p_2(R)$ uniquely. It remains only to determine the value of sales of assets and the size of the bank run.

In the event of a bank run, only the late consumers who withdraw early will end up holding cash, since the early consumers want to consume their entire liquidated wealth immediately. If $\alpha(R)$ is the fraction of late consumers who withdraw early, then the amount of cash injected into the system must be $\alpha(R)D$. For simplicity, we assume that the amount of cash injected is a constant $M$ and this determines the "size" of the run $\alpha(R)$. Since the safe asset and the risky asset are perfect substitutes at this point, it does not matter which assets the representative bank sells to the central bank as long as the nominal value equals $M$. The representative bank enters into a repurchase agreement under which it sells assets at date 1 for an amount of cash equal to $M$ and repurchases them at date 2 for the same cash value.

At the prescribed prices, speculators will not want to hold any of the safe assets, so $y_s = 0$ and $x_s = W_s$.

It is easy to check that all the equilibrium conditions are satisfied: depositors and speculators are behaving optimally at the given prices and the feasibility conditions are satisfied.

To summarize, the central bank can implement the solution to (9.5) by entering into a repurchase agreement with the representative bank at date 1. Given the allocation $\{(y, x), c_1(R), c_2(R)\}$, corresponding to the solution of (9.5), the equilibrium values of prices are given by the conditions $p_1(R)c_1(R) = D < p_2(R)c_2(R)$ for $R > \bar{R}$, and $p_1(R)c_1(R) = D = p_2(R)c_2(R)$ for $R < \bar{R}$. There is a fixed amount of money $M$ injected into the economy in the event of a run and the fraction of late withdrawers who "run" satisfies $\alpha(R)D = M$. The price of the risky asset at date 1 satisfies $p_1(R)R = P(R)$ and the optimal portfolio of the speculators is $(y_s, x_s) = (0, W_s)$.

It can be seen that the central bank intervention ensures that the risky asset's price is always equal to its fundamental value. This means that speculators do not profit and depositors do not lose for $R_0 \leq R \leq R^*$. As a result it is straightforward to show that the allocation is (strictly) Pareto-preferred to the equilibrium of the model with asset markets.

This can be illustrated with the numerical example. Recall that the solution to (9.5) has $(y, x) = (0.514, 0.486)$, $\bar{R} = 1.058$ and $EU = 0.290$. Suppose $D = 1.028$. For $R \geq \bar{R} = 1.058$ then $p_1(R) = p_2(R) = 1$. For $R < \bar{R} = 1.058$ the price levels at the two dates depend on the level of $R$. For the state $R_L = 0.6$, $c_1(0.6) = c_2(0.6) = 0.806$ so $p_1(0.6) = p_2(0.6) = 1.028/0.806 = 1.275$. The lower the value of $R$, the higher $p_t(R)$, so that consumption is lowered by raising the price level. Also $P(R) = 1.028 \times 0.6 = 0.617$. The fraction of late consumers who withdraw from the bank and hold money will be determined by $M$. Suppose $M = 0.1$, then $\alpha(R) = 0.1/1.028 = 0.097$. For the speculators $(y_s, x_s) = (0, 1)$ and their expected utility is $EU_s = 1.86$. The equilibrium with central bank intervention is clearly Pareto-preferred to the market equilibrium without intervention.

## 9.3 CONCLUDING REMARKS

This chapter has argued that monetary policy can have an effect on asset prices in two important ways. The first is that when there is an agency problem between banks and the people they lend to who make investment decisions asset prices can rise above their fundamental. The agency problem means that investors choose riskier projects than they otherwise would and bid up prices. The greater the risk the larger this bubble can become. It is not only the risk that is associated with real asset returns that can cause a bubble but also the financial risk associated with the uncertainties of monetary policy and particularly financial liberalization. The first important conclusion is that the central bank should keep such uncertainties to a minimum. The less uncertainty, the less the magnitude of the positive bubble.

The second problem occurs when asset prices fall. If this fall causes banks to liquidate assets simultaneously then asset prices can fall below their fundamental value. In other words there is a negative bubble. This bubble can also be very damaging. In this case it is desirable for the central bank to step in and provide liquidity and prevent asset prices falling below their fundamental value. They can do this by lending against the banks' assets.

The central bank has a complicated task to prevent both types of bubble. Moreover it is important for it to correctly identify which is the relevant problem and the appropriate policy to solve it otherwise the situation will only be exacerbated.

## REFERENCES

Allen, F. and D. Gale (1998). "Optimal Financial Crises," *Journal of Finance* 53, 1245–1284.

Allen, F. and D. Gale (2000). "Bubbles and Crises," *Economic Journal* 110, 236–255.

Allen, F. and D. Gale (2004). "Asset Price Bubbles and Monetary Policy," in M. Desai and Y. Said (eds.), *Global Governance and Financial Crises*, New York and London: Routledge, Chapter 3, 19–42.

Allen, F. and G. Gorton (1993). "Churning Bubbles," *Review of Economic Studies* 60, 813–836.

Allen, F., S. Morris, and A. Postlewaite (1993). "Finite Bubbles with Short Sale Constraints and Asymmetric Information," *Journal of Economic Theory* 61, 206–229.

Diamond, D. and P. Dybvig (1983). "Bank Runs, Deposit Insurance, and Liquidity," *Journal of Political Economy* 91, 401–419.

Drees, B. and C. Pazarbasioglu (1995). "The Nordic Banking Crises: Pitfalls in Financial Liberalization?" Working Paper 95/61, International Monetary Fund, Washington, DC.

Englund, P. and V. Vihriälä (2006). "Financial Crises in Developed Economies: The Cases of Finland and Sweden," Chapter 3 in L. Jonung (ed.), *Crises, Macroeconomic Performance and Economic Policies in Finland and Sweden in the 1990s: A Comparative Approach*, forthcoming.

Frankel, J. (1993). "The Japanese Financial System and the Cost of Capital," in S. Takagi (ed.), *Japanese Capital Markets: New Developments in Regulations and Institutions*, Oxford: Blackwell, 21–77.

Gorton, G. (1988). "Banking Panics and Business Cycles," *Oxford Economic Papers* 40, 751–781.

Heiskanen, R. (1993). "The Banking Crisis in the Nordic Countries." *Kansallis Economic Review* 2, 13–19.

Jensen, M. and W. Meckling (1976). "Theory of the Firm: Managerial Behavior, Agency Cost and Ownership Structure," *Journal of Financial Economics* 3, 305–360.

Kindleberger, C. (1978). *Manias, Panics, and Crashes: A History of Financial Crises*, New York, NY: Basic Books.

Mishkin, F. (1997). "Understanding Financial Crises: A Developing Country Perspective." *Annual World Bank Conference on Development Economics 1996*, 29–61, Washington, DC: The International Bank for Reconstruction and Development.

Stiglitz, J. and A. Weiss (1981). "Credit Rationing in Markets with Imperfect Information," *American Economic Review* 71, 393–410.

Tschoegl, A. (1993). "Modeling the Behaviour of Japanese Stock Indices," in S. Takagi (ed.), *Japanese Capital Markets: New Developments in Regulations and Institutions*, Oxford: Blackwell, 371–400.

White, E. (1990). *Crashes and Panics: The Lessons from History*, Homewood, IL: Dow Jones Irwin.

# 10

## Contagion

Financial contagion refers to the process by which a crisis that begins in one region or country spreads to an economically linked region or country. Sometimes the basis for contagion is provided by information. Kodres and Pritsker (2002), Calvo and Mendoza (2000a, b) and Calvo (2002) show how asymmetric information can give rise to contagion between countries that are affected by common fundamentals. An example is provided by asset markets in two different countries. A change in prices may result from a common shock that affects the value of assets in both countries or it may result from an idiosyncratic shock that either has no effect on asset values (a liquidity shock) or that affects only one country. Because the idiosyncratic shock can be mistaken for the common shock, a fall in prices in one country may lead to a self-fulfilling expectation that prices will fall in the other country. In that case, an unnecessary and possibly costly instability arises in the second country because of an unrelated crisis in the first.

A second type of contagion is explored in this chapter. The possibility of this kind of contagion arises from the overlapping claims that different regions or sectors of the banking system have on one another. When one region suffers a banking crisis, the other regions suffer a loss because their claims on the troubled region fall in value. If this spillover effect is strong enough, it can cause a crisis in the adjacent regions. In extreme cases, the crisis passes from region to region, eventually having an impact on a much larger area than the region in which the initial crisis occurred.

The central aim of this chapter is to provide some microeconomic foundations for financial contagion. The model developed below is not intended to be a description of any particular episode. It has some relevance to the recent Asian financial crisis. For example, Van Rijckeghem and Weder (2000) consider the interlinkages between banks in Japan and emerging countries in Asia, Latin America, and Eastern Europe. As one might expect, the Japanese banks had the most exposure in Asian emerging economies. When the Asian crisis started, in Thailand in July 1997, the Japanese banks withdrew funds not only from Thailand but also from other emerging countries, particularly from countries in Asia, where they had the most exposure. In this way, the shock of the crisis in Thailand spread to other Asian countries. European and North American banks also reacted to the Asian crisis by withdrawing funds from Asia, but they actually increased lending to Latin America and Eastern Europe. Ultimately, it was Asian countries that were most affected by the initial shock.

The model we describe below has the closest resemblance to the banking crises in the United States in the late nineteenth and early twentieth centuries (Hicks 1989). As we saw in Chapter 1, banks in the Midwest and other regions of the US held deposits in New York banks. These linkages provide a channel for spillovers between the banks if there is a financial crisis in one region.

In order to focus on the role of one particular channel for financial contagion, in what follows we exclude other propagation mechanisms that may be important for a fuller understanding of financial contagion. In particular, we assume that agents have complete information about their environment. As was mentioned above, incomplete information may create another channel for contagion. We also exclude the effect of international currency markets in the propagation of financial crises from one country to another. The role of contagion in currency crises has been extensively studied and is summarized in an excellent survey by Masson (1999).

We use our standard model with a number of slight variations that allow us to focus on contagion through interlinkages. In particular, we assume that the long asset is liquidated using a liquidation technology rather than being sold at the market price. There are three dates $t = 0, 1, 2$ and a large number of identical consumers, each of whom is endowed with one unit of a homogeneous good that can be consumed or invested. At date 1, the consumers learn whether they are early consumers, who only value consumption at date 1, or late consumers, who only value consumption at date 2. Uncertainty about their preferences creates a demand for liquidity.

Banks have a comparative advantage in providing liquidity. At the first date, consumers deposit their endowments in the banks, which invest them on behalf of the depositors. In exchange, depositors are promised a fixed amount of consumption at each subsequent date, depending on when they choose to withdraw. The bank can invest in two assets. There is a short-term asset that pays a return of one unit after one period and there is a long-term asset that can be liquidated for a return $r < 1$ after one period or held for a return of $R > 1$ after two periods. The long asset has a higher return if held to maturity, but liquidating it in the middle period is costly, so it is not very useful for providing consumption to early consumers. The banking sector is perfectly competitive, so banks offer risk-sharing contracts that maximize depositors' ex ante expected utility, subject to a zero-profit constraint.

Using this framework, we construct a simple model in which small shocks lead to large effects by means of contagion. More precisely, a shock within a single sector has effects that spread to other sectors and lead eventually to an economy-wide financial crisis. This form of contagion is driven by real shocks and real linkages between regions. As we have seen, one view is that financial crises are purely random events, unrelated to changes in the real economy (Kindleberger 1978). The modern version of this view, developed by Diamond and Dybvig (1983) and others, is that bank runs are self-fulfilling prophecies. The disadvantage of treating contagion as a "sunspot" phenomenon is that, without some real connection between different regions, any pattern of correlations is possible. So sunspot theories do not provide a causal link between crises in different regions. We adopt the alternative view that financial crises are an integral part of the business cycle (Mitchell 1941; Gorton 1988; Allen and Gale 1998) and show that, under certain circumstances, any equilibrium of the model *must* be characterized by contagion.

The economy consists of a number of regions. The number of early and late consumers in each region fluctuates randomly, but the aggregate demand for liquidity is constant. This allows for interregional insurance as regions with liquidity surpluses provide liquidity for regions with liquidity shortages. One way to organize the provision of insurance is through the exchange of interbank deposits. Suppose that region $A$ has a large number of early consumers when region $B$ has a low number of early consumers, and vice versa. Since regions $A$ and $B$ are otherwise identical, their deposits are perfect substitutes. The banks exchange deposits at the first date, before they observe the liquidity shocks. If region $A$ has a higher than average number of early consumers at date 1, then banks in region $A$ can meet their obligations by liquidating some of their deposits in the banks of region $B$. Region $B$ is happy to oblige, because it has an excess supply of liquidity, in the form of the short asset. At the final date, the process is reversed, as banks in region $B$ liquidate the deposits they hold in region $A$ to meet the above-average demand from late consumers in region $B$.

Inter-regional cross holdings of deposits work well as long as there is enough liquidity in the banking system as a whole. If there is an excess demand for liquidity, however, the financial linkages caused by these cross holdings can turn out to be a disaster. While cross holdings of deposits are useful for reallocating liquidity within the banking system, they cannot increase the total amount of liquidity. If the economy-wide demand from consumers is greater than the stock of the short asset, the only way to provide more consumption is to liquidate the long asset. There is a limit to how much can be liquidated without provoking a run on the bank, however, so if the initial shock requires more than this buffer, there will be a run on the bank and the bank is forced into bankruptcy. Banks holding deposits in the defaulting bank will suffer a capital loss, which may make it impossible for them to meet their commitments to provide liquidity in their region. Thus, what began as a financial crisis in one region will spread by contagion to other regions because of the cross holdings of deposits.

Whether the financial crisis does spread depends crucially on the pattern of inter-connectedness generated by the cross holdings of deposits. We say that the interbank network is *complete* if each region is connected to all the other regions and *incomplete* if each region is connected with a small number of other regions. In a complete network, the amount of interbank deposits that any bank holds is spread evenly over a large number of banks. As a result, the initial impact of a financial crisis in one region may be attenuated. In an incomplete network, on the other hand, the initial impact of the financial crisis is concentrated in the small number of neighboring regions, with the result that they easily succumb to the crisis too. As each region is affected by the crisis, it prompts premature liquidation of long assets, with a consequent loss of value, so that previously unaffected regions find that they too are affected.

It is important to note the role of a free rider problem in explaining the process of contagion. Cross holdings of deposits are useful for redistributing liquidity, but they do not create liquidity. So when there is excess demand for liquidity in the economy as a whole each bank tries to meet external demands for liquidity by drawing down its deposits in another bank. In other words, each bank is trying to "pass the buck" to another bank. The result is that all the interbank deposits disappear and no one gets any additional liquidity.

The only solution to a global shortage of liquidity (withdrawals exceed short assets), is to liquidate long assets. As we have seen, each bank has a limited buffer that it can access by liquidating the long asset. If this buffer is exceeded, the bank must fail. This is the key to understanding the difference between contagion in complete and incomplete networks. When the network is complete, banks in the troubled region have direct claims on banks in every other region. Every region takes a small hit (liquidates a small amount of the long asset) and there is no need for a global crisis. When the network is incomplete, banks in the troubled region have a direct claim only on the banks in adjacent regions. The banks in other regions are not required to liquidate the long asset until they find themselves on the front line of the contagion. At that point, it is too late to save themselves.

## 10.1 LIQUIDITY PREFERENCE

In this section we use the standard elements to model liquidity risk. There are three dates $t = 0, 1, 2$. There is a single good. This good can be consumed or invested in assets to produce future consumption. There are two types

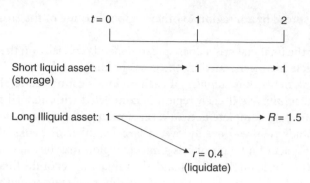

**Figure 10.1.** The short and long assets.

of assets, a short asset and a long asset as shown in Figure 10.1. The short asset is represented by a storage technology. One unit of the consumption good invested in the storage technology at date $t$ produces one unit of the consumption good at date $t + 1$. Investment in the long asset can only take place in the first period and one unit of the consumption good invested in the long asset at the first date produces $R > 1$ units of output at the final date.

Each unit of the long asset can be prematurely liquidated to produce $0 < r < 1$ units of the consumption good at the middle date. Here we assume that liquidation takes the form of physical depreciation of the asset and the liquidation value is treated as a technological constant, the "scrap value." As we have indicated in previous chapters, in practice, it is more likely that assets are liquidated by being sold, in which case the liquidation value is determined by the market price. Introducing a secondary market on which assets can be sold would complicate the analysis without changing the qualitative features of the model.

The economy is divided into four ex ante identical regions, labeled $A$, $B$, $C$, and $D$. The regional structure is a spatial metaphor that can be interpreted in a variety of ways. The important thing for the analysis is that different regions receive different liquidity shocks. Any story that motivates different shocks for different (groups of) banks is a possible interpretation of the regional structure. So a region can correspond to a single bank, a geographical region within a country, or an entire country; it can also correspond to a specialized sector within the banking industry.

Each region contains a continuum of ex ante identical consumers (depositors). A consumer has an endowment equal to 1 unit of the consumption good at date 0 and 0 at dates 1 and 2. Consumers are assumed to have the usual preferences: with probability $\lambda$ they are early consumers and only value consumption at date 1; with probability $(1 - \lambda)$ they are late consumers and only value consumption at date 2. Then the preferences of the individual consumer are given by

$$U(c_1, c_2) = \begin{cases} u(c_1) & \text{with probability } \lambda \\ u(c_2) & \text{with probability } 1 - \lambda \end{cases}$$

where $c_t$ denotes consumption at date $t = 1, 2$. The period utility functions $u(\cdot)$ are assumed to be twice continuously differentiable, increasing and strictly concave. In the example we consider to illustrate the model we have

$$u(\cdot) = \ln(c_t).$$

The probability $\lambda$ varies from region to region. Let $\lambda^i$ denote the probability of being an early consumer in region $i$. There are two possible values of $\lambda^i$, a high value and a low value, denoted $\lambda_H$ and $\lambda_L$, where $0 < \lambda_L < \lambda_H < 1$. The realization of these random variables depends on the state of nature. There are two equally likely states $S_1$ and $S_2$ and the corresponding realizations of the liquidity preference shocks are given in Table 10.1. Note that ex ante each region has the same probability of having a high liquidity preference shock. Also, the aggregate demand for liquidity is the same in each state: half the regions have high liquidity preference and half have low liquidity preference. At date 0 the probability of being an early or late consumer is $\bar{\lambda} = (\lambda_H + \lambda_L)/2$ in each region.

All uncertainty is resolved at date 1 when the state of nature $S_1$ or $S_2$ is revealed and each consumer learns whether he is an early or late consumer. As usual a consumer's type is not observable, so late consumers can always imitate early consumers.

Before introducing the banking sector, it will be convenient to characterize the optimal allocation of risk.

Table 10.1. Regional liquidity shocks.

|  | A | B | C | D |
|---|---|---|---|---|
| $S_1$ | $\lambda_H = 0.75$ | $\lambda_L = 0.25$ | $\lambda_H = 0.75$ | $\lambda_L = 0.25$ |
| $S_2$ | $\lambda_L = 0.25$ | $\lambda_H = 0.75$ | $\lambda_L = 0.25$ | $\lambda_H = 0.75$ |

prob. $S_1 = $ prob. $S_2 = 0.5$

Average proportion of early consumers
  = Average proportion of late consumers
  = 0.5

## 10.2 OPTIMAL RISK SHARING

In this section we characterize optimal risk sharing as the solution to a planning problem. Since consumers are ex ante identical, it is natural to treat consumers symmetrically. For this reason, the planner is assumed to make all the investment and consumption decisions to maximize the unweighted sum of consumers' expected utility.

We begin by describing the planner's problem under the assumption that the planner can identify early and late consumers. The symmetry and concavity of the objective function and the convexity of the constraints simplifies the problem considerably.

- Since there is no aggregate uncertainty, the optimal consumption allocation will be independent of the state.
- Since the consumers in one region are ex ante identical to consumers in another region, all consumers will be treated alike.

Without loss of generality, then, we can assume that every early consumer receives consumption $c_1$ and every late consumer receives $c_2$, independently of the region and state of nature. At the first date, the planner chooses a portfolio $(y, x) \geq 0$ subject to the feasibility constraint

$$y + x \leq 1, \tag{10.1}$$

where $y$ and $x = 1 - y$ are the per capita amounts invested in the short and long assets respectively.

- Since the total amount of consumption provided in each period is a constant, it is optimal to provide for consumption at date 1 by holding the short asset and to provide for consumption at date 2 by holding the long asset.

Since the average fraction of early consumers is denoted by $\bar{\lambda} = (\lambda_H + \lambda_L)/2$, then the feasibility constraint at date 1 is

$$\bar{\lambda} c_1 \leq y \tag{10.2}$$

and the feasibility constraint at date 2 is

$$(1 - \bar{\lambda}) c_2 \leq Rx. \tag{10.3}$$

At date 0 each consumer has an equal probability of being an early or a late consumer, so the ex ante expected utility is

$$\bar{\lambda} u(c_1) + (1 - \bar{\lambda}) u(c_2) \tag{10.4}$$

and this is what the planner seeks to maximize, subject to the constraints (10.1), (10.2), and (10.3). The unique solution to this unconstrained problem is the *first-best allocation.*

The first-best allocation must satisfy the first-order condition

$$u'(c_1) \geq u'(c_2).$$

Otherwise, the objective function could be increased by using the short asset to shift some consumption from early to late consumers. Thus, the first-best allocation automatically satisfies the *incentive constraint*

$$c_1 \leq c_2, \tag{10.5}$$

which says that late consumers find it weakly optimal to reveal their true type, rather than pretend to be early consumers. The *incentive-efficient allocation* maximizes the objective function (10.4) subject to the feasibility constraints (10.1), (10.2), and (10.3), and the incentive constraint (10.5). What we have shown is that the incentive-efficient allocation is the same as the first-best allocation.

**Proposition 1**   The first-best allocation $(x, y, c_1, c_2)$ is equivalent to the incentive-efficient allocation, so the first best can be achieved even if the planner cannot observe the consumers' types.

**Example 1**   To illustrate the optimal allocation, suppose that the asset returns are $R = 1.5$ and $r = 0.4$ and the liquidity shocks are $\lambda_H = 0.75$ and $\lambda_L = 0.25$. The average proportion of early consumers is $\bar{\lambda} = 0.5$. The planner chooses $y$ to maximize

$$0.5 \ln \left(\frac{y}{0.5}\right) + 0.5 \ln \left(\frac{R(1-y)}{0.5}\right).$$

The first-order condition simplifies to $y = 1 - y$ with solution $y = 0.5$. This gives us the optimal consumption profile $(c_1, c_2) = (1, 1.5)$.

It is helpful to consider how the planner would achieve this allocation of consumption in the context of the example, as shown in Figure 10.2. Since there are 0.5 early consumers and 0.5 late consumers there are 0.5 units of consumption at date 1 and 0.75 units of consumption needed at date 1 in total in each region. In order to achieve this first-best allocation, the planner has to transfer resources among the different regions. In state $S_1$, for example, there are 0.75 early consumers in regions $A$ and $C$ and 0.25 early consumers in regions $B$ and $D$. Each region has 0.5 units of the short asset, which provide 0.5 units of consumption. So regions $A$ and $C$ each have an excess demand for

|                  | A                    | B                     | C     | D     |
|------------------|----------------------|-----------------------|-------|-------|
| Date 1:          |                      |                       |       |       |
| Liquidity demand: | 0.75                | 0.25                  | 0.75  | 0.25  |
| Liquidity supply: | 0.5                 | 0.5                   | 0.5   | 0.5   |
| Transfer         | ←0.25 —              |                       | ←0.25 — |     |
| Date 2:          |                      |                       |       |       |
| Liquidity demand: | 0.25×1.5 = 0.375    | 0.75×1.5 = 1.125      | 0.375 | 1.125 |
| Liquidity supply: | 0.5×1.5 = 0.75      | 0.75                  | 0.75  | 0.75  |
| Transfer         | — 0.375→             |                       | — 0.375→ |     |

**Figure 10.2.** Achieving the first-best allocation in state $S_1$.

0.25 units of consumption and regions $B$ and $D$ each have an excess supply of 0.25 units of consumption. By reallocating this consumption, the planner can satisfy every region's needs. At date 2, the transfers flow in the opposite direction, because regions $B$ and $D$ have an excess demand of 0.375 units each and regions $A$ and $C$ have an excess supply of 0.375 units each.

## 10.3 DECENTRALIZATION

In this section we describe how the first-best allocation can be decentralized by a competitive banking sector. There are two reasons for focusing on the first best. One is technical: it turns out that it is much easier to characterize the equilibrium conditions when the allocation is the first best. The second reason is that, as usual, we are interested in knowing under what conditions the market "works." For the moment, we are only concerned with the feasibility of decentralization.

The role of banks is to make investments on behalf of consumers and to insure them against liquidity shocks. We assume that only banks invest in the long asset. This gives the bank two advantages over consumers. First, the banks can hold a portfolio consisting of both types of assets, which will typically be preferred to a portfolio consisting of the short asset alone. Second, by pooling the assets of a large number of consumers, the bank can offer insurance to consumers against their uncertain liquidity demands, giving the early consumers some of the benefits of the high-yielding long asset without subjecting them to the high costs of liquidating the long asset prematurely at the second date.

In each region there is a continuum of identical banks. We focus on a symmetric equilibrium in which all banks adopt the same behavior. Thus, we can describe the decentralized allocation in terms of the behavior of a representative bank in each region.

Without loss of generality, we can assume that each consumer deposits his endowment of one unit of the consumption good in the representative bank in his region. The bank invests the deposit in a portfolio $(y^i, x^i) \geq 0$ and, in exchange, offers a deposit contract $(c_1^i, c_2^i)$ that allows the depositor to withdraw either $c_1^i$ units of consumption at date 1 or $c_2^i$ units of consumption at date 2. Note that the deposit contract is not contingent on the liquidity shock in region $i$. In order to achieve the first best through a decentralized banking sector, we put $(y^i, x^i) = (y, x)$ and $(c_1^i, c_2^i) = (c_1, c_2)$, where $(y, x, c_1, c_2)$ is the first-best allocation.

The problem with this approach is that, while the investment portfolio satisfies the bank's budget constraint $y + x \leq 1$ at date 1, it will not satisfy the budget constraint at date 2. The planner can move consumption between regions, so he only needs to satisfy the average constraint $\bar{\lambda} c_1 \leq y$. The representative bank, on the other hand, has to face the possibility that the fraction of early consumers in its region may be above average, $\lambda_H > \bar{\lambda}$, in which case it will need more than $y$ to satisfy the demands of the early consumers. It can meet this excess demand by liquidating some of the long asset, but then it will not have enough consumption to meet the demands of the late consumers at date 2. In fact, if $r$ is small enough, the bank may not be able to pay the late consumers even $c_1$. Then the late consumers will prefer to withdraw at date 1 and store the consumption good until date 2, thus causing a bank run.

There is no overall shortage of liquidity, it is just badly distributed. One way to allow the banks to overcome the maldistribution of liquidity is by introducing interbank deposits. Using the data from Example 1, we first consider the logistics of implementing the first best using interbank deposits when there is a complete network of interbank relationships. Then we consider the case of an incomplete, connected network.

**Example 2 (A complete network)** Suppose that the interbank network is complete and that banks are allowed to exchange deposits at the first date. This case is illustrated in Figure 10.3. Each region is negatively correlated with two other regions. The payoffs on these deposits are the same as for consumers. For each 1 unit deposited at date 0, the bank can withdraw 1 at date 1 or 1.5 at date 2. We are interested in seeing how the first-best allocation can be implemented. Suppose each bank holds a portfolio $(y, x)$ of $(0.5, 0.5)$. If every bank in region $i$ holds $z^i = (\lambda_H - \bar{\lambda})/2 = 0.25/2 = 0.125$ deposits in each of the regions

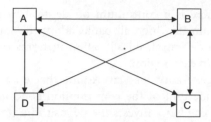

**Figure 10.3.** Complete network.

$j \neq i$, they will be able to supply their depositors with the first-best allocation no matter whether state $S_1$ or $S_2$ occurs. At date 1 the state of nature $S$ is observed and the banks have to adjust their portfolios to satisfy their budget constraints. If the region has a high demand for liquidity, $\lambda^i = \lambda_H = 0.75$, it liquidates all of its deposits in other regions. On the other hand, if it has a low demand for liquidity, $\lambda^i = \lambda_L = 0.25$, it retains the deposits it holds in the other regions until the final date.

Suppose that the state $S_1$ occurs and consider the budget constraint of a bank in region $A$ with a high demand for liquidity as shown in Figure 10.4. The first thing to notice is that its deposit of 0.125 with a bank in region $C$, which also has high demand, cancels with the claim on it of 0.125 from region $C$. In addition it must pay $c_1 = 1$ to the fraction $\lambda_H = 0.75$ of early consumers in its own region for a total of 0.75. On the other side of the ledger, it has $y = 0.5$ units of the short asset and claims to $2 \times 0.125 = 0.25$ deposits in regions $B$ and $D$. Thus, it has enough assets to meet its liabilities. The same analysis holds for a bank in region $C$.

Next consider a bank in region $B$, which has low liquidity demand. It must pay $c_1 = 1$ to a fraction $\lambda_L = 0.25$ of their own depositors and redeem $2 \times 0.125 = 0.25$ deposits from the banks in the regions $A$ and $C$ with high liquidity demand. It has $y = 0.5$ units of the short asset to meet these demands, so its assets cover its liabilities. A similar analysis holds for a bank in region $D$.

At date 2, all the banks liquidate their remaining assets and it can be seen from Figure 10.4 that they have sufficient assets to cover their liabilities. Consider a bank in region $A$ or $C$ first. It must pay $c_2 = 1.5$ to the fraction $1 - \lambda_H = 0.25$ of early consumers in its own region for a total of 0.375. The banks in regions $B$ and $D$ have total claims of $2 \times 0.125 \times 1.5 = 0.375$. The total claims on it are 0.75. On the other side of the ledger, it has $1 - y = 0.5$ units of the long asset that gives a payoff of $0.5 \times 1.5 = 0.75$. Thus, it has enough assets to meet its liabilities. The same analysis holds for a bank in region $C$.

Banks in regions $B$ and $D$ must each pay $c_2 = 1.5$ to a fraction $1 - \lambda_L = 0.75$ of their own depositors so their total liabilities are $0.75 \times 1.5 = 1.125$. In terms of their assets they have 0.5 of the long asset which has a payoff of $0.5 \times 1.5 = 0.75$ and deposits in banks in regions $A$ and $C$ worth

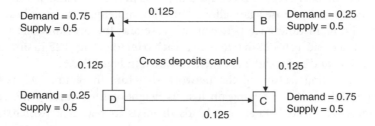

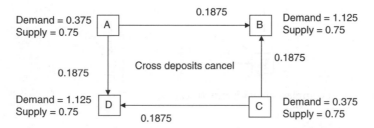

**Figure 10.4.** The flows between banks in state $S_1$ with a complete network structure.

$2 \times 0.125 \times 1.5 = 0.375$. So its total assets are $0.75 + 0.375 = 1.125$ and these cover its liabilities.

Thus, by shuffling deposits among the different regions using the interbank network, it is possible for banks to satisfy their budget constraints in each state $S$ and at each date $t = 0, 1, 2$ while providing their depositors with the first-best consumption allocation through a standard deposit contract.

**Example 3 (An incomplete network)** The interbank network in the preceding section is complete in the sense that a bank in region $i$ can hold deposits in every other region $j \neq i$. In some cases, this may not be realistic. The banking sector is interconnected in a variety of ways, but transaction and information costs may prevent banks from acquiring claims on banks in remote regions. To the extent that banks specialize in particular areas of business or have closer connections with banks that operate in the same geographical or political unit, deposits may tend to be concentrated in "neighboring" banks. To capture this effect, which is crucial in the sequel, we introduce the notion of incompleteness of the interbank network by assuming that banks in region $i$ are allowed to hold deposits in some but not all of the other regions. For concreteness, we assume that banks in each region hold deposits only in one adjacent region, as shown in Figure 10.5. It can be seen that banks in region *A* can hold deposits in region *B*, banks in region *B* can hold deposits in region *C* and so on.

This network structure again allows banks to implement the first-best allocation. The main difference between this case and the previous one is that instead of depositing 0.125 in two banks, each bank deposits 0.25 in one bank. The transfers at dates 1 and 2 are then as shown in Figure 10.6.

One interesting feature of the network structure in Figure 10.5 is that, although each region is relying on just its neighbor for liquidity, the entire economy is connected. Region *A* holds deposits in region *B*, which holds

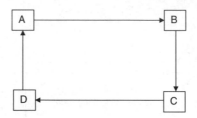

**Figure 10.5.** Incomplete network structure.

Date 1:

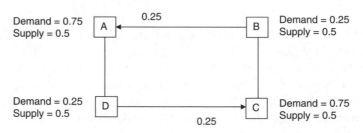

Date 2:

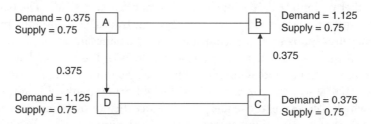

**Figure 10.6.** The flows between banks in state $S_1$ with an incomplete network structure.

deposits in region *C*, and so on. In fact, this is unavoidable given the network structure assumed. Consider the alternative network structure shown in Figure 10.7. Region *A* holds deposits in region *B* and region *B* holds deposits in region *A*. Likewise, region *C* holds one unit of deposits in region *D* and region *D* holds one unit of deposits in region *C*. This network structure is more incomplete than the one in Figure 10.2 and the pattern of holdings in Figure 10.5 is incompatible with it. However, it is possible to achieve the first best through the pattern of holdings in Figure 10.8. This is true even though

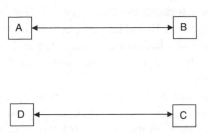

Figure 10.7. A separated incomplete network structure.

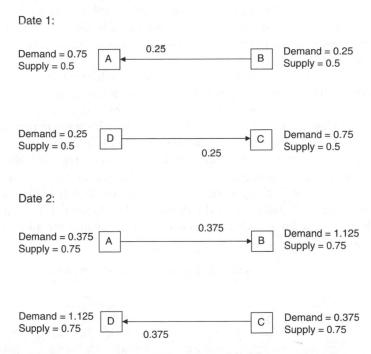

Figure 10.8. The flows between banks in state $S_1$ with a separated incomplete network structure.

the economy is disconnected, since regions $A$ and $B$ trade with each other but not with regions $C$ and $D$ and regions $C$ and $D$ trade with each other but not with regions $A$ and $B$. Again, these patterns do not seem to have any significance as far as achieving the first best is concerned; but they turn out to have striking differences for contagion.

## 10.4 CONTAGION

To illustrate how a small shock can have a large effect, we use the decentralization results from Section 10.3. Then we perturb the model to allow for the occurrence of a state $\bar{S}$ in which the aggregate demand for liquidity is greater than the system's ability to supply liquidity and show that this can lead to an economy-wide crisis.

The network structure is assumed to be given by Figure 10.5. The corresponding allocation requires each bank to hold an initial portfolio of investments $(y, x)$ and offer a deposit contract $(c_1, c_2)$, where $(y, x, c_1, c_2)$ is the first-best allocation. In order to make this deposit contract feasible, the representative bank in each region holds $z = 0.25$ deposits in the adjacent region. Note that $z$ is the minimal amount that is needed to satisfy the budget constraints. It will become apparent below that larger cross holdings of deposits, while consistent with the first best in Section 10.3, would make the contagion problem worse.

Now, let us take the allocation as given and consider what happens when we "perturb" the model. By a perturbation we mean the realization of a state $\bar{S}$ that was assigned zero probability at date 0 and has a demand for liquidity that is very close to that of the states that do occur with positive probability. Specifically, the liquidity shocks are shown in Table 10.2. In state $\bar{S}$, every region has the previous average demand for liquidity $\bar{\lambda}$ except for region $A$ where the demand for liquidity is somewhat higher $\bar{\lambda} + \varepsilon$. The important fact is that the average demand for liquidity across all four regions is slightly higher than in the normal states $S_1$ and $S_2$. Since the abnormal state $\bar{S}$ occurs with negligible probability (in the limit, probability zero) it will not change the allocation at

Table 10.2. Regional liquidity shocks with perturbation.

|  | A | B | C | D |
|---|---|---|---|---|
| $S_1$ | $\lambda_H = 0.75$ | $\lambda_L = 0.25$ | $\lambda_H = 0.75$ | $\lambda_L = 0.25$ |
| $S_2$ | $\lambda_L = 0.25$ | $\lambda_H = 0.75$ | $\lambda_L = 0.25$ | $\lambda_H = 0.75$ |
| $\bar{S}$ | $\bar{\lambda} + \varepsilon = 0.5 + \varepsilon$ | $\bar{\lambda} = 0.5$ | $\bar{\lambda} = 0.5$ | $\bar{\lambda} = 0.5$ |

date 0. In states $S_1$ and $S_2$ the continuation equilibrium will be the same as before at date 1; in state $\bar{S}$ the continuation equilibrium will be different.

In the continuation equilibrium beginning at date 1, consumers will optimally decide whether to withdraw their deposits at date 1 or date 2 and banks will liquidate their assets in an attempt to meet the demands of their depositors. Early consumers always withdraw at date 1; late consumers will withdraw at date 1 or date 2 depending on which gives them the larger amount of consumption. Because we want to focus on essential bank crises, we assume that late consumers will always withdraw their deposits at date 2 if it is (weakly) optimal for them to do so. Banks are required to meet their promise to pay $c_1$ units of consumption to each depositor who demands withdrawal at date 1. If they cannot do so, they must liquidate all of their assets at date 1. The proceeds of the liquidation are split pro rata among depositors in the usual way. If the bank can meet its obligations at date 1, then the remaining assets are liquidated at date 2 and given to the depositors who have waited until date 2 to withdraw. In the rest of this section, we describe the continuation equilibrium at date 1 in state $\bar{S}$, assuming the actions consistent with the first best at date 0.

### 10.4.1 The liquidation "pecking order"

At date 1 a bank can find itself in one of three conditions. A bank is said to be *solvent*, if it can meet the demands of every depositor who wants to withdraw (including banks in other regions) by using only its liquid assets, that is, the short asset and the deposits in other regions. The bank is said to be *insolvent* if it can meet the demands of its deposits but only by liquidating some of the long asset. Finally, the bank is said to be *bankrupt* if it cannot meet the demands of its depositors by liquidating all its assets.

These definitions are motivated by the assumption that banks will always find it preferable to liquidate assets in a particular order at date 1. We call this the "pecking order" for liquidating assets and it goes as follows: first, the bank liquidates the short asset, then it liquidates deposits, and finally it liquidates the long asset. To ensure that the long asset is liquidated last, we need an additional assumption,

$$\frac{R}{r} > \frac{c_2}{c_1} \tag{10.6}$$

which is maintained in the sequel. Since the first-best consumption allocation $(c_1, c_2)$ is independent of $r$ (this variable does not appear in the first-best problem in Section 10.2) we can always ensure that condition (10.6) is satisfied by choosing $r$ sufficiently small. It can be seen that (10.6) is satisfied in our example since $R/r = 1.5/0.5 > 1.5/1 = c_2/c_1$.

Each of the three assets offers a different cost of obtaining current (date 1) consumption in terms of future (date 2) consumption. The cheapest is the short asset. One unit of the short asset is worth one unit of consumption today and, if reinvested in the short asset, this is worth one unit of consumption tomorrow. So the cost of obtaining liquidity by liquidating the short asset is 1. Similarly, by liquidating one unit of deposits, the bank gives up $c_2$ units of future consumption and obtains $c_1$ units of present consumption. So the cost of obtaining liquidity by liquidating deposits is $c_2/c_1$. From the first-order condition $u'(c_1) = Ru'(c_2)$, we know that $c_2/c_1 > 1$. Finally, by liquidating one unit of the long asset, the bank gives up $R$ units of future consumption and obtains $r$ units of present consumption. So the cost of obtaining liquidity by liquidating the long asset is $R/r$. Thus, we have derived the pecking order, short assets, deposits, long assets:

$$1 < \frac{c_2}{c_1} < \frac{R}{r}.$$

In order to maximize the interests of depositors, the bank must liquidate the short asset before it liquidates deposits in other regions before it liquidates the long asset.

The preceding argument assumes that the bank in which the deposit is held is not bankrupt. Bankruptcy requires that all assets of the bankrupt institution be liquidated immediately and the proceeds distributed to the depositors. So the preceding analysis only applies to deposits in non-bankrupt banks.

## 10.4.2  Liquidation values

The value of a deposit at date 1 is $c_1$ if the bank is not bankrupt and it is equal to the liquidation value of all the bank's assets if the bank is bankrupt. Let $q^i$ denote the value of the representative bank's deposits in region $i$ at date 1. If $q^i < c_1$ then all the depositors will withdraw as much as they can at date 1. In particular, the banks in other regions will be seeking to withdraw their claims on the bank at the same time that the bank is trying to redeem its claims on them. *All depositors must be treated equally*, that is, every depositor gets $q^i$ from the bank for each unit invested at the first date, whether the depositor is a consumer or a bank from another region. Then the values of $q^i$ must be determined simultaneously. Consider the representative bank in region $A$, for example. If all the depositors withdraw, the total demands will be $1 + z$, since the banks in region $D$ hold $z$ deposits and the consumers in region $A$ hold 1 deposit. The liabilities of the bank are valued at $(1 + z)q^A$. The assets consist of $y$ units of the short asset, $x$ units of the long asset, and $z$ deposits in region $B$. The assets are valued at $y + rx + zq^B$. The equilibrium values of $q^A$ and $q^B$ must equate the value of assets and liabilities

$$q^A = \frac{y + rx + zq^B}{(1 + z)}. \tag{10.7}$$

A similar equation must hold for any region $i$ in which $q^i < c_1$.

If $q^B = c_1$ then we can use this equation to calculate the value of $q^A$; but if $q^B < c_1$ then we need another equation to determine $q^B$ and this equation will include the value of $q^C$, and so on.

### 10.4.3 Buffers and bank runs

A bank can meet a certain excess demand in liquidity at date 1, which we call the *buffer*, by liquidating the illiquid long-term asset before a run is precipitated. To see how this works consider the following examples of what happens in $\bar{S}$ when there is an incomplete network structure as in Figure 10.5.

**Example 4** $\varepsilon = 0.04$
In this case it follows from Table 10.2 that the proportions of early and late consumers are as follows.

| | Early consumers | Late consumers |
|---|---|---|
| Proportion of Bank $A$ customers | 0.54 | 0.46 |

Since the bank has promised $c_1 = 1$ it must come up with 0.54 of consumption. To do this it goes through its pecking order.

 (i) To meet the first 0.5 of its liquidity needs of 0.54, it liquidates its 0.5 holding of the short asset.
 (ii) It needs more liquidity so next it calls in its deposit from Bank $B$. Now from Table 10.2 it can be seen that in state $\bar{S}$ Bank $B$ has a liquidity demand of 0.5 from its early consumers. It uses its proceeds from the short asset of 0.5 to cover this. When Bank $A$ calls in its deposit then Bank $B$ goes to the second item on its pecking order and calls in its deposit from Bank $C$. Bank $C$ is in a similar position to Bank $B$ and calls in its deposit from Bank $D$, which in turn calls in its deposit from Bank $A$. So overall Bank

*A* is no better off in terms of raising liquidity. It has an extra 0.25 of the liquid asset but it also has an extra demand for liquidity from Bank *D* of 0.25.

(iii) Bank *A* goes to the third item in its pecking order, which is to liquidate its holding of the long asset. Since $r = 0.4$ and it needs 0.04 it must liquidate $0.04/0.4 = 0.1$.

The use of the short-term asset and the liquidation of 0.1 of its long-term asset means that Bank *A* is able to meet its liabilities. It has $0.5 - 0.1 = 0.4$ of the long asset remaining. At date 2 it will have $0.4 \times 1.5 = 0.6$ from this holding of the long asset. It can distribute $c_2 = 0.6/0.46 = 1.30$ to the late consumers. Since this is above the $c_1 = 1$ they would obtain if they pretended to be early consumers, there is no run on the bank. The only effect of the increased liquidity demand is a reduction in the consumption of Bank *A*'s late consumers as it is forced to liquidate some of its buffer.

**Example 5**   $\varepsilon = 0.10$

Next consider what happens if the liquidity shock is larger. Now the proportions of early and late consumers are as follows.

|  | Early consumers | Late consumers |
|---|---|---|
| Proportion of Bank *A* customers | 0.6 | 0.4 |

The sequence of events is the same as before. Bank *A* goes through its pecking order but now it needs an extra 0.1 of liquidity. It must therefore liquidate $0.1/0.4 = 0.25$ of the long asset. At date 2 it would have $0.5 - 0.25 = 0.25$ of the long asset, which would generate a payoff of $0.25 \times 1.5 = 0.375$. It could distribute $c_2 = 0.375/0.4 = 0.94$ to the late consumers. Since this is below the $c_1 = 1$ they would obtain if they pretended to be early consumers, there is a *run* on the bank.

In the run on Bank *A* all depositors, including Bank *D*, withdraw and take a loss. There is a *spillover* to Bank *D*. The key question is whether there is *contagion* so that Bank *D* also goes bankrupt.

Assume initially that there is no contagion and in particular that Bank *A*'s deposit claim on Bank *B* is worth 0.25. We shall check shortly whether this assumption is consistent with what everybody receives. Using (10.7) it can be seen that the pro rata claim on Bank *A* is

$$q^A = \frac{0.5 + 0.5 \times 0.4 + 0.25}{1.25} = 0.76.$$

This means that Bank $D$'s 0.25 deposit claim is worth $0.76 \times 0.25 = 0.19$. They have claims of 0.5 from their depositors and also of 0.25 from Bank $C$'s deposit claim on them for a total of 0.75. Since their total liquidity from their holdings of the short asset and their deposit in Bank $A$ is $0.5 + 0.19 = 0.69$ they need to draw on their buffer and liquidate enough of their long-term asset to give them $0.75 - 0.69 = 0.06$. The total amount they must liquidate of the long asset is $0.06/0.4 = 0.15$. Bank $D$ thus has $0.5 - 0.15 = 0.35$ of the long asset remaining. At date 2 it will have $0.35 \times 1.5 = 0.525$ from this holding of the long asset. It can distribute $c_2 = 0.525/0.5 = 1.05$ to the late consumers. Since this is above the $c_1 = 1$ they would obtain if they pretended to be early consumers, there is no run on Bank $D$ and *no contagion*.

Note that even if $\varepsilon$ was larger, there would still be no contagion. Bank $A$ is bankrupt and all its depositors irrespective of whether they are early or late consumers get 0.76. In order for there to be contagion we need $R$ to be lower than 1.5 so that there is a run on Bank $D$. This is the case we consider next.

**Example 6**   $\varepsilon = 0.10, R = 1.2$

Example 6 is the same as Example 5 except for the last step. At date 2, instead of having $0.35 \times 1.5 = 0.525$ from their holding of the long asset, Bank $D$ will have $0.35 \times 1.2 = 0.42$. It could distribute $c_2 = 0.42/0.5 = 0.84$ to the late consumers. Since this is below the $c_1 = 1$ they perceive they would obtain if they pretended to be early consumers, there is a run on Bank $D$ and now there is contagion. The analysis for Banks $C$ and $B$ is just the same as for Bank $D$ and so all banks go bankrupt.

In the contagion equilibrium all banks go down and are liquidated so $q^i = q$ for $i = A, B, C, D$. Using (10.7) we have,

$$q = \frac{0.5 + 0.5 \times 0.4 + 0.25 \times q}{1.25}.$$

Solving for $q$ gives

$$q = 0.7.$$

So all depositors obtain 0.7 and welfare is lower than when there is no contagion.

It can be seen that there is always contagion provided $R$ is sufficiently low. In fact, there will be contagion whenever $0.35 \times R < 0.5$ or, equivalently, $R < 1.43$.

**Proposition 2**   Consider the model with network structure described in Figure 10.5 and perturb it by the addition of the zero probability state $\bar{S}$. Suppose that each bank chooses an investment portfolio $(y, x, z)$ and offers a deposit contract $(c_1, c_2)$, where $(x, y)$ is the first-best investment portfolio, $(c_1, c_2)$ is the first-best consumption allocation, and $z = (\lambda_H - \bar{\lambda})$. If the liquidity shock $\varepsilon > 0$ is sufficiently large and $R > 1$ is sufficiently low, then, in any continuation equilibrium, the banks in all regions must go bankrupt at date 1 in state $\bar{S}$.

We have illustrated this proposition for a numerical example. A more formal version of the proposition is provided in Allen and Gale (2000).

### 10.4.4 Many regions

So far we have only considered the case of four regions $A, B, C$, and $D$. However, it can be seen from the final step of the example above that there would be contagion no matter how many regions there are. When Bank $D$ goes bankrupt all the other regions also go bankrupt. The same argument would hold with a thousand or many thousands of regions. Thus, even though the initial shock only occurs in one region, which can be an arbitrarily small part of the economy, it can nevertheless cause banks in all regions to go bankrupt. This is why contagion can be so damaging.

**Proposition 3**   Proposition 2 holds no matter how many regions there are.

## 10.5 ROBUSTNESS

The incompleteness of networks is important for the contagion result. In the example we considered last where there was contagion when networks were as in Figure 10.5 it can be shown that if there is a complete network as in Figure 10.3, there is no contagion. The key difference is that now with a complete network, each bank deposits 0.125 in two other banks rather than 0.25 in just one bank.

**Example 7**   $\varepsilon = 0.10, R = 1.2$
The analysis is the same as before except when we are considering whether there is contagion. Bank $B$ and $D$'s deposit claims of 0.125 on Bank $A$ are now worth $0.76 \times 0.125 = 0.095$. Banks $B, C$, and $D$ have claims of 0.5 in total from their early consumers and 0.125 from the three banks that have deposits in them. They have liquidity of 0.5 from their short asset and 0.125 from two of their deposits and 0.095 from their deposit in Bank $A$. They need to liquidate

enough of the long asset to raise $0.125 - 0.095 = 0.03$. Given $r = 0.4$ the amount liquidated is $0.03/0.4 = 0.075$. They thus have $0.5 - 0.075 = 0.425$ of the long asset remaining. At date 2 they will have $0.425 \times 1.2 = 0.51$ from this holding of the long asset. They can distribute $c_2 = 0.51/0.5 = 1.02$ to the late consumers. Since this is above the $c_1 = 1$ they would obtain if they pretended to be early consumers, there is no run on Banks $B$, $C$, and $D$ and no contagion.

The reason there is no contagion in the case with a complete network is that the liquidation of assets is spread among more banks so there are more buffers to absorb the shock. This means that banks do not hit the discontinuity associated with a run when all the bank's assets are liquidated at a significant loss and as a result there is no contagion. We have illustrated this for the example. Allen and Gale (2000) again show that a similar result holds more generally. Complete networks are less susceptible to contagion than incomplete networks.

## 10.6 CONTAINMENT

The critical ingredient in the example of contagion analyzed in Section 10.4 is that any two regions are connected by a chain of overlapping bank liabilities. Banks in region $A$ have claims on banks in region $B$, which in turn have claims on banks in region $C$, and so on. If we could cut this chain at some point, the contagion that begins with a small shock in region $A$ would be contained in subset of the set of regions.

Consider the incomplete network structure in Figure 10.7 and the allocation that implements the first-best allocation for our example, which is shown in Figure 10.8. The allocation requires banks in regions $A$ and $B$ to have claims on each other and banks in regions $C$ and $D$ to have claims on each other, but there is no connection between the region $\{A, B\}$ and the region $\{C, D\}$. If state $\bar{S}$ occurs, the excess demand for liquidity will cause bankruptcies in region $A$ and they can spread to region $B$, but there is no reason why they should spread any further. Banks in regions $C$ and $D$ are simply not connected to the troubled banks in regions $A$ and $B$.

Comparing the three network structures we have considered so far, complete networks in Figure 10.3, incomplete networks in Figure 10.5, and the disconnected network structure in Figure 10.7, we can see that there is a non-monotonic relationship between completeness or incompleteness of networks and the extent of the financial crisis in state $\bar{S}$. With the complete network structure of Figure 10.3 the crisis is restricted to region $A$, with the network structure in Figure 10.5 the crisis extends to all regions, and with the network structure in Figure 10.7 the crisis is restricted to regions $A$ and $B$.

It could be argued that the network structures are not monotonically ordered: the complete network does contain the other two, but the paths in the network in Figure 10.7 are not a subset of the network in Figure 10.5. This could be changed by adding paths to Figure 10.2, but then the equilibrium of Figure 10.7 would also be an equilibrium of Figure 10.5. This raises an obvious but important point, that contagion depends on the *endogenous* pattern of financial claims. An incomplete network structure like the one in Figure 10.5 may preclude a complete pattern of financial connectedness and thus encourage financial contagion; but a complete network structure does not imply the opposite: even in a complete network there may be an endogenous choice of overlapping claims that causes contagion. In fact, the three equilibria considered so far are all consistent with the complete network structure. There are additional equilibria for the economy with the complete network structure. Like the three considered so far, they achieve the first best in states $S_1$ and $S_2$, but have different degrees of financial fragility in the unexpected state $\bar{S}$, depending on the patterns of interregional deposit holding.

What is important about the network structure in Figure 10.5, then, is that the pattern of interregional cross holdings of deposits that promotes the possibility of contagion, is the only one consistent with this network structure. Since we are interested in contagion as an essential phenomenon, this network structure has a special role. The complete network economy, by contrast, has equilibria with and without contagion and provides a weaker case for the likelihood of contagion.

## 10.7 DISCUSSION

The existence of contagion depends on a number of assumptions. The first is that financial interconnectedness takes the form of ex ante claims signed at date 0. The interbank loan network is good in that it allows reallocation of liquidity. But when there is aggregate uncertainty about the level of liquidity demand this interconnectedness can lead to contagion. It is not important that the contracts are deposit claims. The same result holds with contingent or discretionary contracts because the interbank claims net out. Ex ante contracts will always just net out. Spillover and contagion occur because of the fall in asset values in adjacent regions, not the form of the contract. The interbank network operates quite differently from the retail market in this respect.

Note that if there is an ex post loan market so contracts are signed at date 1 rather than date 0 then there can be the desirable reallocation of liquidity but no contagion. The reason that there will be no contagion is that the interest rate in the ex post market must compensate lenders for the cost of liquidating assets but at this rate it will not be worth borrowing. However, there are the usual difficulties with ex post markets such as adverse selection and the "hold-up" problem. If the long asset has a risky return then ex post markets will also not be optimal.

We have simplified the problem considerably to retain tractability. In particular, by assuming state $\bar{S}$ occurs with zero probability, we ensure the behavior of banks is optimal since the interbank deposits and the resulting allocation remains efficient. When $\bar{S}$ occurs with positive probability the trade-offs will be more complex. However, provided the benefits of risk sharing are large enough interbank deposits should be optimal and this interconnection should lead to the (low probability) possibility of contagion. When $\bar{S}$ occurs with positive probability a bank can prevent runs by holding more of the liquid asset. There's a cost to this in states $S_1$ and $S_2$ though. When the probability of $\bar{S}$ is small enough this cost is not worth bearing. It is better to just bear the risk of contagion.

The focus in this paper is on financial contagion as an essential feature of equilibrium. We do not rely on arguments involving multiple equilibria. The aim is instead to show that under certain conditions every continuation equilibrium at date 1 exhibits financial contagion. Nonetheless, there are multiple equilibria in the model and if one is so disposed one can use the multiplicity of equilibria to tell a story about financial contagion as a sunspot phenomenon.

For simplicity, we have assumed that the long asset has a non-stochastic return, but it would be more realistic to assume that the long asset is risky. We have seen at many points in this book, such as Chapter 3 on intermediation, that when the long asset is risky it is negative information about future returns that triggers bank runs. In the present framework, uncertainty about long asset returns could be used both to motivate interregional cross holdings of deposits and to provoke insolvency or bankruptcy. The results should be similar. What is crucial for the results is that the financial interconnectedness between the regions takes the form of claims held by banks in one region on banks in another region.

We have shown in this chapter that a small shock in a single region or bank can bring down the entire banking system no matter how big this system is relative to the shock. What is key for this is the network structure for interbank deposits. If there are relatively few channels of interconnectedness then contagion is more likely. Clearly transaction costs mean it is much too costly for every bank to hold an account with every other bank so networks are complete. However, one low cost equivalent of this is to have a central bank that is connected with every other bank. The theory here thus provides a rationale for central banks.

## 10.8 APPLICATIONS

In this section we try to bridge the gap between the theory developed in the preceding sections and empirical applications. The model we have presented here describes an artificial and highly simplified environment in which it is possible to exhibit the mechanism by which a small shock in one region can be transmitted to other regions. This result depends on a number of assumptions, some of them quite restrictive, and some of them made in order to keep the analysis tractable. In any case, the model is quite far removed from the world in which policymakers have to operate. Nonetheless, although the model only provides an extremely simplified picture of the entire financial system, the basic ideas can be applied to real data in order to provide some indication of the prospects for contagion in actual economies. There have now been several studies of this sort, carried out on data from different countries. An excellent survey of this literature is contained in Upper (2006). Here we start with one particularly transparent example, which will serve to illustrate what can be done in practice.

### 10.8.1 Upper and Worms (2004)

In an important study, Upper and Worms (2004), henceforth UW, use data on interbank deposits to simulate the possibility of contagion among the banks in the German financial system. The UW model is very simple. There is a finite number of banks indexed by $i = 1, ..., n$. Each bank $i$ has a level of capital denoted by the number $c_i \geq 0$. For any ordered pair of banks $(i, j)$ there is a number $x_{ij} \geq 0$ that denotes the value of the claims of bank $i$ on bank $j$. These claims may represent deposits in bank $j$ or bank loans to bank $j$ or some combination. The numbers $c_i$ and $x_{ij}$ represent the data on interbank relationships and that will be used as the basis for the analysis of contagion.

The other crucial parameter that plays a role in the process of contagion is the loss ratio $\theta$. When a bank goes bankrupt, its assets will be liquidated in order to pay off the creditors. Typically, the assets will be sold for less than their "book" or accounting value. The reasons why assets are sold at firesale prices are numerous and well known. Some potential buyers, perhaps those who value the assets highly, may be unable to bid for them because of a lack of liquidity. Or it may be that assets are sold in haste, before every potential buyer is ready to bid on them, leading to a non-competitive market for the assets on which buyers can pick up the assets for less than the fair value. There is also the problem of asymmetric information. If potential buyers have limited information about the quality of the assets (and some bank assets, such as loans, are notoriously hard to value), fear of adverse selection will cause buyers to incorporate a "lemons" discount in their bids. Part of the loss from selling the assets at firesale prices will be absorbed by the bank's capital, but the losses may be so great that the liquidated value of the assets is less than the value of the bank's liabilities. In that case, part of the losses will be passed on to the creditors, who only receive a fraction of what they are owed. The loss ratio $\theta$ measures the fraction of the creditors' claim that is lost because of the liquidation.

The process of contagion begins with the failure of a single bank. If the loss ratio is positive, all the creditors will lose a positive fraction of the claims against the failing bank. If this loss is big enough, some of the affected banks may fail. This is the first round of contagion. The failure of these additional banks will have similar effects on their creditors, some of whom may fail in the second round. These effects continue in round after round as the contagion spreads throughout the financial sector. This recursive description of contagion suggests an algorithm for calculating the extent of contagion from the failure of a single bank.

The first step of the algorithm takes as given the failure of a given bank and calculates the impact on the creditor banks. Suppose that bank $j$ fails and bank $i$ is a creditor of bank $j$. Bank $i$'s claim on bank $j$ is $x_{ij}$ and a fraction $\theta$ of this is lost, so bank $i$ suffers a loss of $\theta x_{ij}$. If the loss $\theta x_{ij}$ is less than bank $i$'s capital $c_i$, the bank can absorb the loss although its capital will be diminished. If the loss is greater than the value of the bank's capital, however, the bank's assets are reduced to the point where they are lower than its liabilities. When assets are less than liabilities, the bank is insolvent and must declare bankruptcy. So the failure of bank $j$ will cause the failure of bank $i$ if and only if the loss $\theta x_{ij}$ is greater than its capital $c_i$:

$$\theta x_{ij} > c_i.$$

The banks that satisfy this inequality constitute the first round of contagion from the failure of bank $j$.

Let $I_1$ denote the set of banks $i$ that failed in the first round of contagion, plus the original failed bank $j$. The failure of bank $j$ has spread by contagion to all the banks in the set $I_1$ but the contagion does not stop there. Banks that did not fail as a result of the original failure of bank $j$ may now fail because of the failure of banks in $I_1$. Suppose that $i$ does not belong to $I_1$. For every $j$ in $I_1$, bank $i$ loses $\theta x_{ij}$ so its total loss is $\sum_{j \in I_1} \theta x_{ij}$. Then bank $i$ will fail in what we call the second round if and only if

$$\sum_{j \in I_1} \theta x_{ij} > c_i.$$

Let $I_2$ denote the set of banks that fail in the second round plus all the banks included in $I_1$. We can continue in this way calculating round after round of failures until the set of failed banks converges. Let $I_k$ denote the set of banks that fail in the $k$-th and earlier rounds. Since there is a finite number of banks, contagion must come to an end after a finite number of periods. It is easy to see from the definition that if $I_k = I_{k+1}$ then $I_k = I_{k+\ell}$ for every $\ell > 0$.

The interesting question is how far the contagion will go. There are various ways of measuring the extent of contagion. UW report various measures, including the total number of failed banks and the percentage of assets in failed banks. The procedure for estimating the extent of contagion is as follows. Choose an arbitrary bank $i$ and assume that it fails, calculate the set of banks that will fail as a result of the failure of bank $i$ (the procedure described above), and then repeat this procedure for every possible choice of the starting bank $i$. The extent of contagion is the least upper bound of the relevant measure, say, the total number of failed banks or the percentage of assets in failed banks, over all starting values $i$. In other words, we choose the initial failed bank to maximize the measure of contagion and call that maximized value the extent of contagion.

The data required for this exercise are not available in completely disaggregated form so UW were forced to approximate it using partially aggregated data. German banks are required to submit monthly balance sheets to the Bundesbank in which they report interbank loans and deposits classified according to whether their counterparty is a foreign or domestic bank, a building society, or the Bundesbank. Savings banks and cooperative banks have to report in addition whether the counterparty is a giro institution or a cooperative central bank. All banks are also required to divide their lending into five maturity categories. What are not reported are the actual bilateral positions between pairs of banks. This information has to be interpolated from the aggregates reported by individual banks. Nonetheless, the division of interbank loans and deposits into so many categories allows UW to construct a number of matrices corresponding to lending between different types of banks in different maturity classes. Since we are ultimately concerned only with the aggregate amount of bilateral lending, these calculations would be of no interest if we could observe bilateral exposures directly. Since we cannot observe bilateral exposures, the additional information on the breakdown of lending by individual banks is useful in estimating the unobserved bilateral exposures. UW use a complex, recursive algorithm which uses the sum of lending and borrowing by each bank in each of several categories (defined by type of counterparty and maturity) to estimate the bilateral exposures for those categories. By applying this procedure to the 25 separate matrices corresponding to lending between different types of banks and in different maturities, UW are able to get more precise estimates of the true bilateral exposures, because many banks are active only in some of these categories. The resulting matrices are then summed to give aggregate bilateral exposures. Since they only have data on domestic banks and domestic branches of foreign banks, UW eliminate exposures to foreign banks, building societies and the Bundesbank. They are left with a closed system in which assets and liabilities sum to zero.

The "full information" method shows that the patterns of lending and borrowing are quite different for different classes of banks. Among their broad conclusions about the structure of lending are the following.

- Banks tend to have larger claims on banks in the same category. For example, commercial banks transact much more with other commercial banks than one would expect from the baseline matrix.

- Similarly, the head institutions of the two giro systems (cooperative banks and savings banks) have a large proportion of the loans and deposits in the individual banks in each giro system. There are almost no deposits held between individual banks at the base level of the same giro system.

- There are therefore two tiers to the banking system, the lower tier consisting of savings and cooperative banks, the upper tier consisting of commercial banks, the head banks of the giro systems (Landesbanken and cooperative central banks) plus a variety of other banks. Whereas the lower tier banks have little exposure to banks in the same tier, the upper tier banks have transactions with a variety of other banks including banks in other categories.

The two-tier system falls between the complete network and the incomplete network emphasized in the theory model. As a network it is incomplete but the hubs in the upper tier play an important role in integrating the system. In addition, the theoretical model assumes that all banks are ex ante identical,

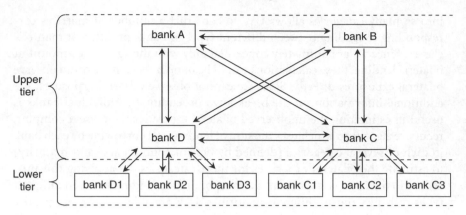

**Figure 10.9.** Two-tier structure of German interbank holdings (Figure 4 in Upper and Worms 2004).

whereas the key to understanding the two tier system in Germany is the difference in sizes and specialized functions of the banks in each tier. A stylized picture of the two-tier system, reproduced from UW, is shown in Figure 10.9.

As mentioned above, the loss ratio is a key parameter in determining the possibility of contagion. Since data on loss ratios applicable to the German banking system are not available, UW consider a range of values of $\theta$ and calculate the incidence of contagion, as measured by a variety of statistics, for each value of $\theta$. Recall that we are referring to the maximum incidence here, that is, the maximum extent of contagion associated with the failure of a single bank. We reproduce in Figure 10.10 the relationship between the loss ratio and both the maximum number of banks and the maximum percentage of total assets affected using the full information matrix of bilateral exposures.

The relationship between the loss ratio and the extent of contagion has several important features that can be seen in Figure 10.10 or in the underlying calculations.

- There is always contagion for any loss ratio. In fact, there are 17 banks that fail in the first round, independently of which bank is chosen to fail first. These are all small banks and the assumptions on which the interpolation of interbank exposures is based may be unrealistic in their case.
- There appears to be a critical value of $\theta$ (around 40%) at which the extent of contagion resulting from a single bank failure increases very sharply.
- For very large values of $\theta$ (possibly unrealistically large values), the contagion extends to most of the financial system.

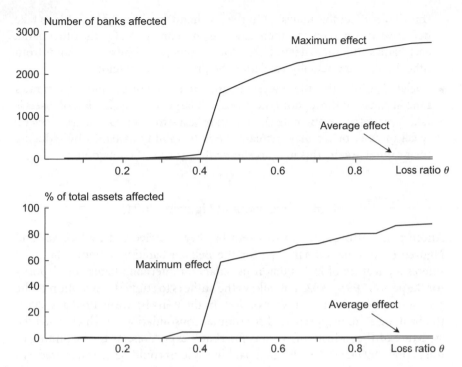

**Figure 10.10.** Loss ratio and the severity of contagion in the absence of a "safety net" (Figure 5 in Upper and Worms 2004).

UW provide a number of other results, relating to the dynamics of contagion and the disparate impact of contagion on different types of banks.

The UW methodology provides a method for estimating the incidence of contagion using hypothetical values of the loss ratio and estimates of bilateral exposures based on available data. It provides a quantitative assessment of the financial fragility of the banking system as well as some interesting insights into the sensitivity of the results to different structural parameters of the system. At the same time, the approach has a number of limitations.

- UW focus on interbank holdings, but there are other sources of instability, for example, shocks originating outside the financial system, that may lead to contagion.

- UW interpret their algorithm for calculating the extent of contagion as a dynamic process in which each round can be thought of as a different time period. In a truly dynamic model, banks would be able to change their portfolios in each period as the contagion progressed. It is not clear how this would affect the analysis. On the one hand, banks might be able to take defensive action to protect themselves against contagion. On the other hand, each bank's attempt to defend itself, for example, by withdrawing funds from other banks, may actually accelerate the process of contagion.

• A related point is that the analysis assumes that asset prices and interest rates remain constant throughout the process. If large scale liquidation of assets is taking place (or is anticipated), there may be a strong impact on asset prices. A fall in asset prices may increase the vulnerability of banks by reducing their capital. Again, this may accelerate the process of contagion.

## 10.8.2 Degryse and Nguyen (2004)

Another interesting study in this vein has been carried out by Degryse and Nguyen (2004), henceforth DN, for the Belgian banking system. The most interesting feature of DN is that it uses data on interbank loans and deposits for the period 1993–2002. This allows the authors to study the evolution of the risk of contagion over a ten year period. In the years between 1998 and 2001, the banking system experienced substantial consolidation which changed the structure of the industry as well as interbank exposures. At the beginning of the period 1993–2002, the Belgian banking system could be characterized as a complete network, in which all banks have more or less symmetric exposures. By the end of the period, it resembled an incomplete network with multiple money centers, in which the money center banks have symmetric links to other banks and the non-money center banks do not have links with each other.

DN simulate the risk of contagion at the beginning and end of the period 1993–2002 using a variety of values of loss given default (LGD), which is their counterpart to the loss ratio $\theta$ in UW. They find that the risk of contagion has fallen over the period and is quite low by the end. Even with an unrealistically high LGD of 100%, they calculate that banks representing less than five percent of total assets would be affected by contagion following the failure of a single Belgian bank. Thus, the banking system has become less complete over the period during which the risk of contagion has fallen. This stands in contrast to the result of Allen and Gale (2000), which suggests that complete financial networks are more stable than incomplete financial networks. It must be remembered, however, that the assumptions of the Allen–Gale result are not satisfied by the Belgian banking system. Allen and Gale (2000) assumes that all banks are ex ante identical, whereas the Belgian banking system contains well capitalized money center banks in addition to smaller banks. Also, the Allen–Gale result claims that greater completeness increased stability *ceteris paribus.* The Belgian banking system by contrast experienced substantial changes between 1993 and 2002 in terms of the number, size, and balance sheets of the banks. Nonetheless, the estimated stability of the banking system is a striking result.

DN make a number of other interesting observations about the structure of the Belgian banking system. They pay particular attention to the international nature of the banking business and the fact that Belgian banks are well integrated in the international banking system. This leads them to distinguish analytically between contagion having a source outside the Belgian banking system from contagion originating in the failure of a Belgian bank. It turns out that the extent of contagion caused by the failure of a foreign bank is somewhat larger than that caused by the failure of a domestic bank. This result has to be qualified, however, because the most important foreign banks are very large, well capitalized and have very high credit ratings, so the probability of failure is correspondingly small.

Another interesting consequence of the integration of Belgian banks in the international banking system is that several of these banks have very large operations outside of Belgium. As a result, their asset holdings are large relative to the size of the Belgian economy. Our discussion of contagion so far has taken no account of the safety net provided by governments and central banks. In the Belgian case, the very size of some of the banks might make it difficult to put together a rescue package for one of these large banks if it were to find itself in financial distress. Although UW estimated that the extent of contagion might be large, at least if the loss ratio were large enough, the existence of a safety net might stop contagion in the early stages, before it reaches the critical mass needed to spill over into a large part of the financial sector. By contrast, small countries with very large international banks may not have the resources to stop this process in the early rounds. As DN show, the risk of contagion appears to be small even in the absence of a safety net; but this may not be true of other small countries, where some banks are literally "too large to save."

### 10.8.3 Cifuentes, Ferrucci, and Shin (2005)

In our discussion of UW we pointed out that no account was taken of price effects, that is, asset prices are assumed to be unaffected by bank failures and the process of contagion. DN and most other studies of this type make the same assumption. We conjectured that if price effects were important, the downward pressure exerted on asset prices by liquidations and/or hoarding of liquidity would reduce bank capital and accelerate the speed and extent of contagion. Cifuentes et al. (2005), henceforth CFS, have developed a model of contagion in which price effects play an important role. In addition to the usual matrix of interbank claims, CFS add an asset market with a downward sloping demand curve for assets. In this market, there are two channels for contagion. The first is through the usual bilateral exposures in the interbank market; the second is through the effect of asset price changes on bank capital. Every bank is assumed to satisfy a capital adequacy requirement. When bank capital is too low relative to the value of assets, the bank must sell some assets in order to satisfy the capital adequacy constraint (it is not possible to raise additional capital, at least in the short run). The bank will first try to sell liquid assets, whose price is assumed to be fixed, but if it still cannot satisfy the capital adequacy constraint it will have to sell the illiquid asset. The market for the illiquid asset has a downward sloping residual demand curve, so the more of the illiquid asset is sold by the banks, the lower the price. Contagion through interbank exposures works in the usual way. One bank failure creates a loss for the creditor banks and reduces their capital. If the loss is big enough, capital becomes negative, assets are less than liabilities, the bank fails, and the losses spill over to other previously unaffected banks. The new channel is different. When one bank fails, other banks suffer losses that reduce their capital. If the capital adequacy constraint was binding, this would put the creditor bank in the position of having to sell assets to reduce the marked-to-market value of its assets. At first, it may be possible to satisfy the capital asset constraint by selling liquid assets, but eventually it will be necessary to sell illiquid assets. If several banks do this, the asset price is reduced and this has an effect on banks in general. Other things being equal, a reduction in asset prices reduces the amount capital in each bank, possibly causing it to violate the capital adequacy constraint. Those banks for whom the constraint is violated will be forced to sell assets themselves, thus increasing the downward pressure on asset prices. This all has a family resemblance to the story told in Chapter 5 and indeed it is very similar. The novelty of the CFS approach is that it combines the asset price channel with the interbank borrowing and lending channel to get a more powerful effect. The two channels run side by side, each reinforcing the other. CFS do not calibrate their model to real world data, but they do simulate the behavior of the model for reasonable parameter values and find that the price effects greatly amplify the extent of contagion for appropriate parameter values. The analysis provides important insights into the factors that can increase the likelihood and extent of contagion and should provide a guide for future research.

## 10.9 LITERATURE REVIEW

There are a number of different types of contagion that have been suggested in the literature. The first is contagion through interlinkages between banks and financial institutions. The second is contagion of currency crises. The third is contagion through financial markets. In addition to the surveys by Masson (1999) and Upper (2006) already mentioned, De Bandt and Hartmann (2002), Karolyi (2003), and Pericoli and Sbracia (2003) contain surveys of this literature. Claessens and Forbes (2001) and Dungey and Tambakis (2005) contain a number of papers on various aspects of international contagion. Given the large number of recent surveys this section will be relatively brief.

Banks are linked in several ways including payments systems and interbank markets. These linkages can lead to a problem of contagion. We start by considering models of payment system contagion. Building on a locational model of payment systems developed by McAndrews and Roberds (1995), Freixas and Parigi (1998) have considered contagion in net and gross payment systems. In a net payment system banks extend credit to each other within the day and at the end of the day settle their net position. This exposes banks to the possibility of contagion if the failure of one institution triggers a chain reaction. In a gross system transactions are settled on a one-to-one basis with central bank money. There is no risk of contagion but banks have to hold large reserve balances. A net payment system is preferred when the probability of banks having low returns is small, the opportunity cost of holding central bank money reserves is high, and the proportion of consumers that have to consume at another location is high. Freixas, Parigi and Rochet (2000) use this model to examine the conditions under which gridlock occurs. They show that there can be gridlock when the depositors in one bank withdraw their funds, anticipating that other banks cannot meet their netting obligations if all their depositors have also withdrawn their funds. Rochet and Tirole (1996a) consider the role of the too-big-to-fail policy in preventing contagion. Furfine (2003) considers interbank payment flows in the US and concludes that the risk of contagion from this source is small.

As discussed above at length, Allen and Gale (2000) focus on a channel of contagion that arises from the overlapping claims that different regions or sectors of the banking system have on one another through interbank markets. When one region suffers a banking crisis, the other regions suffer a loss because their claims on the troubled region fall in value. If this spillover effect is strong enough, it can cause a crisis in the adjacent regions. In extreme cases, the crisis passes from region to region and becomes a contagion. Eisenberg and Noe (2001) derive various results concerning the interconnectedness of institutions. Aghion et al. (1999) also consider a model of contagion through interbank markets. In their model there are multiple equilibria. In one equilibrium there are self-confirming beliefs that a bank failure is an idiosyncratic event and in the other there are self-fulfilling beliefs that a bank failure signals a global shortage of liquidity. Lagunoff and Schreft (2001) study the spread of crises in a probabilistic model. Financial linkages are modeled by assuming that each project requires two participants and each participant requires two projects. When the probability that one's partner will withdraw becomes too large, all participants simultaneously withdraw and this is interpreted as a financial crisis. Rochet and Tirole (1996b) use monitoring as a means of triggering correlated crises: if one bank fails, it is assumed that other banks have not been properly monitored and a general collapse occurs. Dasgupta (2004) uses a global games approach to show how a unique equilibrium with contagion can arise when banks hold cross deposits. Allen and Carletti (2006) show how contagion can occur through the market for credit risk transfer. Van Rijckeghem and Weder (2000) document linkages through banking centers empirically. Iyer and Peydró-Alcalde (2006) consider a case study of interbank linkages resulting from a large bank failure due to fraud.

There is a growing literature on contagious currency crises and international contagion. Masson (1999) provides a good overview of the basic issues. He distinguishes between "monsoonal" effects, spillovers and pure contagion. Monsoonal effects occur when there are major economic shifts in industrial countries that impact emerging economies. Spillovers occur when there are links between regions. Pure contagion is when there is a change in expectations that is not related to fundamentals and is associated with multiple equilibria. Eichengreen et al. (1996) and Glick and Rose (1999) provide evidence that trade linkages are important factors in the spread of many currency crises. Kaminsky et al. (2003) consider a long history of contagion across borders and consider why contagion occurs in some cases but not in other similar situations. Pick and Pesaran (2004) consider some of the econometric issues that arise in distinguishing contagion from interdependence.

There are a number of papers that consider contagion through financial markets. King and Wadwhani (1990) consider a situation where information is correlated between markets. Price changes in one market are perceived to have implications for asset values in other markets. Calvo (2002) and Yuan (2005) consider correlated liquidity shocks as a channel for contagion. When some investors need to obtain cash to, for example, meet a margin call they may liquidate in a number of markets so the shock is spread. Kodres and Pritsker (2002) use a multi-asset rational expectations model to show

how macroeconomic risk factors and country-specific asymmetric information can combine to produce contagion. Kyle and Xiong (2001) present a model of contagion in financial markets due to the existence of a wealth effect. Pavlova and Rigobon (2005) provide a theoretical model of contagion of stock market prices across countries arising from wealth transfers and portfolio constraints.

## 10.10  CONCLUDING REMARKS

Contagion is one of the most important topics in the area of financial crises. The idea that shocks can spread and cause a great deal more damage than the original impact is one that is extremely important for policymakers. It is used to justify much of the intervention and regulation that is observed. As we have seen contagion takes many forms. Although there is a large literature on this topic, much work in this area remains to be done. The same is true of all the topics covered in this book!

## REFERENCES

Aghion, P., P. Bolton, and M. Dewatripont (1999). "Contagious Bank Failures," working paper, Princeton University.

Allen, F. and E. Carletti (2006). "Credit Risk Transfer and Contagion," *Journal of Monetary Economics* 53, 89–111.

Allen, F. and D. Gale (1998). "Optimal Financial Crises," *Journal of Finance* 53, 1245–1284.

Allen, F. and D. Gale (2000). "Financial Contagion," *Journal of Political Economy* 108, 1–33.

Calvo, G. (2002). "Contagion in Emerging Markets: When Wall Street is a Carrier," Proceedings from the International Economic Association Congress, vol. 3, Buenos Aires, Argentina 2002. Also in G. Calvo, *Emerging Capital Markets in Turmoil: Bad Luck or Bad Policy?* Cambridge, MA: MIT Press 2005.

Calvo, G. and E. Mendoza (2000a). "A Rational Contagion and the Globalization of Securities Markets," *Journal of International Economics* 51, 79–113.

Calvo, G. and E. Mendoza (2000b). "A Capital-Markets Crises and Economic Collapse in Emerging Markets: An Informational Frictions Approach," *American Economic Review* 90, 59–64.

Cifuentes, R., G. Ferrucci, and H. Shin (2005). "Liquidity Risk and Contagion," *Journal of the European Economic Association* 3, 556–566.

Claessens, S. and K. Forbes (eds.) (2001). *International Financial Contagion*, Norwell, MA: Kluwer.

Dasgupta, A. (2004). "Financial Contagion through Capital Connections: A Model of the Origin and Spread of Bank Panics," *Journal of the European Economic Association* 6, 1049–1084.

De Bandt, O. and P. Hartmann (2002). "Systemic Risk in Banking: A Survey," in *Financial Crises, Contagion, and the Lender of Last Resort: A Reader*, C. Goodhart and G. Illing (eds.), Oxford: Oxford University Press.

Degryse, H. and G. Nguyen (2004) "Interbank Exposures: An Empirical Examination of Systemic Risk in the Belgian Banking System," National Bank of Belgium, NBB Working Paper No. 43.

Diamond, D. and P. Dybvig (1983). "Bank Runs, Deposit Insurance, and Liquidity," *Journal of Political Economy* 91, 401–419.

Dungey, M. and D. Tambakis (eds.) (2005). *Identifying International Financial Contagion*, Oxford: Oxford University Press.

Eichengreen, B., A. Rose, and C. Wyplocz (1996). "Contagious Currency Crises: First Tests," *Scandinavian Journal of Economics* 98, 463–484.

Eisenberg, L. and T. Noe (2001). "Systemic Risk in Financial Systems," *Management Science* 47, 236–249.

Freixas, X. and B. Parigi (1998). "Contagion and Efficiency in Gross and Net Interbank Payment Systems," *Journal of Financial Intermediation* 7, 3–31.

Freixas, X., B. Parigi, and J. Rochet (2000). "Systemic Risk, Interbank Relations and Liquidity Provision by the Central Bank," *Journal of Money, Credit & Banking* 32, 611–638.

Furfine, C. (2003)."The Interbank Market During a Crisis," *Journal of Money, Credit and Banking* 35, 111–128.

Glick, R. and A. Rose (1999). "Contagion and Trade: Why Are Currency Crises Regional?" Chapter 9 in P. Agénor, M. Miller, D. Vines and A. Weber (eds.), *The Asian Financial Crisis: Causes, Contagion and Consequences*, Cambridge, U.K.: Cambridge University Press.

Gorton, G. (1988). "Banking Panics and Business Cycles," *Oxford Economic Papers* 40, 751–781.

Hicks, J. (1989). *A Market Theory of Money*, New York: Clarendon Press; Oxford: Oxford University Press.

Iyer, I. and J. Peydró-Alcalde (2006). "Interbank Contagion: Evidence from Real Transactions," working paper, European Central Bank.

Kaminsky, G., C. Reinhart, and C. Vegh (2003)."The Unholy Trinity of Financial Contagion," *Journal of Economic Perspectives* 17, 51–74.

Karolyi, G. (2003)."Does International Financial Contagion Really Exist?" *International Finance* 6, 179–199.

Kindleberger, C. (1978). *Manias, Panics, and Crashes: A History of Financial Crises*, New York, NY: Basic Books.

King, M. and S. Wadhwani (1990). "Transmission of Volatility Between Stock Markets," *Review of Financial Studies* 3, 5–33.

Kodres, L. and M. Pritsker (2002). "A Rational Expectations Model of Financial Contagion," *Journal of Finance* 57, 768–799.

Kyle, A. and W. Xiong (2001). "Contagion as a Wealth Effect," *Journal of Finance* 56, 1401–1440.

Lagunoff, R. and S. Schreft (2001). "A Model of Financial Fragility," *Journal of Economic Theory* 99, 220–264.

Masson, P. (1999). "Contagion: Monsoonal Effects, Spillovers and Jumps Between Multiple Equilibria," Chapter 8 in P. Agénor, M. Miller, D. Vines and A. Weber (eds.), *The Asian Financial Crisis: Causes, Contagion and Consequences*, Cambridge, UK: Cambridge University Press.

McAndrews, J. and W. Roberds (1995). "Banks, Payments and Coordination," *Journal of Financial Intermediation* 4, 305–327.

Mitchell, W. (1941). *Business Cycles and Their Causes*, Berkeley: University of California Press.

Pavlova, A. and R. Rigobon (2005). "Wealth Transfers, Contagion, and Portfolio Constraints" NBER Working Paper No. W11440.

Pericoli, M. and M. Sbracia (2003). "A Primer on Financial Contagion," *Journal of Economic Surveys* 17, 571–608.

Pick, A. and M. Pesaran (2004). "Econometric Issues in the Analysis of Contagion," CESifo Working paper Series No. 1176.

Rochet, J. and J. Tirole (1996a). "Interbank Lending and Systemic Risk," *Journal of Money, Credit and Banking* 28, 733–762.

Rochet, J. and J. Tirole (1996b). "Controlling Risk in Payment Systems," *Journal of Money, Credit and Banking* 28, 832–862.

Upper, C. (2006). "Contagion Due to Interbank Credit Exposures: What Do We Know, Why Do We Know It, and What Should We Know?" working paper, Bank for International Settlements.

Upper, C. and A. Worms (2004). "Estimating Bilateral Exposures in the German Interbank Market: Is there a Danger of Contagion?", *European Economic Review* 48, 827–849.

Van Rijkeghem, C. and B. Weder (2000). "Spillovers Through Banking Centers: A Panel Data Analysis," IMF Working Paper 00/88, Washington, D.C.

Yuan, K. (2005). "Asymmetric Price Movements and Borrowing Constraints: A Rational Expectations Equilibrium Model of Crisis, Contagion, and Confusion," *Journal of Finance* 60, 379–411.

# Index

Adams, John Quincy 3
Agénor, P. 296, 297
Aghion, P. 294
Allen, F. 84, 90, 95,103, 124, 128, 147, 172,
    176, 184, 193, 204, 212, 214, 218, 224,
    228, 231, 237, 238, 239, 246, 247, 250,
    252, 262, 280, 281, 290, 293, 294
Alonso, I. 95
Argentina crisis of 2001–2002 17–18
Arnott, R. 214
Arrow securities 146, 150, 42
Arrow–Debreu economy 41
Asian crisis of 1997 1, 15, 260–261, 217–218
Asset price bubbles
    agency problems 237
    banking crises 247
    negative 236
    positive 236
    risk shifting 237
    without Central Bank intervention 254
Azariadis, C. 147

Bagehot, W. 3
Bank capital
    incentive function 193
    risk–sharing function 193
Bank of England 3
Bank of Sweden 3
Bank runs 74
    empirical studies 96
Banking Act of 1935 5
Banking and efficiency 72–73
Bannier, C. 93
Barth, J. 213
Benefits of financial crises 153
Bernanke, B. 147
Bernardo, A. 148
Bertaut, C. 101
Besanko, D. 192
Bhattacharya, S. 94, 95, 192, 214
Bill of exchange 126
Blume, M. 101
Bolton, P. 295
Boot, A. 214
Bordo, M. 2, 3, 9–12, 16

Bossons, J. 125
Boyd, J. 18, 19, 228
Brennan, M. 101
Bretton Woods Period 1945–1971 10
Bryant, J. 20, 58, 59, 74, 84, 94, 95, 96,
    147, 149
Buffers and bank runs 277
Business cycle view of bank run
    82, 95

Call loans 6
Calomiris, C. 83, 94, 96, 147, 231
Calvo, G. 260, 294
Campbell, J. 100
Capital regulation 191
Capital structure
    Modigliani–Miller theorem 203
    optimal 194
    with complete markets 201
Caprio Jr., G. 214
Carey, M. 214
Carletti, E. 294
Carlsson, H. 90, 95
Cash-in-the-market pricing 102,
    110–114
Cass, D. 147
Chang, C. 233
Chang, R. 230, 231
Chari, V. 94, 95, 147
Chatterjee, K. 97
Chui, M. 229, 230
Cifuentes, R. 291
Claessens, S. 293
Competitive equilibrium 159
Complete markets 41, 70
Cone, K. 94
Constantinides, G. 98
Constrained efficiency 182, 198
Consumption and saving 27, 32
Contagion
    asymmetric information 260
    Belgian banking system
        290–291
    currency crises 261, 294
    empirical studies 284–292

Contagion (*contd.*)
    financial markets 294–295
    German banking system 284–290
    incomplete interbank markets 274
    overlapping claims 260
    payments systems 293
    price effects 291–292
Contingent commodities 40
Corsetti, G. 231
Costs of financial crises 18–19, 153
Courchene, T. 215
Crash of 1929 2
Crash of 1987 100
Credit and interest rate determination 243
Crises and stock market crashes 5
Crises in different eras 10
Crockett, J. 125
Currency crises and twin crises 229

Dasgupta, A. 294
De Bandt, O. 293
de Neufville Brothers 126, 147
De Nicoló, G. 231
Deflation 218
Degryse, H. 290
Desai, M. 258
Dewatripont, M. 98, 213, 295
Diamond, D. 20, 58, 59, 74, 94, 95, 96, 130,
    147, 149, 228, 229, 230, 255, 262
Diamond–Dybvig preferences 150, 116
Dollarization 231–232
Dollarization and incentives 226–228
Dornbusch, R. 125
Drees, B. 235
Dungey, M. 293
Dybvig, P. 20, 58, 59, 74, 94, 95, 96, 130, 147,
    149, 230, 255, 262
Dynamic trading strategies 156

Economywide crises 149
Efficient allocation over time 27
Efficient risk sharing 165
Eichengreen, B. 9, 25, 294
Eisenberg, L. 293
Endogenous crises 148
Englund, P. 14, 235
Equilibrium bank runs 76
Essential bank runs 85
Excess volatility of stock prices 100
Exchange Rate Mechanism crisis 229
Extrinsic uncertainty 129, 148

Fama, E. 100
Farmer, R. 147
FDIC 190
Ferrucci, G. 291
Financial Crisis of 1763 126
Financial fragility 126
First Bank of the United States 3
First Basel Accord 191
Fisher, S. 125
Fixed participation cost 101–102
Flood, R. 229
Forbes, K. 293
Forward markets and dated commodities 31
Fourçans, A. 16, 229
Franck, R. 16, 229
Frankel, J. 15, 235
Freixas, X. 94, 213, 293
Friedman, M. 58, 96
Friend, I. 101, 125
FSLIC 190
Full participation equilibrium 120
Fundamental equilibrium 129, 141, 148
Furfine, C. 293
Furlong, F. 192

Gai, P. 229, 230
Gale, D. 84, 95, 103, 124, 128, 147, 172, 176,
    184, 193, 195,199, 204, 212, 214, 218,
    224, 226, 228, 231, 232, 237, 238, 246,
    247, 250, 252, 262, 280, 281, 290, 293
Galindo, A. 231, 232
Garber, P. 229
Geanakoplos, J. 147, 198
General equilibrium with incomplete markets
    147
Gennotte, G. 192
Gertler, M. 147
Glass–Steagall Act of 1933 5, 190
Glick, R. 294
Global games approach to currency crises
    230
Global games equilibrium uniqueness 90, 95
Goenka, A. 147
Gold Standard Era 1880–1913 10
Goldstein, I. 90, 95
Goodhart, C. 296
Gorton, G. 4, 20, 83, 94, 95, 96,147, 231, 239,
    247, 262
Gottardi, P. 147
Gramm–Leach–Bliley Act 190
Great Depression 2, 190, 217

Green, J. 57
Greenwald, B. 214
Guiso, L. 100, 101
Gup, B. 215

Haliassos, M. 101, 125
Hamilton, Alexander 3
Hansen, L. 98
Harris, M. 98
Hart, O. 147
Hartmann, P. 293
Heiskanen, R. 14, 235
Heller, W. 215
Hellman, T. 192
Hellwig, M. 95
Herring, R. 213
Hicks, J. 261
Hoggarth, G. 18
Honohan, P. 25, 233
Hubbard, R. 151, 233

Illing, G. 296
IMF 25
Incentive compatibility and private
    information 71
Incentive compatible 131
Incentive constraint 131
Incentive efficiency 72, 175
Incomplete contracts 154
Incomplete markets 154
Inefficiency of markets 66
Inside money 216
Insurance and risk pooling 48
Interbank network
    complete 263, 269
    incomplete 263, 271
Intrinsic uncertainty 129, 148
Irwin, G. 212
Iyer, I. 294
Ize, I. 233

Jacklin, C. 94, 95
Jagannathan, R. 95
Japanese asset price bubble 15, 235
Jappelli, T. 125
Jensen, M. 241
Jones, C. 6, 26
Jonung, L. 259

Kahn, C. 94
Kajii, A. 147

Kaminsky, G. 230, 231, 294
Kanatas, G. 192
Kanbur, R. 214
Karolyi, G. 293
Keeley, M. 192
Kehoe, P. 147
Keynes, J. M. 216
Kim, D. 192
Kindleberger, C. 2, 3, 20, 58, 126, 147,
    235, 262
King, M. 100, 294
Kiyotaki, N. 147
Klingebiel, D. 25
Kodres, L. 260, 294
Krooss, H. 4
Krugman, P. 229
Kwak, S. 25
Kyle, A. 295

Laeven, L. 25
Lagunoff, R. 148, 294
Leape, J. 100
Leiderman, L. 231, 232
Leroy, S. 100
Levine, R. 214
Limited market participation 100–102,
    114–124
Liquidation pecking order 275
Liquidity insurance 68
Liquidity preference 53, 59–60
Liquidity trading 100
Long Term Capital Management (LTCM)
    16, 127
Lowenstein, R. 16

Magill, M. 147
Mailath, G. 152
Mankiw, N. 100
Marion, N. 229
Martinez–Peria, M. 25
Mas–Collel, A. 57
Mason, J. 96, 147
Masson, P. 261, 293, 294
McAndrews, J. 293
Meckling, W. 241
Mendoza, E. 260
Merton, R. 100
Mikitani, R. 15
Miller, M. 296, 297
Mishkin, F. 236
Mitchell, W. 20, 58, 262
Money and banking crises 228–229

Money and risk sharing 218–223
Moore, J. 147
Morris, S. 90, 92, 93, 95, 230, 259
Murdock, K. 215

Nalebuff, B. 214
National Bank Acts of 1863 and 1864 4
National Banking Era 4, 83
Neave, E. 215
Nguyen, G. 290
Noe, T. 293

Obstfeld, M. 230
Optimal currency crises 223–226
Optimal monetary policy 256
Optimal risk sharing through interbank
    markets 266
Outside money 216
Overend & Gurney crisis 2, 3
Özgür, O. 199

Panic-based runs 94
Parigi, B. 293
Parke, W. 100
Participation and asset-price volatility
    120–121
Pauzner, A. 90, 96
Pavlova, A. 295
Pazarbasoglu, C. 235
Pericoli, M. 293
Pesaran, M. 294
Pesenti, P. 231
Peydró-Alcalde, J. 294
Pick, A. 294
Pigou, A. C. 216
Polemarchakis, H. 198
Porter, R. 100
Portfolio choice 49
Posen, A. 15
Postlewaite, A. 95, 148, 259
Prati, A. 93
Prescott, E. 98
Pritsker, M. 260, 294
Production 36
Pyle, D. 192

Quinzii, M. 147

Rajan, R. 94, 233, 229
Real business cycle 147
Regulation of liquidity 204

Reinhart, C. 230, 231, 234, 296
Reis, R. 25
Rigobon, R. 295
Risk aversion 45
    absolute 46
    relative 46
Risk pooling 55
Roberds, W. 293
Rochet, J. 90, 94, 95, 192, 293, 294
Rogoff, K. 234
Rose, A. 294, 296
Roubini, N. 18, 231
Russian Crisis 127
Russian Crisis of 1998 16

Said, Y. 258
Samuelson, L. 152
Samuelson, W. 97
Santomero, A. 192, 213
Santos, J. 213
Saporta, V. 25, 215
Savastano, M. 234
Sbracia, M. 93, 293
Scandinavian crises 1, 14–15, 235–236
Schnabel, I. 126, 147
Schreft, S. 148, 294
Schwartz, A. 58, 96
Second Bank of the United States 3
Second Basel Accord 191
Separation Theorem 39
Sequential service constraint 94
Sequentially complete financial markets 170
Setser, B. 18
Shell, K. 147
Shiller, R. 100
Shin, H. 90, 92, 93, 95, 126, 147, 230, 291
Smith, B. 25, 228, 233
Sprague, O. 6, 96
St-Amant, P. 215
Starr, R. 215
Starrett, D. 215
Stiglitz, J. 215, 241
Studenski, P. 4
Stulz, R. 98, 214
Sunspot equilibria 129, 140, 147, 148
Sunspots and bank runs 76–77, 94
Sylla, R. 6, 26

Takagi, S. 25, 26
Tambakis, D. 293
Tanaka, M. 215

Thakor, A.  94, 214
Tillman, P.  93
Timberlake, R.  3
Tirole, J.  213, 293, 294
Tschoegl, A.  15, 235
Turnovsky, S.  98
Twin crises  9, 230–231

Uncertain bank runs and equilibrium  76–82
Upper, C.  284, 293

Value of the market  63
Van Damme, E.  90, 95
Van Rijckeghem, C.  260, 294
Vegh, C.  296
Velasco, A.  230, 231
Vihriälä, V.  14, 235
Vines, D.  296, 297
Vissing–Jorgensen, A.  101
Vives, X.  90, 95, 226, 232
Von Neumann-Morgenstern utility
       function  44

Wadhwani, S.  294

Wallace, N.  94, 98
Wealth and present values  20
Weber, A.  296, 297
Weder, B.  260, 294
Weiss, A.  241
Welch, I.  148
West, K.  100
Whinston, M.  57
White, E.  242
Wicker, E.  96
Wilkins, C.  215
Wilson, J.  5–8
Winton, A.  94
Worms, A.  284
Wyplocz, C.  296

Xiong, W.  295

Yuan, K.  294

Zame, W.  186
Zeldes, S.  100